PEACEMAKING

Lessons from the Past,
Visions for the Future

VIBS

Volume 105

Robert Ginsberg
Executive Editor

Associate Editors

A volume in
Philosophy of Peace
POP
Joseph C. Kunkel, Editor

PEACEMAKING

Lessons from the Past,
Visions for the Future

Edited by

Judith Presler
Sally J. Scholz

Amsterdam - Atlanta, GA 2000

The paper on which this book is printed meets the requirements of "ISO 9706:1994, Information and documentation - Paper for documents - Requirements for permanence".

ISBN: 90-420-1552-7 (paper)
ISBN: 90-420-1562-4 (bound)
©Editions Rodopi B.V., Amsterdam - Atlanta, GA 2000
Printed in The Netherlands

For
Henry A. Presler
and
Christopher P. Kilby

CONTENTS

EDITORIAL FOREWORD

Though the cold war is over, serious societal conflicts remain; some would argue that such conflicts have increased. By societal conflicts I mean not only foreign wars fought among and within nations but also school and office shootings within the United States; and racial, gender, sexual, and class systemic injustices. Conflicts are overt and covert, international and domestic; one form flows into and out of the other. Nationalistic ethnic cleansing begins with ethnic intolerance; it is also fueled by an unrestrained global conventional arms trading that values corporate profits over global security. Guns kill when human beings allow insecure individuals to turn deadly weapons upon one another. Guns kill when individuals with guns remain uninformed of and untrained in nonlethal means of resolving ongoing conflicts.

In recent years we have experienced open warfare in the Middle East, the former Yugoslavia, Russia, Africa, Latin America, and elsewhere. By contrast we have also witnessed a new democratic multiracial government in South Africa, the peaceful dividing of Czechoslovakia into two nations, negotiations and a referendum on the future of Northern Ireland, and some progress in the United States and elsewhere on gender, race, sex, and age discrimination. Yet, growing class disparities remain hidden and ignored, to our future peril.

Peacemaking, the topic of this volume, is much broader than secret diplomatic meetings between representatives of two sides that are in shooting wars or armed conflict. Such mediations are sometimes successful, as currently seems to be the case in Northern Ireland and Bosnia, but often they drag on for generations or fail altogether. Armed conflicts continue to dominate troubled areas until one side wins decisively or exhaustion extinguishes the desire of the combatants to continue fighting. Peace conjoined with warmaking was termed by Thomas Hobbes the "absence of war"; this is a type of peace that is coerced by a balance of power among the contending nations or groups. Hobbes views individuals within nations as similarly scrambling for power–in a covert rather than an overt manner–with the most powerful factions dictating the ruling policies for the rest of society, and with the police and judicial system enforcing those skewed policies. In the United States, for instance, federal and state elections are generally determined by wealth and, accordingly, the wealthy oppose any serious effort at campaign finance reforms that might make a democratic government more attuned to the needs of all the people.

The chapters in this volume make only passing reference to this form of "negative" peacemaking. The reasons are several. First, as philosophers most of the authors are trained to challenge reigning assumptions. The soundness of the fundamental Hobbesian aggression principle is generally disputed.

Admittedly individuals within nations and particular nations as political units frequently act out of a power motive; nevertheless not all individuals and nations do. Positing this orientation as the rule for all individual and national actions seems like an inordinately pejorative interpretation of human nature. The evidence is thin that humans are naturally and necessarily at war with one another.

Second, philosophers look at interactive issues from a moral perspective. Political realists who follow Hobbes tend to subordinate morality to power. For example, Henry A. Kissinger, who served from 1969 to 1977 as U. S. National Security Advisor and then Secretary of State, addressed the political-moral distinction on various occasions, but in particular in his 1975 talk "The Moral Foundations of Foreign Policy." Kissinger distinguishes the values and interests of the United States. Values are the principles we espouse, which he enumerates as "freedom, the dignity of the individual, [and] the sanctity of law." Interests are furthered by power and security. To apply values independent of law to the practice of politics, he says, is hopelessly idealistic. Power is the only means, for Kissinger, for making sure that U.S. values are secure.

Morality, in practice, thus becomes limited to whatever is sanctified under the contract of law; all other morality is deemed "hopelessly idealistic." This is a form of contractarian ethics, which most ethicists disavow. Most ethicists view morality as derived from principles that are equitable for all and hence independent of the power of the few. For most ethicists might is not right. Justice in the sense of equity has become the foundation for a more "positive" peacemaking.

Third, peacemaking is generally felt to require a more solid foundation than power and domination. Peacemaking either begins at home or does not succeed. Conflicts occur from birth on; parents, teachers, ministers, sages, counselors, mediators, and even democratic politicians, police, and judges strive to resolve these conflicts in beneficial, caring, and fair ways. The hope is to extend these caring and just forms of conflict resolution to the global community of nations. Hence the subtitle for the book, *Lessons from the Past, Visions for the Future.*

This book is unusual in that the authors addressing the peacemaking theme are practicing philosophers. As such they are not steeped in the strategic thinking of political and military theoreticians or national security advisors. Still they are knowledgeable about public affairs and bring an abiding interest in peacemaking to their writing. Many go back several decades in sorting through themes relating to war and peace, violence and nonviolence. From this broader perspective they challenge the *status quo* of establishment political thinkers. They disagree among themselves on what national and international relations can or ought to be envisioned for the future, but they all expect future generations to be less militaristic than past.

The book has three sections. The first examines various models for peacemaking theory. One criterion that permeates the section is the susceptibility of each proposed theory for moral implementation. Theories that do not coincide with morality or social justice are rejected as inadequate. The authors do not agree on what constitutes morality or justice, so there is flexibility in their judgments. But the need for some type of moral underpinning is generally acknowledged. Politics as power that works is not seen as a sufficient foundation for genuine peacemaking.

The second section takes up international interventions. The first two authors, coming from a realistic perspective, defend contrasting views on the peacekeeping role of the United Nations. The source of their debate is *An Agenda for Peace*, a report by the former U.N. Secretary General Boutros Boutros-Ghali. Two other authors examine nonmilitary approaches to the same kinds of conflict, and the last author expounds a meaning of sovereignty that is congruent with positive peace.

The third section focuses on domestic matters. It opens with an exposition of the views of Jane Addams, who, for pragmatic reasons, opposed the entry of the United States into World War I. Two authors follow who look at the role of mothering and the role of African sages in resolving conflicts. The last three authors examine verbal catcalls, white privilege, and gang violence. These chapters allow readers to compare the goings-on of domestic life with ramifications for global institutions. Social justice is a necessary ingredient for international peacemaking. Relations that succeed at home prevail abroad.

Judith Presler and Sally J. Scholz have performed a highly commendable editing service in molding these chapters into a readable book. Their love of the topic and attention to detail enhances the quality of this publication. The subject matter is timely and usable in a variety of contexts. We hope that the book will reach beyond academic circles to speak to peace lovers around the world. What more could be asked for philosophers who strive to bring their wisdom to bear on problems affecting the larger society?

Joseph C. Kunkel
Editor, Philosophy of Peace

PREFACE

Peacemaking includes a large array of activities ranging from local to global attempts to attain peace. Peacemaking in today's contemporary world encompasses international, interstate, and intertribal conflict resolution. It also entails attempting to bring about social justice within communities. On the international level peacemaking has been understood to entail bringing about peace after a war, making treaties that prevent war or other forms of international conflict, effecting disarmament, creating international organizations that secure order among nations, and deterring war through the possession of nuclear and other weapons. Peacemaking on the local level includes intergroup and interpersonal conflict resolution, race and ethnic group relations, crime and violence prevention, and, in general, efforts to affect social justice.

Philosophers have long been interested in peacemaking and philosophical accounts of peacemaking reflect the variety of perspectives, methods, and activities found in other philosophical enterprises. In some instances, philosophers of peace not only theorize about peace but comment upon the practice of peacemaking. As philosophers examine the concept of peacemaking, they push at the boundaries of what had been traditionally thought of as violence, injustice, and peace. In doing so, they also push at the boundaries of personal responsibility. When we begin to recognize the numerous and varied ways in which we as individuals or groups perpetuate and perpetrate violence, we also begin to recognize how we are morally responsible or blameworthy for injustice.

The next step is the constructive step. That is, how do we move from the recognition of our responsibility for violence and injustice to our responsibility to make peace? As philosophers, part of our role as peacemaker is to propose alternative approaches. For example, the philosopher might critically evaluate an actual peacemaking project. Such an evaluation could help to uncover moral problems or inconsistencies within the peacemaking process or it might function to justify some of the peacemaking activities. Alternatively, the philosopher-peacemaker might offer a new perspective through which to view an unjust situation or a situation in need of peacemaking. Finally, the philosopher-peacemaker might challenge us as global citizens to expand our understanding of violence thereby facilitating a broader range of practices for which we as individuals and groups are responsible. In other words, through critical reflection, the philosopher might facilitate moral action toward more peaceful relations.

As numerous philosophers have noted, peace, in both its negative and positive forms, is a constituent of a just society. The once clear demarcation between positive and negative peace is no longer a significant distinction. In the nuclear age, negative peace or the absence of war, has grown to include new forms of international involvement; and the distinction between justice and injustice seems to become blurred when one nation is involved in the affairs of another nation or when an international governing body is involved in the affairs of a nation. With increasing international involvement in peacemaking, the broader issues of sovereignty, cultural autonomy, and economic interdependence must enter into discussions of peace. Positive peace, traditionally the more extensive form of peace, entails social justice. Positive peace, when it is true peace, cannot occur until there is justice. Thus, justice and peace have a symbiotic relationship.

At the close of the twentieth century, peacemakers increasingly participate in attempts to end ethnic cleansing, reinstate justly elected political leaders, and reach compromises in the ideological differences that perpetuate age-old conflicts. Peacemakers continue to work in our schools, homes, and workplaces. Resolving conflict, as required for negative peace, is often found to be possible only in the presence of social justice. Conversely, unjust social conditions (for example, inadequate or unjust distribution of resources, covert and overt forms of sexism and racism, and neglect of those in need) are often causes of conflict or may at times result from a failure to recognize the importance of social justice in peacemaking efforts. These are some of the many reasons it is imperative for us critically to evaluate the theoretical and practical connections between positive and negative peace–justice and peace– as well as to examine the implications of our peacemaking actions. The chapters in this volume take a step in this direction, examining peace first theoretically, then practically in the global arena, and finally practically in the local arena.

The first section sets out some theoretical arguments for various aspects of peacemaking. The first three chapters by Thomas A. Imhoff, Jerald Richards, and Judith Presler explore moral justifications for peacemaking as conflict resolution. These chapters might prove particularly useful for the student of political philosophy. They provide clear presentations of some canonical political theories while also using examples to illustrate how those theories might be modified or used in political negotiation, global morality, and conflict resolution. Mar Peter-Raoul examines the relationship between positive peace and justice. Donald A. Wells critically evaluates the role religion has played in war. The section ends with two chapters highlighting some insights from feminism. Mary Lenzi and Joseph C. Kunkel each argue that some of the varying theories of feminism might be productively used in formulating a philosophy of peace.

The chapters in the second section examine several practical proposals for alleviating international conflicts; these accounts are necessary for a full understanding of international peacemaking. The first three chapters look at peacekeeping and military and nonmilitary intervention. While Leo Groarke takes a more critical look at international peacekeeping, Robert Litke argues for creating a global peacekeeping force analogous to the local peacekeepers in Canada. William C. Gay's chapter examines military and nonmilitary forms of intervention and proposes his conception of effective nonmilitary intervention. Richard Wendell Fogg explores the possibility and desirability of a nonmilitary response to nuclear threat or attack. Both Gay and Fogg emphasize responsible citizen action. The section ends with Steven Lee's examination of the apparent conflict between maintaining national sovereignty and international positive peace. Although most explicitly addressed in the last chapter, all five of the chapters in Section Two illustrate the importance and difficulty of respecting national sovereignty and cultural autonomy in our peacemaking efforts.

The final section focuses on practical examples of peacemaking in daily life. Many of the examples, presented on a local level of peacemaking, require an individual response to the violence of injustice. The day-to-day peace-maker is the socially responsible and socially responsive self. As the chapters of the third section reveal, individuals who strive for peace and justice in personal relations with family, community, and self confront the issues of power relations, language, social groupings, and distribution of resources–all equally international issues. Thus, reflection upon local peacemaking leads not only to clarity about local peacemaking but also to considerations that are internationally applicable. Just as chapters in Section Two tend to respond to particular historical situations, the chapters in Section Three tend to arise from daily existence or personal narrative. This sort of embeddedness lends the chapters a practical element often absent from traditional philosophy. Marilyn Fischer's chapter provides an explicit link between peacemaking as international conflict resolution and peacemaking as social justice. Fischer finds in the work and thought of Jane Addams not only a theoretical link between justice and peace but also a practical instantiation of that link. In the next chapter, Laura Duhan Kaplan critically examines mothering, revealing both the potential for peace as well as the potential for war in the practice of mothering. Critical examination is the key to being able to develop the peacemaking potential for that practice. This chapter provides an illustrative link with the ethics of care as peacemaking articulated by Kunkel in Section One. Gail M. Presbey offers an alternative, non-Western, model for conflict resolution based on the work and teachings of sages and queen mothers in Africa. As Presbey relates, daily conflict resolution within a community is a necessary and foundational element to peaceful communal living. In the final three chapters of the volume, the social injustices of sexism and racism are variously explored and critiqued. Sally J. Scholz examines verbal violence and offers a pacifist proposal to some instances of sexist verbal violence. In her chapter, Alison Bailey compares the way that the dominant race in our society makes the distinction between white and nonwhite, to the way that war makers make the distinction between us and the enemy. In each case there is a process of enmification. Ron Hirschbein's chapter concludes the volume. He makes use of personal narratives to illustrate the important similarities between warfare on our city streets and warfare among nations. His chapter is a fitting end to a collection of chapters that together propound the idea that our conception of peacemaking must be expanded to include social justice as well as international conflict resolution.

Judith Presler
University of North Carolina at Charlotte

Sally J. Scholz
Villanova University

ACKNOWLEDGMENTS

We thank all of the contributors to this volume. Their work on peacemaking is philosophically interesting and challenging. As editors we express our gratitude to the individual authors for allowing us to publish these essays together. Although each of the chapters could easily stand alone, we believe that together they provide a forceful message for peacemaking that will prove valuable to professional philosophers, students, peacemakers, and seekers after justice.

Many of the chapters in this volume originated at a Concerned Philosophers for Peace conference on peacemaking at Villanova University in the Fall of 1994. Joseph Betz served as the program chair and local host for that conference. This volume owes a great deal to him for his work on that conference and support throughout the compilation of this volume. He continues to work tirelessly as both a professional philosopher and global citizen peacemaker.

We are grateful as well for the guided assistance, and, most of all, encouragement of two long-time leaders of Concerned Philosophers for Peace: Willam C. Gay, past President and Laura Duhan Kaplan, current President.

Joseph C. Kunkel, the Philosophy of Peace Special Series Editor offered indispensable suggestions and assistance with our work on this contribution to the Philosophy of Peace special series of the Value Inquiry Book Series. His insights and commitment to peacemaking continue to serve as an inspiration to both colleagues and students alike. We extend our gratitude to him.

We thank the Brandywine Peace Community of Swarthmore, Pennsylvania for permission to reprint Janice Hill's poem "Letter to a Political Prisoner," from their *Of the Heart and the Bread: An Anthology of Poems for Peacemakers* (1985).

Finally, this book was made possible through generous financial assistance from Villanova University and the University of North Carolina at Charlotte. The editors thank both institutions for their commitment to faculty research and for their support of the editing of this volume on peacemaking. Pam Mullins was invaluable in preparing this manuscript for publication.

Judith Presler
Sally J. Scholz

SECTION I

THEORETICAL MODELS FOR PEACEMAKING

INTRODUCTION

The chapters in this section variously explain, critique, and use theoretical models for peacemaking. The models, offering us lessons from the past, are from as far back in our philosophical heritage as fourth-century BCE Greek texts and as recent as late twentieth-century feminist writings. In all but two of the chapters, hopeful visions for future peacemaking are conceptions developed from instructive inquiry into the theoretical models.

In "Moral Foundations of Political Negotiations," Thomas A. Imhoff examines three theoretical models of negotiation and demonstrates that the model of principled negotiation is defensible on both prudential and moral grounds. Morally, principled negotiation mirrors the contractualist paradigm of moral reasoning. Imhoff also examines some potential problems with principled negotiation. These problems include a significant power differential among negotiating parties, failure to negotiate in good faith, and the case when one of the parties to the negotiation does not wish to negotiate. For these problem cases, Imhoff offers a supplement to principled negotiation that he defends as insuring a moral outcome of the negotiation. His application of this model to international conflict leads him to conclude that coordinated international economic and political institutional arrangements for applying swift and effective pressure to achieve moral results should be created.

Jerald Richards, in "Common Morality and Peacemaking," examines ordinary people's religious, political, and ethical positions embedded in representative cultures around the globe and draws from this examination a universal common morality. The common moral principles are (1) that one do to others what one would wish done to oneself, and (2) the demand that human beings be treated humanely. Presupposed by these two principles is the intuition we have of the worth, value, and dignity of human life. This intuition, while inherent, sometimes wanes in the face of the experience of injustice and cruelty, and needs nurturing. Richards makes seven recommendations of ways to nurture the basic intuition of the preciousness of human life. He is not, however, unrealistically optimistic about human nature; in fact he also makes recommendations of ways to remain aware of the human potential for evil and of ways to respond morally to that evil. Finally, he notes that peacemaking, creating a culture of nonviolence and respect for life, stands little chance of being even minimally successful in the modern world without the acknowledgment of and commitment to this kind of common universal global ethics.

In "Peacemaking and Procedural Justice: A Critique," Judith Presler briefly explicates Stuart Hampshire's theory of procedural justice and examines his sort of procedural justice at work in historical examples of international conflict negotiation. Initially procedural justice seems promising as a model for peacemaking. However, Presler's examination uncovers serious practical and theoretical difficulties. Some of the practical difficulties are that procedural justice comes into play only as a last resort; it establishes only temporary peace; it is suited to resolve only peripheral problems; and it neither pertains to moral considerations nor leads to moral conclusions. Theoretically Hampshire's theory contains within it fundamental conceptual inconsistencies. Presler's conclusion is that this theoretical model is not well-suited to bring international conflict to a peaceful resolution.

In her chapter "Justice as Structure and Strategy of Peace," Mar Peter-Raoul develops a model of justice and a model of peace, and inquires into the relationship between them. As she follows the concept of peace through the chapter she elucidates the depth and complexity of her concept of peace by qualifying it differently from section to section. Peter-Raoul begins by reporting extreme examples of injustice in the world today. The second section is an account of social justice. Here justice is described as grounded in fundamental human rights that guarantee persons the right to human dignity and well-being. Social justice so formed is likely to promote what she calls "positive peace." In the third section of her chapter, Peter-Raoul offers a literary model of her concept of social justice and what she calls "just peace." Lastly, she suggests seven strategies, rooted in a radical revision of values, that together can bring about "emancipatory peace."

In "Ambiguous Roles of Religions in War and Peace," Donald A. Wells examines the relationship between the religious model and peacemaking/ pacifism. He first details numerous examples of how religion has at times offered contradictory dictates with regard to war. Wells then argues that Buddhism, Islam, Hinduism, Judaism, and Christianity have each contributed to the increase in the number of wars while each might also entail an explicit historical message contrary to war. Wells looks both at the religious indi-vidual's involvement in war and the religious sanctioning of war. In the end, although individuals might turn to religion to justify their pacifism, history shows that all of the major world religions have, at best, only an ambiguous relation to pacifism. If Wells is correct, then we will have to turn elsewhere to find a theoretical model for peacemaking/pacifism. The world religions have offered too many contrary messages in both theory and practice.

In "Plato and Echo-Feminism: Platonic Psychology and Politics for Peace," Mary Lenzi takes a broad view of peacemaking in her comparison of models of the soul and the polity according to Plato in *Laws* and according to contemporary ecofeminism. According to Lenzi, ecofeminists "echo" Plato in their forward looking "antimilitarist reconstruction of the human self and democracy." After first showing how Plato and many contemporary feminists view justice as the goal to theory and practice, Lenzi illustrates some of the feminist strands of Plato's social and political writing. Lenzi's account differs from other feminist reclamations of Plato in that it focuses primarily on *Laws* and only by way of comparison appeals to *Republic*. She argues that "in Plato's state, both female and male citizens integrate their shared desires and common goals by conjoining their efforts and pursuits to experience personal and political justice and well being." Plato thereby serves as an historical precursor to many of the contemporary ecofeminist discussions which emphasize the individual's connection to the whole and vice versa. In short, Plato's theory is echoed in the feminist rallying cry "the personal is political." The vision of Plato and the ecofeminists is an extraordinarily positive vision of personal well-being, and an integrated and peaceful polity.

Joseph C. Kunkel's chapter, "Reflections on Caring and Peace Politics," critically examines the ethics of care model in contrast with the justice model. He then points out some criticisms of the ethics of care model, and considers the possibility of an ethics of care supplemented by a system of justice. Even supplemented by a system of justice, Kunkel holds, caring ethics has weaknesses associated with its subjectivity. Kunkel suggests that dialogue when added to an ethics of care provides the critical objectifying factor, replacing an abstract system of assessing moral justification. Appealing to a variety of sources, he argues that dialogue, when carried on in an open and inquiring manner, aids in objectifying moral conflicts while remaining in the mode of caring. Appealing not only to theory but also to his own practice, he argues that friendship enveloped in dialogue enhances moral growth. In the final section he examines the concept of maternal thinking. He argues that maternal thinking alone cannot bring about peace; however he suggests that coupling dialogue with maternal thinking can lead to peace.

One

MORAL FOUNDATIONS OF POLITICAL NEGOTIATIONS

Thomas A. Imhoff

In *Getting to Yes*, Roger Fisher, William Ury, and Bruce Patton defend the idea of "principled negotiations" as a way of constructing agreement without capitulation or appeasement.[1] The central task of principled negotiations is to establish principles that all the parties to a conflict will recognize as objective standards for judging the merits of proposals offered as solutions to the conflict. By definition principled negotiations serve multiple interests and leave each negotiating party feeling fairly treated. Each party feels that it has not been taken advantage of in order to benefit others. In this chapter I examine the method of principled negotiation in order to determine whether this method is defensible not simply on prudential grounds, that is, on the grounds that using principled negotiation results in agreements more appealing than agreements reached using standard negotiation strategies, but also on moral grounds.

I conclude that in negotiations that reach consensus among the negotiating parties, the method of principled negotiation parallels one of the dominant paradigms of moral reasoning, the contractualist paradigm. When principled negotiation works, it results in an agreement that no reasonable negotiator rejects. There is a set of cases in which the method of principled negotiations will not produce a moral outcome. These are cases in which there is a large power differential between the disputants, in which one of the disputants does not want to negotiate, or in which one of the disputants can not be trusted to negotiate forthrightly. In these cases, principled negotiation, I argue, must be supplemented, if it is to result in a moral outcome.

1. Principled Negotiations

Fisher, Ury, and Patton argue against the technique of positional bargaining. Positional bargaining pits negotiators against one another as they each stake out their positions, making offers and counter offers and resorting to mechanical techniques like splitting the difference as a last attempt to resolve an impasse. The problem here is that in focusing on positions rather than on interests, negotiators often fail to create innovative solutions that benefit all sides. The classic arena for positional bargaining is the buying and selling of commodities such as cars or houses. If, for example a prospective home buyer finds a motivated seller who needs to sell a house quickly, the buyer's temptation is to disregard objective measures of the property's value (such as the price for which comparable homes have recently sold) and make an offer substantially lower in hopes of getting a deal. If the seller is quite concerned about the chances of making a quick sale, the seller may give a counter offer that is below the market price. Should this happen, the buyer and seller would be engaged in what Fisher, Ury, and Patton call "positional bargaining." Instead of trying to reach a mutually agreed on fair price based upon widely recognized objective standards for determining value, the buyer and seller throw offers back and forth in an attempt to buy low or sell fast. Fairness is the first casualty of such negotiations, and discontent is often the first consequence of such exchanges. What is lost in positional bargaining is a reasoned attempt to establish value, the value both to the buyer and to the seller of the item being offered. Also lost is any chance at arriving at an exchange in which both buyer and seller feel that they have participated in a fair transaction and in which each has a clear idea of the reasons why the transaction is fair.

Principled negotiation introduces as the central tasks of negotiating, the idea of establishing value, and of giving reasons why some transaction is better, more fair, than another. Being fair is primarily making sure that the various negotiating parties are satisfied with the deal they have made and can explain to themselves why the deal they have struck is superior to the various other deals that were on the table. At the center of this process is the identification of what Fisher, Ury, and Patton call "objective criteria."

Objective criteria vary from negotiation to negotiation. What makes criteria objective is that the negotiating parties agree upon the criteria and thus recognize that the criteria represent an objective standard. Several ways to identify mutually agreeable objective standards exist. One way is to appeal to established practices. For example, in the real estate case previously cited, one criterion used to establish the value of a home would be the price of other comparable homes that have recently sold in a neighborhood. In auto sales, other standards operate–the price of comparably equipped autos with similar mileage; the blue book value for this year, make, and model of auto. The relevant standard depends on the sort of negotiation. If the issue is how to regulate timber cutting in the Pacific Northwest, one relevant standard is the level of timber cutting that could be done while allowing the forest ecosystem to continue to support the variety of plant and animal life that make that ecosystem distinctive. If the issue is how to regulate factory fishing in Alaskan waters, one standard would be how many of one sort of fish could be taken either without harming that species' ability to maintain its population at a stable level or without threatening the food supply of other aquatic life. The importance and appropriateness of these standards is itself a subject for negotiation as well as an issue for scientific study and recommendation. Once negotiations turn toward establishing standards and away from the defense of positions, discussion can focus on the vital and urgent interests of each of the negotiating parties. Focusing on interests, on what the various parties take to be their central concerns, makes it possible to construct creative solutions that take into account those central concerns and help to allay fears that something precious is being lost in the negotiated solution. If all parties to a conflict can leave the negotiation conference assured that their respective situations are improved as a result of having negotiated a plan for managing the conflict, each of the parties will view the negotiations as having been in its interest. Such mutual gain solutions are excluded from consideration when all talk is centered on positions, for example, on the board feet of lumber needed to keep a logging company going at a particular production level, or on how many tons of fish are required to keep a factory trawler operating at peak profitability.

Throughout their explanation of the method of principled negotiation Fisher, Ury, and Patton offer practical suggestions on how to construct mutual gain solutions. They suggest refusing to react to emotional outbursts, listening actively to the concerns of the other side, being open to reasoned persuasion but unmoved by threats or the application of pressure, offering proposals that are consistent with the opposing party's values, refusing to blame the other side for one's problems, and separating the people involved in negotiations from the conflict being negotiated. These suggestions are designed to maximize the chances of developing a working relationship with each of the other negotiating parties, and of constructing a solution to the conflict that each of the parties to the dispute can recognize as protecting its interests while at the same time appearing to be an equitable solution to the dispute. The elaboration of principled negotiations, with its emphasis on reasoned agreement and attention to important interests aiming at a mutual gain solution, suggests obvious parallels with one of the major contemporary ethical paradigms, that is, contractualism.

A major difference exists between the conflict management strategies suggested by a contractualist negotiation and those offered as acceptable by principled negotiation. Principled negotiation is a way of getting the most out of a negotiation position, even when that position is weak. Contractualist theory suggests that the only way to get an ethical result from a conflict that pits a weak negotiator against one much stronger is to equalize the negotiating arena. With radically unequal negotiation positions, principled negotiations may leave one better off than one would be had no negotiations taken place, but they will not result in an ethical resolution of the conflict. If ethics is important, it is important to consider how to turn the prudent suggestions, tactics, and strategies of principled negotiation into ethical procedures with the likelihood of moral outcomes.

2. Informed Contractualist Paradigm

In this section I explain informed ethical contract negotiations and draw out some of the parallels between contract theory and principled negotiation. I do not offer a detailed defense of contract ethics as against other ethical paradigms (such as virtue ethics, consequentialism, or deontology) nor do I offer reasons for adopting my informed version of contract theory over other versions, for example, John Rawls's and David Gauthier's. The contract argument I use derives from the work of T. M. Scanlon.[2] It is a fully informed negotiation (unlike Rawls's version) with normative components built in (unlike Gauthier's version).[3]

To be attracted to contractual ethics is to be something of a moral skeptic and a relativist. The motivation for viewing negotiation as a useful way to settle conflicts ethically is the belief that no party to a dispute has the only accurate description or analysis of the conflict. In human affairs truth is always partial. In human conflict, whether between individuals or groups, each party has a point of view that portrays differently the history of the conflict, the important interests and moral principles at stake, and the preferred solutions. On the supposition that no one has a corner on truth, but all points of view carry some persuasive power, one profitable avenue for settling disputes is negotiation that issues in a contract or agreement that all parties can recognize as minimally acceptable.

Informed contractualism does make one assumption about human beings, namely that human beings have a psychological need to justify their behavior both to themselves and to others. If this assumption is correct, if people actually behave this way, then human beings are naturally motivated to engage in dialogue concerning justification. The offering of persuasive reasons is the primary way people get others to accept their justifications. Persuasive reasons are those that take into account the worries and concerns of those we are trying to persuade. If a person can offer reasons that appeal to the interests and concerns of the adversary, then those reasons will be persuasive. This relationship between justification and persuasion leads to a particular understanding of reasonableness. The contractualist definition of reasonableness is that judgments and views are reasonable if others find persuasive the reasons backing up these judgments and views. This definition amounts to a rhetorical understanding of reasonableness. If others find a person's views to be reasonable, then, by definition, they are reasonable.

The concept of reasonableness is at the center of informed contract theory since the goal of contractualist negotiations is to reach an agreement that it would be unreasonable to reject. The combination of the goal–of reaching a particular sort of agreement–with the contractualist understanding of reasonableness, results in a thoroughgoing proceduralism when it comes to settling conflicts. Conflicts are settled through negotiations. In order for consensus to develop, solutions must universally persuade reasonable negotiators.

Negotiators are persuaded if they can be shown that some solution protects or promotes their most urgent interests, their most central concerns. If all negotiating teams can be shown that a particular solution does a better job than any other of protecting the wide variety of vital interests of concern to the various negotiating teams, then each of the teams has been shown that it would be unreasonable to reject that particular solution. A reasonably unrejectable solution is one that minimizes serious losses to each of the negotiators while offering benefits as well.

To illustrate these ideas let us take the case of the United Farm Workers and their struggle in the 1960s and 1970s with California table grape growers. The United Farm Workers were seeking better working conditions (toilets in the fields, for example), safer working conditions (careful use of herbicides and insecticides), and higher wages. When Cesar Chavez first began his efforts to organize farm workers in the table grape industry, growers were afraid that the United Farm Workers union would take control of the vineyards away from the owners, destroying the profitability and thus the economic viability of the California grape industry. Guided by these fears, growers spent all of their energies for a number of years attempting to destroy the United Farm Workers union. Had the growers instead consulted a practitioner of contractualist ethics, perhaps a local philosopher teaching at California State University, Bakersfield, they would have discovered that there are better ways to deal with opponents than by trying to destroy them.

The philosopher-mediator would have pointed out that both the growers and the farm workers had legitimate worries and that opening up a dialogue might make it possible to discover ways to address many of those worries without destroying the business relationship on which both the growers and the farm workers depended for their livelihood. The contractualist goal is to construct a noncoercive program or process for managing conflict. If each of the disputants agrees that it would be unreasonable to reject the program, negotiations succeed—no coercion is necessary. In the grower-farm worker dispute, the philosopher's advice to the growers would have been for them to talk to representatives of the farm workers as business associates essential to the success of the grape production enterprise. The ideal business arrangement would be a contract according to which the farm workers did not believe they were being asked to work in unsafe, demeaning (no toilets at the job sites) conditions for wages far lower than comparable work done in other sectors of the economy, but a contract according to which growers did not fear that their production costs would run them into bankruptcy or that the contract would strip them of the authority to make legitimate business decisions. It is all but certain that this advice, coming from the philosopher, would have been rejected by the growers. Why, after all, should the growers consult with farm labor about how to operate their vineyards and why should grape growers listen to a philosopher who understands ethics but knows precious little about agribusiness?

But let us suppose that the growers did listen to the counsel of our philosopher-mediator and sat down to talk with Cesar Chavez, the representative of farm labor. Let us suppose that all the concerns had been laid out on the table and a number of proposals dealing with major worries of each side had been put forward. Suppose that the philosopher-mediator, with help from a colleague from the School of Business, had crafted a plan that addressed the worries both of the growers and of farm labor. Suppose further that farm labor had agreed to the provisions of the settlement but that the growers, harboring a hatred of organized labor as usurpers of management authority, had refused to agree to the settlement package, though they had understood and agreed to each of the provisions that make up the settlement package. We have an impasse.

What has just been described is the case of recalcitrance. An interest group (the growers) rejects the judgment that some particular settlement would be unreasonable to reject. It rejects the settlement even though all other parties (farm labor and the mediators) agree that, given each party's stated interests and concerns, the proposed settlement protects each negotiator's important interests and offers to each significant benefits. If the recalcitrant party refuses to sign on to the constructed process, while at the same time giving no persuasive reasons for this recalcitrance, then the recalcitrant party is judged to be unreasonable and can ethically be coerced to comply with the negotiated solution. In the farm labor case, the unwillingness of the growers to sign on to the mediated settlement is, by hypothesis, due to the grower's hatred of farm labor unions. Hatred is not a persuasive reason for rejecting the mediated settlement given that the growers have agreed to each provision in the construction of the settlement as being in their interest. The growers would be saying that though the settlement addresses their major concerns (economic viability and continued productivity), they believe they would be better off not having to deal with the farm workers as an organized body and would prefer to destroy the union and maintain the *status quo*. Such reasoning certainly does not appeal to the central concerns of the farm workers. Consequently, it has no chance of persuading them, and represents an unreasonable rejection of the negotiated settlement according the contractualist definition of reasonableness. If, on the other hand, the growers could persuasively (by appeal to the vital interests of farm labor) argue that it is reasonable to reject the constructed solution, then the negotiated settlement could be thrown out as reasonable to reject and the negotiators would begin again the process of constructing a reasonably unrejectable procedure for managing the labor/grower conflict.

Two requirements remain to fill out this explanation of informed contract theory. Negotiations require full information so that all the negotiators understand the context in which the agreement takes place. A mechanism must exist for insuring that impartial judgments are made during negotiations. The process for insuring impartiality parallels the process for insuring reasonable judgments. If the negotiators agree that a judgment is impartial, that the judgment does not sacrifice the more important interests of one party in order to protect the relatively less important interests of some other party, then, by definition, the judgment is impartial. To construct such impartial judgments, negotiators require a way to rank interests in order of importance and to rank possible conflict management strategies in order of desirability. The most desirable strategies or plans are those which do the best job of protecting important interests while also distributing benefits widely. In the farm labor case, growers would have to consider, for example, the costs of putting toilets in the fields against the costs to farm laborers of having to urinate and defecate squatting under grape vines. How would growers feel if they and their families were forced to relieve themselves in this way at their places of work? Having made such evaluative comparisons, it should be possible to rank losses suffered under various alternative settlements. As might be expected, the procedure for ranking losses, interests, and conflict management plans is the procedure of reasonable negotiations, negotiations that gain their persuasive force, their reasonableness, from their appeal to the interests and concerns of the various negotiating teams.

So there are several parallels between principled negotiations and informed contract theory. The focus in each is on the interests of the various parties and on the offering of reasons designed to demonstrate that a cooperative agreement is better than holding out for an agreement that benefits one side at the expense of others, or to demonstrate that a negotiated agreement is better than no agreement. The objective standards of judgment referred to by principled negotiation theorists parallel the contractualist idea of constructing through dialogue, discussion, and consensus, standards of reasonableness and impartiality by appeal to persuasive reasons. But there are significant differences too.

The problem of transferring informed contract theory from the mind of the philosopher into the world of conflicting interests is that conflicting parties are rarely in equivalent negotiating positions. Grape growers in California's central valley refused to negotiate with farm workers represented by Cesar Chavez's union for a number of years, preferring instead to try to break the United Farm Workers union by hiring nonunion labor. It was not until a national and later international boycott of California table grapes resulted in huge financial losses for California growers that they finally realized they would have to negotiate a labor agreement with farm labor. Until the boycott, California growers were confident that they had the economic resources to outlast the United Farm Workers union. The growers had the advantage when it came to comparative bargaining position strength. This sort of behavior–refusing to negotiate, preferring instead to ignore or destroy an opponent–is perhaps the primary problem for contractualist theory in the real world of economics and politics. What is to prevent the party with the stronger position from attempting to dictate the terms of agreement?

Classic examples of such dictation are relationships between employers and organized labor, and relationships between nation states with significant military or economic power and those without. In these cases contract theory requires breaking through the logic of self-interest, the logic that dictates dispensing with impartiality and disregarding what one's adversaries consider reasonable and valuable.

Principled negotiation has an answer for the disadvantaged negotiator: improve your Best Alternative To a Negotiated Agreement (BATNA). The idea is to protect important interests as much as possible; try to convince the adversary that there are benefits available through cooperation (negotiation) that are not available otherwise; and be willing to walk away from negotiations if it is clear that negotiations are not going anywhere. This is good advice, prudent advice, but following such advice will not result in ethical outcomes.

3. Haiti: The Ethical Inadequacy of Prudence

The case of Haiti offers an example of how prudent negotiations can fail. Jean-Bertrand Aristide was elected President of Haiti in December 1990 only to be deposed by the Haitian military when it became clear that he was actually going to change the way business was conducted in his country. It was not until mid-October 1994 that Aristide returned as president following many months of failed negotiations and a United States military invasion. It is instructive to consider in this case what went wrong. Why was it that negotiations did not yield a workable settlement? Why did the decision to send in the Marines look like a good option?

Haiti represents a case in which negotiations were going nowhere because one side, the Haitian military, believed their BATNA to be better than any negotiated settlement they could hope to achieve. At one point during discussions with the United States State Department concerning the return to power of the democratically elected Aristide government, Haitian military leaders agreed to abdicate power in a gradual process. But this agreement was later exposed as a ploy by the military to gain time. The Haitian military reneged on its agreement to allow United States military trainers into the country as an initial step in the process of handing over of power. It turned out that even when negotiating an end to military rule, the military was negotiating in bad faith. The standoff between Haiti and the United States government had all the problems associated with negotiations likely to fail. First among these problems was a large power differential between the supporters of Aristide and the ruling Haitian military, which deposed him. That power differential could easily be interpreted as weighted in the opposite direction if the United States, along with the international community, had been willing to take more than symbolic action to protest Haitian military rule. Second, when negotiations were in progress, the Haitian military exhibited an unwillingness to engage in serious negotiations, to negotiate in good faith, and to abide by agreements already reached.

The recommendation of principled negotiation theory would be to make the BATNA of the Haitian military much worse, that is, to make it in the interest of the military to begin serious negotiations designed to create a mutual gain solution. There are a number of ways this might have been done. One, of course, is military action–an invasion by the United States Marines. Historically this is the method of choice for the United States in dealing with small countries in its sphere of influence who refuse to act in accordance with its interests. But invasion would not represent a mutual gain solution. For the Haitian people, an invasion would likely be a guaranteed loss solution with possibly thousands of civilians dead and the prospect of a foreign occupying force fighting a guerrilla war against the remnants of a defeated Haitian military. Perhaps it is this scenario which led Aristide himself to advise against an invasion.

There were a variety of military responses that would decrease the attractiveness of the Haitian military's BATNA while at the same time decreasing United States costs measured in the lives of its military personnel. Here is another scenario: a swift and decisive United States invasion designed to destroy the Haitian military, then a quick withdrawal, and the introduction of a police force made up of trained Haitian expatriates whose job it would be to keep order and prevent what was left of the military from retaking power. But even in this scenario massive loss of civilian life and the destruction of the meager Haitian economic and social infrastructure would likely result.

Decreasing the attractiveness of the Haitian military's BATNA need not require a military response. The international community, acting in support of democratic values, could have sealed off Haiti from any except emergency commerce and communication. Assets of the wealthy, whose interests are protected by the military, could have been frozen in their foreign accounts. If countries were unwilling to comply with sanctions of this kind, the scope of sanctions could have been broadened to include countries unwilling to cooperate. The Dominican Republic, which shares a border with Haiti and which was unwilling to cut off fuel supplies to its neighbor, comes to mind here. Sanctions targeting ruling elites were possible and would not have had much of an effect on the majority of Haitians already desperately poor. Such sanctions would have significantly increased the pressure for ruling elites to come in good faith to the negotiating table.

Principled negotiation can work in situations like the standoff over Haitian democracy. The problem is getting the disputing parties to the negotiating table and getting all sides to negotiate in good faith. Principled negotiation recommends settling conflicts by manipulating the context in which negotiations are to take place in such a way as to demonstrate that no side's BATNA is better than a principled agreement. Principled negotiation theory even has strategies for dealing with negotiators who refuse to discuss in good faith, for example, third party mediation in which a mediator listens to the concerns and interests of the disputing parties and constructs a succession of proposals designed to address those concerns and take into account those interests. Whether it is a question of bringing all the parties to the table or of getting all the parties to bargain in good faith, in some cases when one or more parties views self-interest as more important then the creation of an agreeable conflict management process, effective pressure must be brought to bear on the self-interested parties. If nonmilitary pressures are to be effective in the international arena, a more efficient and coordinated set of institutional arrangements and agreements are needed than are at present available.

There is a role for coercion in the moral universe of the contractualist. Coercion may be used for getting unwilling negotiating parties to comply with what negotiations have demonstrated to be a conflict management plan that it would be unreasonable to reject. But even before negotiations have begun, coercion is sometimes morally justifiable, namely, if it is used to get disputing parties to the table in order to begin in earnest to work out a settlement to the conflict. Being cautious, being prudent, engaging in continuing dialogue often will not work without economic and political pressure to break the logic of self-interest.

4. Moral Case for Institutional Supplements

The case of Haiti illustrates the inadequacies of the international system of political commerce. It should have been a simple matter to get the nations with which Haiti had economic ties to freeze the foreign assets of Haiti's wealthy citizens. It should have been a simple matter to impose a tight economic embargo designed to disable Haiti's economic system. It should have been a simple matter to end all international commerce and travel between Haiti and the rest of the world. It should, in short, have been a simple matter to make the Haitian oligarchy pay for its overthrow of a president elected by an overwhelming majority. That it was not a simple matter to do these things suggests that various countries, including the United States, considered the costs of supporting such measures too great to balance the benefits likely to have resulted. What is required to counter such self-interested, cost-benefit calculations is the reconsideration of the costs and benefits from a broader perspective, from the perspective of the reasonable and impartial negotiator. Contractualist theory offers a process for breaking the logic of self-interest.

Contract theory suggests a process for dealing with national and international conflict. That process is one of negotiation. The difficulty of mobilizing the international community on issues of great import like the overthrow of Haitian democracy, even when that community has the United Nations as a forum within which to carry on international dialogue, suggests that better procedures must be created through negotiation for rapidly constructing cooperative responses to international problems, responses which could bring effective economic and political pressure to bear on countries that flout widely accepted values in the international arena. The recommendation of principled negotiation theory for dealing with stalemate and uncertainty over conflict is to negotiate not only the principles on which decisions will be based, but also the procedures by means of which negotiations are undertaken. Such negotiations over general procedures of decision making are long overdue in the modern world. If the community of nations would use the United Nations as a forum to negotiate guidelines for dealing with illegitimate regimes like the Haitian military and if the United Nations would negotiate procedures for creating swift and decisive cooperative responses to situations of international concern, the prospects for peace would be greatly enhanced and the latitude given regimes like the Haitian military would be much reduced. Along with a clear expectation of what is likely to happen to illegitimate regimes at the hands of the international community would come a much less sanguine self-appraisal of the regime's BATNA. Negotiations would have a chance.

It must be said that prudence narrowly defined will never bring about a peaceful resolution of a national or an international conflict. What it may be prudent to do in order to promote national interests, or the interests of the most powerful group in society, is very likely not prudent or ethical when the interests of other countries or other national groups within a country are taken into account. The promotion of self-interest is often imprudent because of the anger and dissatisfaction such promotion creates on the part of those whose interests have been sacrificed. The single-minded promotion of self-interest is always unethical in that it is unreasonable to promote the interests of some by sacrificing the important interests of others. Such a plan could not have broad persuasive appeal. The method of principled negotiation does advise those with weak BATNAs to do what they can to strengthen them and to do what they can to weaken the BATNAs of their adversaries. But in the international arena this is often difficult if not impossible to do without the cooperation of many other nation states. Informed contract theory offers the moral justification for making such cooperation routine. To fail to create an international system which can efficiently mount a coordinated effort to protect, through the application of economic and political pressure, the urgent interests of peoples around the world, is to settle for an international system that it would be reasonable to reject. Both contract theory and principled negotiation theory recommend that we do better than the *status quo*.

Without supplementation, without economic mechanisms for making assets unavailable and for making products unobtainable, without political mechanisms for isolating and ostracizing the economic and political leaders of offending nations, negotiations may yield an outcome that is as good as could be hoped for relying solely on dialogue. But the outcome will likely be immoral. Interests that should not be sacrificed will be sacrificed. This result suggests that in order for negotiations to be more than simply making the best of a bad situation, in order for principled negotiations to be justified by ethics as well as by prudence, it is necessary to set up a variety of institutional arrangements that are likely to lead to outcomes that no reasonable negotiator could reject even in the difficult cases of power imbalance, reluctance to negotiate, or unwillingness to negotiate forthrightly. That coordinated international economic and political institutional arrangements for applying swift and effective pressure are necessary to achieve moral results argues powerfully for their creation.

Notes

1. Roger Fisher and William Ury with Bruce Patton, *Getting to Yes: Negotiating Agreement without Giving In* (New York: Houghton Mifflin, 2nd ed., 1991).

2. T. M. Scanlon, "Utilitarianism and Contractualism," in *Utilitarianism and Beyond,* ed. Amartya Sen and Bernard Williams (Cambridge, U.K.: Cambridge University Press, 1982), pp. 103-128.

3. John Rawls, *A Theory of Justice* (Cambridge, Mass.: Harvard University Press, 1971); and David Gauthier, *Morals by Agreement* (Oxford: Clarendon Press, 1986).

Two

COMMON MORALITY AND PEACEMAKING

Jerald Richards

This chapter develops some preliminary thoughts about the basic principles and primary intuitions of a universal common morality that is a prerequisite for successful peacemaking–the reduction of violent conflict among individuals, groups, institutions, peoples, and nations, and the eventual replacement of violent with nonviolent means of conflict resolution. The basic principles are grounded in thinking about the fundamental principle of reciprocity and fundamental inalienable human rights. The primary intuitions include a recognition of the value, worth, and dignity of human beings, and a sense of the nature of moral wrongness (or human evil) as the violation of persons, understood in terms of the unjustifiable infliction of harm. The concluding section develops some thoughts on how peacemakers might foster and nourish the primary intuition of the worth and dignity of persons, including some thoughts on avoiding unrealistic views of human nature.

The concept of peace is understood in a full and robust sense to include both negative peace (the absence of war) and positive peace (the absence of war plus the existence of social justice). Peacemaking includes (1) efforts to bring about the cessation of armed conflicts among peoples and nations and (2) efforts to eliminate structural or institutional injustices and to bring about just social arrangements among individuals, peoples, and nations. A peaceful world would be one in which violent conflicts have been reduced to a minimum and in which violent means of conflict resolution have been replaced by nonviolent means. A universal common morality is necessary for the achievement of these goals. Without a common morality, peacemakers will be unable to cooperate fully and freely with each other and to deal creatively and effectively with the many types of divisive and discriminatory "isms" that result in violent conflicts and social injustice, including such "isms" as sexism, racism, ethnocentrism, nationalism, and warism.

This understanding of peace and peacemaking is consistent with definitions evolving out of United Nations resolutions and declarations. For example, UNESCO's Medium-Term Plan for 1977-1982 states:

> No international settlement secured at the cost of the freedom and dignity of peoples and respect for individuals can claim to be a truly peaceful settlement, either in its spirit or in terms of its durability. In the resolutions which it has adopted respecting this problem...the General

Conference has associated the struggle for peace with a condemnation of
all forms of oppression, discrimination and exploitation of one nation by
another, not only because they inevitably generate violence but also
because they themselves constitute a form of violence and partake of the
spirit of war.[1]

Subsequent U.N. statements reflect similar concerns about peace. UNESCO's
Second Medium-Term Plan (1984-1989) states:

There can be no genuine peace when the most elementary human rights
are violated, or while situations of injustice continue to exist....Disregard
for the rights of individuals and peoples, the persistence of inequitable
international economic structures, interference in the internal affairs of
other states...are always real or potential sources of armed conflict and
international crisis. The only lasting peace is a just peace based on
respect for human rights. Furthermore, a just peace calls for the
establishment of an equitable international order which will preserve
future generations from the scourge of war.[2]

I do not attempt to set forth a full set of principles for the moral
guidance of human action in all spheres of both individual and collective life.
If human beings can come to a consensus on fundamental intuitions and basic
principles, then there is some hope that the difficult and challenging tasks of
generating secondary and tertiary moral principles, and of appropriately
applying these principles to specific situations can be carried out successfully
in ways that could be universally acceptable. Without agreement on the
foundational intuitions and principles, we have little hope of achieving agreement on morally appropriate behavior in specific contexts. Nor do I attempt to
respond to criticisms coming from nihilism, skepticism, and relativism. However important some of these criticisms may be, they arise from "isms" that at
least in their extreme forms, are false to the realities of human nature, values,
and possibilities. Important distinctions can be made in the realm of values.
We can gain some significant knowledge about the right and the good, and
we can communicate that knowledge to one another. Although there may be a
variety of ways in which human beings apply moral principles in specific
contexts in morally appropriate ways, not everything goes. Some attitudes,
character traits, and actions are universally morally wrong or evil, and other
attitudes, traits, and actions are universally right or good.

I am writing with an increased awareness of the amazing social, economic, political, and cultural diversity that exists among peoples of the world.
According to one expert, currently there are 10,000 human societies on the
planet earth inhabiting some 168 nation-states.[3] This wide diversity and
pluralism must be acknowledged and taken into account by peacemakers concerned about establishing positive peace in the world, especially by those

peacemakers who maintain that a common morality is essential to successful peacemaking.

1. Principle of Reciprocity

The principle that stands the best chance of being universally accepted as the fundamental principle of morality is the principle of reciprocity. The bedrock articulation of this principle can be expressed negatively as "What you do not wish done to yourself do not do to others" and positively as "What you wish done to yourself, do to others."[4]

John Hick understands this principle as "the utterly basic principle that it is evil to cause suffering to others and good to benefit others and to alleviate or prevent their sufferings."[5] This principle of love, compassion, and generous concern for the welfare of others is developed and applied in the moral precepts of all the great traditions.[6] Variations are found in the authoritative writings of Hinduism, Buddhism, Taoism, Confucianism, Zoroastrianism, Judaism, and Christianity.[7]

To get a clearer sense of the scope and nature of the principle, I am setting forth equivalent statements coming from a wide variety of cultural sources. Hans Küng provides the following examples:

> Confucius (c.551-489 BCE): What you yourself do not want, do not do to another person (Sayings 15.23).
> Rabbi Hillel (60 BCE to 10 CE): Do not do to others what you would not want them to do to you (Shabbat 31a).
> Jesus of Nazareth: Whatever you want people to do to you, do also to them (Matt. 7.12; Luke 6.31).
> Islam: None of you is a believer as long as he does not wish his brother what he wishes himself (Forty Hadith of an-Nawawi, 13).
> Jainism: Human beings should be indifferent to worldly things and treat all creatures in the world as they would want to be treated themselves (Sutrakritanga I, 11, 33).
> Buddhism: A state which is not pleasant or enjoyable for me will also not be so for him; and how can I impose on another a state which is not pleasant or enjoyable for me? (Samyutta Nikaya V, 353.35-342.2).
> Hinduism: One should not behave toward others in a way which is unpleasant for oneself; that is the essence of morality (Mahabharata XIII 114, 8).[8]

To the above statements, Hick adds a few others, writing,

> [T]here are several passages in which the Buddha, rebuking those who are ill-treating others, says such things as "Life is dear to all. Comparing others with oneself, one should neither strike nor cause to strike"

(*Dhammapada*, 10:2)....In the Taoist *Thai Shang* we read that the good man will "regard [others'] gains as if they were his own, and their losses in the same way" (3). The Zoroastrian *Dadistan-I-Dink* declares, "That nature only is good when it shall not do unto another whatever is not good for its own self" (94.5).[9]

Secular or secularized versions of the principle of reciprocity, influenced by the humanistic ideals of ancient Greece, the Renaissance, and the Enlightenment, as well as by some of the traditions referred to above, especially the Jewish and Christian traditions, have exerted tremendous positive influence in the past several centuries. The moral philosophies of Immanuel Kant and John Stuart Mill are classic examples of ethical systems that give primacy to the fundamental principle of reciprocity as it evolved out of both secular and religious traditions. Kant's principles of universality and humanity can be viewed as expressions of the principle of reciprocity. The principle of universality calls for acting only in ways in which you would be willing that all persons act in the same or similar circumstances, even if the roles were reversed. The principle of humanity calls for acting only in ways in which you treat human beings, including yourself, always as ends and never as means only. These principles in combination call for impartial action, treating persons equally, respecting persons, and not exploiting or manipulating them as objects or things.[10] Mill writes,

> [T]he happiness which forms the utilitarian standard of what is right conduct is not the agent's own happiness but that of all concerned. As between his own happiness and that of others, utilitarianism requires him to be as strictly impartial as a disinterested and benevolent spectator. In the golden rule of Jesus of Nazareth, we read the complete spirit of the ethics of utility. "To do as you would be done by," and "to love your neighbor as yourself," constitutes the ideal perfection of utilitarian morality.[11]

In estimating the worth or value of this basic common moral principle, it is important to distinguish between the principle as a moral ideal and the specific ways the ideal has been applied. At least three things need to be kept in mind.

(1) The human mind seems to be almost infinitely flexible in the ways in which it is able to use, twist, modify, and reinterpret moral principles in order to provide justification for various types of control, domination, exploitation, and discrimination. Thus, consistent and just application of the principle of reciprocity requires constant vigilance against the egoistic impulse.

(2) Many different kinds of beliefs–metaphysical, empirical, cultural, and political–influence the concrete moral judgments that human beings make. These beliefs often differ widely from culture to culture and from age

to age. Even if persons and peoples can agree on the foundational intuitions and principles of morality, disagreement on morally appropriate behavior in specific contexts may exist on account of these different beliefs. Since these beliefs often contradict each other, some of them are true and some of them are false. It is possible that, with regard to some of these beliefs related to a specific context, all of them are false or at least only partially true. Consistent and just application of the principle of reciprocity requires constant effort in striving to correct erroneous beliefs that influence our moral judgments.

(3) Some disagreements may arise over applications of basic principles and intuitions in particular contexts that are not due to the distorting influences of either the egoistic impulse or erroneous beliefs but to different perceptions of human worth and dignity or how a given action impacts upon human worth and dignity. These different perceptions are due to different levels of grasping human worth in its fullness or different understandings of the nature of the impact upon human beings of the action in question. Consistent and just application of the principle of reciprocity requires constant effort to grasp the full meaning of human worth and dignity and to gain a full understanding of how specific actions are either consistent or inconsistent with that worth and dignity.

So although persons may agree on the foundational intuitions and principles of morality, they may disagree on the moral justifiability of such things, among others, as abortion, euthanasia, capital punishment, assisted suicide, the practice of suttee, and female genital circumcision. These disagreements could be due to the desire to rationalize morally questionable practices, the application of erroneous beliefs to the practice, or an inadequate understanding of human worth and dignity and how particular actions impact upon it. The successful resolution of these disagreements depends upon the willingness of the disputants to work at identifying and eliminating irrelevant egoistic concerns and erroneous beliefs from their moral deliberations, as well as their willingness to gain a full understanding of human worth and dignity and the actual impact of particular actions upon it. In principle, there is nothing that militates against the possibility of doing these things.

2. Human Rights

Another important language (besides the language of the various expressions of the principle of reciprocity and the principles derived from it) that gives expression to or articulates the fundamental demand that "human beings must be treated humanely" is the language of universal human rights. This language and its development has a relatively long history. It may be true that the famous declarations of human rights in previous centuries, such as the Magna Carta, the Declaration of Independence, the Declaration of the Rights of Man, and the United States Bill of Rights, were not declarations of universal human rights, even though they were set forth in universal or pseudo-universal form (for example, by talking about all "men" or all persons).[12] But the important declarations of this century, especially the Universal Declaration of Human Rights (1948), and also subsequent declarations emanating from the United Nations (for example, the 1966 Covenants on Civil, Political, Economic, and Cultural Rights), clearly affirm universal human rights.

According to the prevailing language of human rights, a right is "an entitlement to demand a certain performance or forbearance on pain of sanction for noncompliance...."[13] A moral right is "a right regarded as authoritative in that it takes precedence over other action and is legitimate...for considering the welfare of others...."[14] A human right is a universal moral right that belongs to all human beings *qua* human beings and that protects something of indispensable human importance. Examples of human rights set forth in the Universal Declaration of Human Rights are the rights to life, liberty, and security of person; the right not to be held in slavery or servitude; the right not to be subjected to torture or to cruel, inhuman, or degrading treatment or punishment; the right to equal protection of the law; the right to freedom of thought, conscience, and religion; the right to freedom of opinion and expression; the right to peaceful assembly and association; and the right to a standard of living adequate for health and well-being including adequate food, clothing, shelter, and medical care.[15] Most human rights, whether negative (forbidding certain kinds of treatment) or positive (requiring certain kinds of treatment), are not absolute and could be justifiably suspended or forfeited under certain specific conditions, where there is a conflict with other rights, when individuals voluntarily forgo pressing their rights, or when individuals have violated the rights of others. Some human rights are, or come as close as possible to being, absolute rights, rights to which there are no exceptions and that do not conflict with other rights. In this latter category are such rights as the negative rights not to be tortured, treated in a barbarous manner, brainwashed, exploited, or enslaved.[16] These absolute, or virtually absolute, rights are primary, basic, or "irreducible core" human rights.[17] David Little sees each of these rights as "a fundamental protection against the arbitrary infliction of severe suffering."[18] Violations of these rights are offenses against the "foundations of human life."[19] Joel Feinberg sees these rights as expressions of a right to a kind of respect he calls "an inviolable dignity."[20]

3. Human Worth, Value, and Dignity

The principle of reciprocity, in its many variations and in the many forms of its principles of application, is a principle of love, compassion, and generous concern for the welfare of others. It is, to quote Hick again, "the utterly basic principle that it is evil to cause suffering to others and good to benefit others and to alleviate or prevent their sufferings." Statements of human rights, especially those of primary or basic rights, are making the same kinds of claims. Presupposed by these principles and human rights statements is a fundamental understanding of human beings. This is the understanding, intuition, recognition, sense, perception, grasping, or apprehension of the worth, value, dignity, pricelessness, or preciousness of human life. Without this understanding, the moral necessity of not causing harm to others, protecting others from harm, and promoting the welfare of others, as well as the moral insistence that human beings have rights to this inviolability, these protections and this welfare are left hanging without adequate grounding. This understanding is the source of the generation of these principles and statements.

In talking about this understanding of the worth of persons, I will be using primarily the word "intuition." By using the word "intuition" I am not implying anything about the way intuitions are known or how they are known. I am implying only that the propositions that state what it is we intuit cannot be proved, at least not in the traditional way of understanding proof in terms of statements that follow with logical necessity from true and uncontested premises. It does not follow from this that the intuition of the worth of persons cannot be supported with evidence or reasons. It does follow that this evidence and/or these reasons can be challenged. With the intuition of the worth of persons, we are at an ultimate starting point for, or a beginning foundation of, the generation of basic principles of action and statements of basic human rights.

Philip Hallie offers some interesting and helpful thoughts on the intuition of the worth of persons in his book about the amazing work of the people of the small French village of Le Chambon during World War II.[21] During the years 1940-1944, this small village of three thousand people, committed to the philosophy and practice of nonviolence, rescued from the Vichy government and the Nazis, and smuggled into neutral Switzerland, some five to six thousand persons, mostly Jews, many of them children. In the final chapter of the book that tells this incredible story, the chapter entitled "How Goodness Happened Here," Hallie talks about the primary intuition of the worth of persons that undergirded and informed the rescue efforts of those four years. This intuition or presumption was that all human life is precious. This sense of preciousness was related to a sense of pricelessness. Hallie writes, "the people of Le Chambon would not give up a life for any price–for their own comfort, for their own safety, for patriotism, or for legality. For them, human life had no price; it had only dignity." Hallie goes on to point out that the saving of children was a very important part of the rescue efforts, and then suggests that an exploration of the idea of the preciousness of a child's life may help us to begin to understand the idea of the pricelessness of all human life.[22] Consider the following quotations from Hallie:

For us children are the springtime, the creative burgeoning of human life. They are not only *in* that springtime; they *are* that springtime.

Except when they are ill or hungry or in terror, their faces are fresh, free
of the scars of old passions and enduring responsibilities. They seem to
breathe their own excess of vitality into the things they touch or try to
touch. Their surprise (and they are themselves surprises) sometimes
makes us older ones to draw close to them....

And when they are tortured, when they are deliberately broken and
killed, it is spring that is being attacked. It is as if the living center of
human life were being dirtied and smashed.

Insofar as one can realize what is happening and what is evil about that
murder, one is realizing the pricelessness of a child's life.[23]

It was not just the intuition of the preciousness of a child's life that moved
and motivated the Chambonnais, but the preciousness of all human life. We
also may begin to grasp life's value by reflecting upon our own adult lives,
especially in times of enjoyment, whether times of profound enjoyment or
times of ordinary enjoyment. In these times, we say or are saying "yes" to
life–"yes, life is worth living," "yes, life is worth choosing." In these times,
Hallie suggests, "[w]ithout noticing it, our bodies and our minds are usually
celebrating a conviction deeper than words can express, a conviction that life
is incomparably more valuable to us than death."[24]

Hallie believes that "[t]o realize the preciousness of life is to realize its
value to all of us,"[25] and that "[s]uch a realization, such an imaginative perception of the connection between the preciousness of my life and the
preciousness of other lives, is the vital center of life-and-death ethics."[26] "If
we do not discern that connection," Hallie continues, "the 'laws' of ethics are
empty patterns of sounds and shapes, without meaning or force."[27] I myself
see no reason to limit this realization to life-and-death ethics, that is, to those
regions of human interaction and experience concerned with matters of life
and death. This realization, this intuition, is the vital center of all ethics. The
overwhelming importance of this intuition may be dramatically demonstrated
to us in life-and-death situations, but it is crucial to all regions of human
experience touched by questions of right and wrong, good and evil.

Although many philosophers do not highlight, stress, or articulate this
primary intuition of the worth of persons as they build their ethical systems, it
seems to me that it is the primary pretheoretical intuition behind their efforts
and the necessary recognition that enables them to get their systems going.

A good example is the ethics of Kant. It is possible to see embedded in
his principles of universality and humanity, or presupposed by them, an
intuition of the worth, value, and dignity of human beings. If we ask Kant
why we should be unwilling to treat other persons in ways we would find
unacceptable if we were on the receiving end of the actions, why we should
treat persons as ends and not as means, why we should regard and respect

them as persons in their own right and not manipulate, use, and exploit them as objects or things, Kant essentially answers, because they are the kinds of beings they are, autonomous, self-legislating, free rational beings. What is this answer other than an acknowledgment of a pretheoretical primary intuition of the worth and dignity of human beings? Grounded in this intuition, the principles of universality and humanity emerge. It is this intuition that gets the whole business of morality in general going and the subsequent business of Kant's normative ethical theory going as well.[28]

4. Nourishment of the Primary Intuition

The strength and clarity of the intuition of the preciousness of human beings fade in and out, wax and wane in the light of one's experiences and the experiences of other persons. On the one hand, experiencing unjust, cruel, violent, or harmful treatment leads one to question the preciousness of at least the victimizer and even, sometimes, strangely enough, of oneself.[29] Reading or hearing about the brutal treatment of other human beings (in, for example, the former Yugoslavia, the Middle East, or Rwanda) also raises doubts about that intuition. On the other hand, the experience of just, kind, compassionate, caring treatment, or reading or hearing about the same treatment of others, often brings that intuition into sharper focus and reaffirms it.

The fact that the sense of the value of human life fades in and out in the light of our experiences and perceptions makes it of critical importance that we keep this sense strong and clear. Hallie tells us that the moral leadership of Andre Trocmé (the Huguenot minister of the Protestant Temple in Le Chambon) consisted in keeping the perception of the preciousness of human beings green both in his life and in the lives of other Chambonnais.[30] One of the major tasks of peacemakers is keeping this intuition green in their lives and in the lives of those they seek to influence for good. In many cases, it will not be so much a matter of keeping the intuition green in the lives of others but of helping to bring that greening up out of a deep dark dormancy by providing various kinds of nourishment.

But how do we keep the intuition green? Or bring it back from dormancy? I doubt that there is any list of specific things that will be effective with all human beings in all circumstances. The nourishment must be suited to the particular contexts in which particular human beings find themselves. But there are some general things that can and need to be done. Among them are the following:

(1) Nurturing and encouraging a healthy self-respect. The achievement of self-respect requires honest self-examination, the avoidance of self-deception about one's strengths and weaknesses, self-discipline, and becoming a person of character. Healthy self-respect has little chance of emerging in situations where structures of violence, oppression, discrimination, and injustice tend, and are often designed, to break it down or destroy it. In these

kinds of situations, peacemakers must not be part of these structures, must oppose them, and must strive to replace them with structures of justice. In achieving self-respect one also recognizes one's worth, value, and dignity as a human being. Self-respect is often, if not always, the necessary requisite for respect for others. And in respecting and regarding others, we recognize their worth and dignity.

(2) Encouraging contemplation of and reflection upon the lives, actions, and achievements of human beings, including both moral heroes (or moral saints) and ordinary exemplary human beings. Especially important is introducing persons to examples and models of nonviolent life and action. It also may be necessary to redefine the ideas of hero and saint.

(3) Encouraging awareness of and reflection upon the capacities of human beings. Included here would be the capacities to think, reason, choose, create, discover, work, build, appreciate, love, care, sacrifice, value, and evaluate. Reflecting upon these capacities and their positive and constructive possibilities might lead to a sense of awe and wonder about the kinds of beings we are.

(4) Fostering awareness of a sense of the uniqueness of human life in general but also, most importantly, of individual human beings.

(5) Developing a keener awareness of our "shared fate" on this planet. Several important dimensions of this awareness are the following:

(a) the perception that all human beings have plans, projects, hopes, dreams, goals, needs, fears, anxieties, times of joy and happiness, and times of despair and boredom;

(b) an awareness of the finitude, precariousness, and frailty of human existence, including our vulnerability to disease, accident, chance, circumstance, and death; and

(c) a sense of our dependence upon others to live and to do the things we want to do, understood in terms of mutual dependence or interdependence.

(6) Gaining and helping others to develop the powers of understanding, empathy, and sympathy; a keener sense of justice; and the virtues of caring and love.

In addition sometimes the worth of human beings is intuited or recognized at the same time as, or along with, the intuition of the moral wrongness (the moral inappropriateness) of various types of violent, cruel, harmful, unjust behavior. Part of the process of nurturing the intuition of the preciousness of human life might involve the exposure of persons to a clear description or picturing or imagining of what actually is being done to or happening to persons as victims of various types of harmful action. Once persons recognize the wrongness of certain types of treatment and the worth of human beings, they can be exposed to alternate ways of relating to persons and resolving conflicts with them. It is in these contexts that they are open to a serious consideration of nonviolence and nonviolent alternatives.

5. Realistic Assessment of Human Nature

In all our efforts to bring to consciousness a sense of the worth or value of human life, we must avoid the adoption of unrealistic, overly optimistic, highly utopian views of human nature. Avoidance of these views requires a thorough understanding of the moral weaknesses and failures of human beings as well as of the evils that human beings have perpetrated and continue to perpetrate. We must become aware of and be exposed to the negative side of human nature and behavior, in our own lives as well as in the lives of others. Exposure to such horrors as the Holocaust, warfare, murder, assault, rape, spouse abuse, and child abuse; exposure to such evils as colonialism, racism, and sexism; and exposure to such realities as hatred, the desire for revenge and retaliation, jealousy, and envy is necessary for a realistic assessment of human nature and human possibilities. The recovery and nurture of hope can be achieved only in the face of these realities. And hope must be distinguished from wishful thinking and utopian daydreaming. Nothing is more prone to crush incipient hope than an unrealistic assessment of human nature and possibilities.

We must avoid dwelling upon, becoming morbidly obsessed with, lured by, fascinated with, captured by the evil possibilities of human behavior, lest we become entranced by the sirens of nihilistic, skeptical, cynical, pessimistic, and relativistic thinking. These dangers are not chimerical or imaginary. Having become more fully aware of the negative dimensions of human nature, we must return to concentration upon the positive dimensions and possibilities of our beings but we return in a moderated and duly humbled state of mind, because we remember the evils that have been and are perpetrated by human beings, and we know these evils can be repeated in the future.

In this moderated and reminiscent state, even though concentrating upon the positive dimensions and possibilities of our beings, we may be sorely tempted to bury in the recesses of our subconscious a recognition of the preciousness of human life, at least a recognition of the preciousness of all human beings, especially the human beings who are victimizers, and perpetrators of violence and injustice. If in these latter contexts we can keep green the perception of the preciousness of all human beings, with the concomitant sense that we should treat them humanely, we make (or may make) one or more of a number of mental moves, among which are the following: (1) We can distinguish between persons and their actions and say that the actions are evil but the persons are precious. (2) We can distinguish, perhaps as Kant might do, between good wills and potential good wills. Not all human beings are good wills, but all are potential good wills, and as potential good wills the victimizers are to be respected as persons. (3) We might say that the essential human core, the essential humanity, of the victimizers has been crushed or buried due to extremely harsh treatment or circumstances, and that although, as Aristotle might say, goodness of character might shine through the harshest of circumstances in some few cases, in most cases it does not. (4) We might say that the victimizers do not really know what they are doing, that they are fundamentally or essentially ignorant of what it is to be a human being and what it is to treat others humanely. (5) We might say that the victimizers are acting out of a misguided sense of justice, an irrational commitment to ideals, or a blind sense of loyalty. Hopefully, none of these "moves," in their specific contexts, shake out as rationalizations that we are engaging in to save at all costs our intuition of the value of human beings. They are moves that, in view of our primary intuition, give us perspectives from which we are able to understand how human beings of value and worth can engage in such evil actions, to consider the possibility that the victimizers might themselves be "converted," and to stay our hands in responding to the victimizers in kind and, thus, becoming like them and adding to the amount of evil in the world. But in all this thinking about responding to victimizers and their actions (evil persons and evil actions), we must not forget our primary responsibility to the victims, to protect them from harm and to take what actions are necessary to bring to an end the evil actions directed against them.

A realistic assessment of human nature helps us to see clearly and starkly what peacemakers are up against, how precarious and fragile their gains are, and the necessity of constant vigilance in their respective tasks. Their general tasks are two in number. One is the task of nurturing the recognition of the preciousness of human life. The other is the task of nurturing the subsequent commitment to the fundamental principle of reciprocity and basic human rights. Grounded in this recognition and commitment, we can generate additional principles, guidelines, standards, and directives for the creation and protection of a culture of nonviolence and respect for life. Without the acknowledgment of and commitment to this kind of common universal global ethics, peacemaking stands little chance of being even minimally successful in the modern world.

Notes

1. *UNESCO, Thinking Ahead: UNESCO and the Challenges of Today and Tomorrow* (Paris: UNESCO, 1977), p. 62, quoted in Birgit Brock-Utne, *Educating for Peace: A Feminist Perspective* (New York: Pergamon, 1985), p. 2.

2. *UNESCO, Second Medium-Term Plan* (1981-1989) (Paris: UNESCO, 1983), p. 259, quoted in Brock-Utne, *Educating for Peace,* p. 3.

3. See Elise Boulding, "The Pacifist as Citizen," in *Pacifism and Citizenship: Can They Coexist?,* ed. Kenneth M. Jensen and Kimber M. Schraub (Washington: United States Institute of Peace, 1991), pp. 9-10.

4. See Hans Küng and Karl-Joseph Kuschel, eds., *A Global Ethic: The Declaration of the Parliament of the World's Religions* (New York: Continuum, 1994), p. 23.

5. John Hick, *An Interpretation of Religion: Human Responses to the Transcendent* (New Haven, Conn.: Yale University Press, 1989), p. 312.

6. *Ibid.*, pp. 316-325.

7. *Ibid.*, p. 313.

8. Hans Küng, "The History, Significance, and Method of the Declaration toward a Global Ethic," in *A Global Ethic: The Declaration of the Parliament of the World's Religions,* ed. Küng and Kuschel, pp. 71-72.

9. Hick, *Interpretation of Religion*, p. 313. Brackets are Hick's.

10. See Immanuel Kant, *Fundamental Principles of the Metaphysics of Morals,* in *Classics in Western Philosophy,* ed. Steven M. Cahn (Indianapolis, Ind.: Hackett, 1977), pp. 840-886.

11. John Stuart Mill, *Utilitarianism,* in *Classics in Western Philosophy,* ed. Cahn, p. 902.

12. See Annette Baier, "Claims, Rights, Responsibilities," in *Prospects for a Common Morality,* ed. Gene Outka and John P. Reeder, Jr. (Princeton, N.J.: Princeton University Press, 1993), pp. 150-154.

13. David Little, "The Nature and Basis of Human Rights," in *Prospects for a Common Morality,* ed. Outka and Reeder, p. 82.

14. *Ibid.*

15. See Universal Declaration of Human Rights, in *Basic Documents of Human Rights,* ed. Ian Brownlie (Oxford: Clarendon Press, 1971), pp. 106-112, arts. 3-5, 7, 18-20, and 25.

16. See Little, "The Nature and Basis of Human Rights," pp. 91-92; and Joel Feinberg, *Social Philosophy* (Englewood Cliffs, N.J.: Prentice-Hall, 1993), pp. 86-88 and 94-97.

17. Little, "The Nature and Basis of Human Rights," pp. 91-92.

18. *Ibid.*, p. 92.

19. *Ibid.*, p. 90.

20. Feinberg, *Social Philosophy*, p. 97.

21. Philip Hallie, *Lest Innocent Blood Be Shed* (New York: Harper and Row, 1979).

22. *Ibid.*, p. 274.

23. *Ibid.*, pp. 274-275.

24. *Ibid.*, p. 276.

25. *Ibid.*

26. *Ibid.*, p. 277.

27. *Ibid.*

28. Kant, *Fundamental Principles*, pp. 840-856.

29. Phillip Hallie, "From Cruelty to Goodness," in *Vice and Virtue in Everyday Life,* ed. Christina Sommers and Fred Sommers (New York: Harcourt Brace, 4th ed., 1997), p. 10.

30. Hallie, *Lest Innocent Blood Be Shed,* p. 277.

Three

PEACEMAKING AND PROCEDURAL JUSTICE: A CRITIQUE

Judith Presler

Stuart Hampshire, in *Innocence and Experience*, presents a theory of procedural justice that provides a mechanism for international conflict resolution.[1] Hampshire introduces the book by relating his experience in the 1930s and 1940s as a student of philosophy and an intelligence officer in Britain. He witnessed extremes of poverty and wealth in Wales and sharp political divisions among his classmates in the university. As an intelligence officer, he interrogated German war criminals. Later he was dismayed to discover that some of his own colleagues were double agents.[2] His experiences informed his later reflections upon justice and goodness. He concluded that abstract theorizing about goodness (innocence) is inapplicable to the complex and equivocal situations that arise in political life (experience).[3] In responding to his experience, he develops a theory of procedural justice applicable to the complex reality of political life. His procedural justice, he thinks, unlike philosophers' theoretical accounts of political good, does not entail the evil of imposing one notion of good upon all. He also thinks that his theory avoids relativism. According to Hampshire, relativism leads to the evil of eschewing all goodness and justice. The first evil is a dogmatic imposition that deprives people of the right to define goodness for themselves. The second evil is a reign of darkness that denies the existence of all values, even the universal negative values, that is, the avoidance of pain, slavery, and death. In this chapter I offer a brief account of Hampshire's theory and describe its use in historical cases of international conflict resolution. Then I critique the cases and the theory itself.

1. Hampshire's Theory

Hampshire's purpose is to devise a theory of justice that can apply universally to humankind. His argument has three strands that converge upon a theory of procedural justice. The first strand of the argument is Hampshire's discernment of the common human way of dealing with practical problems. The second strand is his observation that human beings universally eschew the great evils of pain, enslavement, and death. The third strand in the argument is his assertion of the importance of the singularity of human beings.

A. First Strand in the Argument

Hampshire first suggests that all human beings at all times and in all places approach practical decision-making in the same basic way, both publicly and privately. He says: "Wherever and whenever human societies exist...issues of policy will be debated in some assembly of chosen persons....The institution of articulating and reviewing contrary opinions on policy is of necessity species-wide."[4] He offers as an example of an assembly of chosen persons the council of war in Homer's *Iliad*. "The deliberations of the council of war in the *Iliad* are paralleled by the inner discussion preceding action within the soul of any prudent man."[5] He adds later that "the practice of promoting and accepting arguments for and against a proposal" is "the core of practical rationality." He regards this procedure to be as universal as counting. The procedure is both adversarial and judicial. It is adversarial because opposing sides are represented. It is judicial because some arguments will be accepted and others will not, so that "in the end a Solomonic judgment will normally be made."[6]

Hampshire then claims that the canons of rationality in practical reasoning are the canons of fairness. If all the arguments are not heard and considered, "the final judgment is tainted with bias and unfairness, even if, considered in abstraction, it seems to be fair" and to be the one that would have been reached if the argument had been complete and fair. Justice and fairness, he claims, are "always in part procedural notions." A decision is "just and fair only if the reasoning that supports it has been adequate, and the main relevant considerations have in fact been impartially weighed in the balance."[7]

According to Hampshire, then, the methodology of procedural justice and the canons of fairness are written into the very being of humanity, and are familiar to all of us as the very way in which we reason toward decisions in practical affairs and as the very criteria we inherently require and accept in such reasoning. Procedural justice is universally applicable and acceptable.

B. Second Strand in the Argument

Hampshire distinguishes his theory from other theories of justice that rest upon a notion of a "single substantial morality, including a conception of good and of human virtue,"[8] or upon "[s]ubstantial conceptions of justice and fairness" that are "evidently involved in the distribution of absolute goods and in the avoidance of evils."[9] Founders of such theories assume that their notions of good or justice are universal. But, Hampshire argues, they are not. He then argues that, while a positive notion of good is not universal to hu-mankind, a negative notion is. The negative notion is that pain, enslavement, and death are not good; they are evil. No human being desires these things. It is natural to all human beings in virtue of being living creatures with all the needs that are common to living creatures to desire to avoid these things.[10] "In so far as the great evils are man-made, as in a tyranny's domination by killing, imprisonment, and enslavement, they are so far great moral evils, although the Communist leader, or the Grand Inquisitor, will refer to his own conception of the good as redeeming the evil."[11]

In other words, evil is a result of human agency, some humans causing death, pain, and oppression in others, as happens under tyranny. Examples of tyrants are a communist leader such as Joseph Stalin and Fyodor Dostoyevsky's Grand Inquisitor bringing about evil in the service of an ideal, distributive justice and salvation of the soul, respectively.

Given the universal abhorrence of such evils as oppression, misery, and the destruction of life, it is rational for all "to look for a non-divisive and generally acceptable conception of justice, however thin a conception this may be, amounting at its minimum only to fair procedures of negotiation."[12] Hampshire's procedural justice is the universal and nondivisive conception of justice that provides those fair procedures.

C. Third Strand in the Argument

Having established the commonality of the methodology and canons of procedural justice to all human beings and the lack of commonality as concerns a positive notion of good, Hampshire next argues for the singularity of each human being. The implication of his argument is that since each human is unique, a universal concept of good cannot be applied to people, nor should such a single concept be applied to people. Instead, each human being, as a result of his or her unique perspective on reality, unique amalgam of memories, particular imagination, as well as choices and talents, has his or her own particular goals and ends (concepts of good) that are not universalizable. There is not a single good or set of goods common to all human beings.[13]

A universal moral theory cannot be based upon a concept of good, because there is not, nor should there be, a single concept of good applied to all human beings. One person's concept of good very possibly is in conflict with another's; one culture's concept of good, in conflict with another's. To take one concept of good as "The Good" and to attempt to impose it upon persons who do not accept that concept of good, is unjust. To take one concept of perfection and to impose it as the proper end or goal upon those who do not agree with that concept of perfection, is unjust.[14]

His view that there is a variety of concepts of good is not moral relativism, according to Hampshire. It is simply the recognition that people have different concepts of good and that, therefore, the good cannot be the source of universal morality: instead procedural justice is the source of universal morality. Good is a positive moral notion; but there are different legitimate notions of good. There is one moral universal–procedural justice.

Hampshire claims that "observable facts of human nature, evident in history and in introspection," show us that the singularity and individuality characteristic of human beings is valuable and ought to be cultivated. To promote what he refers to as "normality" as a species-wide idea of humanity is to repress the valuable singularity and individuality of human beings. To the contrary, to value individuality and to value procedural justice are "two fundamental invariant elements in the various conceptions of the good which are defensible," serve the interests of individuals, of humanity in general, and of our descendants.[15]

D. Three Strands Come Together

The three strands taken together support the view that only a theory of procedural justice can be universally applicable to all people. Hampshire writes:

> The arguments of this book are throughout directed against th[e] Enlightenment conception of a single substantial morality, including a conception of the good and of human virtue, as being the bond that unites humanity in universal sentiments or in universal moral beliefs. Humanity is united in the recognition of the great evils which render life scarcely bearable, and which undermine any specific way of life and any specific conception of the good and of the essential virtues. The glory of humanity is in the diversity and originality of its positive aspirations and different ways of life, and the only universal and positive moral requirement is the application of procedural justice and fairness to the handling of moral conflicts between them.[16]

He regards conceptions of substantive justice and fairness to be conceptions of distributive justice, different ones of which derive from different conceptions of good. About these conceptions of good there cannot be agreement. "Universal agreement can be expected in the name of rationality, only on the methods of fair argument which will arbitrate between the different answers to...questions" of substantive justice.[17] When writing about the result of an application of procedural justice, he says that even after negotiation, there will still be a conflict of duties. For each of the parties involved in the negotiation, there will be duties following from that party's substantial conception of justice and other duties following from the minimal, procedural notion of justice. It is not the case that one will or must always prefer the duties of procedural justice.

> If your adversary in negotiation obstinately required you to sacrifice a number of the more essential features of the best way of life, as you see it, you might reasonably decide that this is morally impossible and that the

cost of peaceful co-existence on an agreed and fair basis has been set un-acceptably high. But it would be contrary to reason to refuse to abandon some less essential features of your preferred way of life in a reasonable exchange of concessions with your adversary.[18]

Injustice occurs only when conflict could be avoided by fair and equal negoti-ation, and is not so avoided.

In summary, Hampshire argues: (1) Since practical decision-making is common to all human beings, the "procedure" of procedural justice is basic to all people. (2) Since the desire to avoid pain, enslavement, and death is com-mon to all human beings, the minimal negative goods of procedural justice–minimizing harm, slavery, and death–are universal goods. (3) Since no single positive conception of good is common to all human beings, it is unjust to impose the goods of one person or people upon another person or people.

A theory of justice that properly can be applied universally is one that has very minimal goals (negative goals) and very minimal rules (procedural rules). Procedural justice can serve to limit the imposition of suffering and death upon persons involved in conflict while respecting their different positive conceptions of good. There will certainly be situations in which the differences are irreconcilable, even under the aegis of procedural justice; how-ever, in many cases the negative goals of minimizing harm and death can be achieved. For Hampshire, justice is both procedural and the minimizing of harm that results from just procedures.

2. Historical Examples of Procedural Justice at Work

I am at first inclined to conclude that procedural justice, as Hampshire con-ceives it, is an excellent answer to the question, How can we peacefully and fairly resolve international conflicts? Adversaries must sit down together and mutually assert, argue for, and examine the conflicting conceptions of good that are the source of the adversarial relationship. All of the relevant evidence must be heard, all of the points of view aired, and all of the values made clear. The canons of rationality in practical reasoning must be applied throughout the deliberations.[19] Then the participants may attempt to agree upon a fair resolution of the conflict, a resolution that allows each as many of the high priorities as possible for the sake of peaceful co-existence and minimal justice.

Hampshire claims that the council of war in the *Iliad* is an example of human deliberation that is universal and that carries with it the criteria of fairness.[20] He also claims that procedural justice would be intelligible to the great political theorists Thucydides, Aristotle, Plato, Edmund Burke, John Stuart Mill, and Alexis de Toqueville. He claims that these theorists could discuss procedural justice and that "[t]he discussion would touch on the perennial topics of the underpinnings and origins of justice, of the universal and conventional elements in justice, and of the relation of private to public morality."[21] On the other hand, he also says that every experienced political leader from Thucydides onwards has remarked on the unpredictability of political outcomes and on the fact that most political choices are choices between evils. In essence, Hampshire suggests, there is an enormous gap between the virtues discussed by political theorists (innocence) and the virtues of someone actually exercising political power (experience). The former virtues form part of an orthodoxy that does not recognize the actual differences among human beings and the consequent legitimate differences in their various conceptions of good. The latter virtues pertain to competently dealing with conflicts between substantive justice and political expediency. For the person exercising political power, the just choice is determined by procedural justice.[22] Hampshire says:

> I am representing procedural justice as regulating the necessary conflict between chosen roles, with their attached obligations, and not as a means of making these roles coherent within an accepted and overarching whole. Justice is a means of enabling them to co-exist in civil society and, as far as possible, to survive, without any substantial reconciliation between them, and without a search for a common ground. It is neither possible nor desirable that the mutually hostile conceptions of the good should be melted down to form a single and agreed conception of the human good. A machinery of arbitration is needed, and this machinery has to be established by negotiation. Justice can then clear the path to recognition of untidy and temporary compromises between incompatible visions of a better way of life.[23]

Hampshire then is proposing a theory of justice that pertains to the difficult decisions that confront international peacemakers. Let us examine some examples of international conflict.

Because Thucydides heads Hampshire's lists of political theorists and political leaders and because Thucydides, in *The Peloponnesian War*, recounts debates concerning conflicts between or about sovereign states, I first examine two debates from his history. Then I examine two modern conflicts.

A. Thucydides' Account of the Debate about the Mitylenian Revolt

After quelling, in the fifth year of the war, the revolt in the city of Mitylene on the island of Lesbos, the Athenians debated what punishment should be levied against the Mitylenians. Thucydides selected from among the many speeches the two most radical of the opposing views offered by the most articulate speakers, Cleon and Diodotus.

Cleon spoke for the harsh punishment of putting all of the Mitylenian men to death and enslaving all of the women and children, both the aristocrats, who instigated the revolution, and the common people (the *demos*, normally natural allies of democratic Athens), who joined in the revolution. Among his reasons were the following: (1) The radical treatment would serve as a deterrent to other states considering revolution. (2) To show pity, sentiment, and compassion for people who willingly offended the Athenian rulers would be a failing fatal to empire. Such feelings must not be indulged in this case. These people will remain enemies of Athens irrespective of how they are treated. (3) Exacting a harsh penalty demonstrates the rightness of the rule of the empire, whereas not doing so demonstrates that the revolutionaries were right to revolt and that revolution on the part of other states in the empire is also justified and will not be harshly punished.

Diodotus's argument for putting to death only the leaders of the revolution was as follows: (1) Since revolutionaries usually believe when they initiate a revolution that the possibility of success is worth the attempt, the radical punishment would not serve as a deterrent to revolution but as an inducement to each revolutionary to fight to the death, if death is the fate of the defeated. This view would not serve the self-interest of the Athenians, since they would be involved in a longer war against revolutionaries and a war more costly in materials and men. It would further not be in the interest of the Athenians because the ultimate prize of the counter-revolutionary war, the conquered state, would be in ruins. (2) The less harsh punishment derives not from some soft notion of justice, but from self-interest, as described in the prior point. (3) Punishing the common people in this case provides a dangerous precedent. If the natural allies of Athens cannot assume that their natural alliance will provide them protection against death, they will be less likely to aid Athens by fighting against the aristocrats in their own cities.

Diodotus's argument won a slim majority in the assembly, which reversed the harsh punishment for which it had voted on the previous day. [24]

B. Thucydides' Account of the Athenians' Conference with the Melians

In the sixteenth year of the war, the Athenians sent an enormous military expedition to the island of Melos. The Melians, though a colony of Sparta, had remained neutral in the war and wished to continue to be neutral and free, fighting neither on the side of Athens nor of Sparta. The Athenians demanded that the Melians be a part of the Athenian empire. Before attacking, the Athenian generals sent envoys to the Melian magistrates to negotiate.

The Athenians argued, essentially, that might makes right. They explained that by coming to an agreement with the much larger and stronger Athens, the Melians would gain the advantage of not suffering the worst consequences of death and destruction. The Athenians would gain not only a colony not destroyed by war but also the reputation of a strong empire. The Melians remaining free would attest to the weakness of Athens; the colonization of Melos or, if necessary, a battle in which Melos were captured, would attest to the strength of Athens. Thus the Athenians could not allow Melos to remain free.

The Melians averred that they would trust in the gods and in the assistance of the Spartans. The Athenians averred that they too would trust in the gods and that past history did not suggest that the gods were more likely to assist the Melians than the Athenians. They also pointed out that the Spartans were not known for courting danger and, thus, would be unlikely to come to the aid of the Melians.

The Melians decided to fight. They eventually lost and the Athenians put to death every Melian man, enslaved every Melian woman and child, and colonized the island with its own people. [25]

C. Modern Conflict Between the Israelis and the Palestinians

The initial position of the Palestinians (along with all of the Arab states of the Middle East) was that they would reclaim Palestine from the Israelis after pushing the Israelis into the sea. The initial position of the Israelis was to remain a sovereign state in Palestine. At the present time, there is an intermittent discussion going on between the Israelis and the Palestinians. Among the issues that the two parties dispute are the possession of land, such as the Gaza strip, the Golan Heights, and Jerusalem, and the disruptive activities of Israelis (for example, creating settlements and imprisoning terrorists) and Palestinians (for example, committing acts of terrorism and quickly releasing their own terrorists from their prisons). What is referred to as the "peace process" has been slow going. The representatives of the two sides seem to be quite capable of expressing their values and priorities. Each wants to possess more land than is compatible with what the other side wants and each wants to continue activities that the other side finds intolerable. These values are either expressed in peace process discussions or are exhibited in actions. Mediators have been unsuccessful in bridging the gap between the values of the two sides. So long as the peace process has been going on, there has been less violence than previously.

D. Modern Conflict Among the Bosnians

The discussions of the Dayton Peace Accords aimed toward establishing a series of practical steps to be taken by the Bosnians (with the assistance of U.N. forces) to establish peace and order in that country. While some progress has been made in Bosnia, it has been much slower than expected. For example, American President Bill Clinton thought he would be able to order troops home from Bosnia much sooner than he has been able to. Further, one of the original leaders of the fighting in Bosnia instigated battle against another ethic group, the Albanians in Kosovo. Serbian leader Slobodan Milosevic seemed not to have learned about peace from the Bosnia conflict and its aftermath, nor from the peace talks and the order presumably imposed by those talks. Perhaps he has learned that he can make war with impunity.

The conflict in Bosnia was significantly fueled by discourse (rhetoric). The "ethnic groups" in this population–Serbs, Croats and Bosnian Muslims– are, more accurately speaking, culturally distinct, rather than ethnically distinct. The principal distinguishing cultural characteristic of the these mainly secular people is religion. Croats are culturally Roman Catholic Christians; Serbs, Orthodox Christians; Bosnian Muslims, of course, Muslims. The fundamental source of the conflict was the desire for power on the part of the leaders vying for hegemony in the Balkans. They fed the desire in their people for more land. They fanned the flames of ethnic hatred, fear, and the desire for revenge, which resulted in "ethnic cleansing." The leaders of each cultural group convinced their followers that their group had been victimized by the others. In this way they fired up fervent ethnic hatred and aggression against fellow countrymen, former neighbors, former friends, and sometimes relatives. The rhetorical instruments were (1) quasi-mythical accounts of medieval history in which vicious treatment by the other ethnic group or groups was cited in order to account for one's status as victim and to justify current acts of revenge, and (2) vastly exaggerated accounts of more recent crimes (that is, during the Second World War). These mythic justifications took hold in the minds of the foot soldiers, especially those who did the dirty work of ethnic cleansing.[26]

E. Observations on These Examples and Procedural Justice

Ideally, procedural justice is a process in which all parties to a conflict express clearly their positions. The positions are argued for, evaluated, and prioritized according to the canons of reason. The appropriateness of this way of resolving conflict is founded on the fact that persons and groups do approach conflict resolution in this way, though imperfectly.

In four examples of discourse relating to conflict–the Mitylenian Debate, the Melian Dialogue, the Israeli-Palestinian peace process, and the Dayton Accords–are found some elements of the procedural justice to which Hampshire refers; some results are advantageous, some fail to be advantageous. The Mitylenian Debate is not a debate between the Mitylenians and the Athenians, though one of the Athenians represents arguments on behalf of less harshness towards the Mitylenians. The other meetings include the combatants, though in the modern examples other peacemaking agents are also involved.

(1) The Mitylenian Debate resulted in less pain, suffering, death, and destruction for the Mitylenians than they were facing before that debate and vote. This could be counted as an advantage to the Mitylenians. If Diodotus's argument was correct, it could be counted as an advantage to the Athenians also. (2) The Melians did suffer extreme harm, but not until they had rejected a lesser harm the Athenians offered them in a discussion before battle; the

Melians chose to gamble for freedom. (3) The Israelis and Palestinians, being involved in peace talks at the present time, are staving off the pain and harm of all-out war. As regards the common negative values, the negotiation process is advantageous to both sides. (4) The horror of the Bosnian conflict has abated greatly, though the resulting peace is somewhat tenuous and not without some interruptions; and the rebuilding of the polity, economy, and society is very slow. Again, as regards the common negative values, all sides are benefiting from the negotiation.

The Mitylenian Debate is about the best means to achieve the Athenian end of discouraging rebellions. The goal was shared by the two debaters. The immediately beneficial result to a majority of Mitylenians (that is, the avoidance of suffering and death) is a happy accident, not the objective of the negotiation.

The Athenian view of justice in the Melian Dialogue was that might makes right. The Athenians barefacedly admitted it, the Melians knew that that was the Athenian view. Either the Melian leaders miscalculated the Athenian's resolve to fight and thought that they would not attack, or they thought that the Athenians would attack but would not win. Or else the Melian leaders truly believed, as they said, that the gods or the Spartans would help them win. Perhaps their concept of life and nobility entailed fighting for their autonomy even if that fight held the strong possibility of death. The Athenians may have suspected this latter opinion among the Melian leaders, since they pointed out that the Melian leaders did not allow the Melian citizenry to witness the dialogue. Perhaps the leaders feared that the citizenry would not harbor such noble ideals and would wish to surrender Melian autonomy to the Athenians.

The Israeli-Palestinian peace discussions may be credited with preventing a war at this time between the Israelis and Palestinians, though Palestinian terrorists regularly attack Israelis. However, it may also be the case that the Palestinians and their Arab allies are at present unprepared to declare war officially either because of a lack of will or a lack of means. The Israelis also may be disinclined to go to war at present unless attacked. In other words, the peace process may at this time be merely coincident with a time of peace for reasons other than that the discussion is being carried on.

The Bosnians were brought to an uneasy peace as a result of the Dayton peace talks with the aid of agents of other countries. The substance of these peace discussions is agreements about distribution of populations and allocation of political power. The bringing into being of these agreed upon arrangements is difficult.

Hampshire does not specify what considerations are or are not appropriate or relevant in the procedural approach to justice. Inasmuch as different peoples have different goods and different specific notions of justice relating to those goods, and the only common values are the negative values of avoidance of death, slavery, and pain, the talking points for procedural justice need be only whatever the disputants regard as important–in the cases cited, the most efficacious way to quell future rebellions, Athenian ambitions, Melian choices, Palestinian and Israeli land priorities, and population distribution and political power in Bosnia. These examples are, I submit, representative of international conflict–empire builders adding colonies, nations or ethnic groups warring over the possession of land and resources. At issue in these battles is more land and resources–more land (space) for the aggressor, or more resources (fertile land for agriculture or more oil or gold or diamonds, etc.) for the aggressor. The negotiations seem not to be concerned with conflicting notions of substantive justice or good, nor are they about political expediency, as Hampshire would suggest.[27] Rather, the rhetoric appeals to justice or good, while the negotiators undoubtedly make agreements in consideration of their own assessment of political expediency. And so the choices do seem to be between evils, as he says, and a just choice in such a case, he supposes, is determined by procedural justice.[28] In other words, justice is choosing fairly between conflicting claims about possessions in light of what is politically expedient.

I see some difficulties with this notion of justice and with this solution to the problem of international conflict. Some of these difficulties are practical, some are theoretical. I begin with six difficulties discovered in the historical examples of procedural justice. Then, I discuss an inherent inconsistency in Hampshire's theory.

3. Critique of the Theory of Procedural Justice

A. Difficulties Discovered in the Historical Cases.

Six practical difficulties are (1) that procedural justice comes into play only as a last resort, (2) that the peace established by procedural justice is temporary, (3) that procedural justice cannot resolve fundamental differences but only peripheral difficulties, (4) that the rational basis of procedural justice cannot resolve the differences deriving from such passions as patriotism and cultural identity, (5) that the argumentative method of procedural justice may entail that the most persuasive argument wins rather than the best argument, and (6) the considerations to which procedural justice applies and the conclusions reached by procedural justice are not moral considerations nor moral conclusions.

(1) The study of history indicates that nations rarely are willing to sit down at the negotiating table until they are convinced by the death and suffering of war that (procedural) justice is a preferable option to imposing the good of one nation on another. While a weak nation is willing to negotiate, a strong one is not. Hampshire himself would agree that nations are willing to negotiate about minor matters, matters that do not impinge upon their basic ethos or their source of power. Nations are not often willing to negotiate about

their very essence, and might regard the sacrifice of the more essential features of their conception of the best way of life in exchange for peaceful coexistence a cost unacceptably high.[29] For example, during the Cold War many Americans embraced the slogan, "Better Dead than Red"; the Israelis and Palestinians have demonstrated a similar attachment to their own goods. Strong nations are sometimes unwilling to negotiate with weaker nations even when the weaker nations give in and agree to negotiate. For example, in the case of Mitylene, the first vote of the Athenians was not to negotiate with the Mitylenians. Thus, while procedural justice may serve as a way to negotiate a peace when nations, weakened by and tired of war, are ready to sit down at the conference table, procedural justice does not seem to have served to prevent war. For example, the Camp David Accords were framed only after years of conflict. Procedural justice is frequently not the first resort, but the last resort, the resort to which we turn when we are tired of death and destruction, or when we are defeated.

(2) As Hampshire himself recognizes, often the peaceful compromises brought about by negotiation between two inimical positions are impermanent, temporary.[30] Once strength is regained or passions rekindled, the battle is likely to be renewed. Procedural justice helps us to make peace but not necessarily to keep peace. Hampshire holds that justice presides over a series of compromise formations. He says,

> It is [wrongly] assumed [by political philosophers] that there cannot be social stability within nations, and–now perhaps more urgent–peace between nations, unless an implicit consensus is first discovered and then is made explicit and reinforced. The assumption has been that, from the moral point of view, the bedrock of human nature is to be found in self-evident and unavoidable beliefs. But after every attempt the alleged unavoidable beliefs are shown to be either vacuous or, if substantial, dubious, and at least very far from being unavoidable.

> We should look in society not for consensus, but for ineliminable and acceptable conflicts, and for rationally controlled hostilities, as the normal condition of mankind; not only normal, but also the best condition of mankind from the moral point of view, both between states and within states....[J]ustice presides over the hostilities and finds sufficient compromises to prevent madness in the soul, and civil war or war between peoples.[31]

Peace is a state of "rationally controlled hostilities."

(3) As Hampshire himself indicates, sometimes the highest good or goods of a nation are directly contradictory to the highest good or goods of its adversary.[32] An example is the commitment of the Palestinians to push the Israelis into the sea, which obviously is contradictory to the commitment of

the Israelis to inhabit Israel. In such a case, procedural justice will not bring about peace so long as these contradictory goods are held to be of the highest importance. Procedures for discourse can perhaps lead to an ultimate agreement when the initial principles are agreed upon, but, as Iris Marian Young points out in *Intersecting Voices*, such procedures do not themselves provide a way to bring about agreement about first principles or basic goods or values.[33]

(4) In relations between nations as well as in relations between persons, the initial conditions in a conflict of goods or ideals is not merely an intellectual conflict. The conflict entails, as well, passion–extreme attachment to one's values, a feeling of defensiveness in respect of one's values, irrational hatred of the other, or intense anger or frustration. And even if originally the passion is weak, once it is awakened it grows and develops. Passion is infectious or at least co-optive. "As a result, disputants cannot hear the voice of reason instructing them to come together and consider the options and evaluate them." The options cannot be heard. The rationality of the argument cannot be heard.[34]

(5) Procedural justice depends upon the marshaling of arguments for and against positions. As Hampshire himself recognizes, it seems possible, indeed likely in the real world, that the proponents of the worse position may have the better or at least more persuasive arguments than the proponents of the better position.[35]

(6) The considerations to which procedural justice applies and the conclusions reached by procedural justice are not moral considerations nor moral conclusions. The considerations are not the competing notions of good and justice of different cultures, but possession of land, resources, and power. The conclusions of the negotiations may be arrived at rationally, but they are not thereby moral. As I mentioned above, the examples from history and the present are representative of the use of procedural justice in negotiating between warring parties and negotiating about possessions and power.

Two of these cases exemplify the lack of morality in considerations and conclusions. (1) The Mitylenian demos' achievement of negative goods (the avoidance of death, enslavement, and pain) was a result of considerations of how best to preserve Athenian hegemony, the "good" from the perspective of the Athenians. (2) The Athenian's treatment of the Melians was unjust, though it resulted from rational deliberation. Again, in this case, the Athenian's positive good was Athen's hegemony. What counts as a good for Hampshire, namely avoidance of enslavement, was the Melian's good. The Melians lost not only their freedom, but their possessions, their power, and, in the case of the men, their lives. Their rational discourse did not approach an evaluation of these negative goods.

Further, one might say that the Athenians arrived rationally at a conclusion based upon the information that they had. However, they lacked much information, and their campaign against Melos was successful not only because of their reasoning but also because of some other circumstances (including inauspicious sailing conditions that prevented the Spartans from launching an attack that would have put more strain upon the Athenian forces) of which the Athenians could have no knowledge. They were lucky, perhaps. Their decision may have been rational, to a degree, but its rationality was not completely responsible for their success and had nothing to do with justice, unless might does in fact make right.

B. Inconsistency in the Theory

The fundamental inconsistency in Hampshire's theory stems from his explicit denial that there is a universal substantive good that can serve as a basis for a theory of justice. The denial is coupled with an implicit appeal to universal substantive goods. These assumed universal substantive goods are fundamental to his theory. The first assumed good is the practical reasoning. Three other goods are couched in negative terms–the avoidance of pain, slavery, and death.

(1) I find an internal inconsistency as regards Hampshire's attitude toward a universal substantial good. Hampshire, contrary to his own prohibition against accepting some universal good, does accept a certain practical form of reasoning as the universal good, though he does not use the term "good." He finds in human beings a beneficial commonality–practical reasoning and decision-making. He bases his moral theory on the commonness and the beneficial quality of the practical use of reason by which human beings fairly evaluate and decide between opposing positions. Hampshire recognizes that persons do not always evaluate fairly. Fairness is an ideal.[36] Fairness is yet another good, I would say.

At the same time, however, Hampshire actually recognizes that his fair practical use of reason is a universal substantial good inasmuch as he criticizes the liberal free-thinker for holding that the supreme human virtue is to be rational. He says,

> There have always been, and there will continue to be, conceptions of the good, and of the best way of life, in which the disposition to think and to be rational is not the supreme human virtue. For example, there is the conception of the good which makes the desire and ability to preserve one's own way of life, with its traditional duties and obligations, the supreme virtue.[37]

Hampshire elevates practical reasoning to the supreme position in the quest for justice. It is practical reasoning that discovers and promotes justice.[38] At the same time Hampshire denies that there are any positive notions of good universally applicable to human beings. He violates his own prohibition of accepting positive good. He believes he is not asserting a human good, but a mere common human characteristic. But to believe that fair practical reasoning is a procedure applicable to all and one which can attain justice is to believe that such reasoning is universal and is beneficial in practice

(2) Hampshire also claims that, while there are not any universal positive goods, there are minimal universal negative goods–the avoidance of slavery, death, and pain.[39] Procedural justice may regard these negative goods as of the first priority. The negative expression of these goods does not hide the fact that they are the traditionally cited universal positive goods of freedom, the preservation of life, and pleasure. Hampshire is appealing to universal substantive goods. While actually appealing to universal substantive goods, Hampshire assumes somehow that he is not, that there is an inherently natural abhorrence of these negatives, and that the natures of these negatives are common and clear, thus requiring no explanation.

Countless members of the human race would not affirm Hampshire's catalogue of negative goods, positively or negatively expressed. We can name a few of them. Socrates, Plato, Baruch Spinoza, the Stoics, the Epicureans, and Christians would not agree that death is the greatest evil, nor that physical pain is the greatest evil. They would agree that the fear of death and of physical pain are two of the reasons why people do evil acts, and that these fears are grounded in ignorance about the real nature of Good for some, or Reality for others, or God for yet others. For some people the positive goods are grounded in our rational nature, for others they are not. Further, these representatives of humankind would disagree with Hampshire, with other thinkers, as well as with one another about the meaning of the terms "slavery" and "freedom." What Hampshire regards as being negative goods common to all humankind are just not all that common.

What these and many other theorists (such as Thomas Hobbes, John Locke, John Stuart Mill, and Immanuel Kant) have attempted to do is to discern what the universal good or goods for human beings might be. And they have undertaken the difficult task of explicating as fully as possible this good or these goods. They have attempted to provide an evaluative anchor for discourse about justice, supposing that such an anchor is necessary, if the discourse is not to drift aimlessly, leaving us without any clear conclusions about justice and how to achieve it.

Hampshire's fear that a commitment to discerning, inquiring into, and elucidating an ideal would lead to a dogmatic imposition of one party's good upon another for whom it is not a good, is not a necessary outcome of such a commitment. He cites a communist leader such as Stalin or Dostoyevsky's Grand Inquisitor. Many of the great moral teachers have appealed to an ideal, rational or passionate in nature, without supposing that the ideal entitled them to do harm to others and without in fact doing harm to any one else. Their attachment to their good was not dogmatic. Two such moral teachers are Socrates and Jesus.

Socrates represents a rational attachment to the Good. He ever pursued a fuller understanding and embodiment of the Good and urged others to do so. He did not believe that his perspective on the Good entitled him to force others to pursue that good. Rather he regarded himself to be involved in an inquiry that approached knowledge of the Good but never completely achieved that knowledge. He regarded himself and all other people to be infinitely perfectible.

Jesus represents a passionate attachment to God. He urged people to love God, and to love one another, recognizing that our ability to do so was imperfect. Harming others and loving others, according to Jesus' conception of love, are mutually exclusive.

We need not necessarily fear ideals or goods nor the elevation of reason or passion in moral theory. It is the dogmatism of some moral theories that lead to death and destruction in the name of something good. Dogmatism is an especial danger when one thinks one is above dogmatism, when one thinks one's theory is value-free, nondogmatic, only descriptive. I believe that Hampshire's moral theory of procedural justice is just such a dogmatic position.

4. Concluding Remarks

In this chapter I explicated Hampshire's theory of procedural justice, applied it to representative negotiations regarding four international conflicts, and critiqued the theory in respect of both those applications and internal inconsistencies. Examining the application of the theory we find that it is at best an imperfect tool for resolving international conflict because it comes into play only as a last resort, the peace that it establishes is temporary, it cannot resolve fundamental differences but only peripheral difficulties, its rational basis cannot resolve the differences deriving from such passions as patriotism and cultural identity, its argumentative method may entail that the most persuasive argument rather than the best argument wins, and its considerations and conclusions are not moral considerations or conclusions.

To consider this last point further, the moral criteria in procedural justice are that the reasoning be adequate and that the main relevant considerations be impartially weighed.[40] For the reasoning to be adequate, one would suppose that the rules of valid deductive argumentation be observed and that the inductive arguments be strong. Neither of these guarantees truth unless the premises of the arguments are true. The premises would be the main relevant considerations, to which Hampshire refers. These are presumably whatever the antagonists bring to the argument. My representative examples of the international use of procedural justice indicate that the main relevant considerations are desires for possessions and power. Presumably the result of the negotiation is just, if the antagonists present their main desires for possessions and power and if the arguments that proceed from these considerations are logically valid or inductively strong. So, for example, supposing that these criteria were satisfied in the Melian dialogue, Athens's subsequent treatment of the Melians, which was implied by the discussion, was just. Hampshire confirms this when he says,

> If your adversary in negotiation obstinately required you to sacrifice a number of the more essential features of the best way of life, as you see it, you might reasonably decide that this is morally impossible and that the cost of peaceful co-existence on an agreed and fair basis has been set unacceptably high.[41]

The parties to the Dayton Accords and the parties to the Oslo agreement might also come to conclude that the cost of peaceful co-existence on the agreed and fair basis is unacceptably high. This being the case, it is unlikely that Hampshire's procedural justice is an adequate tool for dealing with international antagonists. And, again, it would strike many of us that the Athenian treatment of the Melians was unjust, however procedurally correct the discussion was that led to that treatment. In other words, there is a difference between rational rules of discourse and justice. Justice cannot be reduced to the rules of discourse.

Not only is Hampshire's theory of procedural justice inadequate to deal with international conflict and not only does it seem to not really provide ordinarily recognizable moral principles, it is also internally inconsistent in itself. My critique demonstrated that Hampshire explicitly eschews, but implicitly appeals to universal substantial goods. Hampshire confusedly appeals to goods he refuses to acknowledge. Hamp-shire attempts to develop a theory of justice that has no foundation for moral judgment.

Notes

1. Stuart Hampshire, *Innocence and Experience* (Cambridge, Mass.: Harvard University Press, 1989).
    2. *Ibid.*, pp. 4-16.
    3. *Ibid.*, pp. 161-189.
    4. *Ibid.*, pp. 51-52.
    5. *Ibid.*, p. 52.
    6. *Ibid.*, p. 53.
    7. *Ibid.*
    8. *Ibid.*, p. 107.
    9. *Ibid.*, p. 108.
    10. *Ibid.*, p. 106.
    11. *Ibid.*, p. 107.
    12. *Ibid.*, pp. 77-78.
    13. *Ibid.*, pp. 113-114.
    14. *Ibid.*, p. 109.
    15. *Ibid.*, p. 124.

16. *Ibid.*, pp. 107-108.
17. *Ibid.*, pp. 108-109.
18. *Ibid.*, p. 154.
19. *Ibid.*, p. 53.
20. *Ibid.*, pp. 51-52.
21. *Ibid.*, p. 157.
22. *Ibid.*, pp. 170-171.
23. *Ibid.*, p. 109.
24. See Thucydides, *The Complete Writings of Thucydides: The Peloponnesian War,* trans. R. Crawley (New York: Random House, 1951), bk. III, ch. ix, ll. 36-51, pp. 163-173.
25. See *ibid,* bk. V. ch. xvii., ll. 85-116, 330-337.
26. See David Rieff, *Slaughterhouse: Bosnia and the Failure of the West* (New York: Simon and Schuster, 1995).
27. Hampshire, *Innocence,* pp. 170-171.
28. *Ibid.*
29. *Ibid.*, p. 154.
30. *Ibid.*, p. 189.
31. *Ibid.*
32. *Ibid.*, p. 154.
33. Iris Marion Young, *Intersecting Voices: Dilemmas of Gender, Political Philosophy, and Policy* (Princeton, N.J.: Princeton University Press, 1997), pp. 72-73.
34. *Ibid,* pp. 63-71
35. Hampshire, *Innocence,* pp. 53-54.
36. *Ibid.*, pp. 51-53, and *passim.*
37. *Ibid.*, p. 155.
38. *Ibid.*, pp. 51-53, and *passim.*
39. *Ibid.*, pp. 78 and 107.
40. *Ibid.*, p. 53.
41. *Ibid.*, p. 154.

Four

JUSTICE AS STRUCTURE AND STRATEGY OF PEACE

Mar Peter-Raoul

> It will take a great act of imagination
> to save the world.
> I want to begin.
>
> We will travel the way of love
> and leave behind us a trail of seeds
> to root between the rocks.
> They will arrest us
> for littering their battlefield
> with life.
> But no matter.
>
> Janice Hill[1]

Throughout the twentieth century, subject peoples across the world have struggled to free themselves from repression and rank injustice. Breaking through to liberation, resisters have attempted to restructure terrains of terror into territories of democracy and human rights. In just the last decade, transformation has happened in Eastern Europe, Chile, El Salvador, Haiti, and South Africa. A few years ago in a Nobel Debate, Desmond Tutu commented, "It would seem that freedom is breaking out all over." In contrast to this affirmation, global observers count sixty-four present warfares.[2] Today, both oppression and resistance still struggle for power—even after a century of two world wars of catastrophic proportions! In a world context of both struggle and transition, the declaration of war and the declaration of human rights seem to define the contradictory character of the world itself. At the same time, massive militarization sustains dictatorships and most democracies. Given this complex reality, the question upon entering the twenty-first century is: Will the world significantly overcome the repressive use of power, and restructure the planet into broad-based, participatory, regional democracies founded on the systematic guarantee of human rights? The answer to this question will determine both the character of the twenty-first century and the very hope for peace.

The position of this chapter is that the possibility of an enduring, authentic, participatory peace rests on a radical revision of values, a revision affecting the very psychic and spiritual roots of the world community. These radical values, giving rise to an all-encompassing social justice and the hope of a realistic utopia, are at once the spirit, structure, and strategy of peace. A society that structures abiding values into its social, political, economic, cultural, and religious system, structures into this system a just and emancipatory peace, and, in turn, affects the possibility of a world peace. The governing assumption of this position is that deeply rooted structures of justice engender a positive peace. In this chapter, I will (1) report upon the extremity of injustice in the world today, (2) characterize justice as fundamental human rights, (3) offer a literary model toward a just peace, and, (4) suggest seven strategies for peace rooted in a radical revision of values.

1. Injustice and Rank Moral Evil

The world is rife with injustice. Cruel child labor, forced prostitution, virtual slavery, inhuman working conditions (when there is any work at all), ghetto housing, and chronic hunger mark the lot of millions across continents. Socio-political power structures sustain this misery through suppression, surveillance, censorship, interrogation rooms, disappearances, rape, and–throughout Latin America, imported from Brazil–the *"pau d'arara."* Chilean poet Ariel Dorfman describes the *pau d'arara* in *Last Waltz in Santiago: And Other Poems of Exile and Disappearance*. With hands and feet tied together, the victim is suspended naked on a pole. Unspeakable things then happen, says Dorfman. Exiled for his own resistance, Dorfman writes,

> Two inextricably linked experiences in today's Latin America...are *pau d'arara* and *companero*....Too often, it is those who try to make the world into a place where we could all be *companeros*, it is those dreamers of the future, who wind up on the *pau d'arara*.[3]

These dreamers who want to create a wide community of *companeros*, are found throughout the world. A great many pay a terrible cost for their commitment. In Latin America well over a thousand religious and many more civilians, all working for justice, have been murdered over the past few decades. A feature in *The New York Times Magazine*, "Testifying to Torture," recounts the brutal treatment of a young activist, Ines Murillo, in a clandestine, Honduran prison. Her "interrogators," trained in Texas by the Central Intelligence Agency, serve a state apparatus that between 1980-1984 (and still in force) operated there for the purpose of maintaining control of state power and systematically eliminating opposition, whether this opposition was organizing for human rights or forming guerrilla units.[4]

A similar report by Holly J. Burkhalter, a representative of the human rights organization America Watch, reveals that with legislation enacted in the 1970s the United States helped

> the Guatemalan security forces become a giant computerized death squad. Victims were selected at secret meetings in the National Palace and plainclothes policemen tortured, executed and abducted political opponents, trade unionists, students, peasant leaders, teachers and lawyers by the thousands. A telecommunications center in the palace annex...was the headquarters of death squad activity.[5]

In El Salvador, in 1980, four United States churchwomen on their way to the airport were stopped by government patrols, raped and murdered; earlier in 1980, Oscar Romero, an archbishop, after imploring the United States to stop supporting the murderous regime there, was assassinated while saying Mass; in 1989, six Jesuit priests, all committed to the El Salvadoran people's liberation, were executed.

Also in 1989, Diane Ortiz, a nun, was kidnapped in Guatemala, raped, tortured, burned, and then "lowered into an open pit packed with human bodies–bodies of children, women, and men, some decapitated, some lying face up and caked with blood, some dead, some alive–and all swarming with rats."[6] She was kept there for several hours.

In her critical article, "Silencing the Social Critics: An Untold Story in Columbia," Leslie Wirpsa reports that between 1988 and 1995, there were 28,332 political killings in Columbia. "In terms of human rights atrocities," states Wirpsa, "Columbia is El Salvador, it is Guatemala, it is Honduras and Chile and Peru, it is Brazil and Argentina, all revisited today." As elsewhere in Latin America, Wirpsa finds the United States government complicitous in this tragedy "against members of grassroots organizations, religious and laity, political activists, union leaders, teachers, peasants, indigenous lawyers, journalists...."[7]

The examples of murder and repression could be repeated across regions and countries, both East and West. Just one example: the Truth and Reconciliation Commission in liberated South Africa has heard testimonies of state terror practiced during the state system of apartheid. The litany of atrocities recorded by the Commission echoes the examples from Latin America.

At home in the United States, militarization, poverty, and racism (the three evils identified as interrelated by Martin Luther King, Jr.) continue, in force. "The fangs of the Trident nuclear submarine system are less visible today," says activist Jim Clune at a Catholic Worker meeting at Zacchaeus House, "but just as ready, just as deadly."[8] A study released in December 1996 by the National Center for Children in Poverty at the Columbia School of Public Health, finds that the number of poor children in the United States, under the age of six, rose between 1979 and 1994 from 3.5 million to 6.1 million. Segregation of people of color, if not by official policy, continues as a consequence of poverty and racism. Children are bitten in their beds by rats while huge military budgets take priority over rebuilding slum neighborhoods. We have to ask: Is the exorbitant expenditure for policing the world and attempting to develop an impenetrable defense shield, the Strategic Defense Initiative, justified when racking poverty for one in four to five of all American children is the price? With present national priorities, we are committing, in social critic Jonathan Kozol's words, "social homicide."[9]

In this century, there is a wounding at the heart of humanity. Extremities of evil–the killing fields, the Holocaust, Hiroshima, the *pau d'arara*–haunt the horizon. There is no precedent, said philosopher Simone Weil, for the evil of our times. In the United States and across the world, both throughout the century and today, we find an iron course of injustice.

2. Justice as Human Rights

As a broad-based, participatory response against the moral evil of twentieth-century injustice, a world consensus has identified fundamental human rights. As the substance of social justice these rights guarantee the right to human dignity and well-being. Although the precise content of justice may differ from one culture to another, human rights as listed in such documents as national constitutions, the United States Catholic Bishops' Letter on Economic Justice, the seminal 1948 United Nations Declaration of Human Rights, subsequent United Nations covenants, the 1975 historic Helsinki Accords, and the 1976 Eastern European dissident document, Charter 77, express the understanding of a significant part of humanity of the essential right of every person to possess what is needed for personal, political, social, and cultural wholeness. These rights give sustenance to the poor and marginalized, enabling them independently to seek a better life. These rights ensure that resources are distributed equitably. Politically, these rights guarantee the freedom to immigrate and emigrate, to exercise agency, to associate freely with others, to publish poetry and pamphlets, to picket, to pray openly, to ask searching questions and seek unfettered answers. Embodied in all categories of human rights is a situated freedom, a freedom constrained only by the rights of others.

In substance, human rights are related to a positive peace. Close in meaning to the Hebrew word for peace, *shalom*, a positive peace "means such things as wholeness and health, prosperity and security, political and spiritual well-being." In *Making Peace in the Global Village*, Robert McAfee Brown finds *shalom* "shockingly materialistic." He writes, *shalom* "has to do with having adequate shelter; it has to do with a security that is physical as well as spiritual. It is very earthy." As Brown points out, *shalom* is not only about stopping warfare, but about people having enough to eat, able to go to bed at night without fear that someone will spirit them off to prison; that the society will be so planned that there is food enough to go around; that the politics of the country (and of the world) are so arranged that everybody's basic needs are met. Otherwise, no *shalom*.[10]

Brown holds that action

to alleviate world hunger (including that down the block) is peace-making; seeking to reverse the arms race is peacemaking; action on behalf of human rights is peacemaking; working for an economic order that narrows the disparities between rich and poor is peacemaking. Whatever enhances the well-being of the human family is peacemaking, the spreading of *shalom*.[11]

Reflecting on her work as co-founder of the Catholic Worker movement, Dorothy Day, the pacifist, anarchist, early communist, concludes, "After so many years of work in the Peace movement, I had come to the conclusion that basic to peace was the struggle for education, job opportunity, health, and recognition as human beings."[12] For Day, human well-being and peace are interconnected.

Similarly, political advocate, Stanley Kober, links how we treat human beings with our staving off of nuclear war. During the Cold War he held that respect for human rights was the best form of arms control. His point was that how a country treats its citizens–to what extent human rights are respected–indicates how it will act in the international arena.

Structuring human rights, that is, spreading *shalom* into the substantive workings of a society, affects the character of this society and, in an interrelated world, becomes a creating force. From diverse sources, including scientific Chaos theory, Eastern thought, sociology, psychology, and tribal traditions, evidence accrues that every thought and every action has an effect. From a butterfly's wing motion to a nuclear blast, from unspoken thoughts to words spoken, the continuous present and near future of the world is being created. Still, again across a spectrum of sources, comes the realization of contingency and indeterminacy, from the lower forms of life to the higher. In tension with physical laws and the probable effects of action and thought, the phenomenon of freedom is writ large in the heart of the universe. From the unpredictable action of a single electron to the unpredictable action of a single human being, there is only probability. David Lindley puzzles this unpredictability in the scientific world, the tension between physical laws and the single unit. He asks, "If we can't trust a single electron to be precisely in one place at one time, how can we trust a throng of electrons to invariably represent the letter 'a' on my computer screen...?"[13] But we do. Studying single cells, scientist Rodolfo Llinas claims, "They have a point of view, a personality, so to speak."[14] On the human level, there is likewise no guarantee that any one person, or a people, will invariably act in a particular way, whatever the situation or influence. Yet, with some probability, one can predict the outcome of those given certain life chances, those cared about, or not. We know that children nurtured, educated, and taught enduring values, are far more likely to grow into mature, contributing adults than those abused and abandoned. The Harvard University sociologist William Julius Wilson, in a World of Ideas interview with Bill Moyers, claims that he can go into any hospital nursery and, given the data of neighborhood, class, and family situation, tell, in general, where these babies are likely to be in twenty years. The point is, we may not be able to predict the future behavior of any one person, or any one nation, but we can predict a likely outcome. Enough evidence exists to expect that given respect for their own rights, people will respect the human rights of others. When persons receive physical sustenance, moral teaching, and respect for their human dignity and agency, they are likely to take responsibility to support the rights and well being of those in the wider world. Thus, a society grounded in the substantive justice of human rights is a society likely to promote positive peace.

Understanding that peaceful democracies are less prone to go to war, President Woodrow Wilson tried to establish the League of Nations. Wilson's efforts were based on two factors: first, historically, democratic nations are more peaceful; and, second, leaders prone to going to war in democratic countries are constrained by the decisions of the citizenry.

Earlier in United States history, Thomas Jefferson held up an ideal that needs to be recovered for today. For Jefferson, a democracy could not be a true democracy without a democratic foreign policy (pursued through support and persuasion, not force). A democratic people had to contribute in peaceful and concrete ways to democracy around the world. This included a concern for the needs of the citizens of other countries, not only for the needs of one's own citizens. Perhaps one of the best examples for Jefferson's theory is found today in Scandinavian countries, one of the few places where there is respect for both political and social human rights. These social democratic Scandinavian countries contribute more of their gross national product to third world peoples than do most industrialized, democratic countries. Caring about the well-being of their own people is extended to caring about the well-being of other, poorer peoples.

Irrespective of whether respect for human rights will bring about lasting peace in the world, there are those who resist injustice out of a singular sense of solidarity with those whose rights are denied. Breyton Breytonbach, a writer exiled from South Africa during apartheid, writes,

I need not believe or trust in the possibility of obtaining the objective in order to keep moving....Besides, continued commitment may just succeed in being perceived as a form of solidarity and support–by those in... transit areas and prisons who need to feel some human concern in order to survive.[15]

3. Literary Model

Lionel Burger was one of those in prison who had acted in solidarity with the oppressed majority in South Africa, those systematically denied human rights. In *Burger's Daughter*, novelist Nadine Gordimer presents the community of Burger and his associates as a model for creating what political theologian Jurgen Moltmann calls a community of wider loyalty. It is a community that reaches beyond narrow nationalities and arbitrary racial and class divisions. In the context of apartheid, the polarized social system of strict separation of races, Burger, a prominent and respected physician, risks reputation and resources to create with his activist wife, and their daughter named "Rosa," after Rosa Luxemburg, a kind of counter-culture. Out of the center of their comfortable home, the Burgers establish an interracial, interpersonal, politically active extended family/community. Challenging the legitimacy of apartheid, the Burgers live their lives "clearly responsive to 'a standard of justice...beyond that...in existing institutions.'" Burger insists that "South African blacks and whites make a revolution based not on terrorist activities but on strikes, fellowship meetings, and open refusal to honor the color barrier."[16]

A summer tradition in the Burger house is to keep open house around the swimming pool on Sundays. Embracing white and black radicals and their sprawling families (some of whom live in the house from time to time), Burger makes each person feel "liked, honored, understood."[17] It is a family of associates, white, African, colored, Indian. The Burgers and the people around them think always about social justice, work to create just political institutions, and reach out inclusively to different kinds of persons. Always primary is the force of their personal convictions. Their political goals, says critic Robert Boyer, "always have more to do with making a better world in which to live than in securing power." They know they must wrest power, "but they seem as much involved in cultivating fellow feeling as in devising subversive strategies." According to Boyer, the central view of Gordimer's novel is the "view of politics as the concerted activity of an extended though intimate family...based on a conception of the necessary interpenetration of public and private in the quest for a better world."[18]

Sorting out her life and political commitments after her mother's death and her father's trial for treason, with its subsequent life sentence, Rosa Burger remarks, "We belonged to other people....And other people belonged to us."[19] In a later reflection, she affirms,

The political activities and attitudes of that house came from the inside outwards....[P]eople in that house had a connection with blacks that was completely personal...a connection without reservations on the part of blacks or whites...spluttering the same water together in the swimming pool, going to prison after the same indictment....They had the connection because they believed it possible.[20]

What the people of the Burger house create is the beginning structure of an emancipatory peace rooted in social justice. From out of its center of connectedness, this nascent structure sprawls out toward the wider world. A realistic utopia is lived out in the immediacy of the present, in the interpenetration of political and personal relations. Acting on their radical values, those of this house community refuse to wait for a less costly and more propitious time.

In resisting the unjust structures of apartheid, structures solidified into law and protected by the courts, the Burgers persist in continual political activity even at the risk of prison. They create in the present an interpersonal counter-culture of community and caring. With their family of associates, they live out social justice as the measure and meaning of their lives. Creating a center of belonging-to-each-other and extending this belonging outward to include all who would join them, they set in motion a counter-force to the tanks and tear gas of the white regime.

As the Burgers live out the radical values of a community of wider loyalty, countering apartheid in the immediacy of their personal and political lives, how, in the midst of the evils of our own time, do we stake out a radical structure of justice, a realistic utopia? How, beyond the artificial terrain of national boundaries, do we create communal circles and collaborations, regionally and across regions, a global community centered in the presiding values of human well-being? How, in creating this community of wider loyalty, do we make root changes in the world's thinking, so that if the arms are dismantled they will not be remantled?

4. Restructuring, Reconstituting the World, Strategies for Peace

> My heart is moved by all I cannot save:
> so much has been destroyed
> I have to cast my lot with those
> who age after age, perversely
> with no extraordinary power,
> reconstitute the world.[21]

In essence, how do we create a wide and enduring peace? In his book on rebuilding America, Amitai Etzioni, professor at George Washington University, contends that what we need is a change in our basic orientation.

He writes, "What America needs, above all, is a change in the way we approach things, what we value and what we devalue, *a change of heart*." In his call for communitarianism, a movement dedicated to "social responsibility, public and private morality, and the public interest," Etzioni advocates a new spirit.[22] Writing in the wake of the Holocaust, the German, political theologian, Johann Baptist Metz, addressing the world context, also advocates a new spirit. He asks, "How can we achieve a fundamental revision which will affect even the psychic foundations of [public] life?" He asks further, "Where should this change of heart...begin to operate? Where can we initiate a transformation of priorities and change of perspectives?" The aim of these questions, for Metz, "must be...a concrete and fundamental revision of our consciousness." What is imperative for this fundamental revision is that it "must take root in the people as a whole, in...everyday life."[23] I suggest that the following strategies for peace resonate with Etzioni's and Metz's call for a new spirit and a change of heart. They also seek to reconstitute world-consciousness by way of a radical revision of values. In offering these strategies I am mindful of critic Jacques Derrida's statement in his essay, "Racism's Last Word." He points out, "[N]o one strategy is sufficient; there is...no ideal and absolute strategy. We have to multiply the approaches...."[24] Not attempting to be comprehensive, I outline seven strategies toward a revision of values. This revision is set toward affecting the psychic and spiritual foundations of human consciousness and creating a community of wider loyalty. I draw from peace theologians, activists, educators, social critics, and others who have contributed to thought and action in the on-going struggle for a profound and structured peace. All the strategies interrelate with one another, and interpenetrate the personal and public.

A. Realistic Utopia

In the particularity of our personal and public lives we must act on the potential for altering the social context, or at least, some part of it. Alert to possibilities within our own situations, we must commit ourselves to constructing, as did the Burgers, an immediate community toward a realistic utopia. And from this created center, participate in an ever-widening circle of coalitions and larger inter-community projects, for example, Sister Cities and Sister Churches, and link our work with an aspiring global community.

One example of acting at one's own site is found at Green Haven, a federal, maximum security prison. Prisoners who have taken college courses, structure discussion groups and tutor other inmates. Going even further, Siddiq Najee and Raymond Cornwell, both graduates of the New York Theological Seminary Masters in Professional Studies program at Sing Sing prison, worked with William Webber of the Seminary, Sister Marian Bohen of the Seminary's program at Sing Sing Prison, and Greg Moses of Marist College to create for fellow prisoners a certificate program in theology.

Subsequently, several former prisoners opened a center in Brooklyn to counsel and provide a support system for others newly released. One of the founders of the center, Lateef Islam, is today the executive director of the Family Partnership Center in downtown Poughkeepsie, New York. His commitment to helping reclaim those in trouble continues at this new site. In particular, he is concerned with the youth gathering on street corners, where he once gathered himself. "You want to throw away those kids hanging out?" asks Lateef. "Well, I have a passion for those kids. I want to see them have a reason to stay in school, to see a future for themselves."[25]

The great voice for peace, William Lloyd Garrison, advocated "at whatever site" in his Declaration of Sentiments adopted in 1838 by the Peace Conference in Boston. In his Declaration, Garrison fervently proposes to speak and act boldly, in a moral and spiritual sense, "in high places and in low places, to apply our principles to all existing civil, political, legal and ecclesiastical institutions." Further, he insists, "We shall employ lecturers, circulate tracts and publications, form societies, and petition our state and national governments, in relation to the subject of universal peace." Resonate with the call for a change of heart, Garrison concludes, "It will be our leading object to devise ways and means for effecting a radical change in the views, feelings and practices of society, respecting the sinfulness of war and the treatment of enemies."[26]

B. Conversion to the Neighbor

Peruvian theologian Gustavo Gutierrez who lives among the poor in Lima, calls for a fundamental conversion to the neighbor, to begin to feel our neighbor's distress as our own distress. Affirming the interconnectedness of life perceived by all the great religious traditions, conversion to the neighbor requires an identification with others on the sole ground of our common humanity. Metz believes that on this conversion to the neighbor, "world peace depends."[27] Allan Boesak, black South African theologian and former activist says against apartheid, "If human life is broken in South Africa or Indonesia or El Salvador, there is no way that life can be whole in the United States."[28]

In a letter from his cell in a Birmingham jail, Martin Luther King, Jr. agrees, "We are caught in an inescapable network of mutuality, tied in a single garment of destiny. Whatever affects one directly, affects all indirectly...."[29] King advocated this conversion to the neighbor when telling his followers, "It is time for the Negro haves to join hands with the Negro have-nots, and, with compassion, journey into that other country of hurt and denial."[30]

When peace activist Barbara Deming died, Grace Paley, her friend, was given an envelope containing shards and stones from the rubble of a

Vietnamese town. Both had protested the war with a deep sense of solidarity for the burned and fleeing Vietnamese. On the envelope were the words "endless love." They were words of shared remembrance "of another people's great suffering," an example of feeling another's pain as one's own. Paley writes, "I thought Barbara was saying,–Send those words out, out into the...mortal fact of the world, endless love, the dangerous transforming spirit."[31]

Conversion to the neighbor is when the welfare of others matters, and when we realize, in Deming's words, "we are part of one another." It is then that our policies, foreign or domestic, will reflect this identification and hold out against imperialism and privilege. Conversion to the neighbor is a radical understanding that the well-being of others is a requirement for our own well-being, and a fundamental requirement for peace. A Hanukkah poem expresses this perception.

> Throughout history, dictators
> large and small
> have tried to darken, diminish,
> and separate people by force
> But always in the end they fail
> For always somewhere in the world
> the light remains
> We must remember:
> a candle alone is a small thing
> a person alone is a small thing
> a nation alone is a small thing
> Remembering this we must recognize
> something much more
> than our indispensability to others
> We must remember their indispensability
> to us
> We cannot hope either as individuals
> or nations
> to reach our highest capability
> until we help those around us
> reach theirs.

C. Transformative Pedagogy

Paulo Freire, a Brazilian educator, developed the concept of "conscientization" in a context of repression and terror. Conscientization is the process of becoming aware of the workings of an oppressive society. By asking critical questions, the teacher seeks to lay bare structural injustice as it affects the subjugated, those exploited by political and economic systems. Freire inspired a new pedagogy for the oppressed, a pedagogy that reaches now around the world, into make-shift learning sites, into prisons, and even into the most elite college classrooms. It is a method of critical inquiry starting with the social location, language, concepts, and situations of those oppressed. And from there linking to a larger, more global analysis. In his Introduction to Freire's *Pedagogy of the Oppressed*, Richard Shaull writes,

> There is no such thing as a *neutral* educational process. Education either functions as an instrument which is used to facilitate the integration of the younger generation into the logic of the present system and bring about conformity to it, *or* it becomes the practice of freedom, the means by which men and women deal critically and creatively with reality and discover how to participate in the transformation of their world.[32]

In *The Dialectic of Freedom*, Maxine Greene writes that it is through an education for freedom, an education leading to conscientization, that individuals can be provoked to reach beyond their intersubjective space to think about the wider community. Yet, in our educational institutions, says Greene, there "is almost no serious talk of reconstituting a civic order." Where there should be impassioned dialogue about connectedness and being together in community, there is "a widespread speechlessness." Greene finds little, if anything, done "to render problematic a reality that includes home-lessness, hunger, pollution, crime, censorship, arms build-up...." At a time of tragic lack in American society, a time of "some of the saddest instances of de-humanization," educators offer "promises of 'career ladders,' 'board certification,' and decision-making power." Greene decries the fact that in preparing students for a high technology society, few provocative questions are asked about the poorly paid third-world workers who will do the assembly line work.[33]

In agreement with Freire and Greene, Frank Lentricchia writes in *Criticism and Social Change*, "He comes down on the side of those who believe that our society is mainly unreasonable and that education should be one of the places where we can get involved in the process of transforming it."[34] For Lentricchia, this means that the specific intellectual (as identified by Foucault) is "one whose radical work of transformation, whose fight against repression, is carried on at the specific institutional site where he finds himself."[35] Presently, he sees educational institutions in the United States reinforcing the current hegemony and ideology of Western capitalism.[36] Lentricchia suggests that we need a "theory of reading that will instigate a culturally suspicious, trouble-making readership."[37] The ultimate point, he concludes, "is to create a new social center."[38]

Related radical educator, Henry Giroux states, "Contemporary forms of critical educational theory need to make new connections, take up new paradigms, and open up different spaces with new allies in order to work simultaneously on changing the schools and the wider social order."[39]

At the site of education a pedagogy of conscience can affect the world view of upcoming generations. Such a pedagogy is a crucial strategy toward the psychic foundations of world consciousness.

D. Praxis

Beginning from an individual's location and with conscious commitment to social justice, praxis enters into partnership with the oppressed other, works alongside, shares goods, offers assets and abilities, and, most critically, recognizes the assets and abilities of those rendered "anonymous," "invisible," "superfluous."[40]

It is here, in partnership with those who suffer injustice, that the work of praxis comes to know the truth of a social order. Freire holds that a "qualitative change in the perception of the world can only be achieved in the praxis."[41] Moving beyond activism alone, praxis includes critical reflection on the world. Praxis is an epistemological moment. It finds that the situation of the powerless is a privileged vantage point for viewing the oppressive structures of a particular society. Ignacio Martin-Baro, one of the six Jesuits killed in the 1989 massacre in El Salvador, a doctor of psychotherapy, writes, "We know from the sociology of knowledge that what is seen of reality, and how it is seen, depends essentially on the social location from where it is viewed."[42]

Praxis, as distinguished from volunteerism and community, is a continual, interpretive reflection on one's practice. Participating at a soup kitchen, a shelter, or a downtown center is the starting point for analysis. Reflecting on the experience, one begins to ask, why are poor people poor? Why is poverty increasing in America? Why are one out of every four to five children in the United States poor? What is the psychological effect on an abused child, a child not cherished, read to, attended? Why does the United States incarcerate more of its people than any other industrialized nation, approaching one and one-half million? What are the social arrangements whereby one community in the society eats well, is relatively safe from violence and vermin, supports well-supplied schools, and is largely a professional class? And what are the socio-political structures whereby an adjacent, poorer community struggles with undersupplied schools, substandard housing, drug use in peeling and peed-in stair wells? How does this disparity play out in life chances, aspirations, self-worth, achievement, responsibility? Politically, who has power? Whose values prevail? How are resources distributed; who gets to eat, go to college, go to the beach?

The above questions arise out of the at-site experience of praxis. The Venezuelan sociologist Otto Maduro, insists, "It is not enough to be solidly committed to a struggle in order for it to have a successful outcome. No, all this is insufficient. We have to come to know–to know how and why things have come to this pass...in society. We have to learn what changes are possible."[43] One task of analysis is to become aware of the workings of ideology, ideology as our interpretive apparatus. We might compare ideology to a computer program. On one dimension, we are the human computers, programmed by parents, sit-coms, commercials, social location, teachers, social texts all around, by the whole appreciative mass that informs our perceptions. Our view of the world is mediated by this received way of knowing–the values we grow up with, the ideas expressed in our presence, the attitudes so subtly communicated, and fervent concepts, such as "the land of the free and the home of the brave."

Ruling ideologies conceal self-interest without raising too much suspicion, often through language. A telling example was the progressive rephrasing of its ideology of apartheid (rarely using the term itself) by white South Africa, concealing the unequal power relations in the historically progressive terms of "separate development," "multinationalism," "self-determination," and the last, "democratic federalism."[44]

Analysis needs to penetrate beneath the naturalness of ideology, the-way-things-are. Only when this order of things is problematized through critical inquiry, does the smooth, natural, even friendly face of state power reveal its fangs–and sometimes the *pau d'arara*. Greene writes, "[T]here is no consciousness of obstruction, no resentment or restraint when a person experiences no desire to change or to question."[45]

In *Behind the Veil of Economics*, Robert L. Heilbroner asks, "What does the complicated subject matter of economic analysis conceal from view?" He answers, "Vision and ideology,...our deep-lying...notions concerning human nature, history,...and the various disguises by which we come to terms...with the primary but hidden sources of social orchestration."[46] For Heilbroner, behind the veil of economics, including the economics of the marketplace, "stands a social organization embodying a set of values that have large social and moral implications."[47]

The Czech poet-president and former prisoner Vaclav Havel holds that to disclose the truth of ideology, both economics and democracy require a "spiritual or religious base." Reminding us that what is needed is spirit, he pictures "democracy as the triumph of life over ideology, of the broad view over the narrow...of personality over banality–democracy as the individual's responsibility to himself and the universe."[48]

To affect change in the root thinking of the planet, we must in critiquing ideologies, reveal their inherent contradictions and lift them to view. Repressive cultures almost always have some cracks in their ideology, often professions of justice that, when held against the actual conditions of a people, subvert its rhetoric (for example, as democratic federalism was held against Bantustans in South Africa). One of the ways we can penetrate an ideological lens is to entertain hermeneutical (interpretive) suspicion. Even of the Burger model we might be a little suspicious. Seen through feminist models of more communal leadership, we might consider that as beneficent and inclusive as Burger was the community of associates revolved around the force of his personality. Without question, he was the center of the Burger house.

We are not computers; and ideology is rarely, if ever, hegemonic. It takes only one voice to bear witness to something else, to speak otherwise, and an alternative course comes into view. Pietro Spino, the revolutionary priest in Ignazio Silone's *Bread and Wine*, is a literary example of the lone individual who chooses a counter course as a simple act of conscience. Spino's act of resistance challenges the reigning ideology in fascist Italy prior to World War II, and bears witness to an alternative truth. His example is a critical praxis. In continuous interaction, he speaks out, resists, acts in conscience, takes the side of the *cafoni* (the oppressed of his country), analyzes structures of power, and further acts upon his knowing. Spino's struggle for justice, in a circle of action, analysis, and interpretive reflection, is a praxis attempting to bring about in his native region a realistic utopia.

E. Resistance/Refusal

In the small Italian village where he is in hiding, Spino, under the assumed name, "Don Paulo," gets up in the night and in protest to the impending war against Ethiopia, takes a piece of charcoal and scrawls on walls and the steps of a church, "DOWN WITH THE WAR." Paulo later confides,

> The dictatorship is based on unanimity....It's sufficient for one person to say no and the spell is broken....Under every dictatorship,...one man, one perfectly ordinary little man who goes on thinking with his own brain is a threat to public order. Tons of printed paper spread the slogans of the regime,...thousands of priests in the pulpit repeat these slogans....But it's sufficient for one little man, just one ordinary, little man to say no, and the whole of that formidable granite order is imperiled.[49]

Today, perhaps, the peace movement needs to take pieces of charcoal and write impolitely across Pentagon pronouncements our "NO" against national policy when that policy dehumanizes Native Americans, refugees, poor people, single mothers, and when it trains interrogators for Latin American operations. In *The Dark Night of Resistance*, poet and priest Daniel Berrigan, who spent years in United States jails for his own active resistance to policies of war, reflects,

[Resistance is] the wounds suffered day after day in the struggle to remain human and to vindicate life,...[to resist] the canker and spur and itch toward violence....[T]he ante,...prison, exile, the edge....It has to do with the beginnings, following the first stirrings of conscience, the first serious step as a consequence, the first march, the first legal jeopardy, the first trial attended. And everything serious after.[50]

The Civil Rights movement in the United States exemplified such resistance. With the method of nonviolence, the movement refused to accept the structured injustice of Jim Crow, and the violent racism of rope, hoses, and dogs. The intention of the movement was to restructure American society into one of a reconciled and inclusive community. King believed that the moral power of nonviolence is primarily found in what it does to the souls of those committed to it. But the power of nonviolence also appeals to the heart and conscience of the oppressor, essentially appealing to the values held in common with the oppressed, for example, the Bill of Rights of the United States Constitution. The task, perceived by King, is, finally, to save the soul of the United States, ultimately affecting the spiritual essence of social being. King's vision crossed the United States and beyond to a transformed world-house community. The community articulated by King was the beloved community–one that included all races, classes, religions, ethnic groups, and, ultimately, all nations. Transcending economic, social, political, and cultural lines, the vision of the beloved community, carried forth by King and others, is a vision of a world transformed. The vision is one of justice as the spirit and substance of peace.

Resistance on behalf of this vision of justice affects the moral ground of a people. Asian philosophy reminds us that human deeds generate an invisible force. Every thought, every action contributes to world consciousness. Between rank moral evil and heroic self-sacrifice, the moral composition of any society is a sum total of ideals and practice, the character of what visions hold sway, and the whole mix informing public choice, public consciousness, public conscience. Entering this mix, resistance announces in the flesh the compelling vision of a just peace. For Gutierrez, to bear witness to this vision sets in motion a dynamic and mobilizing projection into the future. Resistance lays claim to the subversive power of hope and places us in a wider horizon of expectation. This expectation for King, "sees in this generation's ordeals, the opportunity to transfigure both ourselves and society."[51]

F. Healing the World

Rabbi, psychotherapist, and cofounder of the politics of meaning movement Michael Lerner sees a deep need for healing among not only the dispossessed, but of those caught up in work that characterizes most of American life.

Lerner says that in harried, competitive work, people close off the spiritual essence of their being for negative values: being number one, profits before people, and making it. Advocating a new bottom line, Lerner calls for "psychologically sensitive and caring human beings who can maintain long-term, loving, personal and social relationships." His vision is to "create a society that encourages and supports love and intimacy, friendship and community, ethical sensitivity and spiritual awareness among people." He insists on the "primacy of spiritual harmony,...mutual recognition, and work that contributes to the common good."[52]

Going even further, Mohandas K. Gandhi, King, Day, Gutierrez, and others teach that given the interconnectedness of all humanity, we must not exclude from our love even our enemies. We belong to one another in some essential way. We may stand our ground, resist oppressive power, and refuse to participate in evil purposes, but we must always hold open the possibility of even our enemies' conversion to the neighbor. Explaining his theory of soul-force, or *Satyagraha*, Gandhi writes, "The *Satyagrahi's* object is to convert, not to coerce, the wrongdoer."[53]

The appeal is to the heart. Forbidden to retaliate or humiliate, we must try rather to appeal to the better part within even those who would injure us. King made this appeal to the heart of the oppressor central to his method of nonviolence. Gutierrez teaches that it is not a question of not having enemies, but of not excluding them from our love. It is love of enemies, he claims, that challenges the whole system and becomes subversive.

In the Gospels, Jesus tells us to love our enemies. This itinerant healer, telling us to love our enemies while his own nailed him to the cross, is subversive of both state and synagogue. Preaching a radical love, he threatens Roman hegemony with an alternative kingdom. "But seek first his kingdom and his righteousness," he teaches.[54] He subverts religious rules when eating and drinking with prostitutes and tax collectors (the undesirables of that day). Jesus's kingdom requires that one feed the hungry, care for the sick, visit those in prison. In the Sermon on the Mount, Jesus supersedes the Hebrew understanding of an eye for an eye. He calls his followers to non-retaliation, teaching, "Love your enemies and pray for those who persecute you."[55] Even from the cross, Jesus cries, "Father, forgive them: for they know not what they do."[56] Shifting the locus of loyalty, from Caesar's court and the religious hierarchy, Jesus subverts the powers of his day with a new power of the spirit, the spirit of radical love. For Jesus, it is this spirit of love that heals. When criticized by the Pharisees for his supping with sinners, Jesus answers, "Those who are well have no need of a physician, but those who are sick."[57] Lerner reminds us that the sick are among us, that our society, itself, is sick. What is needed is an attitude of radical love, of giving and forgiving, for the healing and repair of the world, of ourselves.

G. Chosen Exile

The seventh strategy is the chosen exile, an exile chosen in solidarity with those on the edge, the afflicted, the injured. As identified by Jewish theologian Marc Ellis, the chosen exile is an act of radical identification.[58] Choosing to relocate ourselves to the periphery of public life, we enact a radical identification with the exiled and excluded. In some real way, the chosen exile lets the iron of these circumstances enter our own flesh by sharing in some substantial way the lot of those who have no escape. *In extremis*, the chosen exile is an act of love that is transforming, that turns the world towards the beloved community and, within our own hearts, is itself a turning. We come to know what can only be known in the praxis of a chosen exile.

King lived out a chosen exile when, during the Chicago campaign of 1966, he moved to a hot, vermin-infested, walkup, tenement apartment. In one of his last books, he remarks,

> I doubt if the problems of our teeming ghettos will have a great chance to be solved until the white majority through genuine empathy, comes to feel the ache and anguish of the Negroes....[T]he white man must begin to walk in the pathways of his black brothers and feel some of the pain and hurt that throb without letup....[59]

Our presence and close proximity with the poor in acts of advocacy and solidarity, puts into motion a spirit which profoundly speaks to the very psychic foundations of our common humanity. By our presence with the undesirables of our day, with those least regarded among us, we declare the irrevocable value of every human being. When those hoping to create an enduring and just peace situate themselves at the periphery where the tired and troubled, the truant and injured are found, this site becomes the locus of the radical revision of values needed to save our world. Yes, it is still working at all levels of government, and at whatever site, to establish social and political structures for a just peace. But all these levels of effort must be connected to the periphery; the consciousness of the poor must be present at every conference table. Through our solidarity, we must begin to see the truth of our social, political, economic, cultural, and religious arrangements from the perspective of those who feel their consequences.

The chosen exile is a radical response to a time of mechanization and surplus people. Kurt Vonnegut's Eliot Rosewater (described as a Utopian dreamer, a tin-horn saint) enacts a chosen exile upon inheriting the Rosewater Foundation. He moves himself into a storefront and proceeds to share his wealth. "How can we help you?"[60] Eliot writes across the front window. Eliot is not only concerned with redistributing his fortune. He intends "to love these discarded Americans, even though they're useless and unattractive." With sudden conviction, Eliot declares, *"That* is going to be my work of art."[61]

Weil, a French Jew during the rise of Nazism, and a professor and idealist, articulated a new saintliness for her time. Coming from comfort and the position of a settled professional family, Weil sought out her country's lowest strata–the unemployed, the exploited worker, the farm hand, the refugee–and attempted to share their condition. She once said to a factory manager that, without much hope, she had chosen deliberately to adopt the point of view of those at the bottom. Turning from the affluence and privilege into which she was born, she took upon herself the affliction of those who suffered severe deprivation. With all her heart she longed for the most sweeping transformation of the present order. She worked incessantly so that after the war, France would be rebuilt on the concern for love of neighbor. Her singular, and some would say absurd, route toward realizing this hoped-for transformation was to share radically the life of the poor. It was here, at this site-of-exile that she expected to learn how society could be transformed, from the bottom up.

Weil's was an exile chosen *in extremis*, in response to the extreme suffering she knew to be the lot of so many in the world. The center point of her exile was the year she spent working in three factories. With a leave of absence from her professorship, she lived the day-to-day hunger and exhaustion of an unskilled worker. She wanted to understand just how it really was. Subjecting herself to the full force of this oppressive work, she sought to know, to know the actual experience of the worker, and to learn how the oppressiveness of the work could be changed. In his Introduction to Weil's collection, *Waiting for God*, Leslie Fiedler asks, "To what then does she bear witness?" To his own question, he answers, "To the uses of exile and suffering,...to the unforeseen miracle of love."[62]

And then we remember Oxford-educated Gandhi made the untouchable caste of India–whom he renamed the *harijan*, the people of God–the heart of his movement. Day, when not in jail for direct action protest, lived out her calling to peace on the Lower East Side of Manhattan, among the derelicts and destitute. King not only lived in a Chicago slum, but also cast his lot with the striking sanitation workers of Memphis, which cost him his life. Warned of the danger, King replied that the question was not what would become of him if he stopped to help the workers, but rather, "If I do *not* stop to help...what will happen to them? *That's* the question."[63] Jesus in his profound identification with the poor told his followers, "I was hungry and you gave me food, I was thirsty and you gave me drink; I was a stranger and you welcomed me;...naked and you clothed me,...sick and you visited me,...in prison and you came to me." Asked when they had seen him thus, Jesus answered, "In so far as you did this to one of the least of these my brethren, you did it to me."[64]

5. Radical Choice of a Just Peace

In the face of global mortars and missiles, and raging disparities between the affluent and poor, the strategies for building a community of wider loyalty, the beloved community of an emancipatory peace, is the radical choice before us. "The choice is ours," King reminds us, "and though we might prefer it otherwise, we must choose in this crucial moment of human history."[65] The question put to Rosa Burger by her friend in the South African struggle may be our own question: "What choice: Rosa? In this country, under this system, looking at the way blacks live....What else could you choose?"[66]

Burger, Paulo, Rosewater, King, Day, Gutierrez, and Weil all bear witness to the radical choice of a just peace. Alongside the uprooted and tortured, at the cost of their own comfort, they choose to resist the forces of abusive power and to cast their lot with those at the edge. Enacting a chosen exile, they envision a realistic utopia as they work to reconstitute the world. They know the lived reality of those who suffer injustice and they know that it is not disappearances and death squads that ensure peace, but the deep structures of justice.

And what of the spirit called for by Etzioni and Metz? Is there a power of the spirit, a power little studied, yet recognized by all the world's great religions, by artists, songwriters, novelists, a power on the side of life? Is the deepest substratum of existence humanity's power for love and healing? For philosopher Paul Ricoeur, goodness is more primordial than evil. Evil "is the staining, the darkening, the disfiguring of an innocence, a light."[67] For King, the moral arc of the universe is long, but it bends toward justice. Is there finally a power of the spirit, an ineffable power able to penetrate the most oppressive state power, and even able to convert the enemy to the neighbor? In the deep springs of reality, is there a transformative spirit, a spirit of justice that constitutes a fundamental option of human conscience? For mythologist Joseph Campbell, the hero's supreme task is to reclaim from all the dark forces the power of a transfiguring love. This, it would seem, is the task and radical choice for each one of us, in both our personal and public lives, at whatever site. The task is to resist evil, to support, at cost to ourselves, a true democracy constituted by human rights, to feel the pain of the afflicted as our own, and tikkun–to heal and repair. Through a radical revision of values, the task is nothing less than to affect world consciousness. It is to enact a radical praxis of justice, a transformative justice as the spirit, structure, and strategy of peace.

Notes

1. Janice Hill, "Letter to a Political Prisoner," in *Of the Heart and the Bread: An Anthology of Poems for Peacemakers,* ed. Brandywine Peace Community (Swarthmore, Pa.: Plowshares, 1985).

2. "Many Groups try to Put Number on Global Wars," *Press & Sun-Bulletin* (30 December 1996), p. A2.

3. Ariel Dorfman, Author's note, *Last Waltz in Santiago: And Other Poems of Exile and Disappearance*, trans. Edith Grossman (New York: Penguin, 1988).

4. James LeMoyne, "Testifying to Torture," *The New York Times Magazine* (5 June 1988), p. 44.

5. Holly J. Burkhalter, "Guatemala Asks the U. S. for Trouble," *The New York Times* (30 March 1987), p. A19.

6. Jack Nelson-Pallmeyer, *The School of Assassins: The Case for Closing the School of the Americas and for Fundamentally Changing U. S. Foreign Policy* (Maryknoll, N.Y.: Orbis, 1997), p. 11.

7. Leslie Wirpsa, "Silencing the Social Critics: An Untold Story in Columbia," *The National Catholic Reporter* (4 July 1997), p. 11.

8. Jim Clune at Zacchaeus House, Binghamton, New York, on 1 May 1994 (conversation with author).

9. Jonathan Kozol, *Amazing Grace: The Lives of Children and the Consciousness of a Nation* (New York: Crown,1995), p. 109.

10. Robert McAfee Brown, *Making Peace in the Globel Village* (Philadelphia: Westminister, 1981), p. 14.

11. *Ibid.*, p. 15.

12. Robert Ellsberg, ed., *By Little and by Little: The Selected Writings of Dorothy Day* (New York: Alfred A. Knopf, 1983), p. 328.

13. Quoted by Christopher Lehmann-Haupt in his review of David Lindley's *Where Does the Weirdness Go?*, "How Strange is Small and Vice Versa," *The New York Times* (1 August 1996), p. C16.

14. Quoted in Philip J. Hilts, "Listening to the Conversation of Neurons," *The New York Times* (27 May 1997), p. C1.

15. Breyton Breytonbach, *End Papers: Essays, Letters, Articles of Faith, Workbook Notes* (New York: Farrar, Straus and Giroux, 1986), p. 32.

16. Robert Boyer, *Atrocity and Amnesia: The Political Novel since 1945* (New York: Oxford University Press, 1985), p. 127.

17. Nadine Gordimer, *Burger's Daughter* (New York: Viking, 1979), p. 86.

18. Boyer, *Atrocity and Amnesia,* p. 131.

19. Gordimer, *Burger's Daughter*, p. 84.

20. *Ibid.*, p. 172.

21. Adrienne Rich, "Natural Resources," *The Dreams of a Common Language: Poems 1974-1977* (New York: W. W. Norton, 1978), p. 67.

22. Amitai Etzioni, *The Spirit of Community: Rights, Responsibilities, and the Communitarian Agenda* (New York: Crown, 1993), pp. 18 and 20.

23. Johann Baptist Metz, *The Emergent Church*, trans. Peter Mann (New York: Crossroad, 1986), pp. 9, 13, and 30.

24. Jacques Derrida, "Racism's Last Word," in *"Race," Writing, and Difference,* ed. Henry Louis Gates, Jr. (Chicago: The University of Chicago Press, 1986), p. 357.

25. Lateef Islam, orientation presentation for the Ballard & Bard Project for City Youth, 9 October 1996, Marist College.

26. Wendell Phillips Garrison, *William Lloyd Garrison: The Story of His Life Told by His Children* (New York: Century, 1883), vol. 2, p. 230.

27. Metz, *The Emergent Church*, p. 91.

28. Allan Boesak, *Black and Reformed: Apartheid Liberation and the Calvinist Tradition*, ed., Leonard Sweetman (Maryknoll, N.Y.: Orbis, 1984), p. 46

29. Martin Luther King, Jr., *Why We Can't Wait* (New York: New American Library, 1964), p. 77.

30. Martin Luther King, Jr., *Where Do We Go from Here: Chaos or Community?* (Boston: Beacon, 1967), p. 132.

31. Grace Paley, "Introduction: Thinking about Barbara Deming," in Barbara Deming, *Prisons that Could Not Hold* (San Francisco: Spinsters Ink, 1985).

32. Richard Shaull, "Foreward," in Paulo Freire, *Pedagogy of the Oppressed,* trans. Myra Bergman Ramos (New York: Herder and Herder, 1972), p. 15.

33. Maxine Greene, *The Dialectic of Freedom* (New York: Teachers College Press, 1988), pp. 12 and 13.

34. Frank Lentricchia, *Criticism and Social Change* (Chicago: The University of Chicago Press, 1983), p. 2.

35. *Ibid.*, p. 6.

36. *Ibid.*, p. 20

37. *Ibid.,* p. 11.

38. *Ibid.*, p. 34.

39. Henry Giroux, *Border Crossings: Cultural Workers and the Politics of Education* (New York: Routledge, 1992), p. 2.

40. See John P. Kretzmann and John L. McKnight, *Building Communities from the Inside Out* (Chicago: ACTA Publications, 1993).

41. Freire, *Pedagogy*, p. 151.

42. Ignacio Martin-Baro, *Writings for a Liberation Psychology*, ed. Adrienne Aron and Shawn Corne (Cambridge, Mass.: Harvard University Press, 1994), p. 46.

43. Otto Maduro, *Religion and Social Conflict* (Maryknoll, N.Y.: Orbis, 1982), p. xxv.

44. See Anne McClintock and Rob Nixon, "No Names Apart: The Separation of Word and History in Derrida's *Le Dernier Mot du Racisme,*" in *"Race," Writing, and Difference*, ed. Gates, pp. 339-353.

45. Greene, *Dialectic*, p. 11.

46. Robert L. Heilbroner, *Behind the Veil of Economics* (New York: W. W. Norton, 1988), p. 185; see also p. 65.

47. Elizabeth Wolgast, "All Bosses Are Tyrants," review of Robert L. Heilbroner, *Behind the Veil of Economics: Essays in the Worldly Philosophy, The New York Times Review of Books* (26 June 1988), p. 13.

48. Paul Berman, "The Philosopher-King is Mortal," in feature, "The Poet of Democracy and His Burdens," *The New York Times Magazine* (11 May 1997), p. 37.

49. Ignazio Silone, *Bread and Wine,* trans. Eric Mosbacher (New York: New American Library, 1986), pp. 209-210.

50. Daniel Berrigan, *The Dark Night of Resistance* (New York: Doubleday, 1971), pp. 11, 19, and 27.

51. Martin Luther King, Jr., *Stride toward Freedom* (San Francisco: Harper and Row, 1958), p. 220.

52. Michael Lerner, *The Politics of Meaning: Restoring Hope and Possibility in an Age of Cynicism* (New York: Addison-Wesley, 1996), p. 56.

53. Mohandas K. Gandhi, *Nonviolent Resistance (Satyagraha)* (New York: Schocken, 1961), p. 87.

54. The Gospel according to Matthew, in *The New Oxford Annotated Bible*, Revised Standard Version, ed. Herbert G. May and Bruce M. Metzger (New York: Oxford University Press, 1977), 6:33.

55. *Ibid.*, 5:44.

56. The Gospel according to Luke, in *The New Oxford Annotated Bible*, ed. May and Metzger, 23:34.

57. The Gospel according to Mark, in *The New Oxford Annotated Bible*, ed. May and Metzger, 2:17.

58. Marc Ellis, Maryknoll School of Theology (Maryknoll, N.Y., Summer 1982, course lecture).

59. King, *Where Do We Go from Here*, pp. 101-102.

60. Kurt Vonnegut, *God Bless You, Mr. Rosewater* (New York: Dell, 1965), p. 49.

61. *Ibid.*, p. 36.

62. Leslie Fiedler, "Introduction," in Simone Weil, *Waiting for God*, ed. Leslie Fiedler (New York: Harper Colophon, 1951), pp. 9-10.

63. Stephen B. Oates, *Let the Trumpet Sound: The Life of Martin Luther King, Jr.* (New York: Harper and Row, 1982), p. 485.

64. The Gospel according to Matthew, 25:35-41.

65. James M. Washington, ed., *A Testament of Hope: The Essential Writings of Martin Luther King, Jr.* (San Francisco: Harper and Row, 1986), p. 242.

66. Gordimer, *Burger's Daughter*, p. 127.

67. Paul Ricoeur, *The Symbolism of Evil*, trans. Emerson Buchanan (New York: Harper and Row, 1967), p. 156.

Five

AMBIGUOUS ROLES OF RELIGIONS IN WAR AND PEACE

Donald A. Wells

The distinguished historian W. E. H. Lecky concluded:

> In looking back, with our present experience, we are driven to the melancholy conclusion that, instead of diminishing the number of wars, ecclesiastical influence has actually and very seriously increased it. We may look in vain for any period since Constantine, in which the clergy, as a body, has exerted themselves to repress the military spirit.[1]

He then remarked that with the possible exception of Islam no religion has done so much to produce war as was done by the religious leaders of Christendom. If Lecky is correct, what are we to conclude, not merely about Christianity and Islam but about other major religions, such as Judaism, Hinduism, and Buddhism? All who have maintained that religion has played or at least should play a significant role in determining action, should wonder whether Lecky's observation is a function of a radical distortion of religion or whether "onward Buddhist, Muslim, Hindu, Mosaic, or Christian soldiers" represents a fair picture of an essentially warlike message and ministry of their founders.

Popular folklore asserts that religious beliefs generate moral sensitivity and that the loss of religion accounts for decline in basic values. The inference is so firmly believed that one religious group in America calls itself the "moral majority," giving the impression that their religious beliefs entail certain moral actions. If something about religion does serve this function of providing the basis for higher moral action, then we should be able to identify what it is about religion that generates these higher morals. A larger question is whether religion is supposed to affect everything that we do and whether it does. Some may expect that religion will make them better husbands or wives, fathers or mothers, better politicians, plumbers, or doctors, but virtually no religion ever listed the moral steps to those ends.

We will concentrate on a simpler question. Does some causal relationship exist between the various religions and how their members believe or behave, specifically with respect to war? In order that the moral attitude toward war not be as vacuous as the expression, "I hate war" or "Thou shalt not kill," let us see whether conscientious objection to war or at least some critique of war has religious roots for the objector and, if so, what those roots might be. We may raise the same query concerning religious supporters of war. Does their support for war come from their religion? We also want to know if religious persons who support war draw different limits as to what is permissible in war from the limits drawn by nonreligious persons. The bombings of Hiroshima and Nagasaki serve as an example. Christians need to know whether Jesus would have praised the action and whether, even if he personally would not have dropped the bomb, he might have been a chaplain to bless the event. Jews need to know whether Moses would have opposed the Intifada militarily. Buddhists need to know whether the Buddha would have supported the Korean War. Muslims need to be able to answer whether Mohammed would have joined the Croatian army. Would we expect that the religion of the pilot and bombardier of the "Enola Gay" would have influenced their willingness to drop the bombs on Hiroshima and Nagasaki? Would Christians differ from Jews, Muslims, or Buddhists with respect to that act? My own ethical autobiography on war and peace began ambiguously when I became convinced that Jesus was a socialist-pacifist-religious-philosopher. I got this idea, understandably, from a socialist-pacifist-religious-philosopher, who incidentally called my attention to a tract titled, *Would Jesus Join a Labor Union*? The answer was, of course, in the affirmative. Sadly for him and for me he died before explaining whether his pacifism came from his Methodist religion, his socialism, his philosophy, or from some other source. This is the problem before us.

Several facts complicate the answer to this question. First, every major religion is fractured into denominations differing radically from each other, both in beliefs and in practices. It is clear from this that not all believers can claim to be followers of the plans of their founder. On the other hand, this diversity may suggest that the founders had no specific moral advice and that each denomination has always been on its own when it comes to moral choices. A current volume lists over 1,200 separate religious bodies in the United States alone and notes 22 different branches of Presbyterians exist, as well as 54 Baptist, and 52 Seventh Day Adventist, but also 34 different Jewish, 20 Muslim, 52 Hindu, and 57 Buddhist groups all meeting and worshipping separate from each other. [2] This means that we cannot speak in general about any of the larger groups, like Christian, Muslim, or Buddhist, or about what even smaller denominations like Lutherans or Methodists believe about war. Many Protestant groups praise both their members who become soldiers and those who become conscientious objectors. A reasonable inference is that if both are praiseworthy neither is implied from any basic religious premise. Historically, however, conscientious Christian soldiers have far outnumbered conscientious Christian objectors. In World War I in America, for example, the War Department in 1918 reported that fewer than 4,000 out of 2.8 million inducted men claimed to be conscientious objectors.

All but about 350 were Jehovah's Witnesses, Mennonites, and Quakers. The 500 objectors to World War I who served time in prison came from 345 different church denominations, meaning that no denomination had more than a handful.[3]

In the second place, many of the current conflicts pit religions against each other. Muslims and Hindus fought in Kashmir; Catholics and Protestants in Ulster; Christians and Muslims in Sudan; Buddhists and Hindus in Sri Lanka; Shiite and Baha'i in Iran; Christians and Muslims in Cyprus; Sikhs and Hindus in Punjab; Indonesian Muslims and Roman Catholics in Timor; Armenian Christians and Azerbaijani Muslims; and Jews and Muslims in Israel. The size of the defense industry, the strategies of the armies, and the general aggressiveness of national foreign policies seem unaffected by whatever domestic religious claims are made. No religion seems to have made any difference in the frequency that their nations go to war. Whatever moral religious claims Christians or Jews may make, their national war making policies are indistinguishable from those of Hindu, Muslim, Buddhist, or so-called secular countries. Those who claim that the United States is a Christian nation and a peace-loving one need to explain why the United States leads the world in arms manufacture and sales and has the largest military.

In the third place, religions are complex affairs and it is not obvious what it is about them that is supposed to generate moral commands. We might emphasize: (1) what the relevant beliefs may be; (2) what religious experiences consist of; (3) what acts may be considered religiously obligatory; and (4) if religion rests on feelings, what these feelings might be. If religion does generate ethical views on war, from which aspect of religion does the inference come? Evangelical Christians commonly quote scripture to justify whatever they endorse, and both supporters and opponents of war have found scriptural support. Such biblical citing, however, is not an intellectual option for most mainline Christian denominations, which do not view scripture as much of a guide of any sort. Vague generalizations about the fatherhood of God or the brotherhood of man suffice for some as a basis for war protest, but few contemporary theologians make any explicit inferences from belief to action relevant to our problem. It will be sufficient for our purposes to determine whether certain common attitudes toward war and peace are asserted by persons of common religious denominations. Few religious groups were ever explicit on objection to war as were Quakers, Mennonites, Schwenkfelders, or Brethren who interpreted "Thou shalt not kill" as implying conscientious objection to all and any war. Indeed, in a volume giving the religious creeds of over 1,500 American churches only those four groups gave any advice on war objection.[4] Most religions have a general commandment against killing, but it has rarely been interpreted as a mandate to conscientious objection. Because most religious devotees have consci-

to conscientious objection. Because most religious devotees have conscientiously endorsed war, given the right circumstances, we need to know whether this was inferred from some religious commitment.

In the fourth place, we need to come to some conclusion whether the initial presumption might rest on a mistake. Do religious persons deduce moral conclusions from religious premises? Several hypotheses are possible to account for the obvious lack of unanimity. (1) Some religions speak essentially to private matters and they emphasize primarily inner feelings. No particular moral acts seem entailed as a consequence. A considerable amount of religious observance does deal with advice about self contemplation rather than social action. In spite of well-known commandments many religions have no particular social message, no particular view on war, no particular view on capitalism or socialism, or on any other social issue. Occasionally clergy may urge the members of their congregations to vote a certain way, but most advice is more general such as the advice of Polycarp of Smyrna, "Little children, love one another." Some religions attract persons with personal rather than social concerns. Many devotees have the kind of private conviction that produces a Simon of Stylites or an isolated Eremite. Some religions develop meditation centers, and celibate monks or nuns, whose primary function is to pray, spin prayer wheels or contemplate in isolation. (2) Perhaps in the absence of any specific ethical system deriving from their religion, believers have historically tended to adopt the mores of the societies in which they exist. The Protestant "two-sword" theory is a case in point. Christians only worry about the godly sword of the spirit, while the material sword is left to the prevailing Caesar. But this means that worldly ethics does not derive from religion. In cases where killing was required, consciences were sometimes assuaged by the creation of just war theories administered by the secular power. Saint Augustine thought that Christian soldiers would be more humane than heathen soldiers, but he did not expect them to be pacifists. The major denominations in the United States have usually supplied chaplains for the soldiers in war although not all religious persons are comfortable with that role.[5] (3) For a variety of reasons and sometimes with the connivance of the powers that be, religions have been used in the way characterized by Karl Marx as an opium providing social stability. Because the major religions developed in powerful and warlike nations, it may be no surprise that "Thou shalt not kill" was commonly a tribal mandate against taking life within the group, as it was for those Jews who first entered the promised land. To keep the issue within manageable limits, I will comment on some of the major faiths but concentrate primarily on Christianity. The question is, "Do religious persons infer their views on war from their religion?"

1. Buddhism

Both of the major branches of Buddhism (Mahayana and Theravada) urge their devotees not to kill, but to forgive their enemies. Both assert the Five Precepts to abstain from killing, lying, stealing, intoxicants, and sexual misconduct. According to Theravada Buddhism, one of the ten duties of a ruler is to promote peace and prevent war. Some sects of Buddhism have a long history of nonviolence, and Buddhism was said to have modified the warlike characteristics of the Mongols and the Tibetans. Indeed, a Turkish Khan was advised to keep away from Buddhists, if he wished to remain militarily strong. Yet at the end of the Sung dynasty orthodox monks fought against the Mongols under the banner, "Crush the demons."

From ancient times martial prowess was one of the traits of greatness. Although many believed that to kill or to be a soldier was an offense, Buddhist clergy and laity, like their Christian counterparts, commonly fought wars with each other. For 2,000 years Buddhists found scriptural justification for going to war. Kings went to battle with a relic of the Buddha on their spears, just as Christians went to battle with the emblem of the cross on their shields. In 515, Fa-ch'ing led 50,000 troops in rebellion against the Northern Weiu and announced that soldiers would become bodhisattvas as soon as they had killed one of the enemy. Was this a misreading of the message of the Buddha?

Under Mao Tse-tung many monks were eager to show that as religious leaders they were not reactionaries and they found religious justification for the Maoist movement. When China entered the Korean war a meeting of 2,500 Buddhist monks, nuns, and devotees in Wuhan (20 January 1951) condemned United States imperialism as more murderous than fascism and concluded that such imperialism and Buddhism could not coexist. Even monks and nuns went off to the Korean war and it was said that to fight the American imperialist demons who were breaking world peace was, according to Buddhist doctrine, not only blameless but gave rise to merit. Some Chinese Buddhists raised money for a fighter plane (1951-1952) which they named "The Chinese Buddhist." At the same time, Thich Nhat Hanh remarked: "Men cannot be our enemies. Our enemies are intolerance, hatred, and discrimination." These lie in the hearts of man.[6] Also with his reputation for peace the Dalai Lama received the Nobel Peace Prize in 1989. Who really spoke for Buddhism? In Japan from the tenth to the sixteenth century, monks were also soldiers. Monks trained in the art of war, and the emperor Shirakawa was recorded as saying that he could not control the flooding of the river Kame or the turbulence of the Buddhist monks. Monasteries fought each other and they persecuted new sects, especially Zen. The current militant sect, Sokagakkai in Japan, emerged as a lay organization of the Nichiren sect. What can a contemporary Buddhist conclude? If Buddhists had made the decision and if they had the means, would they have dropped the bombs on Hiroshima and Nagasaki? We know that pacifist Buddhists have existed but so also have Buddhist soldiers. Are the two options coincidental? If both are acceptable, does this not mean that neither is entailed? A tradition also exists in Japan for conscientious objection based on either religion or socialism.[7]

2. Islam

Pacifism was never an integral part of the Muslim religion. While intertribal warfare within the brotherhood or community of Islam was banned, Mohammed supported wars for defense as well as pre-emptive raids against infidel tribes in Arabia. After Mohammed's death, Islam was occasionally spread by military conquest and the concept of *jihad* (striving in the way of Allah) was interpreted as war against unbelievers and enemies of the faith. This position was supported by Ayatollah Ruhollah Khomeini in 1942: "Those who know nothing of Islam pretend that Islam counsels against war. Those who say this are witless. Islam says: 'Kill all the unbelievers just as they would kill you all.'"[8] In 1986, Mohammed Taqi Partovi Sabzevari wrote, "A people that is not prepared to kill and to die in order to create a just society cannot expect any support from Allah. It is Allah who puts the gun in our hand. But we cannot expect Him to pull the trigger as well, simply because we are faint-hearted."[9] Yet, in the context of the call of Saddam Hussein for a united Muslim front in the Gulf War, the responses of Muslims in Iran, Jordan, Egypt, Algeria, and Pakistan gave little evidence of any such unanimity.[10]

Four kinds of holy war were recognized: (1) defensive war; (2) war against People of the Book; (3) wars against polytheists; and (4) wars against apostates, dissenters, and bandits. Muslim jurists formulated rules comparable to Christian just war theory. Examples of their rules are (1) only a caliph can declare war, (2) the war must be waged with good intentions, and (3) non-combatants should be spared unless they were helping the enemy cause. Early Muslim jurists raised the issue of proportionality in the means of waging war and attempted to formulate rules limiting damage to civilians, the poisoning of wells, and the cessation of war during holy days. Current Islamic militancy has supported the advocacy of holy war against Western influences, the assassination of Anwar Sadat by the radical al-Jihad group, and the exploits of the Hiozb-Allah (Party of God) in Lebanon. Would devout Muslims know from their beliefs that limits to permissible violence existed and that the bombing of Hiroshima and Nagasaki exceeded the limit? Some Sufi Muslims have interpreted *jihad* as emphasizing personal mastery and self-purification rather than military conquest. The somewhat pacifist Ahmadiyya movement claims over ten million followers; this needs to be balanced against the militant tradition. Currently, conscientious objection does not appear to be a live option for Muslims.[11] I suggest that conscientious support for war does derive from Muslim religion.

3. Hinduism

In the *Bhagavad Gita*, Arjuna reported that, on the eve of battle, he had misgivings about killing, and he initially proposed to cast his weapons aside. However, Krishna said to Arjuna, "There is nothing more welcome for a man of the warrior class than a righteous war," and "it is only the lucky who get such an unsolicited opportunity for war, which is an open door to heaven"(2:31-32). Krishna persuaded Arjuna to go into battle using two familiar religious arguments: (1) Physical death does not touch the essential soul and (2) No greater good exists for a Kshatriya than war required by duty. Krishna concluded, "If you do not engage in this lawful battle, then you will fail in your duty and your glory and incur sin" (2:33). If one were a Brahmin, then nonviolence would be appropriate.

Jains practiced *ahimsa* (reverence for life) to such a degree that they became vegetarians, and some would not even be farmers because they would have to pull carrots violently from their ground. In spite of this, Jainism produced men of violence and great military commanders. Hindus have fought Muslims throughout much of their history. Although Mohandas Gandhi urged nonviolence, he also said that every person must find his or her own light, and that it was better to be a sincere soldier than an insincere pacifist.[12]

Hindus have not agreed about how to interpret the *Gita* story. Gandhi, for example, considered that the *Gita* account was not a report of an actual battle so much as a doctrinal portrayal of the human conflict between the higher and lower selves, and that it gave no moral advice about how Hindus should behave in war. Does this mean that Krishna has no advice to contemporary Hindus about war? Swami Ranganathananda insisted that Hindus have traditionally not engaged in aggressive wars outside India. K. Shridharan observed that legends praising nonviolence are plentiful in folklore.[13] Many Western religious pacifists were inspired by the ideas of nonviolence asserted by Gandhi. It is not clear whether Gandhi was a pacifist because he was a Hindu or a pacifist and incidentally a Hindu as well. Followers of Hinduism have been both conscientious objectors to and conscientious supporters of war.

4. Judaism

All religions have paid a moral price for having a homeland. Pentateuchal Judaism believed in holy war and their God supported their first wars against the Canaanites. The concept of a holy war was shared by the Islamic *jihad* and the medieval Christian crusaders. The idea of holy war for a homeland resurfaced in the recent Palestine-Israel conflict in the form of Gush Emunim, a radical settlers movement whose leaders substituted the Palestinian Arabs for the Canaanites and insisted that they be dealt with in the same harsh way. Other Jewish groups, however, like the Oz Veshem and Netivot Shalom, urged compromise and an end to the *Intifada*.

Pacifist clergy in America were rare in World War I. R. H. Abrams reported that only seventy pacifist ministers were known to exist, and three of these were rabbis.[14] A small number of Jewish conscientious objectors in America were imprisoned in World War I and World War II. A survey of pacifism in Canada during the 1930s mentioned Maurice N. Eisendrath, Rabbi of Holy Blossom Temple in Toronto.[15] He was a Reform Jew and the first president of the Toronto Fellowship of Reconciliation (FOR) in 1930 and, in that capacity, represented Canada at the World Assembly of the FOR. He said that his pacifism was not derived solely from his Judaism, although he cited as support for his position the Old Testament book Micah about beating swords into plowshares. At a meeting at Riverside Church in New York City on 4 May 1935, over 200 clergymen, including some rabbis, announced they would not support another war. These few cannot be said to speak for Judaism.

Understandably few Jewish conscientious objectors surfaced in World War II. Obviously the existence of the Holocaust was primarily influential. Some Jewish objectors reported that their scarcity was also due to the bad publicity from religious conservatives that this was a "Jewish war," and that this publicity prompted them to keep a low profile. Current Israeli law makes no provision for conscientious objection, although the Bret Shalom and Kedma Mizracha groups in Israel promoted Arab-Jewish rapprochement and their members refused both combatant and noncombatant service in the Israeli army.[16] Developments since the 1940s prompted some Jewish leaders to question the presumption that any war can be just.[17] Consistent with this opposition to war, a group of 2,500 Jewish veterans of the 1982 war against Lebanon refused to serve again as soldiers (a kind of selective objection). On the other hand, a British Jewish legion fought in World War I and another in World War II. Although the major Jewish leaders (like the major Christian leaders) supported the United State's role in the Vietnam War, others, like Alfred Lilienthal, even criticized the wars in which the Israelis had engaged since 1948.[18] Representatives of Reform Judaism, the Orthodox Congregations, and the Synagogue Council of America opposed the nuclear policies of Ronald Reagan, then President of the United States, and a few rabbis, like Stephen Wise, joined Protestant and Roman Catholic clergy in opposing all war. Judaism does not, however, appear to have any univocal position on conscientious objection and it is not apparent that what Jewish pacifists there are derive their position from their religion. Albert Einstein once observed,

"My pacifism is an instinctive feeling, a feeling that possesses me because the murder of men is disgusting. My attitude is not derived from any intellectual theory."[19] With regard to the bombing of Hiroshima and Nagasaki, Jews might take a lesson from the question of Abraham to Jehovah recorded in Genesis 18:23 when Jehovah contemplated the destruction of Sodom and Gomorrah, "Wilt thou also destroy the righteous with the wicked?" and infer that the bombs should never have been dropped. In any event, no current shortage of conscientious Jewish soldiers exists.

5. Christianity

Some scholars, like C. J. Cadoux and G. M. C. MacGregor, claimed that Jesus could be understood only from a pacifist presumption.[20] Cadoux commented that the vast number of Christians stayed out of all political involvement including armies, and he noted that the evidence was "exceedingly slight" for the existence of even a single Christian soldier between 60 and 165 CE[21] Even after the conversion of Constantine, the Roman armies were said to be the primary refuge of pagans.[22] As late as 299, Eusebius noted that a certain general Veturius attempted to purge Christians from the army under his command because they made poor soldiers. What inferences may we draw from this? Augustine believed that the Christian religion would make a crucial difference. He observed in *The City of God* that, with respect to war, the advent of Christianity would banish barbarity and introduce humanness. He concluded, "Whoever does not see that this is to be attributed to the name of Christ and the Christian temper, is blind; whoever sees this, and gives no praise, is ungrateful; whoever hinders anyone from praising it, is mad."[23] On the other hand, Celsus (second century) asserted that Christians were so uninvolved in worldly matters that the question of military service did not occur to them. Justin Martyr (100-165) claimed that becoming a Christian entailed altering those actions associated with hating and killing.[24] Christians would not go to war. Tertullian (160-230), after his conversion, stated that it was not proper for a Christian to make a profession of the sword.[25] But who, if any, of these speaks for Christianity and what is their inference?

Paul Ramsey believed that the Christians of the first two centuries were universally pacifists but that this was a function of the times and not of their religion.[26] Roland Bainton reminded his readers that historically Christians were assumed to be pacifists and the early Church Fathers' attitude toward pacifism ought not to be lightly dismissed.[27] The distinguished historian, Kenneth Scott Latourette, claimed that no Christian writing for the first three centuries had survived that condoned Christian participation in war.[28]

On the other hand, Umphrey Lee insisted that the effort to find Jesus speaking to the modern issues of war was misguided. He claimed that "there is in the Gospels no ethical system, no moral code."[29] John Bennett said that he wrote against a background of Christian ethics when he concluded that the dominant Christian traditions opposed pacifist solutions.[30] Adolf Harnack said of Jesus that he was not a revolutionary and had no political program.[31] Indeed, the United States Draft Board during World War II may have been prescient when they allowed Conscientious Objector status only if it had religious roots. Christian objectors were a rare breed, while objectors on socialist or generally humane grounds were common.

From the middle of the third century, military metaphors for the Christian life became standard. Christians were soldiers; Christ was a general; the church was a camp; and baptism was a military oath of allegiance. In 314, the Council of Arles condemned conscientious objectors and Louis the Pious of France said that the best answer to a contentious pacifist Jew is to run a sword into him as far as it will go.[32] By the fifth century non-Christians were excluded from the military profession.[33] After centuries of Christian military crusades, it was no surprise that Martin Luther was able to adjust Christian conscience to war in his essay, "That Soldiers, Too, Can Be Saved." Although Christians were to turn the other cheek in church, they were urged to use the sword outside. The hand that wielded the sword was not theirs, but God's.[34]

Christian religious objections to war were revived in the twelfth century by the Waldenses of Southern France and Northern Italy; later in Bohemia under Petr Chelcicky; in Switzerland, Germany, and the Netherlands by anabaptist Brethren and Mennonites.[35] Some objected to war chiefly because they believed that shedding blood prevented the achievement of salvation. Some, for example, Christadelphians and Jehovah's Witnesses, objected to war as an interim ethic while reserving the need to go to war at some final day of reckoning. Other Protestant groups argued that war was inconsistent with the Fatherhood of God, the early role of the church, and the moral order of the universe. Christian pacifism reappeared later with Hugo Grotius, the great Dutch jurist, who wrote in his major work: "It does not seem right that Christians should be compelled to serve against their will."[36] The implication was that Christian conscientious objectors existed. Erasmus (1466-1536) affirmed that "the man who engages in war by choice...is a wicked man: he sins against nature, against God, and against man."[37] Mennonites, Anabaptists, Hutterites, and Quakers emerged. The Mennonite Articles of Faith of 1632 (known as the Dort Confession) stated in Article 14 that Jesus had forbidden his followers to be soldiers. A group of high English churchmen listed this as an "Anabaptistical error." The treatment of pacifists was a varied one. In Prussia under Frederick I (1711), Mennonites were exempted from military service. Under Frederick William (1713), Mennonites were forced into the army. Under Frederick the Great (1740), Mennonites were again exempted. But by the time of Frederick III in the 1860s, pacifist sects were denied common civil rights.[38]

In America, the Puritans and most New England clergy rejected pacifism as "smacking of Arminianism" and asserted that pacifists were no better than Anabaptists who sapped the will for self-defense. Military sermons were preached on most colonial occasions. The general theme was that wars were the result of sin and that the profession of soldiering was consistent with the Christian life. Many Puritans carried Native American scalps at their belts. So many Presbyterians were in the continental army that it was commonly referred to as "the Presbyterian army." Yet a Presbyterian business man, David Low Dodge, wrote one of the first pacifist tracts, *War Inconsistent with the Religion of Jesus Christ.*

An unseemly militarism took over the churches during World War I. The Bishop of London urged young English soldiers to "kill Germans...kill the good as well as the bad....[I]t is a war for purity, I look on everyone who dies in it as a martyr."[39] In Oregon in 1918, a Methodist minister told a Portland Rotary Club, "There is no place on the top side of the American soil for a Pacifist.... If you have one shoot him."[40] The Reverend Charles E. Locke said that pacifists were worse than pro-Germans and should all be exported to Berlin. At a peace conference at Long Beach (1918), three ministers were sentenced to 6 months in prison and fined $1,200 for publicly quoting the scripture, "Love your enemy." Edward Pell of Virginia wrote, "We must fight pacifism, because it is contrary to the teachings of Christ." Lynn Harold Hough, professor at Garrett Theological School, wrote *The Clean Sword* to prove that the Bible did not support pacifism. Former Disciples clergyman Harold Bell Wright wrote for the YMCA a pamphlet, *The Practice of Friendship*, assuring the readers that Jesus himself would enlist. The picture on the cover showed Jesus with a grenade at his waist thrusting a bayonet into a German soldier. Albert Dieffenbach, editor of the *Unitarian Register*, editorialized that Jesus would have been happy to carry a bayonet. The religious journal, *Living Church*, said that Quakers were not entitled to be called Christians; the editor of the Methodist *Zion's Herald* affirmed that the scriptures did not allow "standing room" for Quakers.[41] According to the War Department, in World War I only 3,989 out of 2,810,286 made any claim for conscientious objection. Most of these were Jehovah's Witnesses, Mennonites, or Quakers.

The ambiguity was illustrated in a study conducted in 1932 at the University of Chicago to determine whether religious conservatism or liberalism affected either the pacifism or militarism of the members. The investigator concluded that Catholics and Lutherans were the most militaristic while Jews, Christian Scientists, Methodists, and those who identified themselves simply as Protestants were the most pacifistic. No evidence was provided that either pacifism or militarism was consciously inferred from religious premises, although the author concluded the general rule: "The more conservative a church is the more militaristic it will tend to be, and the more liberal a church is the more pacifistic it will profess to be."[42] This conclusion seemed to be challenged by a report in 1939 by the Jesuit weekly, *America*, of a survey of 54,000 Catholic students of both sexes that asked whether they would be conscientious objectors. Their polls showed that twenty percent would volunteer in the military, forty-four percent would accept if conscripted, and thirty-six percent would be conscientious objectors.[43]

The leadership of Christian churches presented a fractured front during World War II. In December 1941, nineteen months after the Methodist Church had announced that it would never officially support or endorse war, its bishops voted that the Methodists of America would loyally support the President and the nation. The president of the Northern Baptist Convention stated that Baptist ministers were all out to win. The National Catholic Welfare Conference agreed. Overwhelming support emerged for Christian and Jewish chaplains. The historic peace churches endeavored with some success to hold to their traditional pacifism. Mennonites had the best record although only three out of five of their eligible young men filed as conscientious objectors. Fewer than one eighth of the Brethren young men rejected military service, and sixty-two percent of the Brethren churches dropped the pacifist pledge as a condition of membership. Most Quaker colleges accepted ROTC and three-fourths of all Quakers drafted did not claim to be conscientious objectors.[44] Of the objectors who served time in prison, most were Mennonites, Church of the Brethren, Society of Friends, and Jehovah's Witnesses. Sibley and Jacob reported that of those still in prison in 1945, 2,724 were Jehovah's Witnesses, 475 from other religions, and 1,504 non-religious objectors.[45] This latter datum suggests that religion was not a necessary condition. No theological Christian dogma clearly or consistently condemns military necessity as a justification for the deliberate killing of the innocent.

Christian theologians did not agree whether World War II deserved Christian sanction. Karl Barth criticized the British church for not fighting the war "unequivocally in the name of Jesus Christ."[46] Bennett stated that while we cannot say that the war is "holy" we can say that it is "righteous."[47] Beginning 4 December 1940, *The Christian Century* ran a series titled, "If America is drawn into the war, can you as a Christian participate in it or support it?" Bennett, Reinhold Niebuhr, Henry Pitt VanDusen, Charles B. Taft, and Francis J. McConnell said, "Yes." John Haynes Holmes, Albert E. Day, Albert W. Palmer, Harry Emerson Fosdick, and Ernest Fremont Tittle said, "No."[48] In 1948 the World Council of Churches sanctioned three disparate positions as Christian options: (1) Support for national wars, (2) nuclear pacifism, and (3) total pacifism. In 1950 a commission of the federal Council of Churches of Christ in America issued a report, "The Christian Conscience and Weapons of Mass Destruction," that rejected pacifism, calling it "irresponsible," and denied that nuclear weapons were forbidden by any Christian concern.[49] Gordon Zahn remarked that he was the only pacifist writer among the nine Catholic contributors to a much publicized volume on religion and modern warfare.[50]

This is a very confusing story whose conclusion is, at the least, that religious leaders have not agreed whether any particular social action seems implicitly required from religious commitments. The acceptance of just war theory, urged by Augustine and Thomas Aquinas, did not enable Christians to find any clear stand on war, although it did seem to make absolute pacifism untenable. Religious people do not seem to possess any univocal advice on such matters. Many religious persons accepted Immanuel Kant's belief in the absolute worth of persons. Unlike Kant, they claimed that it was rooted in their theology.[51] How do religious supporters of dropping the bombs on Hiroshima and Nagasaki explain to the descendants of the victims that the nuclear oven that obliterated their relatives was on a higher moral plane than that which obliterated the helpless Jews in Nazi ovens? John C. Ford once concluded that, if we have to resort to nuclear weapons to wipe out the communists or be wiped out by them, "I would consider that we had arrived at the point where absolute moral imperatives were at stake, and the followers of Christ should abandon themselves totally to divine Providence rather than forsake these imperatives."[52] Arthur Compton, who assisted in the development of the bombs and advised U.S. President Harry S. Truman to use them, asserted: "I think that not only did God condone our act in dropping the bombs, but that it was only with His help and inspiration that the job was done."[53] On the other hand, in 1958 the British Campaign for Nuclear Disarmament demanded that Great Britain abandon the hydrogen bomb in the name of "Christianity, humanity, morality and sanity."[54] Paul Tillich claimed that the first use of such a weapon could not be justified, but that a limited nuclear response could have a Christian defense.[55] The Roman Catholic ethicist, John Courtney Murray, justified a Christian use of nuclear weapons.[56] It does not appear that most religious believers made formal inferences from their beliefs to any specific moral acts. Many Christian theological beliefs, such as the divinity of Jesus, the Trinity, the immaculate conception of Mary, or immortality, do not seem to imply any moral response in this world of space and time. Most religious groups have a special social action commission that does assert specific moral positions on many matters, including war. It is, however, an odd fact that only a small fraction of the members of churches with such social action pronouncements ever support them. Local congregations of typical groups normally distance themselves from any specific social stand of their social action groups, let alone of their hierarchies.

Many Catholic, Jewish, and Protestant conscientious objectors and conscientious supporters appeared during World War II and Vietnam, independently of the general absence of any specific positions of their respective hierarchies.[57] Few on either side ever believed that they lacked denominational support. With the probable exception of Islam, the major religions all have conscientious objectors and conscientious supporters of war, and both groups usually insist that their religious premises support their actions. It is also evident that objection to war has not required religious roots.

Notes

1. W. E. H. Lecky, *History of European Morals* (New York: D. Appleton, 1929), vol. 2, p. 254.

2. J. Gordon Melton, *Encyclopedia of American Religions* (Wilmington, N.C.: McGrath, 1978).

3. Ray H. Abrams, *Preachers Present Arms* (New York: Round Table, 1933).

4. J. Gordon Melton, *The Encyclopedia of American Religious Creeds* (Detroit, Mich.: Gale Research Company, 1988).

5. Robert E. Klitgaard, "Onward Christian Soldiers: Dehumanization and the Military Chaplain," *The Christian Century*, 87 (18 November 1970); Willard L. Sperry, ed., *The Religion of Soldier and Sailor* (Cambridge, Mass.: Harvard University Press, 1945); and Eugene Debs, *Writings and Speeches* (New York: Hermitage, 1948), p. 49.

6. Thich Nhat Hanh, *Vietnam: The Lotus in a Sea of Fire* (London: SCM Press, 1967), p. 119.

7. Nobuya Bamba and John F. Howes, eds., *Pacifism in Japan: The Christian and Socialist Tradition* (Vancouver: University of British Columbia Press, 1978).

8. See Amir Taheri, *Holy Terror: Inside the World of Islamic Terrorism* (Bethesda, Md.: Adler and Adler, 1987), p. 242.

9. See *ibid.*, p. 255.

10. James Piscatori, ed., *Islamic Fundamentalisms and the Gulf Crisis* (Chicago: The American Academy of Arts and Sciences, 1991).

11. Habib Boulares, *Islam: The Fear and the Hope* (London: Zob Books, 1990).

12. Peter Brock, "Was Gandhi Ready to Become a Combatant in the Summer of 1918?" *Studies in Peace History* (York, G.B.: William Sessions, 1991).

13. K. Shridharani, *War without Violence* (New York: Garland, 1972).

14. Abrams, *Preachers Present Arms*, p. 197.

15. Thomas P. Socknat, *Witness against War: Pacifism in Canada, 1900-1945* (Toronto: University of Toronto Press, 1987).

16. Penny Rosenwasser, *Voices from a Promised Land* (Willamantic, Conn.: Curbstone, 1992); and Colin Schindler, *Ploughshares into Swords* (London: Y. B. Tauris, 1991).

17. See Donald H. Bishop, "Judaism and War," in *An Encyclopedia of War and Ethics*, ed. Donald A. Wells (Westport, Conn.: Greenwood, 1996), pp. 250-252.

18. Alfred Lilienthal, *The Zionist Connection* (New York: Dodd, Mead, 1978).

19. Peter Mayer, ed., *The Pacifist Conscience* (New York: Holt, Rinehart and Winston, 1966), p. 235.

20. Cecil J. Cadoux, *The Early Christian Attitude to War* (London: Headley Brothers, 1919); Cecil J. Cadoux, *The Early Church and the World* (Edinburgh: T. and T. Clark, 1925); and G. M. C. MacGregor, *The New Testament Basis for Pacifism* (London: James Clarke, 1936).

21. Cadoux, *The Early Church and the World*, pp. 115 and 275.

22. G. R. Watson, *The Roman Soldier* (Ithaca, N.Y.: Cornell University Press, 1969), p. 133.

23. Saint Augustine, *The City of God* (New York: Macmillan, 1950), bk. 1, sec. 7.

24. Justine Martyr, *The First Apology*, in *The Ante-Nicene Fathers*, ed. Alexander Roberts and James Donaldson (New York: Christian Literature, 1890), vol. 1, ch. 14, p. 167.

25. Tertullian, *Apology*, in *The Ante-Nicene Fathers*, ed. Roberts and Donaldson,vol. 3, ch. 42, p. 49; Tertullian, *On Idolatry*, in *The Ante-Nicene Fathers*, vol. 3, ch. 19, p. 73; and Tertullian, *The Chaplet*, in *The Ante-Nicene Fathers*, vol. 3, ch. 1, p. 93.

26. Paul Ramsey, *War and the Christian Conscience: How Shall Modern War Be Conducted Justly?* (Durham, N.C.: Duke University Press, 1961), p. 1.

27. Roland H. Bainton, "Christian Pacifism Reassessed," *The Christian Century*, 75 (23 July 1958), p. 847.

28. Kenneth Scott Latourette, *A History of Christianity* (New York: Harper and Brothers, 1953), p. 242.

29. Umphrey Lee, *The Historic Church and Modern Pacifism* (Nashville, Tenn.: Abingdon-Cokesbury, 1943), pp. 151, 37.

30. John C. Bennett, ed., *Nuclear Weapons and the Conflict of Conscience* (New York: Charles Scribner's, 1962), p. 93.

31. Adolf Harnack, *What Is Christianity?* (New York: Harper and Row, 1957), p. 102.

32. W. R. Inge, *Christian Ethics and Modern Problems* (New York: G. P. Putnam's Sons, 1930), pp. 318 and 319.

33. Sydney D. Bailey, *War and Conscience in the Nuclear Age* (New York: Saint Martin's, 1987), p. 10.

34. Martin Luther, *Works* (Washington: The Carnegie Institution, 1917), vol. 3, p. 36.

35. Peter Brock, *Freedom From Violence: Sectarian Nonresistance from the Middle Ages to the Great War* (Toronto: University of Toronto Press, 1991), pp. 269-270.

36. Hugo Grotius, *The Law of War* (Oxford: Clarendon Press, 1925), bk. 2, ch. 26, sec. 5.

37. Inge, *Christian Ethics*, p. 320.

38. Lawrence J. Baack, "Frederick William III, the Quakers, and the Problem of Conscientious Objection in Prussia," *Journal of Church and State*, 20:2 (Spring 1978), p. 306.

39. Roland Bainton, *Christian Attitudes Toward War and Peace* (Nashville, Tenn.: Abingdon, 1960), p. 207.

40. George M. Marsden, *Religion and American Culture* (New York: Harcourt Brace, 1990), p. 176.

41. Ray H. Abrams, "Preachers Present Arms," *The Christian Century*, 57 (3 January 1940), p. 15.

42. D. D. Droba, "Churches and War Attitudes," *Sociology and Social Research*, 17 (July-August 1932), p. 550.

43. Patricia McNeal, "Catholic Conscientious Objection during World War II," *The Catholic Historical Review*, 61:2 (April 1975), p. 225.

44. Lawrence S. Wittner, *Rebels against War* (Philadelphia: Temple University Press, 1984), pp. 37 and 45.

45. Mulford Q. Sibley and Philip E. Jacob, *Conscription of Conscience* (Ithaca, N.Y.: Cornell University Press, 1952), p. 498.

46. Editorial: "Barth Says Britain's War Is Christian," *The Christian Century*, 58 (17 September 1941), p. 1132.

47. John C. Bennett, "If America Is Drawn into the War, Can You, as a Christian Participate in It, or Support It?" *The Christian Century*, 57 (4 December 1940), p. 1508.

48. See *The Christian Century*, 57 (4 December 1940) to 58 (5 February 1941).

49. "The Christian Conscience and Weapons of Mass Destruction," Report of a Commission of the Federal Council of Churches of Christ in America, *The Christian Century*, 67 (13 December 1950), pp. 1489-1491.

50. William J. Nagle, ed., *Morality and Modern Warfare* (Baltimore, Md.: Helicon Press, 1960).

51. Charles Chatfield, *For Peace and Justice: Pacifism in America, 1914-1941* (Knoxville, Tenn.: University of Tennessee Press, 1971), pp. 329-330.

52. John C. Ford, "The Hydrogen Bombing of Cities," in *Morality and Modern Warfare*, ed. Nagle, p. 103.

53. Arthur H. Compton, "God and the Atom," *American Magazine* (October 1950), p. 118.

54. See Vera Brittain, "British Peace Movements Today," *The Christian Century*, 75 (19 November 1958), p. 1334.

55. Paul Tillich, "The Nuclear Dilemma: A Discussion," *Christianity and Crisis*, 21 (13 November 1961), p. 204.

56. John Courtney Murray, "Theology in Modern War," in *Morality in Modern Warfare*, ed. Nagle, p. 75.

57. Gordon C. Zahn, "Catholic Opposition to Hitler: The Perils of Ambiguity," *Journal of Church and State*, 13:3 (Autumn 1971), p. 424; Thomas E. Quigley, ed., *American Catholics and Vietnam* (Grand Rapids, Mich.: William B. Eerdmans, 1968); and McNeal, "Catholic Conscientious Objection, pp. 222-242.

Six

PLATO AND ECHO-FEMINISM: PLATONIC PSYCHOLOGY AND POLITICS FOR PEACE

Mary Lenzi

1. Why Plato Now?

Contemporary feminist theory and practice inherit critical roots and aims from Plato. Both Plato and feminists radically re-envision the psychology and politics of gender, justice, war, and peace. In similar ways, their philosophical projects focus on redirecting humanity's individual, natural impulses toward creative, peaceful political society and ways of life, rather than destructive, warring ones. Moreover, both demonstrate that the outward projections of conflicted inner selves clearly warrant substantive restructuring of society and government. In fact, the standard of government in Plato's *Laws* is no less than "the highest good," that is, "peace with one another and friendly feeling."[1]

Ecofeminists, particularly politically focused ones, "echo" Plato; those engaged in political programs advocate far-reaching antimilitarist reconstructions of the human self and democracy, in order that we may engage in peace and harmony with others and with nature.[2] Yet both Plato and the ecofeminists must work with a conflicted conception of humanity: humans are rationally sexless and instinctively social/political in seeking the company of others, while, at the same time aggressively competitive, individually sexed and typecast. Despite this, both demonstrate that any programmed alienation and exclusion of others due to gender harms the self and society in part and whole.

Plato was the first Western philosopher to counsel social/political human selves organized in society to make love and music, not war. But do not take my word for it, let us go to the text.

> – '[Cultivate and] make music.'
> – [Before now, I had imagined that this was only intended to exhort and encourage me in the study of philosophy, the pursuit of my life, and the noblest and best of music.][3]

Before his court-ordered death Socrates recalls these words from his recurring dream, still musing about its meaning and import. So too in his last dialogue, the *Laws*, Plato leaves his listeners with a curious vision of a new democratic government. It is a government forged and nurtured by creative forms of education, law, and leisure, and in which both men and women (by law) share and participate. Plato's final vision in the *Laws* radically departs from his mid-life vision of the best state in the *Republic*, in which democracy was deemed only a notch above tyranny, and henceforth banished.[4] This government's most novel form of leisurely education includes a legal education for all citizens. By their active social/political participation, citizens learn the underlying rationale of the laws that bind them. Laws, for Plato, musically convey the rules and rhythms of everyday social/political life. In fact, the state's primary muse is the law.

With the *Laws's* alternative vision of a peace-loving, gender-equal, musical society in the background, I hear Plato's voice echoing in modern voices of feminism.[5] The ecofeminist, like Plato, centrally focuses on and re-envisions the diverse part-whole relationships in which an individual is embedded.[6] I quote: "Feminist approaches to peace will be as varied as the feminisms from which they take their inspiration, but gender will always be the organizing concept of analysis."[7] Next let us reword Alfred North Whitehead's statement: "The safest general characterization of the European philosophical tradition is that it consists of a series of footnotes to Plato."[8] Let us say: "All Western Philosophy is a series of echoes from Plato." These words aim to invoke missed connections critical to contemporary feminist voices. Regrettably missing in feminist etiology is the discussion of Plato on the whole, but above all of his last work, the *Laws*.[9]

Because the proposed government in the *Laws* is in significant part a participatory democracy, it is unlike any other Platonic vision of state and government. Rather than echoing his mid-life political diagnosis in the *Republic*–that the open democratic society is the harbinger of personal and political disaster–his last dialogue offers a substantially new look at justice, gender equality, and peace. Simply put, Plato's *Laws* manifests that eco-feminists did not invent antimilitarist, participatory democracy–the Greeks did.[10]

In order to consider this comparative stance at least two caveats are in order:

First, although Plato and ecofeminists share the broader focus of examining the self's engagement in nature and in the larger universe (our one song), the present analysis does not attempt to show Plato's feminist tendencies in these other dimensions. Instead we restrict our discussion to Plato's vision of an individual as part of the larger social, political whole, namely, the state.

Second, Plato's novel form of government includes under its leisurely education a general civic and legal education for all its citizens. Part 4, below, details the significance of this connection in regard to Plato's own contributions to the broad Greek vision of education and leisure in the daily lives of citizens. The Greek ideal of citizenship further presupposes and requires that one live primarily a life of leisure to taste the good life. Surely without the freedom from continual daily labor and commerce, someone would not be free to participate in citizenship or in the so-called good life. Yet, in Plato's day, the lowly, disenfranchised positions of both slaves and women made them by law subordinated to the education and leisure of Athenian male citizens in preparation and practice for good lives.

Given these qualifications, Plato and feminists essentially share the view that justice is a mainspring and impetus for their theorizing. They may well differ, however, in their respective gender definitions, and specifically in the weight they attach to gender equality in the theory and practice of justice. To illustrate this, as a linchpin is a device used in a shaft to keep something, like a wheel, from slipping off, so too gender is the linchpin and primary controller of feminism. For Plato, justice is the linchpin. Plato uses justice to weigh and to evaluate theories and practices of government, gender equality, happiness, war, and peace. Consequently, at any point in Plato's analysis it is fair to ask: Is this equality, happiness, war, or peace just? If not, it must be abandoned in order to proceed in a more promising direction.

To begin, Plato and feminists both uphold gender equality and peace as indispensable conditions for egalitarian justice. They also share a more fundamental core belief that theorizing about such issues requires reconstructing society. Plato and feminists begin their philosophies by reversing the usual logic and order of business. Rather than making practice the test and gold standard for their theories, they appear to make their primary objective the principle: If it does not work in theory, it cannot work in practice. For instance, consider the advice of one contemporary, active political ecofeminist Noel Sturgeon: Let us avoid "creat[ing]...an opposition (between feminist theory and feminist practice) [that] prevents an analysis of the practice of feminist theory or the theory of feminist practice."[11] In actuality, practice and theory become interwoven, even interchangeable entities in an unbreakable loop. As we shall see, Plato's philosophy shares with ecofeminism the "intention of all radical social/political movements: To change, systematically, structures that produce inequality and injustice."[12] Let us turn now to Plato's proposals for change.

Plato's feminist spirit commits him to rebuilding human society from the ground up, constructing a new world piece by piece. He must tear away old definitions, structures, and customs if they prove to breed and feed unhealthy traditions, governments, and laws.

Plato thereby chooses to begin his philosophic enterprise by overturning the traditional male-engendered views of sexuality, psychology, virtue, law, and government. He redefines humanity's vision of justice and happiness in the process.

Plato makes the following three bold moves, to be discussed in the three-part analysis that follows:

(1) By making the philosophic life of peace, wisdom, and friendship the apex of a human life, Plato overturns Homeric militaristic views of manhood, courage, war, and peace, almost in a single stroke. [13]

(2) Plato laments the moral horror of injustice and suffering due to the exclusion of fifty percent of humanity from legal citizenship and political society. He says,

> The most senseless of all things [is], namely, that men and women should not all follow the same pursuits with one accord, and with all their might. For there arises...half a State only, instead of a whole one, in nearly every instance, yet surely this would be a surprising blunder for a lawgiver to commit! [14]

Hence in Plato's state, females are to be legal citizens and, in significant areas of daily life, equal to their male counterparts in the eyes of the law. [15] To reinvent democratic society and government along the lines of gender parity, first Plato must provide a new psychology of the human self (*psyche*) in terms of male and female gender.

(3) Plato broadens and radicalizes ordinary notions of friendship, individuality, and citizenship by integrating a detailed schema of leisure for males and females alike. In the *Laws* this plan calls for new forms of music, poetry, and law as the preparations for, and living of, the good life, in opening up the state for the good life for female as well as male citizens.

Plato first cites these "three waves" in his mid-career work, the *Republic*, surely radical for his day. [16] Until the twentieth century, John Stuart Mill, was the only other Western philosopher to propose legal, political equality of the sexes. Martha Nussbaum, offering contemporary agreement with Plato's life-long project, claims that the following insights hale from Plato:

> Convention and habit are women's enemies here, and reason their ally. Habit decrees that what seems strange is impossible and "unnatural"; reason looks head on at the strange, refusing to assume that the current status quo is either immutable or in any normative sense "natural." The appeal to reason and objectivity amounts to a request that the observer refuse to be intimidated by habit, and look for cogent arguments based on evidence that has been carefully sifted for bias. [17]

In his final, and more novel, vision in the *Laws*, Plato designs and constructs an entire political society founded on democratic legal principles of justice, liberty, and equality. Considerable parallels to Plato's theoretical philosophy are found in his own personal and career choices: founding and heading the first Academy of higher education, as well as risking his life to implement his theories during his Sicilian expeditions. Along with participatory democracy and its system of law, Plato's new society is fueled by friendship and peace, and designed to be enjoyed by all in a drama-like existence.[18]

The evidence here details a Plato radically different from the Plato of the *Republic*. He depicts in broad, often outlandish strokes, human society as more widely open than our own in the respects mentioned above. If we can grant Plato his own definitions of virtue, gender, citizenship, and law, we can make sense of his social/political design and agenda.

2. Redefining Virtue to Make Peace, Not War, from Within

Plato centrally positions at the beginning of the *Laws* the question, Why war? The speakers ask the Athenian Stranger if war is inevitable. The Stranger ripostes that competition and conflict underlie human affairs because it is a personal struggle for someone to be in self-harmony.[19] Inner discord becomes writ large in society because of the inner discord in each of us.[20] If we do not use reason and self-knowledge in regulating ourselves, how can we expect ourselves, or others, to accept government control and comply to law?

Plato chooses to begin his philosophic enterprise by overturning the traditional male-engendered (Homeric) views of sexuality, psychology, virtue, law, and government. His ongoing dialogue contends with the model of the ideal human person, relative to the arena of war and peace, a model traditionally conceived as a Homeric male: the polite gentleman, wily hero (like Odysseus), and noble warrior. From his early Socratic dialogues to his last dialogue, the *Laws*, Plato deals persistent and sometimes fatal blows to the conventional ideal of human virtue as primarily war-like and competitive. Plato portrays this sort of courage as sustaining an unsuitable and potentially disastrous model for male and female human beings.

To achieve personal (and political) justice and peace in Plato's society first requires redefining traditional manliness.[21] Only then may we see how his proposals and practices, presented below in Part 4, could work in redirecting inborn competitive desires for reputation, honor, and success toward the objectives of a peace-loving society. For his own purposes, Plato takes up another competing line of common sense–that the whole point of war is peace. Without peace people would be unable to enjoy any human goods, such as wealth, friendship, and culture. A militaristic society and militaristic courage are not good and desirable in themselves, but, as Plato argues, dire means unsuited to achieve the goals and virtues of justice and peace. Any acts of military aggression (in contrast to unavoidable defense of the survival of the state) must be banned. Although a lawmaker first must grasp the natural strife inherent in society, he or she must go on to make and implement laws that lead society in a more peace-promoting and cooperative direction.[22]

Hence, "friendship, wisdom, and freedom" become key legislative goals for the *Laws*.[23]

Throughout his philosophy Plato proposes and elaborates broader, philosophical forms of courage. Plato's state in the *Laws* envisions social and political ideals, duties, and responsibilities neither in the military mode, nor in the philosopher king and queen roles (as in the *Republic*), but in the mode of active democratic citizenship. As in a participatory democracy, political officials are drawn from the citizenry at large by lot and by election, so too for Plato (and Aristotle) citizens must take turns in "ruling and being ruled."[24] Plato believes that a citizen's personal, ongoing political involvement is required in order to maintain a state founded on democratic ideals and virtues of a participatory nature for justice, equality, and peace. Such embedded forms for democracy serve not only a person's individual virtue and well-being, but also a peace-promoting, democratic society that fosters these individual goods and values for all citizens.

More specifically the *Laws* builds upon Plato's premise that "each person is his or her own enemy."[25] The victory over the self then appears as the sweetest of all, the inner core and true mark of courage.[26] Such self-command entails self-knowledge and restraint over the desires that lead to self-enslavement.[27]

Regarding Plato's view of personal courage, contemporary feminists again echo Plato: "Radical feminist peace researchers are among the most aggressive in redefining traditional male definitions of power as dominance or 'power over'...to power as competence or 'power to' and 'power within' (or, empowerment)."[28] As I discuss below, by extricating ourselves from destructive expressions of natural impulses and aims, we may find virtues in inner harmony and joy in self-liberation. Only then would someone be capable of living in peace and justice with others.

3. "Male" and "Female" Faces of Peace with a Difference

Surprisingly, Plato's last work, the *Laws*, stands as the only dialogue in which Plato explicitly ranks the virtues, and ranks courage last. Accordingly, wisdom is first, justice second, inner self-harmony (*sophrosyne*) third, and courage, fourth and last.[29] The significance and implications of this ranking for Platonic philosophy may be far-reaching, as Plato does not clearly explain and justify this ordering in the text of the *Laws*. Similarly, Platonic scholars and commentators seem uncertain about its weight in Plato's overall theory of the virtues. However, as we see below, this ranking conveys special significance for our present analysis.

Plato's ranking of the virtues makes psychic harmony and inner peace (conveyed in the broad Greek ideal and virtue of *sophrosyne*) a higher form of virtue than courage.[30] The explanation for Plato's valuation may be found in his psychological account of a well-blended and balanced temperament, and resulting character, as opposed to a simply courageous one. For Plato, the opposition between the spirited (courageous) temperament and the gentle (harmonious) temperament is thoroughly fundamental: "The very classes 'energy' and 'moderation' are ranged in mutual exclusiveness, and in opposition to each other."[31]

Facing this entrenched schema, Plato rejects and transcends traditional stereotyping of women and men.[32] By reasoning in the *Laws* that psychic harmony represents, even in its incipient form, a more valuable disposition than the courageous one, Plato overturns custom and convention.[33] Generally Plato links the courageous nature with recklessness, self-assertion, aggression, and license; he ties the harmonious nature to civil and philosophical qualities, such as natural self-control and mindfulness. In Plato's metaphysical scheme, the moderate female invokes a resemblance of the female principle with rest, being, form, and law, while the spirited male calls to mind motion, becoming, and disorder. The actual existence of immoderate females or complacent males, does not invalidate Plato's theory. One need only note here that female and male represent essential psychological aspects of human, (as, for instance, in Carl Jung's psychology). If one grants my depiction of Platonic metaphysics and psychology, an individual becomes unbalanced when either the female or male side of the self gets the upper hand.

Plato reasons further in the *Laws* that a naturally courageous temperament, if untethered by justice, right opinion, or philosophic wisdom, may easily lead someone toward vice.[34] In sharp contrast, Plato maintains a person's psychic harmony makes all other goods valuable and enjoyable.[35] By essentially associating the female with order, law, and reason, and maleness with disorder, lawlessness, and irrationality, Plato thereby (inadvertently) reverses the customary classical tropes for light and darkness. If we accept this proposed reading of Plato's psychology in both its moral and metaphysical aspects, the essence and virtue of the female emerge out of (the idea and image of) darkness to light!

Plato seems to favor a naturally peace-loving temperament. It is the basis for psychic harmony. Still, this form of harmony is, like natural boldness, often unreliable and inconsistent. It has yet to embody and manifest the requisite stability produced by true opinion or philosophical and political wisdom. Such fledgling virtue may yield harm to someone who uses natural restraint for irrational and selfish purposes, heedless of or mindless to the overall good for that person or any other.

4. Music and Law in Stately Drama to Make and Play Peace

According to Plato, the love of war and glory can be traced to a central psychological facet of the human self (*psyche*), namely, spirit (*thumos*)– defined here as an inborn "competitiveness and the desire for self-esteem and esteem by others."[36] In the *Republic* the human spirit in the *psyche* indicates the aggressive tendency in the soul, anger at injustice, and love of honor.[37]

For Plato, political society would serve its members well by educating and creatively redirecting this self-centeredness and self-assertion toward a life of peace, justice, and well-being.[38] Plato holds:

> In relation to one's State and fellow-citizens that person is by far the best who, in preference to a victory at Olympia, or in any other contest of war, would choose to have a victorious reputation for service to one's native laws, as being the one above all others who has served them with distinction throughout one's life.[39]

Rather than seeking fame and glory largely through sport, war, and career, people would better attain the objects of desire, by finding honor and self-respect from a common ground of mutual respect and regard for all in the law.

From the start of this analysis, I highlighted Plato's rallying points for better political government of human society: that peace, cooperation, and justice be primary legislative goals; moreover, that "the highest good" be "peace with one another and friendly feeling."[40] As an illustration in presenting these foundational theories, he resorts to an analogy, one between rivaling siblings and warring citizens, to advance his view of a political official and legislator. Such elected leaders are to make judgments and edicts on behalf of peace and reconciliation, as opposed to war and estrangement:

> We can...[foresee] a better judge–the one who will take this single quarreling family in hand and reconcile its members without killing any of them; by laying down regulations to guide them in the future, this judge will be able to ensure that they remain on friendly terms with each other.[41]

Strikingly, these broad legislative goals of friendship, wisdom, and freedom, target male-female harmony in everyday living and activities.[42] Novel and leisurely ways for advancing such goals include the following: females and males exercising, sporting, and wrestling together publicly in the nude; dining daily at communal meals, where adult men and women break bread together, before and after marriage;[43] and frequent festivals, technically of a religious nature, where more diverse and varied forms of socialization may occur. A festival seems to occur almost every day of the year.[44]

Taken as a whole, these radically new proposals reveal the state's underlying vital function: it is to make justice and happiness open to all its members, regardless of age, class, and gender. In Plato's state, both female and male citizens integrate their shared desires and common goals by conjoining their efforts and pursuits to experience personal and political justice and well-being.

Plato broadly depicts the art of lawmakers (*demiurgy*) to be as creative as that of the poets. Unlike poets, lawmakers are charged with the weightiest task of all–to produce the finest drama for citizens to live, share, and enjoy.[45] Conceived as a drama, life in Plato's state is only an artistic image of the best life. Plato's original punning of law-tune (*nomos-nema*) indicates that he deems lawmaking to be the highest social/political form of music and art. It is not out of character that he alleges the collapse of the Athenians was due to their lawlessness. According to Plato, Athenians displayed excessive license and lack of self-discipline not only in personal and political behavior, but in their music, and in other choices of pastimes.[46]

In Plato's diagnosis, social/political corruption and chaos arose and burgeoned in the Athenian people due to perversion of their leisure. This process gradually transformed an open, peace-loving people into an imperialist, military empire, constantly feeding itself on war. Plato believes that even the best poetry is second-best to the highest and best of human lives, namely, the life of philosophy. Both the *Republic* and the *Laws* consistently envision the life of the average citizen as second-best to the life of the philosopher. Thus Plato argues that only the philosopher would be capable of enjoying the best kind of human happiness.[47]

Also noteworthy is Plato's analysis of the Nocturnal Council, consisting of a select group of old and young officials and legislators of the state, assigned the highest task of investigating, among other topics, the "connection therewith [of philosophy] and its Muse." They must strive to "apply [such knowledge] harmoniously to the institutions and rules of ethics."[48] Here, Plato's pun of education-play (*paideia-paidia*) works cleverly to capture his vision that learning to be just is the highest form of play; yet, paradoxically, justice is the most serious of human aims.[49]

We may extrapolate from this analysis that, in Plato's world, individuals internalize and live the just or unjust laws and policies of their own government. This occurs above all in a democracy, because citizens participate in a drama of their own making, played and produced by all, for all.[50] Above all, because Plato's final stately vision is, in significant part, that of direct, participatory democracy, individual identification (male or female) to the larger social/political group becomes more accessible. It is mandated by government that they participate in an actively formed and fostered state of affairs. It forms their personal and political daily routines and education.

A person's private satisfaction and personal fulfillment seems more likely attainable from such a significant sense of belonging. By means of small group Choruses and *symposia*, the State grooms youthful members into a personal and political life shared and enjoyed in peace with others.[51] In a long, provocative discussion, in *Laws* Books I and II, Plato calls for the regular convening of Choral groups arranged by age and purpose.[52] He also elaborates on the nature, methods, and purpose of wine-drinking dinner parties (*symposia*) for the young and old.[53] The young are to acquire the arts of self-knowledge and civic camaraderie through self-control at wine-drinking parties conducted by concerned older chaperons.[54] Plato metaphorically speaks of a symposium commander (*strategos*) who fosters unity and friendship in a state of peace and good will at wine-drinking parties.[55] He states that the symposium commander should "be wise about social gatherings. For this person must both preserve the friendliness which already exists among the company, and see that the present gathering promotes it still further."[56]

In the above passage, Plato seems purposefully to use the term "*strategos*," "military commander or general," to describe the commanders of these peace-time, friendly parties. Plato incites his listeners to put the great amount of thought, energy, and detailed strategic efforts toward promoting peace and justice instead of planning and executing war. Such parties therefore serve to promote and to preserve a just government and way of life. Equally surprisingly, a so-called Dionysian Chorus, which shares the helm of this government as optimally wise officials and lawmakers, also regularly gather at wine-drinking parties. For these elders, wine-parties serve to generate their inspired, oracular story-telling. As Plato writes, the "music they have mastered is nobler than the music of the choruses and the theaters," for they "possess the highest capacity for the noblest and the most useful song...law."[57]

Overall such elaborate proposals and practices originate a plausible comparison between Plato and many radical feminists, purportedly showing that, for both, the personal is political.[58] Plato, like contemporary eco-feminists, intently focuses on, and directly questions, the psychological and moral quality of the individual's connection as a participant part and member of the social/political whole: Does the state serve to repress, or to promote, an individual's goodness and happiness? Does the good blend together well with the good of the state? Does the state protect and promote the good of its citizens, regardless of class and gender? Conversely, does an individual citizen protect and promote the public interest and good of others belonging to the larger complex whole of state?

5. Concluding Remarks

This analysis shows that just as no one can make and wage war without others, so too no one can confront and supersede conflict and war without others. Human individuals are conceived from the biological difference of parents, born into a world of conflict, and expected to fight conflict while the inner self is also in conflict. Winning peace is not something for which anyone is solely responsible; it requires community effort. Personal and political peace and well-being are sorely and hard won.

From Plato to Jung, Albert Einstein to many contemporary feminists, we hear echoing that the nature of the interplay between the inner self and the outer world psychologically spawns and determines the moral and psychological quality and well-being of our social/political arrangements.[59] So too from Plato to Henry David Thoreau to feminists, we hear echoing that the personal is the political. This interplay between self and society accounts for ever-alternating currents of war and peace. In their respective discussions, Plato and ecofeminists find that these outward manifestations of our inner selves clearly warrant continual re-envisioning and redesigning of gender roles on behalf of our shared political world. Especially in this shared political world, our individual natural impulses and acquired genders may be redirected toward creative, peaceful ways of sustaining life, rather than destructive, warring ways of ruining lives.

To promote an enduring, just peace, Plato and ecofeminists demonstrate that we must first produce an organic body politic, one that promotes harmony between the different genders, rather than conflict. Planned and controlled conflict among diverse people and groups, whether they be an entire class or gender, is not only painful but destructive of self and society, especially self and society as conceived within this analysis–as an organic whole growing itself in its many member-parts. This re-envisioned democratic society is ever opening itself to justice and equality for more of its members.

This analysis thereby shows that human beings will achieve a longer-lasting peace, if and when we seek happiness through the justice of enjoining the many diverse psychological and political parts of ourselves and others in a pluralistic society. The victory prize for seeking a holistic personal and political self and society is a just peace. Such peace is a way of life experienced not by further splitting apart but by coming together, growing individually by reaching out toward others in political movement, as in theory, transforming ourselves by extending this living, just society to others.[60]

Notes

1. Plato, *Laws,* trans. R. G. Bury, *The Loeb Classical Library,* vols. 10-11 (Cambridge, Mass.: Harvard University Press, 1967-1969), 628c5.

2. Karen J. Warren, "A Feminist Philosophical Perspective on Ecofeminist Spiritualities," in *Ecofeminism and the Sacred,* ed. Carol J. Adams (New York: Continuum, 1993), pp. 119-132.

3. Plato, *Phaedo,* trans. H. N. Fowler, *The Loeb Classical Library,* vol. 1 (Cambridge, Mass,: Harvard University Press, 1914), 60e-61a (with my alterations of translation indicated in brackets).

4. Mary Lenzi, *The Virtues of the "Laws"* (Ph.D. dissertation, Department of Philosophy, The University of Pennsylvania, 1989); Harvey Yunis, *Taming Democracy: Models of Political Rhetoric in Classical Athens* (Ithaca, N.Y.: Cornell University Press, 1996); Trevor Saunders, "Plato's Later Political Thought," in *The Cambridge Companion to Plato,* ed. Richard Kraut (New York: Cambridge Univeristy Press, 1992), pp. 464-492.

5. William Cowling and Nancy Tuana, "Plato and Feminism: A Review of the Literature," *American Philosophical Association Newsletter on Feminism and Philosophy,* 90:1 (Fall 1990), pp. 110-115; and Karen J. Warren and Duane L. Cady, "Feminism and Peace: An Overview," *American Philosophical Association Newsletter on Feminism and Philosophy,* 93:1 (Spring 1994), pp. 108-121.

6. Val Plumwood, "Plato and the Philosophy of Death," *Feminism and the Mystery of Nature* (New York: Routledge, 1993), pp. 69-103; see also Mary Lenzi, "Platonic Polypsychic Pantheism," *The Monist,* 80:2 (April 1997), pp. 232-250.

7. Noel Sturgeon, "Positional Femisism, Ecofeminism, and Radical Feminism Revisitied," *American Philosophical Association Newsletter on Feminism and Philosophy,* 93:1 (Spring 1994), p. 41. See also Karen Warren and Duane Cady, "Feminism and Peace: An Overview," *American Philosophical Association Newsletter on Feminism and Philosophy,* 93:1 (Spring 1994), p. 41.

8. Alfred North Whitehead, *Process and Reality* (New York: Free Press, 1969), p. 53.

9. Bat-Ami Bar On, ed., *Engendering Origins* (Albany, N. Y.: State Univeristy of New York Press, 1994); and Nancy Tuana, ed., *Feminist Interpretations of Plato* (University Park, Penn.: Penn State Press, 1994).

10. Sturgeon, "Positional Feminism," p. 45.

11. *Ibid.,* p. 42.

12. *Ibid.,* p. 46.

13. Plato, *Laws,* 693c-d and 628c5.

14. *Ibid.,* 804d-805b.

15. *Ibid.,* 805c-d.

16. Plato, *Republic,* trans. by Paul Shorey, *The Loeb Classical Library,* vols. 5-6 (Cambridge, Mass.: Harvard University Press, 1930 and 1935), 450c-473b.

17. Martha Nussbaum, "Feminists and Philosophy," review of *A Mind of One's Own: Feminist Essays on Reason and Objectivity,* ed. L. M. Antony and Charlotte Witt, *The New York Times Review of Books* (20 October 1994), pp. 59.

18. Plato, *Laws*, 803a-804b.

19. *Ibid.*, 626d8-10.

20. See Sigmund Freud, *Civilization and Its Discontents*, trans. James Strachey, in *The Standard Edition of the Complete Psychological Works of Sigmund Freud*, vol. 21 (London: The Hogarth Press and the Institute of Psycho-Analysis, 1930); and *Why War?: Einstein and Freud, 1932-1933*, trans. J. Strachey and Joan Riviere, in *The Collected Papers of Sigmund Freud*, vol. 25 (London: The Hogarth Press and The Institute of Psycho-Analysis, 1957); see also Mary Lenzi, "Freud: The Mind/Body of the Eroticist," *Psychoanalytic Studies*, 1:3 (September 1999), pp. 315-326.

21. J. C. B. Gosling, *Plato* (London: Routledge and Kegan Paul, 1973), p. 81.

22. Plato, *Laws*, 628c5.

23. *Ibid.*, 693c-d.

24. *Ibid.*, 643e4-10 and 767e10-768a: see also Aristotle, *Politics*, trans. By H. Rackham, *The Loeb Classical Library*, vol. 21 (Cambridge, Mass.: Harvard University Press, 1977), II. 5. Ch. 25, and III. 11. Ch. 3.

25. Plato, *Laws*, 626d1.

26. *Ibid.*, 840b4-c6.

27. *Ibid.*, 633c8-d8 and 836d8-e2; Plato, *Laches*, trans. W. R. M. Lamb, *The Loeb Classical Library*, vol. 7 (Cambridge, Mass.: Harvard University Press, 1924), 191c-d; and Plato, *Republic*, 413d-e and 429c4-d2.

28. Sturgeon, "Positional Feminism," p. 40.

29. Plato, *Laws*, 631b-d.

30. *Ibid.*, 710a5-b3; Plato, *Charmides*, trans. W. R. M. Lamb, *The Loeb Classical Library*, vol. 12 (Cambridge, Mass.: Harvard University Press, 1927), 159b6-160d3.

31. Plato, *Statesman*, trans. H. N. Fowler, *The Loeb Classical Library*, vol. 8 (Cambridge, Mass.: Harvard University Press, 1925), 307c and 308b2-4; see also Plato, *Republic*, 375c5-d1.

32. See Plato, *Laws*, 802e6-10.

33. *Ibid.*, 696b-c; and Plato, *Republic*, 376b9-c3.

34. Plato, *Laws*, 630b3-7 and 641b-c.

35. *Ibid.*, 696b8-697b6; 728e-729a; and 709e7-710a2.

36. John Cooper, "The Psychology of Justice in Plato," *American Philosophical Quarterly*, 14:2 (April, 1977), pp. 151-157.

37. Plato, *Republic*, 411a-b and 375a-b; 440c8-d3 and 440a9-b; 439e-440c and 441b-c; 581a9-b.

38. *Ibid.*, 581a9-b and 550b7.

39. Plato, *Laws*, 729d7-e1.

40. *Ibid.*, 628c5.

41. *Ibid.*, 527e-628a2.

42. *Ibid.*, 693c-d.

43. *Ibid.*, 780a-b; 781a-d; 783e-784b; 806e-807a; 823b1-4; and 653c-d.

44. *Ibid.*, 828a-1-835b5 and 643e4-10.

45. *Ibid.*, 817a-d and 806d-807e; see also 803c3-e and 653a6-c4.

46. *Ibid.*, 700a-701c; Plato, *Republic*, 376e-403e; 605a-608b; and 395b-396e.

47. Plato, *Laws*, 667b5-670c8 and 812bc.

48. *Ibid.*, 967d-968a.

49. *Ibid.,* 803c3-e and 653a6-c4; and Plato, *Apology,* trans. H. N. Fowler, *The Loeb Classical Library,* vol. 1 (Cambridge, Mass.: Harvard University Press, 1914), 24c and 25c.

50. Plato, *Laws,* 957c3-8; 822e5-823a9; and 857e.

51. *Ibid.,* 649-650; see also 655e-656b.

52. *Ibid.,* 664-674.

53. *Ibid.,* 637-650 and 639d1-653a4.

54. *Ibid.,* 647c; 648d-e and 666e-667a; see also, Plato, *Apology,* 20a-b.

55. Plato, *Laws,* 640b.

56. *Ibid.,* 640c-d.

57. *Ibid.,* 667a-b and 665d.

58. See Sturgeon, "Positional Femisism," p. 40; and Plato, *Laws,* 803a-804b.

59. See Otto Nathan and Heinz Norden, eds., *Einstein on Peace* (New York: Simon and Schuster, 1960).

60. I thank my colleague, Martha Lee Osborne, for her editorial help on my first draft, Chris Crittenden for suggesting the work of Val Plumwood, and my coeditors, Judith Presler and Sally J. Scholz.

Seven

REFLECTIONS ON CARING AND PEACE POLITICS

Joseph C. Kunkel

The ethics of caring has inaugurated a new approach to moral thinking. Instead of sharply criticizing various facets of the developing theory, I prefer to understand the direction the methodology is taking for evaluating human actions. I am fascinated by the potentiality of this way of moral thinking and by the contribution caring can make to issues of war and peace. I find myself slowly backing into this approach to ethics after having found other approaches to war and peace unsatisfactory.

I begin the chapter with a brief description of the ethics of caring. I then examine some of the controversial components of this moral approach and explain why, for me, some aspects seem more beneficial than others. I am particularly interested in dialogue as a methodological aid for lending more objectivity to the moral justification of caring. In the last section I examine how caring as maternal thinking has been and can be consistently applied to endeavors associated with the politics of peace. In my assessment I again find a role for dialogue.

1. An Ethics of Caring

Carol Gilligan, in *In a Different Voice*, argues that many women think differently than men.[1] Her jumping-off point is a series of studies beginning with Sigmund Freud. The studies set a developmental standard for all humans that is based upon research on the male experience alone. With the male as the human norm, certain feminine qualities have been relegated to an inferior status.

At issue is describing model human beings as separate, independent, and autonomously free. Humans are said to be aggressive, seeking to achieve success and to avoid failure. Moral rules are viewed as universal and abstract, based on a theory of justice and individual rights that entails impartial application of these norms.

Gilligan finds that many women are, by contrast, intimate and nurturing. They associate with others and feel guilty about being too competitive; they do not wish to advance at another's expense. They feel responsible for relationships and are thus more interdependent, less isolatedly free.

Morality for these women is contextual and involves evaluating conflicting responsibilities.

Following Nancy Chodorow's work, Gilligan argues that these dichotomous traits begin early.[2] Since women and men often do not share equally in their children's care, there is a difference in the way boys and girls are reared. Women are the major caregivers. Thus, girls identify with the sex and roles of their maternal caregivers, while boys forge their identities by separating from their mothers. Girls become attached; boys, detached. For the female, development becomes associated with a web of relationships; for the male, with physical and sexual isolation from the caregiver.

Chodorow's theory is one approach to childhood gender development. Boys may be said to detach from their mothers or they may begin to identify with their fathers and other men who are socially detached from one another.[3] According to either theory boys have different gender identities than girls.

Many boys play competitive sports in large groups.[4] When arguments arise, boys learn to refine their debating skills by quoting rules to decide the controversy; when this fails the contested play is repeated and the game goes on. By comparison, many girls play in smaller gatherings, often playing turn-taking games such as hopscotch or jump rope, wherein one girl's success is not another's defeat. When quarrels erupt, girls stop the game to preserve the relationship.

Deborah Tannen has written a bestseller on adult male and female conversations called *You Just Don't Understand*. She says that many men engage one another in a social order that they see as hierarchical, in which they are "either one-up or one-down."[5] In this world they converse by negotiation, striving to gain the upper hand, to remain independent, and to avoid regression. Many women, on the other hand, envision the world as individuals connected with one another. In their conversations they look for support and consensus so as to achieve closeness.

Take for example troubles talk.[6] Many women, when confided in by another person about some troubles, match the difficulty with one of their own. That disclosure shows understanding and empathy, according to their worldviews. Many men, however, reply with a solution. The male response may work for physical or mechanical problems, but hardly for emotional ones. The male solution also involves a one-upmanship, in that the problem-solver knows the answer about which the problem-holder is ignorant. For this reason, too, men are usually reluctant to reveal that they, as individuals, have any troubles. Most women, living in a connected community, know everyone has troubles, and sharing them is not degrading.

Gilligan describes human reality as a web of relationships, a network of connections, and a process of communication.[7] Many women are drawn to these connections, rather than to isolation. Isolation is loneliness. Gilligan quotes an eight-year-old girl talking about her friends. The girl says, "But like if someone's all alone, I'll play with them."[8] That is an example of caring.

Caring informs relationships. Caring people share a responsibility for one another because of this web of connections that encircles us all. If someone is hurting, then the caring person is hurting also. Caring is communicated by verbal and nonverbal language. A caring person naturally expects that if a problem arises, then communication will resolve the conflict.

To illustrate caring, Gilligan cites the familiar example of the Heinz dilemma. This dilemma was used by Lawrence Kohlberg to determine the level of an individual's moral development.[9] Heinz's wife is dying of a disease that only a particular drug can cure. The drug however is very expensive and Heinz cannot afford to pay the price. The moral question turns on whether Heinz should steal the drug to save his wife's life?

An eleven-year-old boy argues in the standard moral way that human life is worth more than money and therefore Heinz ought to steal the drug to save a life. Stealing may be against the law but "laws have mistakes." Moreover the boy argues that the judge would probably agree with Heinz's actions.

An eleven-year-old girl, by contrast, wants to resolve the dilemma without hurting anyone. She is not going to sneak in and steal the drug from a pharmacy to save her dying spouse's life if she can find a way to talk with the pharmacist or a loan officer and in the process meet everyone's needs. She also understands that landing in jail for stealing the drug to save the dying person's life today is not going to help the sick person tomorrow.

The boy uses logical reasoning to conclude that stealing in this instance is morally acceptable. The girl uses caring in search of a more reconciling intervention than stealing. The web of relations, for her, embraces the dying spouse and the pharmacist. All three stand in need of a beneficial resolution.

The ethics of caring involves people in relationships. Out of these networks of relational contexts arise responsibilities. Among these responsibilities are loving others, being compassionate in responding to the specific needs and at times misdeeds of others, and not harming one another. How one acts morally in any given setting starts more with an intuitive and empathetic sensitivity toward others than with abstract rules and rights.

Gilligan lists three stages in the development of the ethics of care.[10] First is "caring for the self in order to ensure survival." Upon further development this view is rejected as selfish. Second is a concept of responsibility which fuses with "a maternal morality that seeks to ensure care for the dependent and unequal." A person cares for others but with a self-sacrificing component. The third and highest stage sees self on a par with others among those needing to be cared for.

The completeness of these three stages is debatable. However, I shall not debate that issue here. My concern is with the ethical. If one maintains that ethics is purely subjective, then, however a person cares about self and others, that person's choices are always ethically right. So whether I care for myself alone, for others alone, or for myself and others equally I am ethical. But is simply caring a sound basis for ethics?

Without getting into the arguments for and against subjectivity and emotivism in ethics, I wish to see whether there are objective and reasonable–using these terms in a broad sense–criteria for an ethics of care. What makes caring ethical? It is not principles, rights, and judgments as found in justice ethics. Caring is more contextual. Nel Noddings says that the ethics of caring begins with a positive feeling that arises out of a condition of natural caring.[11] Mothers, with their caretaking endeavors on behalf of their children, are the primary examples of natural care.

Ethical caring goes beyond natural caring. Noddings says with ethical caring we remember "our own best moments of caring and being cared for," and feel an "I must" care in a given situation.[12] "I must" is the basis for moral obligation. An "I must," perhaps arising with someone we do not like, can be rejected. But subsumed under the moral ideal of maintaining a caring relation with others, "I must" carries some obligation. This obligation, however, may still be premoral.

Noddings contends a fully ethical caring is relational.[13] Ethical caring has two modes: the one-caring and the cared-for. Individuals move in and out of each mode in the course of experiencing caring. So without a cared-for there is no moral caring. If the other in relationship is capable of responding as the cared-for, then I have an obligation to be the one-caring with that other. In this regard we do not have a responsibility to care for everyone in the world, but only for those within our web of connectedness. To be ethical an action has to be in tune with maintaining the caring relation.

2. Problems with an Ethics of Caring

For purposes of reflecting upon the ethics of caring we can grant that men and women generally have distinct upbringings that somewhat affect their moral reasoning.[14] Must this developmental difference impact upon the equality of the two genders? Essentially, no. Factually, however, one perspective has traditionally dominated the other with serious implications for trusting the gender neutrality of our culture. The male worldview has been dominant in our nation since its founding in 1776. Women, for instance, were not given the right to vote until the ratification of the Nineteenth Amendment in 1920. A woman has never been nominated for president by a major political party.

Women's ways of acting have been dismissed *en bloc* as too domestic, overly emotional, partial to particular relations, insufficiently aggressive, and second-rate. Two variant examples from a catalog of offenses bear out this sexual discrimination. *Business Week* listed the CEOs for America's 1000 largest corporations in 1991, and the group included no women.[15] Only in 1997–twenty-five years after passage of the federal Title IX law prohibiting gender discrimination in high school and college sports–have women athletes been taken seriously enough to have, in basketball, a professional group sport "league of their own."

The history and persistence of patriarchal values has occasioned a gaping split in feminist ranks. Katha Pollitt describes two camps as equality feminism and difference feminism.[16] She opposes Gilligan's difference feminism for stressing traits that are culturally subordinate. Pollitt argues that women will never achieve equality with men by glorifying an oppressive condition. Difference feminism, to Pollitt, is a blueprint for maintaining women's inferiority.

Equality feminists challenge male bastions of power, forcing concessions and, they hope, eventual equality in every aspect of public and private life. They argue that women, using the power strategems of men, have forced their way into military services, powerful political offices, corporate boardrooms, athletic competitions, professional occupations, and a host of other previously male-dominated areas. In this regard, who can deny the genuine appeal of equality feminism, wherein women successfully compete on seemingly masculine terms?

The problem for difference feminism comes in the catchy title attached to Pollitt's essay: "Are Women Morally Superior to Men?" While comparative statements of this type do appear in the literature, that is not what Gilligan's work is about. Gilligan began her work in response to the downgrading of some women's views under male norms. The thrust of her work has been to demonstrate that women, starting from a position of caring, have a morality, but not one that is rule- and justice-oriented, as is the dominant morality within our culture. Gilligan is thus disputing the moral inferiority placed upon the ethics of caring, not affixing a superiority over justice morality. Women practicing the ethics of caring, for Gilligan, are not subservient, but equal, to men and women emulating the justice system.

Neither is the issue men versus women. Many women, like Pollitt, prefer to be measured under the reigning justice morality; that is one portion of equality for them. Still, numerous women embrace the ethics of caring. While women are the predominant promoters of caring, some men too–Martin Luther King, Jr., Leo Tolstoy, and Martin Buber come quickly to mind–have preferred this ethical approach.[17] I trust that in a pluralistic world there will be multiple *bona fide* ethical orientations, and that women and men will be allowed to choose their moral standards from among these approaches.

Turning to the ethics of care, I will compare the ethical approaches of caring and justice to see how caring holds its own as a complete ethical approach. Virginia Held spells out several contrasts between justice and caring ethics.[18] First, caring ethics seems to stress the private, family domain while justice ethics emphasizes public, nation-state issues. The prototype for caring is the mother-child relationship, whereas the paradigm for justice is the business contract. The question is can caring be extended to situations of diplomacy? We will examine this issue in the next section.

Secondly, there is the presumed distinction between basing morals on abstract reasons *versus* basing morals on emotions and feelings. Justice ethics, whether of the deontological or utilitarian form applies abstract rules to concrete situations. Caring, by contrast, is a matter of the heart before involving the reasoning mind. Reasoning enters into caring decisions, but the weighing that goes on is contextualized within varying and conflicting desires, feelings, and willings. The moral experience for Held is "the experience of consciously choosing, of voluntarily accepting or rejecting, of willingly approving or disapproving, of living with these choices, of acting and of living with these actions and their outcomes."[19]

Lastly, justice ethicists stress the self-interested self in the drawing up of moral rules, which rules are then universally applied to all individuals. In justice ethics, the rulemaking agent is impartial or perhaps stands behind a veil of ignorance. This approach contrasts with the moral agent who is in relationship with, and cares about, the needs of "particular others," and accordingly applies caring differently in various connections. Selves in caring relationships are particularized; issues are contextual. In caring, the moral self is partial to personal relationships, whereas in justice, family relations supposedly count for nothing in the fair application of abstract rules.

With these comparisons in mind, there are some grounds for criticizing the ethics of care. Claudia Card and Sarah Lucia Hoagland criticize the mother-child relationship as hardly reciprocal when involving dependent children.[20] In mother-child relationships caring appears to be unidirectional and as such furthers the oppressive conditions of the self-sacrificing mothers. Using mothering as a model says little about reciprocal adult caring, and hardly confronts the serious problem of intimate partner abuse. Barbara Houston voices the concern as follows: "My worry is that if the one-caring sees her moral worth as wholly dependent upon her capacity to care for others, or contingent upon being in relation, then she may opt to remain in relations which are harmful to her."[21] So simply having an ideal of maintaining caring relations does not illuminate for the one-caring what is and what is not ethical behavior in a living contextual caring relationship. There has to be more, since caring may be harmful, for example, in situations involving male violence and substance abuse. In such cases women need to get outside their subjective selves and "objectify" their situation in order to act morally.

In her response, Gilligan points to her highest level of caring which places one's self on a par with others as needing to be cared for. A caring person at this stage is no longer caught up in a sense of responsibility directed only toward others and toward not wanting to hurt others. A new, more mature ethic takes over that "evolves around a central insight, that self and other are interdependent."[22]

Noddings responds by pointing out that in relationships parties may contribute differently.[23] This inequality poses no problem since the carers and the cared-fors are not set in their positions. A caring mother in one context is a breadwinner, a partner, and the cared-for in other situations. The mother-child relationship models caring but does not indicate that mothers as persons are never in need of mothering themselves. An adult caring relationship that is equal balances out the carer and cared-for roles.

In yet another approach, Marilyn Friedman describes the caring/justice distinction less starkly, viewing the two ethical approaches as complementary in both private and public realms.[24] Thus, in Lawrence Kohlberg's justice-oriented Heinz example, a husband steals an expensive drug in hopes of saving his wife's life. The justice hierarchy of values has human life universally overriding property. Friedman asks whether the abstract requirements of a system of justice are not factually different for a caring husband than for an unrelated stranger?[25] If not, then justice obligates the implausible, that every person is morally required to steal expensive drugs in hopes of saving the lives of poor, terminally ill persons who are unrelated by family or national origin, and in effect perfect strangers.

Similarly, caring affinities are not without a need for justice. A person who cares for others is vulnerable to harm.[26] When a caring person is oppressed or exploited as in sexual harassment or wife battering, it is the impartiality of justice more than the partiality of caring that is needed to rectify the wrong that has been done. When a private caring relationship ends, like marriage with divorce, an impartial system of justice is needed to ensure fairness in the proceedings.

Caring ethics can be supplemented by a system of justice. Moving in this direction, however, does not mitigate weaknesses in the ethics of caring. One of these weaknesses is its relativist and emotivist leaning. Feminists have not settled on a process inherent in caring for lending an element of objectivity to ethical decision-making in particular situations. Reverting to a justice ethics with an analysis of duties or results resolves the problem only by accepting a set of criteria that is removed from the inner experience of caring.

Alison Jaggar says there has been a "relative lack of attention to moral justification given so far by theorists of care ethics."[27] Jaggar asks how we can sort out ethical caring from caring that becomes spoiling or overindulgence and caring that is seriously abused.[28] Similarly, using Gilligan's three stages of moral development, we can ask whether all three levels are caring, or mainly the middle level, or only the highest level. We can ask, how, in a given context, we can distinguish between true care and pseudo-care.

These are not easy questions, given the contextual nature of caring ethics. Caring is presented in a web of human relations. There regularly occurs inner conflict over priorities among these various relationships. Moreover, some individuals feel more responsible for helping those in need, while others feel little or no responsibility. Is there a proper balance for caring within our relationships and how is that discerned?

Joan Tronto speaks of attentiveness.[29] She quotes Noddings in saying one needs "to be receptive to the needs of others."[30] This approach reminds me of the listening mode developed by the noted psychologist Carl Rogers. Rogers gives some principles of listening that are applicable to the carer. Among these principles are the following: "In my relationships with persons I have found that it does not help, in the long run, to act as though I were something that I am not." "I have found it of enormous value when I can permit myself to understand another person." "I have found it highly rewarding when I can accept another person." "The more I am open to the realities in me and in the other person, the less do I find myself wishing to rush in to 'fix things.'"[31] Expanding upon this attentiveness, Margaret Urban Walker writes of a narrative that has the lives (stories) of carer and cared-for intersect.[32] The carer communicates with the story of the person who is in need of caring. A dialogue replaces an abstract system of assessing moral justification.

I believe dialogue is the critical objectifying factor. I am thinking not merely of the conversation between the carer and the cared-for. Dialogue also occurs among caregivers as when nurses confer with other professionals and when doctors call in specialists. Dialogue helps caregivers learn boundaries. When carers make mistakes they generally talk through situations in order to learn how to rectify those relations in which caring has failed.

By talking out feelings, concerns, and needs, we open the inner-self for examination, modification, and approval. Others observe and comment upon our states of mind. In the Rogerian therapeutic method of listening, even though the carer only carefully repeats what the cared-for says, the cared-for is hearing her mental condition unpacked and reflected back, and this smoothes the way for re-evaluation and change. The cared-for, for example, might say, "Not exactly," and then rephrase her thought in a manner new even to herself.

This process does not label actions good or evil; it does not draw a line in the sand. Neither does it simply accept what the cared-for is saying. My wife, for example, who is a natural carer, used to bother me when she was on the phone in her caring mode. After a call I would ask her, "Why didn't you come right out and say you disagreed?" She would respond that the caller did not need her advice. I was frustrated. Only recently have I come to understand that my wife was right. Her friends know where she stands but they are not seeing the situation through my wife's eyes. They are entangled in their relationships, and my wife in hers. In the process of dialoguing, learning occurs.

Dialogue aids in objectifying moral conflicts while remaining in the mode of caring. Dialogue is at the heart of most humanistic therapeutic practices. When done in an open, inquiring manner, it allows individuals to check their subjective feelings and personal thoughts against the attentive observations of trusted friends. This checking with others begins with what Tannen describes as "troubles talk."[33] An in-depth processing of troubles talk occurs in therapy, and there are a host of dialogical types lying between troubles talk and therapy. When carers and cared-fors talk through their troubles, caring loses some of the sting of emotivism and relativism while retaining the contextual nature of the web of its interrelations.

In *What Are Friends For?* Friedman discusses how friendship enhances our moral growth.[34] Growth is especially possible when we choose some friends who challenge us. Much of the challenge, I believe, is the nature of the dialogue that envelopes our relationships. By talking openly about real situations we observe patterns of acting and reacting that can then be released and re-evaluated.

My wife and I have discussed many personal issues in our thirty-nine years of marriage. As part of our own growth, each of us has undergone therapy, and in the past few years we have chosen to have sessions together. At times we misinterpret one another, but we are more open to hearing the other's comments. We understand the other's personal history, and respect and love one another. I believe our growth has come about as a result of our openness to dialogue.

About ten years ago I committed myself to a men's group that meets twice a month. As a white male I also started having dinner with an African American member of the group prior to the men's meeting. We have dialogued on all sorts of issues, public and private, and have confronted one another during intervening national, cultural, and racial events.

I can truthfully say that I have been challenged by these deliberations and, as a result, have altered behaviors and grown immensely. I have had to learn that liberal views on values are not a panacea for all society's ills. I have learned that we share the most when we care about each other's personal lives.

3. Caring and Peace Politics

Before taking up peace politics we need to discard what Tronto calls a "moral boundary."[35] Boundaries are limitations placed upon ways of thinking that exclude certain types of actions. One of these boundaries differentiates the private from the public. Held pointed out, as we saw, the apparent contrast between care ethics as centering on private, family issues and justice ethics dealing with public, nation-state issues.[36] When caring is limited to private issues and excluded from the public sphere, applying caring to peace politics is impossible.

By contrast, caring helps bond relationships. Each person has a web of relationships. We are not isolated selves but individuals conjoined in family and community. In a community of interrelating members I have special ties with family and friends, as well as ties with others at work, at church, in my neighborhood, in associations, and elsewhere. Some thinkers expand upon these interconnections to envision a global community. Politics is part of the relating that goes on in society, which, when seen as community, makes politics an area that includes caring.

Caring in society is grounded in trust. Annette Baier has written extensively on trust.[37] Babies in the arms of their parents unconsciously trust their caregivers. Babies are decidedly unequal in power with their parents, and hence are not the independent, autonomously free, aggressive human beings that are characteristically male adults. Parents have no explicitly written contracts nor sets of universal moral rules according to which their relationships with their children are set forth. The mother-child relationship, in particular, begins in loving trust.

Held, in *Feminist Morality*, has an insightful chapter on "Preconceptions of Birth and Death."[38] She argues that giving birth is not a natural, biological phenomenon in the sense of reproducing "more of the same." Giving birth is a freely chosen human experience, and as such is empowering. Choosing to give birth is thus a distinctive human action. Honoring giving birth and nurturing as empowering is in contrast to those philosophies, like Hobbes, that stress risking life and the militarist tradition as characteristic of human living. Choosing to care for a child ought to be at least equal in human distinctiveness, Held says, as being willing to die for one's country.

With growth, a child's trust in parents continues, says Baier, for such necessities as "nutrition, shelter, clothing, health, education, privacy, and loving attachment to others."[39] Trust in others is part of dating and loving relationships. It also underpins other significant human interactions, such as, employment, business deals and team work, health care delivery, social services, participation in religion-charitable institutions, the building of community, and national and international affairs. Then at the twilight of life as adults move into their increasingly vulnerable senior years, the trusting relationship reverses–the elderly rely upon younger caregivers, and the process continues with a new generation.

Trust is primary and distrust is secondary. Trust is not built upon agreements, but agreements upon trust. It is mutual trust that undergirds promises, contracts, and treaties. When distrust occurs, trust has failed. Trust is the force that holds relationships together. When hurt and pain supplant trust, only healing can restore the original balance.

A recent national example of the primacy of trust over the Hobbesian view of aggression can be found in the north-western province of Somalia, hundreds of miles from Mogadishu.[40] The cities of Hargeisa and Burao had been utterly destroyed in 1988 by forces loyal to the former dictator Mohammed Siad Barre. After Barre was overthrown in 1991, intra-party feuding erupted and what was left of city life was crushed. Afterwards, the elders of the local clans, over a period of two years, went from person to person and met with the people in small groups in order to restore a modicum of trust. The politicians were unable to restore order.

Cities like these in Somalia have been described as examples of the Hobbesian condition of nature. But I believe Hobbes is wrong. Human life does not begin with every person an "enemy" to every person, but in people trusting one another. Sometimes this basic trust is lost because of an earthly disaster or as a result of the frightening things humans do to one another. A breakdown of that natural human trusting occurs, and is replaced by a heightened subhuman anxiety. At such times the caring adults among us give comfort till the nightmare is over, the fears are subdued, and we return to our truly original condition of trust.

When we return to caring, we need to dwell for a moment on its reciprocal nature. If the mature caring role model is described as reciprocal, then, among adults, there is no obligation for being the carer when the cared-for is unwilling or unable to exchange roles. This limitation on the ethics of care effectively eliminates the passive, self-sacrificing role in which many carers find themselves. At the same time, however, it delimits the extent to which the ethics of care can be used with strangers in peace politics.

Noddings originally thought there would be no obligation for entering into a caring relationship with nonspecific unconnected distant persons. Noddings said, "I am not obliged to care for starving children in Africa, because there is no way for this caring to be completed in the other unless I abandon the caring to which I am obligated."[41] She later modified this viewpoint to include a chain of trust that would pass her American contribution along until the starving are reached and someone is able to complete the act of caring in Africa.[42]

This chain of trust is one approach to connecting caring with peace politics. Another has been developed by Sara Ruddick in her ground-breaking and controversial work, *Maternal Thinking*. Ruddick focuses on mothering rather than the more expansive activity of caring work. She separates mothering from bearing and giving birth to babies, and describes mothering as the practice of caring for and raising children. Maternal practice is also distinguished from fathering, which generally means providing material support for others to do the caregiving.[43] While caring for children is undertaken by some men, mothering is usually performed by women.

Maternal practice for Ruddick has three essential components, namely, the protection, nurturance, and training of children.[44] Protection or preservative love embodies all efforts a mother makes to ensure the health of her child. Nurturance is helping a child unfold gradually in body and mind. Training usually begins with a societally acceptable model but gradually is changed and challenged by the independence of the child; ultimately the process seems to involve conscience. Mothers do not go through the daily concerns of child caregiving without being changed themselves.

Ruddick construes maternal thinking as a central part of a feminist standpoint. Out of a feminist standpoint, the more dominant masculine ways of knowing are revealed as being "in [Nancy] Hartsock's words, 'partial and perverse.'"[45] A particular dominant way of knowing which Ruddick opposes is militarist thinking, and she tries to show from several angles that a feminist standpoint is in opposition to violence.

She contrasts a warrior's death with a child's birth. "If war is 'masculine' and 'abstract,' peace seems 'feminine,'" she says.[46] Again she states, "All of women's work...is threatened by violence."[47] Yet Ruddick admits the "masculinity of war and women's peacefulness" is a myth.[48] She readily admits that individual men differ from one another, and many are not militaristic. She admits too that violence, including violence by women, is a part of life. Nevertheless, for Ruddick, nonviolence is the goal, although not always the practice, of maternal thinking. Maternal peace politics is thus "a truth in the making," for Ruddick.[49]

Several criticisms of Ruddick's philosophy have been offered.[50] One view notes that adults who do not have children are left outside this caring experience. Also, equality feminists, as we have already seen, oppose Ruddick for idealizing in the face of male dominance a traditional feminine relationship that is nonreciprocal.

Alison Bailey faults Ruddick for not sufficiently taking into account the myriad mothering practices of women of color.[51] Bailey is particularly concerned about the growing power differences between mothers of color and white mothers. Bailey quotes bell hooks's claim that white women "have been quite violent, militaristic in their support and maintenance of racism."[52] Unless this oppressive relationship is addressed there remains a covert institutional racist violence enforcing a separation of middle-class and upper-class white mothers, who are privileged by association with white males, from powerless poor mothers and mothers of color.

My own criticism of Ruddick's maternal thinking concerns the transference of a caring attitude toward one's children to people seen as inimical to the mother-child relationship. In particular, I am thinking about people who might be described as directly or indirectly hurting or killing those children. Ruddick has not established that mothers do not use violence to protect their children from violence perpetrated by strangers. While maternal practice can be identified with mothers preserving the lives of their children, Ruddick has not shown that this practice extends to loving the enemy's children (and adults) with the same nonviolent orientation. She does talk about mothers getting together "to protect the neighborhoods they have made."[53] Joining together with other caring people is a step in the right direction, but not the entire answer.

In *From Warism to Pacifism,* Duane Cady describes six different kinds of pacifism.[54] The most extreme, held only by a few pacifists, is Tolstoy's view of using no force against another person. Most of the positions are much weaker and even justify some forms of lethal violence. Thus, among pacifists– those holding that "war, by its very nature, is morally wrong"–there is no agreement about fully adopting nonviolence and never killing in self-defense.[55] Maternal thinking, I believe, would be consistent with any of these kinds of pacifism, as well as with some of the views Cady describes as part of a just-war continuum.[56]

As Ruddick describes maternal thinking, protection for one's children may ideally be nonviolent. However such a position is not inconsistent with violence used in defense of those children. The problem, not taken up by Ruddick, is the difference between innocent life and the life of a person caught in the act of using violence to destroy life. Many mothers are both pro innocent life, say for instance on the highly debated abortion issue, and yet in favor of the death penalty and in support of a "defensive" military. Ruddick appears to dismiss the latter position as inauthentic, a remnant of a failed male dominant culture. Perhaps it is, but without further argument, the essential link between maternal thinking and nonviolence in national defense seems tenuous at best.

In Ruddick's defense, I must state that she is arguing for a goal or an ideal, not a universal practice. Nonviolent maternal thinking is a truth in the making, a view into the future. Ruddick admits that many women do not fit her description of a feminist standpoint. Nevertheless she finds many examples of women who do, and so she continues to see her perspective as "a" but not "the" feminist standpoint.

Ruddick is seeking to transform the caring feminist standpoint through nonviolence. It does not matter that some women are violent, that some mothers encourage their sons to join the military, or that some women themselves join the military.[57] As Ruddick says, "My hope–and belief–is that there are enough maternal practices that are sufficiently governed by principles of nonviolence to offer one model for nonviolent relationships."[58]

As an ideal for maternal thinking, I do not find that Ruddick has made a sufficient connection between mothers caring for their children and loving their enemies. I believe it is loving our enemies, not caring for our children, that is the primary link to nonviolence. Ruddick circumvents this point by recognizing the universality of mothering and by extending the mothering relationship to all humanity, friend and foe. In essence, she appears to be saying, if all human beings cared for one another in the ideal manner of a mother nonviolently caring for her children, then there would be no enemies and the question of loving one's enemies would be a moot point.

In this ideal way of thinking Ruddick is consistent. If this ideal were to become a realizable goal we would need to consider how we can get from here to there. One way would be to demand that dialogue replace engaged military forces in international relations. Nation-states would be required to submit their differences to international negotiation rather than, as in the Hobbesian manner of *Realpolitik*, to have military forces resolve differences on the battlefield. Dialoguing through differences is a significant way in which mothers train their children. There are models for applying this type of approach to nation-state disputes.[59]

Let me briefly describe two contrasting examples. On 2 August 1990, Saddam Hussein invaded Kuwait. George Bush, then the U.S. President, drew a line in the sand and said to Hussein either withdraw your forces or we will force you out. The United Nations set 15 January 1991 as a deadline for Iraq to withdraw. On 17 January, the United States started bombing Iraq.[60] One hundred thousand Iraqi soldiers were killed and at least twice that number of Iraqi civilians have died in an ensuing economic boycott that still is not over.

By contrast, in Haiti on 29 September 1991, the military overthrew a democratically elected government.[61] First Bush and William Clinton, when President, negotiated with the military for a return of the Haitian President, Jean-Bertrand Aristide. Negotiations lasted two years. A ten-point Accord was signed at Governors Island on 3 July 1993, and then broken in October by the military dictatorship. More negotiations occurred.

Finally Clinton set a deadline for either the Haitian military leadership to leave Haiti or United States troops to intervene. Afterwards Clinton went a step further and announced a three-person negotiating committee consisting of Jimmy Carter, a former U.S. President; Colin Powell, a former chair of the U.S. Joint Chiefs of Staff; and Sam Nunn, a distinguished U.S. Senator. The three men flew to Haiti and negotiated until the final hour of the 18 September 1994 deadline. With U.S. airplanes in the air the Haitian military leaders at last relented and U.S. troops were allowed to enter peacefully. No one was killed on account of the negotiations. Aristide returned to Haiti to serve the final year of his presidency.

Dialogue in international affairs is not a panacea. The international scene cannot move from a warrior mentality to maternal thinking overnight. Powerful nations are quite capable of making forced situations resemble negotiations. We have to be wary of false substitutions.

Moreover, the present United Nations structure would need to be democratized in order for smaller nations to have confidence that their poor voices will be heard. At the least this new structure would entail a general assembly that is empowered to enact laws, a security council without major power vetoes, a world court with the power to override the major nations, and United Nations representatives–at least in one body–elected by the peoples of the world. Building such a representative international governing body would itself take dialogue. In the United States such dialogue runs counter to the conservative mentality that the international body ought to be disbanded, so that the United States and state's rights can reign unimpeded.

If we are going to dialogue about caring and peace politics at home and abroad, then we must discuss specific proposals for getting at the causes of violence before violence overtakes us all. That is a contribution I believe practical peace philosophers, feminist thinkers, and political theorists can make at this time. We have these pioneering women philosophers to thank for moving the caring position forward.[62]

Notes

1. Carol Gilligan, *In a Different Voice* (Cambridge, Mass.: Harvard University Press, 1982).

2. *Ibid.*, pp. 7-8; and see Nancy Chodorow, *The Reproduction of Mothering* (Berkeley, Calif.: University of California Press, 1978).

3. See, for example, Warren Steinberg, *Masculinity: Identity, Conflict, and Transformation* (Boston: Shambhala, 1993), pp. 12-17.

4. See Janet Lever, "Sex Differences in the Games Children Play," *Social Problems*, 23 (1976), pp. 478-487; and "Sex Differences in the Complexity of Children's Play and Games," *American Sociological Review*, 43 (1978), pp. 471-483.

5. Deborah Tannen, *You Just Don't Understand: Women and Men in Conversation* (New York: Ballantine, 1990), p. 24.

6. *Ibid.*, pp. 49-73.

7. Gilligan, *Different Voice,* pp. 32 and *passim.*

8. *Ibid.*, p. 33.

9. *Ibid.*, pp. 24-32; and see also Lawrence Kohlberg, *The Philosophy of Moral Development* (San Francisco: Harper and Row, 1981).

10. Gilligan, *Different Voice*, pp. 73-74.

11. Nel Noddings, *Caring: A Feminine Approach to Ethics and Moral Education* (Berkeley, Calif.: University of California Press, 1984), pp. 79-81.

12. *Ibid.*, pp. 79ff.

13. See *ibid.*, pp. 86-90.

14. See Marilyn Friedman, *What Are Friends for?: Feminist Perspectives on Personal Relationships and Moral Theory* (Ithaca, N.Y.: Cornell University Press, 1993), pp. 119-126.

15. Monica Roman, Robert Mims, and Fred Jespersen, "A Portrait of the Boss," *Business Week* (25 November 1991), p. 180.

16. Katha Pollitt, "Are Women Morally Superior to Men?", *The Nation*, 225:22 (28 December 1992), pp. 799-807.

17. See, for example, Martin Luther King, Jr., *Where Do We Go from Here: Chaos or Community?* (New York: Harper and Row, 1967); Leo Tolstoy, *The Kingdom of God Is within You: Or, Christianity Not as a Mystical Teaching but as a New Concept of Life*, trans. Leo Wiener (New York: Farrar, Straus, and Cudahy, 1961); and Martin Buber, *I and Thou*, trans. Ronald Gregor Smith (New York: Charles Scribner's Sons, 2nd ed., 1958).

18. Virginia Held, *Feminist Morality: Transforming Culture, Society, and Politics* (Chicago: University of Chicago Press, 1993), pp. 43-90.

19. *Ibid.*, p. 68.

20. Claudia Card, "Caring and Evil," *Hypatia*, 5:1 (Spring 1990), pp. 101-108; Sarah Lucia Hoagland, "Some Concerns about Nel Noddings' *Caring*," *Hypatia*, 5:1 (Spring 1990), pp. 109-114.

21. Barbara Houston, "Caring and Exploitation," *Hypatia*, 5:1 (Spring 1990), p. 117.

22. Gilligan, *Different Voice*, p. 74.

23. Nel Noddings, "A Response," *Hypatia*, 5:1 (Spring 1990), pp. 120-126.

24. Friedman, *Friends*, pp. 91-183.

25. *Ibid.*, pp. 94-110.

26. *Ibid.*, pp. 130-131.

27. Alison Jaggar, "Caring as a Feminist Practice of Moral Reason," in *Justice and Care: Essential Readings in Feminist Ethics*, ed. Virginia Held (Boulder, Colo.: Westview, 1995), p. 189.

28. *Ibid.*, p. 192.

29. Joan Tronto, "Women and Caring: What Can Feminists Learn about Morality from Caring?", in *Justice and Care*, ed. Held, pp. 101-115.

30. *Ibid.*, p. 106.

31. Carl Rogers, "This Is Me: The Development of My Professional Thinking and Personal Philosophy," *On Becoming a Person: A Therapist's View of Psychotherapy* (Boston: Houghton Mifflin, 1961), pp. 3-27.

32. Margaret Urban Walker, "Moral Understandings: Alternative 'Epistemology' for a Feminist Ethics," in *Justice and Care*, ed. Held, pp. 141-143.

33. Tannen, *You Just Don't Understand*, pp. 49-61.

34. Friedman, *Friends*, pp. 187-206.

35. Joan Tronto, *Moral Boundaries: A Political Argument for an Ethic of Care* (New York: Routledge, 1993), pp. 4-11.

36. Held, *Feminist Morality*, pp. 54-57.

37. See Annette Baier, "Trust and Antitrust" *Ethics*, 96 (1985-1986), pp. 231-260, and "What Do Women Want in a Moral Theory?", *Nous*, 19 (1985), pp. 53-63.

38. Held, *Feminist Morality*, pp. 112-137.

39. Baier, "Trust and Antitrust," p. 242.

40. See Rakiya Omaar, "One Thorn Bush at a Time," *New Internationalist*, no. 256 (June, 1994), pp. 8-10; and Joseph Kunkel, "Somalia: Humanitarian Aid or Business as Usual?", in *From the Eye of the Storm: Regional Conflicts and the*

Philosophy of Peace, ed. Laurence Bove and Laura Duhan Kaplan (Amsterdam: Rodopi, 1995), pp. 297-300.

41. Noddings, *Caring*, p. 86.

42. Noddings, "A Response," p. 121.

43. Sara Ruddick, *Maternal Thinking: Toward a Politics of Peace* (New York: Ballantine, 1989), pp. 42-45.

44. *Ibid.*, pp. 61-123.

45. *Ibid.*, p. 129; and Nancy Hartsock, "The Feminist Standpoint: Developing the Ground for a Specifically Feminist Historical Materialism," in *Discovering Reality*, ed. Sandra Harding and Merrill Hintikka (London: D. Reidl, 1983), pp. 283-310.

46. Ruddick, *Maternal Thinking*, p. 146.

47. *Ibid.*, p. 148.

48. *Ibid.*, pp. 143-156.

49. *Ibid.*, pp. 160-184.

50. See, for example, Rosemarie Tong, *Feminine and Feminist Ethics* (Belmont, Calif.: Wadsworth, 1993), pp. 148-155.

51. Alison Bailey, "Mothering, Diversity, and Peace Politics" *Hypatia*, 9.2 (Spring 1994), pp. 188-198; see also Alison Bailey, *Mothers, Birthgivers, and Peacemakers: The Problem of Maternal Thinking in Feminist Peace Politics* (Ph.D. dissertation, Department of Philosophy, University of Cincinnati, 1993).

52. Quoted in Bailey, *Mothers, Birthgivers, and Peacemakers*, p. 10.

53. Ruddick, *Maternal Thinking*, p. 80.

54. Duane L. Cady, *From Warism to Pacifism: A Moral Continuum* (Philadelphia: Temple University Press, 1989), pp. 57-75.

55. *Ibid.*, p. 4.

56. *Ibid.*, pp. 21-38.

57. See Linda Forcey, *Mothers of Sons* (New York: Praeger, 1987).

58. Sara Ruddick, "Fierce and Human Peace," in *Just War, Nonviolence and Nuclear Deterrence: Philosophers on War and Peace*, ed. Duane L. Cady and Richard Werner (Wakefield N.H.: Longwood Academic, 1991), p. 125.

59. Roger Fisher and William Ury with Bruce Patton, *Getting to Yes: Negotiating Agreement without Giving In* (New York: Penguin, 2nd ed., 1991).

60. See "Section III: Desert Storm Assessments," in *From the Eye of the Storm*, ed. Bove and Kaplan, pp. 107-186.

61. Paul Farmer, *The Uses of Haiti* (Monroe, Maine: Common Courage, 1994); and see Steven Lee, Howard H. Harriott, Sally J. Scholz, and Joseph C. Kunkel in *Concerned Philosophers for Peace Newsletter*, 14:2 (Fall 1994), pp. 4-11.

62. I wish to thank Alison Jaggar, Alison Bailey, Judith Presler, Sally J. Scholz, and the reviewer for this chapter for very helpful comments on improving an earlier draft of this chapter.

SECTION II

INTERNATIONAL INTERVENTION AND DEFENSE

INTRODUCTION

The contributors to Section II approach the making and keeping of peace from widely divergent perspectives on international intervention and defense. The perspectives range from noninvolvement to military intervention to nonmilitary intervention. The lessons from the past applied in these chapters come from theoretical teachers Plato, Theophrastus, and Immanuel Kant in the West to Lao Tsu in the East. Lessons are also taken from present-day theories, practices, and actual peacemaking and peacekeeping efforts.

In "Ancient Thoughts on Peacekeepers and Other Busybodies," Leo Groarke distinguishes between peacemaking and peacekeeping and then argues that the United Nations should radically limit its peacekeeping activities. Boutros Boutros-Ghali's United Nations report *An Agenda for Peace* is the occasion for Groarke's argument. Boutros-Ghali's report recommends an expanded United Nations that can undertake greatly increased peacemaking and peacekeeping activities. Groarke makes an analogy between a modern international peacekeeper and Theophrastus' description of a busybody. Theophrastus suggests that the busybody does not have the requisite historical knowledge of a conflict that would enable him to intervene appropriately. So also, Groarke argues, the international peacekeeping body may lack the full cultural and historical understanding of a conflict, and thus its interference in a conflict would be unjustified. He draws out of this analogy the problems associated with international peacekeeping, namely, (1) its uncertain outcome, (2) the uncertainty of its process, and (3) its limited scope. While Groarke is not opposed to peacemaking and does not reject all peacekeeping, he does recommend an extremely limited form of peacekeeping following the advice of Lao Tsu.

Robert Litke's "Peacekeeping, Peacemaking, and Military Force" also responds to Boutros-Ghali's *An Agenda for Peace*. Litke focuses on military contributions to peacemaking and peacekeeping. Litke argues that appropriate use of force is justified in international peacekeeping and peacemaking actions, just as it is in civic policing. That is to say, use of force is justified and necessary in intervening in genocide in the same way as it is in intervening in homicide. Litke proposes a schedule of increasing levels of dominance or coercion by military agents of the United Nations. His schedule of increasing force is modeled on the schedule for police use of force in the civil setting. A realistic view of our world, Litke argues, reveals that use of force is sometimes needed to protect international victims of violence. Thus, we must give serious consideration to the conditions under which international military force should be used and how that force should be regulated.

William C. Gay, in "Kant's Noninterventionalism and Recent Alternatives of Nonmilitary Intervention," describes a middle ground between the

Kantian responses of "silence" or "violence" to injustice in other nations and to international conflict; that is, there is a third alternative between the silence of nonintervention and the violence of military intervention. Silence, or nonintervention sanctions acts of injustice just as violence commits acts of injustice. Gay argues for intervention that is morally justifiable, being nonviolent, but does not sanction injustice. Gay examines two alternative responses that go between the horns of Kant's dilemma, namely, (1) the world federalist apprehension of individuals responsible for state violence, and (2) the citizen defense nonviolent response to injustice. To these two he adds a third response, diplomacy. He describes how a thoughtful use of all three of these alternatives is an effective humanitarian intervention that offers a moral alternative to silence or violence.

In "Nonmilitary Responses to Nuclear Threat or Attack," Richard Wendell Fogg argues that a complete and detailed nonviolent response to nuclear threat or attack can be a more successful deterrent than a military response. Fogg applies Thomas Kuhn's notion of a paradigm shift to his approach to nonmilitary defense. A paradigm shift occurs when a new paradigm answers a central question that the old paradigm cannot. Fogg argues that deterrence theory does not satisfactorily answer the question of how to defend if deterrence fails and counterstrike is unwise. Fogg proposes a nonmilitary response that amounts to a double paradigm shift. The first shift is away from destroying the aggressor's military forces to reducing the aggressor's support from top leaders on down. The second shift is away from the global belief that nuclear weapons are the most powerful defense to the belief that nonmilitary weapons and positive incentives are the most powerful defense. Fogg's position is supported by a complete set of strategies and applications that he develops into an organized system.

Steven Lee's "Sovereignty and Positive Peace" is another approach to nonviolent resolution to international conflict. In his chapter, Lee first distinguishes between negative and positive peace, then draws out some distinctions relating to sovereignty, and lastly interconnects his clarified notions of positive peace and sovereignty to show their bearing upon our post-cold-war world. Negative peace is simply a lack of conflict. Positive peace is frequently understood as a lack of conflict with the addition of justice. Lee points up some difficulties in this notion of positive peace. He understands by positive peace, nonviolent resolution of conflict. This peaceful condition, he argues, supports justice but avoids the difficulties in the notion of peace that explicitly entails justice. Lee's discussion of sovereignty leads to a resolution of the thorny problem of how a state can maintain its sovereignty and still conform to international law. Sovereign states that conform to international law impose upon themselves constraints that entail adjudication of conflicts. Such international adjudication and agreement is positive peace.

Eight

ANCIENT THOUGHTS ON PEACEKEEPERS AND OTHER BUSYBODIES

Leo Groarke

The title of this chapter might seem unduly negative. I should therefore emphasize that it is not meant as a universal condemnation of peacekeeping. This caveat being noted, I will argue that international peacekeeping should play a secondary role in peacemaking, and that it should be viewed in a more critical, negative, and circumspect way than is frequently the case.

In order to prevent possible misunderstandings, I want to begin by defining "peacemaking" and "peacekeeping." I take the goal of peacemaking to be agreements–or, more generally, understandings–that eliminate or mitigate the causes of violent confrontation. Peacekeeping has the more immediate goal of stopping or preventing violence. In the international arena, peacekeeping employs military and civilian personnel in order to stop or contain violent action by opposing sides. Peacekeeping may prepare the way for peacemaking–or may be its final outcome–but peacemaking is a broader process which has much deeper aims.

We must not confuse either peacemaking or peacekeeping with the attempt to prevent or end war or violence by subduing an aggressor. Especially in cases of blatant human rights violations, this may be a more reasonable course of action than attempts at peacemaking or peacekeeping. In a case of genocide, straightforward military defeat may be the morally preferable way to put an end to crimes against humanity. How such defeat should be constrained by moral imperatives is an interesting question, but I will not address it here. Instead, I want to consider cases in which peace-keeping is seen as a viable way to end a conflict.

The analysis I propose is in part motivated by a negative reaction to an expanded international commitment to United Nations peacekeeping. The attitudes that have propelled this commitment receive their most significant expression in *An Agenda for Peace*, a United Nations report presented by Boutros Boutros-Ghali shortly after he was appointed Secretary General for a five-year term beginning in December 1991.[1] It proposes an expanded United Nations specifically designed to serve the purposes of peacemaking and peacekeeping. According to *An Agenda*, this new United Nations should be achieved by (among other things), (1) expanded United Nations fact-finding activities in perpetuity; (2) a more frequent and more extensive use of the security council, the general assembly, and the secretary general; (3) a larger international role for the world court; (4) a new United Nations mechanism for administering international aid; (5) the creation of permanent stand-by troops available for United Nations use; (6) new peace-enforcement units; and, above all else; (7) a greater financial commitment to the United Nations on the part of member states.

I believe that some of these suggestions have merit, but that the attitude which inspires them is wrongheaded. It has fostered an increasing emphasis on United Nations peacekeeping operations during the last decade. The extent of this trend is reflected in the fact that it took forty-three years (from 1945 to 1988) to establish the first thirteen United Nations peacekeeping operations, but forty-three *months* to establish the next thirteen.[2] By the end of 1996 there were 26 completed missions and 17 missions under way.[3]

I believe we need to question the attitude to peacekeeping reflected in Boutros-Ghali's report and in the recent expansion of United Nations operations. To some extent, my concerns reflect a more skeptical–and, I believe, more realistic–attitude to peacekeeping I have found in ancient thought. Because I will use it to raise questions about contemporary attitudes which are founded on the very best of intentions, my prodding may seem uncharitable. I can only answer that it is offered as healthy skepticism, and that such skepticism is not out of place when the head of a large corporation like the United Nations tells us that the solution to a pressing social problem is an enormous expansion of its powers and greatly increased financial support. His views are popular ones, but in this and similar cases in other contexts, we will do well to follow Socrates' example and think twice before acceding to popular convictions.

1. An Alternative Point of View

In criticizing Boutros-Ghali, I will focus on his underlying attitude to peacekeeping rather than the specific policies he proposes. To this extent, this chapter is philosophical and conceptual rather than empirical. The importance of the questions I raise are a function of the popularity of the attitudes that I criticize–attitudes that are not limited to United Nations reports. The contemporary assumption in favor of peacekeeping derives much of its appeal from the *Bible*, which forever sanctifies peacemakers as "blessed" in Jesus Christ's "Sermon on the Mount."[4] I do not want to reject these sentiments entirely, but I think that they are exaggerated, and that it is especially important to distinguish peacemaking from peacekeeping. Because too positive an attitude to the peacekeeping undermines the circumspection which is the first prerequisite of legitimate peacemaking.

Like the positive attitude to peacemaking reflected in the *Bible*, the negative attitude to peacekeeping I want to advocate is ancient. It is most clearly reflected in an admittedly peculiar work of Aristotle's successor, Theophrastus. He is best known for his commentaries on Aristotle and his scientific work, but he had many other interests. His *Characters* is a rhetorical work that can best be described as a catalogue of positive and negative character types.[5] The negative types that it describes include "the ignoramus," "the flatterer," and "the busybody." It is the section on the busybody that is relevant here, for Theophrastus' paradigm of a busybody is a man who tries to break up a fight between men he does not know. According to Theophrastus, such a man is meddling in other people's affairs and should be roundly chastised. A person of this sort is, in microcosm, the peacekeeper.

Such views raise some intriguing questions. Why should Theophrastus, the ancient rhetors who used his book, and their ancient audiences, criticize someone as laudable as the peacekeeper? And why do they dismiss the attempt to stop a fight as meddling in someone else's affairs? This is a condemnation of peacekeeping in the personal rather than the interstate arena, but this is not because the ancients think that the latter is more feasible. Indeed, the idea of interstate peacekeepers seems too peculiar to be taken seriously in ancient political discussion, even when it addresses (as it often does) issues of war and peace.

The ancient attitude to busybodies we find in Theophrastus is entertainingly reflected in an ancient biography of Aesop, originally called *The Book of Xanthus the Philosopher and his Slave Aesop*.[6] In keeping with this title, a major theme in the book is a series of "philosophical" battles between Aesop and his philosopher owner, Xanthus. At one point, Aesop accuses one of Xanthus' friends of being a busybody. Xanthus answers that everyone is a busybody and challenges Aesop to prove otherwise by inviting to dinner someone who is not. There follow hilarious incidents in which Xanthus tests the candidates that Aesop brings home. Judging by Theophrastus, the first seems to be a textbook example of someone who is not a busybody, for Aesop finds him sitting quietly, reading a book, ignoring a brawl between two men in the town square. In the process he demonstrates an impressive ability to ignore the call of peacekeeping, but Aesop's guest fails to pass muster when Xanthus purposely pretends to be a boor at dinner, threatening to beat the cook for no reason at all. When this finally prompts the man's protests, Xanthus triumphantly declares that he has proven that his guest is a busybody.

This incident is exaggerated for the sake of humor, but it underscores an ancient suspicion of anyone who intervenes in others' affairs, even when they do so in the cause of peace. Theophrastus and *The Book of Xanthus and...Aesop* do not explain the reasons behind such an attitude, but it is not difficult to reconstruct them. Three problems with peacekeeping warrant explanation in this regard.

A. The Uncertain Outcome of Peacekeeping

The first problem with peacekeeping is its uncertain nature. We can never be certain of the outcome of any action in the world of human affairs but we can still distinguish between outcomes that are and are not reasonably predictable. When I chair a meeting in my department, I can reasonably take many things for granted, and can predict which issues will be controversial and which will probably be agreed upon. I know my colleagues well and share with them a mutual understanding of procedure, etiquette, and how to resolve or live with disagreement. This allows us to run the department smoothly, not without disagreement and conflict, but without anything that approaches violent confrontation.

Suppose in contrast that I come across Theophrastus' two men brawling in the street. Assuming I do not know them or why they fight, it is extraordinarily difficult to judge how I should intervene in a situation which is already characterized by extreme behavior. With superior physical force–force I may not have at my disposal–I may be able to subdue the men momentarily, though I run the risk of embroiling myself in the dispute. Even if I succeed in stopping the fight, this does not mean that I will be able to prevent it from recurring. Establishing a long term truce is a difficult prospect given that it may have to be achieved in circumstances that are characterized by fear, anger, and exaggeration, and without the kind of mutual understanding that is the proper basis for a peaceful resolution of a conflict.

The difference between my departmental meeting and Theophrastus' two men brawling makes it easier to understand ancient skepticism about peacekeeping, and its unwillingness to countenance it in the case of war, for the problems that it highlights are exacerbated in the case of war. War occurs when peaceful methods of resolving conflict break down. The impediments that make it hard to reestablish these methods (assuming they once existed) are magnified because war takes destruction, fear, anger, and hatred to new levels, and because states are more complex entities than individuals. This is reflected in the causes of war, which are inevitably tied to the history, the politics, and the social circumstances of millions of people within the states in conflict. An outside body like the United Nations may in some sense know these states, but not in a way that allows it easily to decide how agreement can be reached, or who is right or wrong or reasonable. In some cases, taking one or both parties to the world court may be possible but this is a vastly more complex, expensive, and questionable proposal than taking an individual to court, especially as the international court has (as it is now constituted) no ability to enforce its decisions. Even if it did, we cannot end a war by placing a state in jail.

We might answer that this is stating the obvious: international peacekeeping is difficult. But it is not just difficult. In cases where one or more of the antagonists is determined or recalcitrant and the resources available to restrain them are limited (as they invariably are), peacekeeping may simply be impossible. The inherent contradictions it must overcome even in the best of circumstances are curiously evident even in Boutros-Ghali's claim that peacekeeping works. "If conflicts have gone unresolved," he says, "it is not because techniques for peaceful settlement were unknown or inadequate. The fault lies first in the lack of political will of parties to seek a solution to their differences...."[7] This is a peculiar defense of peacekeeping given that an unwillingness to compromise political objectives for the sake of peace (that is, "a lack of political will") is precisely what produces violence and a need for peacekeeping in the first place. Boutros-Ghali thus defends peacekeeping by claiming that it works in situations which are not characterized by the conditions that create a need for it.

According to Boutros-Ghali, a second reason why peacekeeping sometimes fails is "the lack of leverage at the disposal of a third party."[8] But leverage is expensive and difficult to exert. The best proof of this expense is the continual funding problems that beset United Nations operations. Shashi Tharoor, the Special Assistant to the United Nations Under Secretary General for Peacekeeping has summarized these problems as follows.

> [T]here is the important question of finance....[W]hen every operation is set up, an assessment letter goes to Member States....The average collection rate, three months after this letter goes out, has been 36.7 percent; at the end of six months, 50 percent. Without money coming in, how can we run the kind of large-scale ambitious peacekeeping activities that we're talking about today?[9]

By the closing months of 1998, United Nations members were in arrears 1.6 billion dollars for peacekeeping operations.[10]

Even if it were possible to garner the resources necessary to give United Nations forces the leverage necessary to stop international conflict, such leverage is a two-edged sword that can undermine the goals of peacekeeping. For too much leverage turns peacekeeping into rule by force, which is no longer properly described as peacekeeping. The limits on peacekeeping this implies are poignantly expressed in the following banner which welcomed the United Nations peacekeepers into Gaza on 12 March 1957:

> WELCOME MEN OF PEACE
> WELCOME, HONORABLE GUESTS
> ACT AS PEACEMAKERS BUT NOT AS RULERS[11]

This is a powerful message because the line between ruling and peacekeeping is a fine one that can be difficult to walk.

There are many circumstances in which the best way to prevent belligerence on the part of states (or individuals) is by acting as a ruler. This may be appropriate but it implies something above and beyond peacekeeping. Real peacekeeping is an attempt to "work out" differences between two states–an attempt that inevitably relies on good will and the positive participation of the parties to a conflict. In many cases we cannot rely upon them. In United Nations operations, such circumstances raise the difficult question whether it is legitimate (as in Bosnia-Herzegovina) to use force to protect peacekeeping forces. The answer may be that it is legitimate but that it is questionable whether this qualifies as peacekeeping.

Looked at from an ancient point of view, the pitfalls of peacemaking make it too uncertain to sit well with an ancient emphasis on moral aims and goals that are *achievable*. Perhaps the best expression of this emphasis is Epictetus' *Enchiridion*, which opens with the claim that we must recognize what we can and cannot control, and should achieve happiness through the former. Among other things, Epictetus concludes that we should be indifferent to those external things–wealth, fame, good fortune, and so on–that most people seek, for they are things which depend on circumstances that lie beyond our own control.

Considered from the point of view of what can be achieved, it is hard to think of a more problematic activity than peacekeeping. To be successful, it requires that we exert our influence, not only on the physical manifestations of war, but also on the hearts and minds of citizens in conflicting states. Such influence is difficult at the best of times, but especially in circumstances of war, which are characterized by anger, hostility, and suspicion–emotions that make agreement, reconciliation, and compromise difficult and sometimes impossible. Opposing states are of limited help in this regard, for they invariably believe that God is on their side, and they have tremendous human and other resources that they use to prevent or obstruct any peace that is not to their advantage. It need not follow that we should never practice peacekeeping, but it does mean that the decision to practice peacekeeping must be based on full recognition of its limits and precariousness.

B. The Uncertainty of the Peacekeeping Process

A second problem with peacekeeping is implicit in both Theophrastus' *Characters* and *The Book of Xanthus and...Aesop*. Both are written from the point of view of ancient rhetoric, which is founded on a commitment to the possibility of arguing on any side of any question. This commitment may be exaggerated, but it usefully underscores the epistemic difficulties that arise when one attempts to sort through debates that surround violent confrontation. Peacekeeping is difficult because it must be carried on in circumstances that are characterized by radical disagreements, and by argumentative battles as well as military ones. In the midst of the propaganda war that this implies, it is difficult to assess competing points of view, and difficult to resolve the differences of interest and opinion that fuel the war effort.

Even in Theophrastus' example, the attempt to stop a fist fight is likely to produce impassioned arguments and accusations on both sides. Most opponents will offer views that are a mix of truth and falsehood. In the process they will exaggerate the faults of their opponent and minimize their own. In the midst of these opposing points of view, it is difficult for an outsider to understand the conflict, especially as particular acts of aggression are probably open to competing interpretations and a more convincing argument may reflect more finely honed rhetorical skills rather than a superior point of view. Even in a fist fight, a real understanding of a conflict may require an in-depth understanding of a history that precipitates it.

The confusion that naturally attends a fight is exacerbated in contexts of war and military conflict. As Lieutenant-General E. L. M. Burns, the Chief of Staff of the United Nations peacekeeping forces in the Middle East from 1954-1956, writes:

> When an armed conflict is in progress it is difficult to tell what is actually happening. Both sides put out their own versions of events, usually censored and sophisticated....Observers and observation groups are therefore an essential part of any peacekeeping machinery which the United Nations is likely to set up. However, their effectiveness will depend on co-operation received from the country in which they are observing....Unfortunately, such co-operation on the part of the host countries has seldom been experienced....[12]

In his tour of duty, Burns found that opposing sides in a dispute were likely to twist and bend accepted agreements and played on vagaries and ambiguities in ways that supported their own political objectives.

Similar problems characterize the situation within adversarial states themselves. Genuine peacekeeping must ultimately be built on a commitment to peace on the part of the people in such states, but they may not have access to detailed facts, unbiased reporting, and consensus-building points of view. In real world politics, public opinion in conflict situations is greatly influenced by leaders, media, and other interests that are happy to exploit simplistic arguments, propaganda, and patriotic zeal at the expense of cool and collected attempts to establish careful compromises and assess what is and is not fair.

Such themes are stressed in an interview with Branislav Canak, a Serbian opposition leader. He explains Serbian President Slobodan Milosevic's successful attempt to rouse nationalist support for military intervention in Croatia and Bosnia.

> There were too many people in our [union's] ranks who were at least confused whether they should support Milosevic, or not him, but the idea that he proposed, which was a very simple idea,...the idea that our brothers in Croatia and Bosnia are in trouble–we must help them. They didn't ask what kind of trouble–"Is it real trouble?" "Is it possible for that trouble to be solved in a peaceful way?"–because the propaganda was very strong.
>
> If you don't have the opportunity to look around and read an alternative paper and watch alternative television, to see what is the other point of view of the situation, you must be caught....Otherwise the alternative is, as it was in the beginning, if you don't support that policy you are a national traitor....
>
> I think it is...very confusing....[13]

It is easy to see how one-sided appeals of this sort–appeals which are endemic in the debates that characterize international conflict–are a serious impediment to peacemaking and peacekeeping. In view of them, peacekeepers must often operate in a situation of epistemic deprivation, in which they do not have the ability to distinguish what is true and false, fact and fiction, information and disinformation, and half truth and whole truth.

To some extent, Boutros-Ghali recognizes such problems. It is in view of them that he emphasizes the need for an increased investment in United Nations fact finding. But even if this investment was forthcoming–something which is unlikely–it would be difficult to overcome the problem of epistemic deprivation that characterizes peacekeeping situations. However much money one spends, conflict situations are intrinsically open to different interpretations. What is to one side an act of aggression will inevitably be seen by the other as an act of self-defense or understandable retaliation. In such circumstances, confusion is inevitable, especially within warring states where citizens will not have open access to opposing points of view. Opposing points of view are inevitably dismissed as propaganda (witness the stubborn popular support for leaders like Milosevic and Saddam Hussein).

C. The Limited Scope of Peacekeeping .

A third fundamental problem with peacekeeping can be explained against the background of ancient political views, which tend toward realism: the view that war and conflict are an inevitable product of competing interests. When Plato presents his ideal state in the *Republic*, for example, he matter-of-factly declares that his state's desire for greater wealth will require that it take a slice of its neighbor's land and that it have a military that makes this possible. Considered from this point of view, Plato is much closer to the physiophists' claim that might makes right than is normally allowed.

In the present context, the point is that peacekeeping as we understand it is a partial and superficial attempt to deal with the competing interests that produce conflict situations. It is partial because it focuses on the outward manifestations of conflict, not on the underlying causes that create them. Peacekeeping in and of itself does not, for example, address historical rivalries and injustices, political desires for more economic wealth and power, and complex ethnic and religious differences that we see in those areas of the world in which peace has proved difficult to establish or sustain–in Somalia, Bosnia, Iraq, the Middle East, Ireland, and so on.

The proponents of peacekeeping will say that it allows us to resolve such issues by creating a situation in which they can be addressed. There may be occasions when this is true, but the opposite may also be true. Peacekeeping is a military exercise. This means that it is necessarily driven by the empirical realities of the day–by what is possible and effective from a military point of view. There is no guarantee that the peace that this makes possible will last. It may easily be one that is inherently unstable or that compromises an attempt to redress injustices and inequities. In these circumstances, economic or military action may well be a morally preferable way to end a conflict.

More generally, it is questionable whether the international peace-keeping organization, the United Nations, is an effective mechanism for dealing with the issues that are the root causes of international conflict. However well-intentioned, it is in the end a political organization that is constrained by political maneuvering and the interests of member states. The United Nations Charter expressly prohibits interference in the affairs of member states. In practice this means that the United Nations is frequently unable to address the underlying causes of international tension. Because independent groups (whether social movements or international organizations like Peace Brigades International) are not constrained by similar political realities, they may be able to work more effectively and creatively on the fundamental issues that must be the basis of lasting peace.

2. Limited Peacekeeping

What is to be said of peacekeeping in view of, (1) its uncertain outcome, (2) the uncertainty of its process, and (3) its limited scope? I do not believe it follows that we should reject every attempt at peacekeeping, but it does follow that peacemaking is inherently problematic, and that its ability to establish stable peace is limited. In any particular case, we must assess the prospects for peacemaking by asking the questions suggested by our previous dis-cussion. "Is there a serious commitment to peace on the part of opposing states?" "Are there good reasons for believing that the leverage necessary for peacekeeping is possible?" "Is this a case of peacekeeping or a military intervention?" "How serious is the problem of epistemic deprivation?" "Can a fair and enforceable peace be established?" "Is there good reason to believe that peacekeeping will enshrine serious injustices that may be a barrier to lasting peace?" "Are there alternative courses of action–military or otherwise–that are preferable?"

Applying these questions to particular situations is a complex matter and I will not attempt any case studies here. But these questions suggest that Boutros-Ghali, the United Nations, and their supporters have exaggerated the prospects for peacekeeping. The result has in too many cases been peacekeeping operations that deal with states that lack a serious commitment to peace, that are characterized by extraordinary logistical difficulties, and that are more preoccupied with military realities than with the fundamental causes of conflict. Tharoor writes:

> One of the fundamental difficulties...is that of deploying United Nations peace-keepers in countries or situations where there is really no peace to keep....The success of the peace-keepers has almost always been predicated upon the co-operation of the conflicting parties. In situations where there are no peace agreements–Bosnia or Somalia, for instance,...how do we function? For international peace-keepers to work in the midst of a raging war; to negotiate their way daily; to cope with irregular political authorities and shadowy chains of command; to base their actions upon commitments which are violated as routinely as they are signed; to deal with armed elements whose discipline is nonexistent or brutal; to be shot at themselves, sometimes by the very people they are there to protect and assist–all this is largely unfamiliar territory.[14]

Such problems have been compounded by a well meant United Nations commitment to impartiality which has in practice resulted in many accusations that it condones "the actions of warlords and thugs of various sorts who have otherwise received the censure of the international community."[15]

Tharoor's answer to such problems is more muscular peacekeeping. Boutros-Ghali also leans in this direction. Their implicit goal is, therefore, a mammoth United Nations that would exert control over international conflict and the forces that produce it, by means of peacekeeping. There is a great deal that might be said in favor of such a goal, but it is double-speak to call the more muscular military action it envisages "peacekeeping." When peacekeeping means enforcing peace without consent, it can more properly be called "enforcing the international order" or "international policing," or, more misleadingly, "keeping the international peace." This may be a commendable and necessary endeavor, but it would have to be studied in its own right in order to establish whether it is feasible or reasonable. In the present context, I believe it does not constitute the process of mutual mediation that is properly called "peacemaking."

Even if a more muscular international police force is desirable, it is doubtful whether it can be effectively instituted by a body like the United Nations. A real police force must have the power to take action, bring a case to court, and impose and enforce sanctions. Even if one assumes that one could put in place the system this requires and sort out the tremendous complexities it involves, United Nations action is necessarily constrained by its commitment to national sovereignty–a commitment that Boutros-Ghali stresses.[16] In practice, it means that a United Nations international police force would have to operate without the power to arrest or impose sanctions. The result is likely to be a paper tiger that does not have the teeth necessary to militarily enforce international order.

Questions about international policing take us beyond the problems of peacekeeping (and busybodying) that are the subject of this paper. In this context, there is no general solution to the inherent difficulties that accompany peacekeeping as we understand it, and it is misleading to write as though the only things needed to turn it into a generic means of conflict resolution are more resources and an expanded United Nations. Because we think so highly of peacekeepers, it is easy to be seduced into thinking that peacekeeping is a panacea for international conflict. We will do better to adopt a more realistic, and more negative, attitude toward peacekeeping–one that recognizes it as a very limited mechanism that is in many, and perhaps most, cases not a workable alternative.

3. Postscript

I want to end by trying to capture the spirit of limited peacekeeping that I have proposed. Peacekeeping can be done by returning to ancient philosophy, but this time to the Chinese tradition, to the *Tao Te Ching*.[17] The crux of Taoism is an acceptance of the "way" which rejects interference with the underlying forces of the world. The ideal master therefore seeks to accommodate or harness what is, in some deep sense, natural, instead of opposing, restricting, or governing it. One might put this point by saying that Lao Tsu radically rejects busybodying. The busybody is virtually the opposite of the master.

Consider the following passages from the *Tao Te Ching*:

> When the Master governs, the people are hardly
> aware that he exists.
> Next best is a leader who is loved.
> Next, one who is feared.

The worst is one who is despised.[18]

True mastery can only be gained by letting
   things go their own way.
It can't be gained by interfering.[19]

If you want to be a great leader,
   you must learn to follow the Tao.
Stop trying to control.
Let go of fixed plans and concepts,
   and the world will govern itself.[20]

Governing a large country is like frying a small fish.
You spoil it with too much poking.[21]

The *Tao Te Ching* does not reject all interference in the world's affairs. In Passage 31, it even advocates the use of military force. It is only that interference should be minimal. We must bear in mind its costs, and exercise it in a way that harnesses natural forces.

How does this relate to peacekeeping and peacemaking? It does not mean that they are always mistaken, but it does suggest a negative attitude to peacekeeping, which is always a form of interference. Such interference may have a role to play in circumstances in which peacemaking can harness the existing social, political, and economic forces to make peace possible, but we should not be naive about these possibilities, especially in a world in which different nations, ethnic groups, and so on have vastly different points of view. Considered from this perspective, peacekeeping by itself is a remarkably superficial way to deal with conflict, and interferes with it without addressing its root causes. For reasons I have already enumerated, I think that this raises serious questions about contemporary assumptions in favor of so many peacekeeping operations.

Notes

1. Boutros Boutros-Ghali, *An Agenda for Peace* (New York: United Nations, 1992). (On the world wide web at <http://www.un.org/Docs/SG/agpeace.html>).

2. Shashi Tharoor, "Peacekeeping: Principles, Problems, Prospects," *Naval War College Review* (Spring 1994), p. 9.

3. See United Nations, Peace and Secuirty, U. N. Peacekeeping Operations, on the world wide web at <http://www.un.org/Depts/dpko/>.

4. Matthew 5:9.

5. Theophrastus, *Characters*, ed. and trans. J. N. Edwards (New York: G. P. Putnam, 1929).

6. Lloyd Daly, *Aesop Without Morals: The Famous Fables and a Life of Aesop* (New York: Thomas Yoseloff, 1963).

7. Boutros-Ghali, *An Agenda for Peace*, p. 20.

8. *Ibid.*

9. Tharoor, "Peacekeeping," p. 20.

10. United Nations, Press Release, (<http://www.un.org>, 18 March 1999).

11. E. L. M. Burns, *Between Arab and Israeli* (Toronto: Clarke, Irwin, 1962), p. 192.

12. *Ibid.*, pp. 277-278.

13. "Social Democrats, U.S.A., Interview by Larry Specht with Branislav Canak, "Democratic Forces in the Balkans" (Washington, October 1995). See the world wide web at <http://www.socialdemocrats.org/canakint.html>.

14. Tharoor, "Peacekeeping," p. 16.

15. *Ibid.*

16. Boutros-Ghali, *An Agenda for Peace*, p. 17.

17. Lao Tsu. *Tao Te Ching*, trans. Stephen Mitchell (New York: Harper Perennial, 1988).

18. *Ibid.*, 17.

19. *Ibid.*, 48.

20. *Ibid.*, 57.

21. *Ibid.*, 60.

Nine

PEACEKEEPING, PEACEMAKING, AND MILITARY FORCE

Robert Litke

1. Antidomination

An antidomination perspective has become fashionable. The suggestion is often made that much of the violence in the world today would disappear if we would ban domination from our lives. My view is that condemning domination is no more reasonable than eliminating the use of electrical power to prevent children from electrocuting themselves.

One may doubt that intelligent authors have said such things. They have. Consider the following by the Norwegian philosopher of peace, Birgit Brock-Utne:

> Radical feminist thinkers have tried to deal with the concept of power by pointing out that there really are two separate kinds of power: the normal male-defined power concept–power as dominance–and a female-defined power-concept–power as competence; the first is a power over, the second a power to....Feminist thinkers see power-as-dominance as inextricably linked to violence....Patriarchy is a form of social organization founded on the force-based ranking of the male half of humanity over the female half. Patriarchy has to do with power over other people, mostly power to control women and nature.[1]

Brock-Utne argues that a shift away from domination is a critical element in peace education. In her book, she reviews a body of research which suggests that males are socialized into their affinity for domination through highly competitive sports and games. Her hope is that if we change the games we can transform the culture.

An even broader prospectus has been recommended by the cultural historian, Riane Eisler:

> If we stop and think about it, there are only two basic ways of structuring the relations between the female and the male halves of humanity. All societies are patterned on either a dominator model–in which human hierarchies are ultimately backed up by force or the threat of force–or a partnership model, with variations in between. For example, from a conventional perspective, Hitler's Germany, Khomeini's Iran,

the Japan of the Samurai, and the Aztec of Meso-America are radically different societies of different races, ethnic origins, technological development, and geographic location. But from the new perspective of cultural transformation theory, which identifies the social configuration characteristic of rigidly male-dominated societies, we see striking commonalities. All these otherwise widely divergent societies are not only rigidly male dominant but also have a generally high degree of social violence, particularly, warfare. Conversely, we can also see arresting similarities between otherwise extremely diverse societies that are more sexually equalitarian. Characteristically, such "partnership model" societies tend to be not only much more peaceful but also much less hierarchic and authoritarian....The larger picture that emerges indicates that all modern, post-Enlightenment movements for social justice, be they religious or secular, as well as the more recent feminist, peace, and ecology movements, are part of an underlying thrust for the transformation of a dominator to a partnership system. Beyond this in our time of unprecedentedly powerful technologies, these movements may be seen as part of our species' evolutionary thrust for survival.[2]

Eisler argues that our very survival may depend upon our willingness to progress or evolve from a dominator to a partnership perspective. As indicated in the quotation, her view is that the feminist, peace, and ecology movements share in the conviction that we must move away from destructive forms of control. I think she is correct; mainstream thinkers in a variety of fields agree that such kinds of control or domination are wrong and should be eliminated from the culture.

Ecofeminists Karen J. Warren and Jim Cheney put the abolitionist perspective very succinctly: "Ecofeminists acknowledge up front their basic feminist value commitments: the twin dominations of women and nature exist, are wrong, and ought to be eliminated."[3] Similar formulations of the view that dominating power is inherently wrong, are so widespread in the intellectual climate of these times that it is generally accepted as both intelligible and correct. In this paper I shall swim against the stream.

I often prefer partnership relations to relations of dominance with people and nature. I certainly enjoy power as competence as much as power as dominance in myself and others, to return to Brock-Utne's way of putting the matter. But a number of contexts we can achieve reasonable goals only through the use of force or some other form of dominating power. I understand wishing it were otherwise. But it is foolish and dangerous to pretend that it really is otherwise. In this chapter, I show that if we want peace at home and abroad we must be prepared to use dominating force. The interesting work is to determine how to structure and control this use of power so that it serves rather than victimizes us.

2. Police Forms of Dominance in the Service of Civil Peace

Peace officers are civil officers appointed to preserve the public peace. This category can include by-law officers, parking meter attendants, park wardens, court security guards, customs officials, private security officers, sheriffs, and of course members of police forces. Although useful information about the need for domination in various contexts may lie with all members of this class, I shall restrict my attention to police officers.

We understand that police have three primary functions: (1) maintaining peace and order, (2) preventing crime, and (3) law enforcement.[4] In a "Background Document" the Solicitor General of Canada suggests the following as a mission statement for police forces in Canada:

> As part of the criminal justice system and in accordance with the Canadian Charter of Rights and Freedoms, the police are responsible for maintaining peace, order, and public security, for preventing crime and other offenses, for apprehending offenders and bringing them to justice, and for addressing the fears and concerns of the public with respect to crime and disorder.[5]

While all citizens are expected to contribute to the maintenance of public peace, crime prevention, and law enforcement, police officers are the most rigorously trained and the most heavily armed to serve these functions. It is natural for us to think of the police, like the military, as constituting an organized force with strict chains of command, explicit rules of engagement, and with the authorized capability for wielding various kinds of dominating power on our behalf, including deadly force. It is the conceptual organization of these forms of dominance that I wish to focus on.

First, the overall aim of a police force is the maintenance of peace and security, as noted above. Second, police officers are expected to use the least violent/most peaceful means possible in the course of their duties. The following is a sketch of explicit guidelines for use of force issued to the police officers serving in my community, specified in order of increasing force or domination:

(1) Officer presence;
(2) Tactical communications (use of one's voice);
(3) Soft impact weapons (empty hand techniques);
(4) Hard impact weapons (aerosol spray, night stick);
(5) Police challenge ("Police! Don't move");
(6) Firearms (drawing a firearm or discharging it).

It is understood that every use of force by a police officer is subject to federal (the Criminal Code) and provincial (the Police Act) provisions as well as local by-laws. All officers are expected to have detailed knowledge of how these constrain their conduct while on duty. Every time a use of force results in injury police officers are required to notify their superiors and to file a formal occurrence report of all relevant circumstances. The same is true whenever a firearm is drawn or discharged, other than at an authorized firing range. This is designed to ensure that the use of force does not become cavalier or routine. Finally, citizen review boards and explicit complaints procedures make the use of force subject to appropriate review.

Such are the ways in which dominating power is structured and controlled at the level of the individual officer in my community. Sometimes officers must amplify their capability for dominance by calling for additional help. We are familiar with the need for increased police presence which can arise at political rallies, sports celebrations, and the like. Such presence requires sufficient numbers. We are also familiar with intensification at the other end of the spectrum, namely, the use of riot squads, emergency response officers, SWAT teams, and so on for responding to riots, barricade situations, and hostage takings. And beyond that, the civil authority usually has the option of calling for a military response to those situations which exceed the capability of the police force. The fundamental responsibility of the police is to dominate or be in control of those situations which could threaten civil peace and security. Their mandate is to use the minimum level of dominance required to do so, but that dominance does include deadly force.

In ordinary civil society we do not simply dream of a world without domination, although that would surely be our preference. Rather we anticipate the possibility of wanting the enhanced control that police intervention may provide. To that end we conceptualize and authorize the regulated use of force. We require that the amount of force be modulated to the demands of the situation. We structure it as a schedule of increasing levels of dominance. At every level we constrain the use of force with complex sets of rules and procedures. This we do for the sake of civil peace in communities around the world. I would say that a substantial burden of proof falls to those who glibly advocate the end of domination. With what would they replace a police force and how would they ensure that such organized structures of dominance would no longer be needed?

3. Military Forms of Dominance in the Service of Global Peace

For all its shortcomings, the United Nations represents humanity's best attempt to date to realize for the world the benefits of governance or the rule of law that we routinely enjoy in civil society. To this end we have begun to conceptualize and authorize the regulated use of military force. I will briefly describe its conceptual organization, as it is outlined in an official document *An Agenda For Peace*, by Boutros Boutros-Ghali, his report to the members of the United Nations in June 1992, as requested by the Security Council. He noted that with the end of the cold war the number of requests for United Nations intervention increased dramatically.[6] I would add that escalating conflict and violence in Europe, the Middle East, and Africa since then suggest that we must creatively structure and control the kinds of intervening force we would like the United Nations to employ on humanity's behalf. The following is what was in place in 1992.

Boutros-Ghali's agenda for peace revolves around definitions he gives of four terms: preventive diplomacy, peacemaking, peacekeeping, and post-conflict peacebuilding. Here is how they are related to each other:

> Preventive diplomacy seeks to resolve disputes before violence breaks out; peacemaking and peacekeeping are required to halt conflicts and preserve peace once it is attained. If successful, they strengthen the opportunity for post-conflict peace-building, which can prevent the re-occurrence of violence among nations and peoples.[7]

My focus will be on proposed military contributions to peacemaking and peacekeeping. Peacekeeping is defined as "the deployment of the United Nations presence in the field."[8] This presence may consist of civilians, police personnel or military forces. Notice that this list is ordered by increasing levels of dominance. The members of a peacekeeping operation do not have the mission of coercively preventing the outbreak of hostilities nor are they sufficiently armed for such a task. The hope is that their *presence* will be an adequate buffer between hostile parties or a sufficient dissuasion to those who might otherwise come to blows and ruin the peace. Their mission is to implement peace settlements but not to create or enforce them. The function of military peacekeepers is to patrol troubled areas, to establish demilitarized zones, to clear landmines from former combat zones, and to monitor disarmament arrangements. Like "officer presence" in the context of police work in a civil setting, peacekeeping is the least coercive, least dominating form of United Nations military activity. Great skill and constant vigilance is required of military personnel to restrict themselves to the least violent, most peaceful means possible in the conduct of their peacekeeping duties. The more assertive tasks of creating and enforcing peace settlements fall under the category of peacemaking.

Peacemaking is defined as "action to bring hostile parties to agreement."[9] Naturally, as in civil society, the background assumption is that this is to be done by such peaceful means as mediation and negotiation, the world court, relevant assistance programs, and the imposition of economic sanctions. If peaceful means fail to restore international peace and security, the

United Nations Charter provides for the security council to use military force. Boutros-Ghali states that the credibility of the United Nations as a peace-maker requires that it have this military option available.[10] Why would the world at large be more law-abiding than civil society? To date, the security council has never exercised this option. Boutros-Ghali is proposing that this more assertive military option now be given serious consideration.

He describes the use of military force for two peacemaking functions. Peace-enforcement units would be used to ensure compliance with cease-fire agreements, which are all too often ignored. He notes that the training and weaponry required by such a force would exceed that for peacekeeping forces, and that member states would have to make them explicitly available for such use. [11]

Enforcing compliance requires more than merely establishing a presence in both police and military contexts. The second function is to respond to "outright aggression, imminent or actual."[12] I take this to mean to threaten, and if necessary, to attack the aggressor with disabling or lethal force. Evidently this function would require additional training and more weaponry than that needed for peace enforcement. Again, explicit undertakings by member states would be required.

As for the case of police work in a civil setting, the use of force is conceptualized by the United Nations as a schedule of increasing levels of dominance or coercion:

(1) United Nations civilian presence;
(2) United Nations police presence;
(3) United Nations military peacekeeping forces;
(4) United Nations military peace-enforcement units;
(5) United Nations military responses to aggression.

As noted above, only the least coercive (1-3) of these options have been employed by the security council. But in anticipation of the need for enhanced levels of military control the Charter provides for the fourth or fifth levels of domination. Like the case for civil police domination, the overriding assumption is that the use of force or dominance will be our last resort and that we will utilize the least robust forms first, if possible. Lethal force is the last of the last resorts. We would do well to continue giving serious consideration to the conditions under which such force will be used and the kinds of constraint by which it should be regulated. Dreaming and scheming of avoiding all forms of dominance is not enough.

4. Prodomination

In the beginning, I noted the current fashion of expressing wholesale rejections of dominating power. I have outlined two examples of domination at its best: police and military forms of dominance. Given what humans are like at their worst, I cannot realistically imagine life without such forms of domination or their functional equivalent. Consider domestic violence, that is, violence among those who are closest to each other. If my neighbors are mercilessly beating their child or each other and I do not feel capable of stopping them on my own, I want to be able to dial 911. I fervently wish we could do the same in response to the butchery and other outrages taking place in these times in Europe and Africa or wherever newspaper headlines next take us. In view of such examples, I do not find responsible or even intelligible the prevailing view that domination is inherently wrong. Those advocating it condemn the only means we have for dealing with urgent human problems. I doubt that victims of domestic abuse or ethnic slaughter would deem them credible.[13]

Notes

1. Birgit Brock-Utne, *Feminist Perspectives on Peace and Peace Education* (New York: Pergamon, 1989), pp. 25-29.
2. Riane Eisler, *The Chalice and the Blade* (New York: Harper Collins, 1988), pp. xix-xx.
3. Karen J. Warren and Jim Cheney, "Ecological Feminism and Ecosystem Ecology," *Hypatia* 6:1 (Spring 1991), p. 186.
4. See "police" in *The Random House Dictionary of the English Language* (New York: Random House, 1969).
5. A. Normandeau and B. Leighton, *A Vision of the Future of Policing in Canada* (Ottawa: Police and Security Branch, Solicitor General Canada, 1990), p. 52.
6. Boutros Boutros-Ghali, *An Agenda for Peace* (New York: United Nations, 1992), p.7.
7. *Ibid.*, p.12.
8. *Ibid.*, p. 11.
9. *Ibid.*
10. *Ibid.*, p. 25.
11. *Ibid.*, p. 26.
12. *Ibid.*
13. I would like to thank John Dolby, Waterloo Regional Police Service, for his valuable help.

Ten

KANT'S NONINTERVENTIONALISM AND RECENT ALTERNATIVES OF NONMILITARY INTERVENTION

William C. Gay

1. War Culture and Military Intervention

A standing military organization is seen by many as necessary for an effective deterrent against attack against one's nation and for an effective instrument for the correction of injustices around the world. The use of military force for purposes of humanitarian intervention has received increased attention, especially since the demise of the Soviet Union has eliminated one of the major checks on intervention. However, because intervention may occur without the risk of escalation into a superpower conflict does not mean that it is effective or appropriate.

Many questions need to be raised in relation to humanitarian intervention. Here are a few such questions: Should the global community simply rely on diplomacy and economic sanctions as a response to political repression in Haiti and to ethnic slaughter in Bosnia and Rwanda? Would humanitarian intervention to relieve such injustice and suffering be effective and appropriate? Was humanitarian intervention in Somalia an effective and appropriate response to widespread starvation?

The effectiveness of military intervention is somewhat mixed. For example, while the Gulf War did liberate Kuwait, it did so at the price of rather high civilian casualties. In addition, neither Kuwait nor Iraq has subsequently made major advances in social justice. To decide whether intervention is appropriate or justified raises several philosophical questions. In relation to the situations I have cited, philosophers have already addressed some of the key questions. In relation to the Gulf War, the most frequently raised philosophical question has been whether the criteria of just war theory were satisfied. This is especially important because George Bush, while President of the United States, explicitly appealed to this tradition when he sought congressional and international support for this military operation. Both Douglas P. Lackey and James P. Sterba particularly argue that just war criteria were not satisfied.[1] In relation to Bosnia and Somalia, the questions were different but also concerned the issue of what intentions actually governed intervention or nonintervention. Robert L. Holmes and Joseph C. Kunkel have asked what roles nationalism and capitalism played, while Duane Cady has raised questions about the degree to which the United States takes responsibility for its actions abroad and Robert Paul Churchill has asked what it is about us that keeps us from stopping torture and genocide.[2]

I share with these philosophers a disinclination to use military force, but I want to affirm a nonmilitary approach to intervention based on moral principles. To make this argument, I present what I take to be the imprudence of the noninterventionalism in Immanuel Kant's philosophy and, in a more limited way, the insufficiency of the interventionalism of some world federalists. I argue that under some conditions the protection of human rights and achievement of social justice should be placed above the sovereignty of the state. Nevertheless, while I argue for intervention, I call for nonmilitary forms of intervention in cases where the failure to intervene is tantamount to a tacit sanctioning of unacceptable levels of injustice.

For several centuries, almost all of the nations of the world have relied on war–and rarely as a last resort. For the modern nation state, peace is merely a longer or shorter lull between wars. I use the term "war culture" to characterize this orientation in which peace initiatives involve managing and refining military arsenals, not questioning and eliminating them. In contra-distinction, I use the term "peace culture" to characterize the position that regards peace as the negation of war.[3] By defining peace culture as the negation of war, I am disassociating it not only from negative peace, which is a mere lull between wars, but also from the privation of war, understood as the total absence of war. By peace culture, I mean a positive peace which includes justice. Even on this expanded basis, a long-standing criticism of such a peace culture is its supposed inability to undertake humanitarian inter-vention. Peace and justice may be achieved domestically in a peace culture, while internationally, injustices continue to abound. A peace culture which rejects war may appear to have nothing beyond traditional diplomacy as a means of response.

Even advocates of a world without war have often accepted noninter-ventionalism as one of the costs of global peace. While advocates of a world without war hope that in the long run all nations will eventually achieve adequate humanitarian protection for their citizens, they reject in the short run any forceful intervention into the internal affairs of a sovereign nation. In this chapter, I review Kant's contribution to this understanding of the require-ments for a global peace culture and, as alternatives, I examine the forms of interventionism supported by world federalism and civilian defense. In exam-ining these alternatives, I propose that it may be possible to pass between the horns of the dilemma which Kant bequeathed to the philosophy of nonvio-lence, namely, either reluctantly accept complicity with injustice in another country or reluctantly accept a military intervention which violates principles of just war such as ones concerning proportionality.

2. Kant's Critique of War

Kant developed one of the early and still influential critiques of war. In this section I trace how Kant's critique of war presents the needed distinction between negative and positive peace. However, I show where his approach still falls short of what we need in order to respond to injustice within other nations. Kant develops his critique of war from within the tradition of modern political philosophy. Drawing on social contract theory, Kant notes in his philosophy of history that just as the "unsociable sociability" of people led to civil society, even so the "unsocial sociability" of nations may lead to international federation.[4] For people living since the formation of civil societies and before the formation of international federation, Kant sees war as a central problem, if not the primary one. His most extensive discussion of war is found in *Perpetual Peace,* where he presents war as a lapse into the state of nature.[5] Nevertheless, because war is an instrument and not an end, Kant upholds what are today termed "war conventions" (*jus in bello*) and repudiates what he terms "dishonorable stratagems." He gives several examples of dishonorable stratagems: use of assassins or poisons, breach of surrender, and instigation of treason in the opposing nation. Unless such stratagems are rejected, Kant contends, "no peace can ever be concluded and the hostilities would become a war of extermination (*bellum internecinum*)."[6]

Long before the popularization of terms such as "genocidal," "biocidal," and "omnicidal" war and even before Carl von Clausewitz's citation of "absolute war," Kant foresaw and forbade wars of such magnitude. War at such a level, Kant claims, "would permit perpetual peace to occur only in the vast graveyard of humanity as a whole. Thus, such a war, including all means used to wage it, must be absolutely prohibited."[7]

On the question of peace, Kant carefully distinguishes two methods, namely, a regressive and a progressive method. A regressive method takes a science, a model, or a practice at face value. The regressive method does not question whether what it is examining is adequate. Instead, the regressive method investigates how a science, a model, or a practice arose. However, if one applies the regressive method to a pseudo-science or a pseudo-peace, one will obtain a faulty definition of science or peace; that is, the "conditions of possibility" will have been abstracted from an inadequately "conditioned actuality" and the accidental can be confused for the essential. (In Kant's own work, his hasty acceptance of Newtonian science and Euclidean geometry illustrates the prospect that the regressive method can lead to faulty definition via interpreting the accidental as the essential.)

A progressive method tries to establish on what principles a science, a model, or a practice should be based. A progressive method does not take for granted the current conditions. Instead, the progressive method proposes when a science, a model, or a practice will be adequate. Thus, the progressive method is appropriate when one argues about a pre-paradigmatic discipline or a not yet realized peace. Kant is concerned with "the conditions under which public peace is possible."[8] He regards genuine peace as a *Noch Nicht* ("Still Not"), which is not to be confused with merely "the suspension of hostilities."[9] The latter is pseudo-peace and is associated with a "treaty of peace" (*pactum pacis*), which merely ends a particular war and not the state of war (war culture).[10] Genuine peace, for Kant, is not only not actual, it is also not natural. For this reason, he claims that peace must be founded and that whenever the consent of citizens is not necessary for waging war, genuine peace is not possible. Kant presumed that, for this end, republican states are preferred.[11]

Peace culture (the still unachieved negation of war) is termed by Kant a "league of peace" (*foedus pacificum*).[12] In considering the transition from war culture to peace culture, Kant returns to the point he made in his philosophy of history and asserts that the transition by individuals into civil society and by nations into international federation is governed by law and requires giving up lawless freedom.[13] Kant stresses the importance of the possibility of peace culture, even if it is unlikely; otherwise, if we knew we absolutely could not achieve it, any duty to try to advance peace culture would be eliminated. Morality, which is the theoretical science of ethics, does not conflict with politics, which is the practical science of right; instead, because it can be, politics should be guided practically by moral theory.[14]

Kant concludes his essay as follows:

> If it is a duty to make the state of public right actual, though only through an unending process of approximation to it, and if at the same time there is a well founded hope that we can do it, then *perpetual peace*, which will follow the hitherto falsely so-called treaties of peace (but which are really only suspension of war), is no empty idea, but a task that, gradually completed, steadily approaches its goal (since the times during which equal progress occurs will, we hope, become ever shorter).[15]

Understood in Kant's framework, *Realpolitik* as practiced by most nations today would be a pseudo-political science, if not an outright immoral political practice.[16] *Realpolitik* is a pseudo-political science because it takes for granted that international politics is an amoral state of nature. By making power the determining factor, *Realpolitik* will use any means that is effective for achieving its goal. Consequently, the prospects for immoral political practices are great. Elsewhere, Kant speaks even more bluntly. Beyond the ever increasing devastation of war and ever prolonged recovery from war, the escalating costs of preparing for war will eventually compel people to find means to stop war culture; until then, Kant contends we cannot expect any moral progress.[17]

3. Kant's Critique of Intervention

The first section of *Perpetual Peace* provides six theses, which Kant terms "articles" or "principles." Kant's second article rejects the acquisition of one nation by another nation because such action would turn a nation into a thing.[18] This ground relies on his moral principle that we should always treat persons as ends and never as means. In other words, Kant wants each nation to regard every other nation as an end in itself and never as a mere means to satisfy its own narrow national interest. While it is obvious that this moral principle leads to a rejection of acquisition of another nation, it also entails a critique of mercenaries since such a system treats soldiers as things as well. In his fifth principle, Kant explicitly states, "No nation shall forcibly interfere with the constitution and government of another."[19] Kant argues that "a foreign power's interference would violate the rights of an independent people struggling with its internal ills."[20] Kant was thinking about forceful interference, but nonviolent intervention would also be a form of interference that violates a nation's self-understanding of its independence. Just as a military intervention introduces troops or weapons into a foreign nation, even so a nonviolent intervention introduces individuals prepared to engage in disruptive activities.

According to W. B. Gallie, Kant did not expect that internal problems of politics would be solved domestically before the external relations among nations were solved internationally.[21] In characterizing Kant's position as both statist and noninterventionalist, Gallie states:

> Complete non-interference in the internal affairs of every signatory state seemed to him an essential precondition of faithful adherence, by any sovereign state, to the treaty which he proposed. Kant, the first systematic internationalist, was thus also one of the most steadfast of "statists" in the history of political thought.[22]

Gallie does not question the adequacy of Kant's internationalist perspective *per se*; instead, he questions the adequacy of Kant's peculiar version of statism.

Gallie is quick to point out that, in this regard, Kant is simply an heir to the Western tradition. Gallie contends:

> All political philosophy since Plato, has been directed to articulating the criteria of good–or at least of tolerable–political life *within* a given state or city....The good state, therefore, has meant the state that is good

vis-à-vis its subjects or citizens, for all that, in fact, every state that ever existed has had to face not only its own citizens but other neighboring and probably rival states, and indirectly the citizens of those states as well. The result is that no political philosopher has ever dreamed of looking for the criteria of a good state *vis-à-vis* other states....[23]

Despite this tradition, Gallie stresses that Kant at least recognized that questions about relations among nations need to be faced. In particular, he says that Kant concerned himself more than any other philosopher with the question of how morally nations should interact. However, because of Kant's noninterventionalist position on the response of one nation to a perceived injustice in another nation, Gallie contends that Kant's position is "disappointingly negative and palpably incomplete."[24]

4. Interventionism of World Federalism and Civilian Defense

Within the traditions of world federalism and civilian defense, some more positive and more complete responses can be found to Kant's concern about how a nation should properly conduct external relations. Both of these traditions find ways to support limited interventions that do not qualify as war. However, they differ in focus, method, and scope. The world federalist response focuses on individuals and may use the weapons and force of a police action, but these actions are fairly limited in their scale. Civilian defense, on the other hand, focuses more on the nation itself and eschews the use even of the weapons and force of a police action. Nonetheless it does so in a manner that can require large-scale nonviolent intervention.

In his discussion of world federalism, Ronald J. Glossop makes clear that in relation to any intervention into a sovereign nation, an action is to be directed toward individuals, not national governments.[25] By focusing on individuals, the sovereignty of the nation is not being questioned. The claim is that an individual, not a government, acted irresponsibly. The aim is not to disestablish a government but to punish a criminal. While the apprehension of Panama's General Manuel Noriega by the United States presents a recent example of an action in response to purported crimes of an individual, questions can be raised regarding its legitimacy, since it was conducted by the United States rather than by the United Nations, and regarding its scale, since the level of collateral damage was not marginal.

However, even when criteria of legitimate authority and proportionality are met, a further problem with the world federalist approach is that each nation state would be free to have whatever kind of political system and whatever kind of economic system it wants within its borders.[26] For this reason, unless such systems were in clear violation of international law, systematic internal injustice could be protested verbally but would ultimately have to be tolerated if diplomatic protests and sanctions failed. Until recent internal changes, the system of apartheid in South Africa offers a conspicuous example of a political and economic system that perpetuated social injustice but against which, on the world federalist model, systemic intervention by external parties would be unjustified. While the "long run" in this case lasted "only" decades, in other cases the "wait" has been much longer. As the severity of the injustices and the length of their perpetuation increase, the viability of waiting decreases. So even if there are cases when action can be taken against individuals who violate international law, there are times when direct action against institutionalized practices of a national government are needed.

Civilian defense offers a nonviolent model of national security and provides another alternative in relation to intervention.[27] Civilian defense, which is sometimes referred to as civilian-based defense and civilian resistance, includes a prior pledge and subsequent performance by citizens of organized nonviolent resistance toward an aggressor nation.[28] Since a potential invader knows in advance that it will be difficult, if not impossible, to control the sociopolitical life of that nation, a system of civilian defense functions like a system of military defense, except that it is nonviolent. While some advocates of civilian defense claim that it has the moral advantage that it can be used only defensively, such a characterization is no more accurate than that which states that a nation's military forces are only for defense. The greatest advantage of civilian defense is that, like any credible system of defense, it does not forsake the moral obligation to defend the innocent. Moreover, civilian defense has a further advantage over both the use of military force and the world federalist attempt to apprehend individual criminals. In contradistinction to the use of military force, civilian defense can avoid large-scale destruction of human life and the environment. It may also be more effective than the world federalist focus on individual criminals when the perpetuation of social injustices within a nation is both institutional and widespread, as in the case of apartheid in South Africa.

Actually, the use of civilian defense for intervention–hopefully used for humanitarian intervention–functions more like military intervention than does the world federalist's limited police actions against individuals. Military intervention can range from small-scale strikes (which may or may not introduce any troops into the nation being struck) to full-scale invasion and occupation. The offensive use of civilian defense can range from various forms of intervention against a nation (such as what occurs under protest within a nation by representatives of another nation) to the introduction of sufficiently large numbers of civilian defenders to disrupt the ability of the government to control the nation.[29] Yet another way in which the offensive use of civilian defense is closer to traditional military defense is that the actions of each violate the sovereignty of another nation. Technically, the difference is that a military offense seeks to depose the government by bringing to bear on it violent force introduced from the outside, while civilian defense seeks to delegitimate the government by cultivating nonviolent noncooperation from the inside. By contrast, world federalist police action against an individual neither deposes nor delegitimates a government. Instead, it seeks the prosecution of individual offenders against international law. In this sense, the world federalist approach is less radical in its actions than military or civilian interventions.

Kant and many advocates of peace through international law or peace through a federation of nations would reject either of these types of offensive action because they involve an unsolicited intervention into the internal affairs of another nation. Nevertheless, nations from whom an individual is extricated for criminal prosecution may likewise regard the apprehension of such individuals as a violation of national sovereignty.

From a moral point of view, intervention—whether military or non-military—may be justified if certain principles of human rights and social justice are held higher than the autonomy of the state. In the case of military action, just war theory often provides the moral grounds for intervention or for demonstrating the lack of sufficient moral grounds for intervention. In the case of a world federalist police action or the use of civilian defense for inter-vention, the moral requirements are easier to meet, even if their current feasibility for success is rather remote. From a practical point of view, how-ever, it is important that alternatives to militarism, such as those found in world federalism and civilian defense, can be used for morally justifiable interventions. Until such nonmilitary forms of intervention were developed, advocates of military defense had a basis for arguing that military responses to injustice were unavoidable for the moralist in a world in which governments continue to do great harm to their own people.

One of the lessons of the twentieth century might be that the super-powers were correct in refusing to remain silent about what they took to be in-justices in other nations. To remain silent and refuse to intervene is tacitly to sanction injustice. Such noninterference is a shortcoming in any philosophy of nonviolence. However, the use of large-scale violent intervention—war—also is one of the major shortcomings of the use of military force for the pursuit of global justice as much as for national security. War itself, even if waged to eradicate an injustice, involves injustice since the innocent are virtually never entirely spared and because war and destruction go hand in hand.[30]

My argument rejects the view, which is implicit in Kant's analysis, that we are caught between the horns of a dilemma. Kant was right that military intervention may itself cause injustice and violate principles of proportion-ality, but he too quickly glossed over the prospect that the silence and inaction of noninterventionism can involve complicity in crimes against humanity. In the face of injustice, silence is violence, but not all interventions against injustice are violent or, at least, not all such interventions qualify as war or as the use of military force.

The global community needs an approach to national security and global justice that lies between silence and violence. When we recognize that diplomacy properly functions within this continuum, we may begin to see that more appropriate and potentially more effective complements to diplomacy are found in world federalist intervention against individual perpetrators of injustice and the use of civilian defense for nonviolent intervention against injustice. Diplomacy is by design both vocal and nonviolent. Many times it serves as an instrument by means of which one nation may seek to correct the injustice in another nation, though its purposes are much broader than its capacity to foster greater international justice. World federalist apprehension of international criminals can function as a police action that stops short of war, while civilian defense in all its uses may be viewed as a nonviolent response to injustice. In contradistinction to Clausewitz's characterization of war as "politics by other means," these nonmilitary forms of intervention have the moral advantage of pursuing "politics by the same means."[31]

Notes

1. Douglas P. Lackey, "Bush's Abuse of Just War Thoery," and James P. Sterba, "War with Iraq: Just Another Unjust War," *Concerned Philosophers For Peace Newsletter,* 11:1 (Spring 1991), pp. 3-4 and 4-5.

2. Robert L. Holmes, "Bosnia: Resurgent Nationalism and the Need for Nonviolent Responses," Joseph C. Kunkel, "Somalia: Humanitarian Aid or Business as Usual?," Duane Cady, "Accepting Responsibility for U.S. Action Abroad," and Robert Paul Churchill, "Bosnia and Somalia: Why Is It So Hard to Stop Torture and Genocide?," *Concerned Philosophers For Peace Newsletter,* 13:1 (Spring 1993), pp. 1-2, 3-4, 5-7, 8-9, and 10-17. See also Laurence F. Bove and Laura Duhan Kaplan, *From the Eye of the Storm: Regional Conflicts and the Philosophy of Peace* (Amsterdam: Rodopi, 1995), pp. 293-315.

3. William C. Gay, "Militarism in the Modern State and World Government: The Limits of Peace through Strength in the Nuclear Age," in *From the Eye of the Storm,* ed. Bove and Kaplan, pp. 5-16.

4. Immanuel Kant, "Idee zu einer allgemeinen Geschichte in weltbürgerlicher Absicht," *Gesammelte Schriften, Band 8, Abhandlungen nach 1781* (Berlin: G. Reimer 1902), pp. 20 and 24. See Kant, "Idea for a Universal History with a Cosmopolitan Intent," *Perpetual Peace and Other Essays,* trans. Ted Humphrey (Indianapolis, Ind.: Hackett, 1983), pp. 31-32 and 34.

5. Carl Joachim Friedrich, *Inevitable Peace* (New York: Greenwood, 1948).

6. Immanuel Kant, *Zum ewigen Frieden, Gesammelte Schriften, Band 8, Abhandlungen nach 1781* (Berlin: G. Reimer, 1902), p. 346. See Kant, *Perpetual Peace,* p. 110.

7. Kant, *Zum ewigen Frieden,* p. 346; and Kant, *Perpetual Peace,* p. 110.

8. Kant, *Zum ewigen Frieden,* p. 368; and Kant, *Perpetual Peace,* p. 126.

9. Kant, *Zum ewigen Frieden*, p. 349; and Kant, *Perpetual Peace*, p. 111.

10. Kant, *Zum ewigen Frieden*, p. 355-356; and Kant, *Perpetual Peace*, p. 116-117.

11. Kant, *Zum ewigen Frieden*, p. 349; and Kant, *Perpetual Peace*, p. 112. See John Somerville, "Democracy and the Problem of War," in *Moral Problems in Contemporary Society: Essays in Humanistic Ethics*, ed. Paul Kurtz (Englewood Cliffs, N.J.: Prentice-Hall, 1969), pp. 268-278.

12. Kant, *Zum ewigen Frieden*, p. 356; and Kant, *Perpetual Peace*, p. 117.

13. Kant, *Zum ewigen Frieden*, p. 357; and Kant, *Perpetual Peace*, p. 136.

14. Kant, *Zum ewigen Frieden*, p. 370; and Kant, *Perpetual Peace*, p. 135.

15. Kant, *Zum ewigen Frieden*, p. 386; and Kant, *Perpetual Peace*, p. 139.

16. See Laura Duhan Kaplan, "A Liberal Feminist Critique of Political Realism," Joseph C. Kunkel, "Power Politics, Human Nature, and Morality," I. I. Kravchenko, "Morality or War? Hobbesian Alternatives in Global Politics," and Robert Litke, "Why Domination Defeats Us: A Hobbesian Analysis," in *On the Eve of the 21st Century: Perspectives of Russian and American Philosophers*, ed. William Gay and T. A. Alekseeva (Lanham, Md.: Rowman and Littlefield, 1994), pp. 15-27, 29-48, 49-65, and 67-81.

17. Kant, *Idee*, p. 26; and Kant, *Idea*, p. 36.

18. Kant, *Zum ewigen Frieden*, p. 344; and Kant, *Perpetual Peace*, p. 108.

19. Kant, *Zum ewigen Frieden*, p. 346; and Kant, *Perpetual Peace*, p. 109.

20. *Ibid.*

21. W. B. Gallie, *Philosophers of Peace and War: Kant, Clausewitz, Marx, Engels, and Tolstoy* (Cambridge, U.K.: Cambridge University Press, 1978), p. 13.

22. *Ibid.*, p. 21.

23. *Ibid.*, p. 140.

24. *Ibid.*, pp. 140-141.

25. Ronald J. Glossop, *Confronting War: An Examination of Humanity's Most Pressing Problem* (Jefferson, N.C.: McFarland, 3rd ed., 1994), p. 349; and Glossop, *World Federation?* (Jefferson, N.C.: McFarland, 1994).

26. Glossop, *Confronting War*, p. 352.

27. William C. Gay, "The Prospect for a Nonviolent Model of National Security," in *On the Eve of the 21st Century*, ed. Gay and Alekseeva, pp. 119-134.

28. See Glossop, *Confronting War*, pp. 306-309; Anders Boserup and Andrew Mack, *War without Weapons* (London: Frances Pinter, 1974); Norman Freund, *Nonviolent National Defense: A Philosophical Inquiry into Applied Nonviolence* (Lanham, Md.: University Press of America, 1989); Adam Roberts, ed., *Civilian Resistance as a National Defense* (Baltimore, Md.: Penguin, 1969); Gene Sharp, *The Politics of Nonviolent Action* (Boston: Sargent, 1973); and Gene Sharp with Bruce Jenkins, *Civilian-Based Defense: A Post-Military Weapons System* (Princeton, N.J.: Princeton University Press, 1990).

29. See Beverly Woodward, "Nonviolent Struggle, Nonviolent Defense, and Nonviolent Peacemaking," *Peace and Change*, 7:4 (Fall 1981), pp. 62-63.

30. Glossop, *Confronting War*, esp. pp. 22-25.

31. Carl von Clausewitz, *On War*, ed. and trans. Michael Howard and Peter Paret (Princeton, N.J.: Princeton University Press, 1976).

Eleven

NONMILITARY RESPONSES TO NUCLEAR THREAT OR ATTACK

Richard Wendell Fogg

Should nuclear war ever come, in
whatever form, statesmen will surely be in
urgent need of organizing paradigms. I
applaud your work and wish you well.
General George Lee Butler[1]

The specter of nuclear attack still haunts many countries. Many people believe that the chance of a city being destroyed with nuclear weapons is greater
now than it was during the cold war. Nuclear weapons can be delivered by
ship to most major U. S. cities and to many cities in other countries. More
nuclear proliferation looms. Future enmities may put some regions of the
world in danger of major nuclear attack. So far, enough weapons to mount a
major attack are in the hands of six nations: China, France, Israel, Russia, the
United Kingdom, and the United States. These countries are now friends and
some of them are democracies, which at least virtually never attack other
democracies.[2] However, history is the story of shifting enmities and of democracies becoming dictatorships. George Rathjens of the Massachusetts Institute of Technology believes that, if in the foreseeable future there is another
major war, it might be between China and the major Western powers.[3] It
could be nuclear. Thus, the end of the cold war may not have reduced the
likelihood of small nuclear attacks in the short term or large ones in the long
term. Anyone who believes that nuclear threats are a thing of the cold war
past need only note that in 1990 James Baker, the U.S. Secretary of State,
carried the clearly implied threat to Iraq: if Iraq were to use poison gas in the
Gulf War, the United States would use tactical nuclear weapons in Iraq.[4] (In
his memoirs, Baker says that the threat was a bluff.)

If nuclear attacks occur, as is likely sometime, nuclear counterstrike
would be prone to error (as when used against an accidental attack), would
destroy too much, and would probably escalate the war.[5] Overall, military
defense has failed 68% of the time in the wars since 1815.[6] It has failed
nearly always in immediately repulsing an attack. J. David Singer, a political
scientist who heads the Correlates of War Project at the University of
Michigan, has affirmed this observation of mine, as has Trevor Dupuy, a
military historian at Data Memory Systems in Fairfax, Virginia. Military
attacks succeed right away or the war escalates. Indeed, some authorities can

think of no case of immediate repulsing of an attack. Nuclear counterstrike would generally have to succeed immediately to avoid doing more damage than it is worth. Like conventional counterattack, it might not. (In simulations over the years, an escalation of destruction has generally followed.)[7] An escalating counterstrike would not be likely (1) to avoid provoking preemption, (2) to cause de-escalation, (3) to address the causes of the attack, (4) to minimize the number of casualties, (5) to require only a modest budget, or (6) to retain the counterstriking state's respect with other nations. If nonmilitary defense proves sound, it could satisfy all of these criteria.

The specter of nuclear threat or attack–and counterstrike–means that we must seek ways to provide options besides counterstrike and we must work to abolish nuclear weapons. That is, nuclear defense can certainly be supplemented; also, eventually it actually may be possible to replace these weapons with a safer defense against nuclear attack. Replacement of nuclear weapons is a unique concept but, on the other hand, has been the way weapons traditionally have gone out of use.

I propose the hypothesis that a prepared, rehearsed combination of political, economic, psychological, and all other relevant forms of nonmilitary strength, applied by as many parties as possible, could induce the perpetrators of an immediate nuclear threat–or even an ongoing nuclear attack–to desist or else induce others in their country to depose the perpetrators and then de-escalate.

No matter how unlikely this hypothesis will prove to be, it is worth studying because the dangers of nuclear counterstrike are so great. To increase the chances that the proposal will succeed, some aspects of it will require that changes be made in culture, education, and institutions.

The proposed approach involves a double paradigm shift. First, in place of destroying the opponent's military forces, nonmilitary defense uses the traditional nonviolence paradigm of reducing the aggressor's support from top subordinate leaders, the military, bureaucrats, the public, and allies.[8] This paradigm has been used mainly by underfunded dissidents, often spontaneously. As a nonmilitary defense, it should be well organized. Its potential can be sensed by asking, what if nonviolence were given the five advantages of (1) organization by governments, (2) vast amounts of resources, (3) planning, (4) training, and (5) allies? Military action usually has had all these advantages; nonviolence never has had all of them.[9] The second paradigm shift moves away from the belief that nuclear weapons are logarithmically more powerful than any other weapons and are therefore irreplaceable for defense. The second paradigm shifts to the belief that, in the minds of the aggressor and fellow nationals, a combination of other nonmilitary weapons and positive incentives could be as strong as or stronger than a nuclear counterstrike, and therefore could lead to de-escalation. The approach proposed here is unique.

Thomas Kuhn showed that paradigms shift when a new one answers a central question that the old one could not.[10] Deterrence theory does not satisfactorily answer the question of how to defend if deterrence fails and counterstrike is unwise.[11] Nonmilitary defense theory offers an answer worth full study.

By the mid-1980s, therefore, four decades after the destruction of Hiroshima and Nagasaki, the nuclear strategists had still failed to come up with any convincing methods of employing nuclear weapons should deterrence fail that did not wholly offend common sense....[12]

It is a good time to move away from the deterrence paradigm since dozens of generals and admirals from many nations have called for the abolition of nuclear weapons. Among these high-ranking military leaders are General Alexander Lebed, who may one day be president of Russia, and George Lee Butler, former supreme commander of the U.S. Strategic Air Command.[13]

1. Components of Nonmilitary Defense

In this section, I develop three levels of strength, or power. First I describe and chart strategies and tactics of nonmilitary defense for nuclear crises and give a scenario of how they might be applied in response to a nuclear threat or attack. After describing these specific forms of strength, or power, I describe some at the general level, such as economic strength and political power. Lastly, I describe a level in between, namely methodologies, such as nonviolent action and creative conflict resolution. Following those subsections, I show how these three levels of strength, or power, relate. Then I show how the defense could be organized.

A. Strategies, Strategic Objectives, and Tactics

Chart 1 spells out prepared steps that show chronologically how nonmilitary defense might work to end a nuclear threat or attack. The head of the victim nation and the secretary general of the United Nations could manage the defense. The chart applies to threatened or attacked countries that are armed with nuclear weapons or, with obvious omissions of steps, to countries that are not so armed. Qualitatively, the steps in the chart go from tender to tough, but the reverse also could be done. Quantitatively the chart applies to small or large threats or attacks. The main criteria for choosing which steps to take are a (1) minimum of violence and (2) little authoritarianism. Since women use less of each, they have a strong role to play in this move away from militarism.[14] No matter how extreme an attack, there would be survivors be-

Chart 1. Some Steps in Nonmilitary Defense by Chronology and Severity

Strategies	Strategic Objectives	Tactics
I. Reduce the opponent's fear.	A. To achieve I, avoid cornering the opponent.	1. To achieve A, avoid nuclear retaliation initially.
		2. Fly prominent people to opponent's capital to negotiate issues and to show that you will not fire nuclear weapons there.
II. Remove inappropriate pressures that may have caused the attack.	B. Establish whether the attack was defensive or offensive.	3. Satisfy the opponent's just grievances.
		4. Using mediators, seek win/win solutions to other grievances.
III. Get opponent nationals to de-escalate the attack.	C. Establish communication with every possible person and organization in the opponent's country or group.	5. Use all forms of communication, including computers, television, and ballooned messages.
	D. In the opponent's country, call out higher, antinuclear loyalties in the people than their loyalty to the initiators.	6. Use the facilities in 5 to appeal to loyalties, such as religion, ideology, common decency, legitimacy, law, country, faction, social class, sensible military doctrine, and identity.
	E. If the reason for the initiators' nuclear attack is a fabricated threat, show its falsity.	7. For the present, avoid placing nuclear weapons on alert and publicize this decision.
		8. Reveal evidence of the threat's falsity even if the evidence is classified.

III. Get opponent nationals to de-escalate the attack.(cont.)		
	F. If no reasons for the attack are given, the victim group or country can show that it is not a threat by nonviolently discomforting itself.	9. Publicly destroy a few of your own nuclear weapons.
		10. Ask the president to invite all who believe that their country does not pose a severe threat to the adversary to hold a discomforting, short general strike to convey lack of a threat. Televise the general strike.
	G. Draw upon and establish bonds.	11. For reconciliation, re-establish past bonds, such as people-to-people programs.
		12. Urge people with whom bonds have been made and who have ties with the initiators to work for de-escalation.
		13. Use propaganda domestically and in opponent's area to avoid dehumanizing each other.
	H. Counter the initiators' arresting and killing of their domestic opposition.	14. In opponent's area, encourage security procedures normally used by *coup d'état* plotters.
		15. Encourage opposition by organization leaders who can arrange nonsupport by their entire organization.
		16. Encourage nonsupporters to seek protection from their country's sympathetic military personnel.

Chart 1 (Continued)

Strategies	Strategic Objectives	Tactics
IV. Add pressures.	I. Show how much other countries or groups oppose the attack.	17. Poll countries and groups.
	J. Ostracize the opponent.	18. Remove the opponent's influence on countries and international organizations.
	K. Employ economic pressures.	19. Suspend trade with opponent except for food and medicine.
		20. Exert pressure through international instruments, such as the World Bank and foreign influences on national banks.
		21. Show how the attack could harm the attacker's nationals and their property.
	L. If the initiators demand capitulation enforced by the threat of nuclear attack, counter-threaten with strategies III-V all at once.	22. Broadcast a simulation of strategic objective L to the opponent.
V. If domestic opposition in opponent area has become strong, encourage them to bring about de-escalation.	M. Encourage the opposition to depose, arrest, and replace the initiators.	23. Give domestic opposition resources to depose the initiators through constitutional procedures, nonviolence, or a coup d'état.
		24. Offer attractive terms for peace.

yond the periphery who could struggle. This assertion is approved by Richard Betts, a specialist in nuclear war who is on the staff of the Brookings Institution, although he has not read this chapter.[15] The charted steps are surprisingly adaptable to many types of nuclear threat or attack, including large and small (regional) ones.

If a threat of nuclear attack–or even an actual attack–occurs, the United Nations and the victim country or group would be the best entities to organize the response. I call them the defenders. They should take several steps in making a comprehensive, prepared, rehearsed defense. (Chart 1 sorts these into strategies, strategic objectives, and tactics.) Part of the preparation should be to place an infrastructure in every agreeable country to be used ubiquitously to counter nuclear threats and attacks. This infrastructure should include measures for prevention, preparation, detection, reporting, and treatment. (These are explained in section 2F.) New leaders initiating a nuclear attack would, however, suppress this infrastructure in their own country. To counter that, efforts should be made to help participants in the infrastructure to go underground and hide their resources when a nuclear crisis begins.

If a national leader were to order a nuclear attack, he or she probably would hope for capitulation by the victim after the first volley but would have an overwhelming fear of nuclear retaliation. This fear is likely to encourage such a leader to strike out irrationally, which, in a nuclear conflict, would be extremely dangerous. If the attack were completely irrational, nationals of the attacking country who were not directly involved could be counted on to depose the initiator. Can any nonmilitary steps reduce the initiator fear? Perhaps.

Indeed, the defenders' first strategy should be to reduce this fear so as to discourage immediate, irrational escalation. To achieve a reduction in fear, the defenders should order their forces to avoid nuclear retaliation, at least initially, and should threaten penalties for renegade military figures who disobey. To further assuage the attacker's fear, the victim should appeal to fifty legislators and other prominent people to risk their own lives to save millions of others–by flying to the adversary's capital, without invitation, to negotiate all outstanding issues. This bold action would demonstrate that nuclear weapons would not be fired at the attacker's capital, due to the risk of killing the fifty prominent people. Even if they were held hostage, their presence would demonstrate that their government would not use nuclear weapons on the adversary's capital.[16] The idea is to get the attacker and the defenders talking.

Probably the attack would be caused by strong pressure, so the defenders' second strategy should be to remove any inappropriate, unjust pressures that may have helped cause the attack. Clearly, the defenders would have to determine whether the nuclear attack were a defensive reaction to an inappropriate pressure or were offensive aggression. Perhaps the attacker is an upcoming country that is wrongly denied essential trade in hegemonies of other, more powerful countries, as was Japan before World War II. (In one of history's greatest ironies, Japan secured that trade after unconditionally surrendering! Could the Pacific war, with so much death, have been prevented if the West had given Japan fair trading rights before the conflict erupted?) If inappropriate pressures have caused the attack, the defenders should remove them and seek win/win solutions. It would be hard for the victim to remove a pressure under the threat or actuality of a nuclear attack, but that loss of face would be worth the price of an escalating nuclear war. Could loss of face be avoided? The United Nations already should have established an international mediation service to negotiate grievances about pressures. If the attack were not offensive aggression, the military crisis should be over at this point.

If aggression motivated the attack, many people–even highly placed leaders–in the offending country probably would not want their nation to initiate the use of nuclear weapons. Therefore, in their third strategy, the defenders would try to influence these people to demonstrate, tie up the country, and otherwise persuade the few initiators of the attack to de-escalate. Particular attention should be given to organization leaders who can arrange nonsupport of the attack by their entire organization. This strategy is a reverse of the tradition divide and conquer; the defenders will divide and defend.

To reach these dissenting members of the attacking country, the defenders should establish communication with every possible person and organization in the opponent country concerning the defenders' peaceful intentions. Also, the defenders should appeal to common human feelings, such as avoiding the slaughtering of children. Another appeal of the message is that it may call out higher, antinuclear loyalties than the citizens' loyalty to the initiators. Thus, the defenders will appeal to religion, profession, ideology, common decency, legitimacy, law, country, faction, social class, sensible military doctrine, and identity. Some of these messages should be spontaneous; others should be aesthetically crafted in order to have more impact. Members of these categories around the world can appeal to their counterparts in the aggressing country to work for an end to the crisis. In some countries, to use this communication strategy, it would be necessary to ignore existing laws against communicating with an enemy or to consider the recipients of the message as nonenemies.

The defenders should reach people in the adversary country by telephone, mail, computer, and border crossings. The communicators should also use television, official and ham radio, millions of messages in balloons that shower down to the people, and written messages posted at the border. Billions of dollars should be spent on this communication. The bottom line is to clog the opponent's espionage channels with the de-escalation message. The initiator's colleagues could see the espionage traffic and realize the peaceful intentions of the defenders.

To facilitate these communications, the defenders should keep anti-broadcast-interference technology ahead of broadcast technology. The adversary leaders cannot entirely isolate their people from outside communication, because, to govern, the leaders must communicate abroad and domestically by telephone, computer, radio, and television. To some extent, these can be used by outsiders to reach the adversary, even when resisted.[17]

Since the initiators probably would try to win support by fabricating or exaggerating a brutal threat facing their country, the defenders should reveal evidence of the falsity of the threat, even if the evidence is classified. But what if the defenders do not know the ruse justifying the attack and told only to adversary leaders? Then the defending country should show that there is no significant threat to the aggressor country. But how could the defenders show that they are credible? To do so, the victim country's citizens should undertake the traditional use of nonviolence that discomforts themselves, like Mohandas K. Gandhi's fasting. Their government should direct this discomforting. To achieve it, the defending leaders of the country–or, if it is a non-nuclear state, leaders of the nations protecting it–should publicly destroy a few of their own country's nuclear weapons–not proof of peaceful intent, but not the behavior of a hostile country either. As well, the head of state of the victim nation should appeal to its own citizens who believe that their country does not pose a severe threat to the adversary. He or she would invite these citizens to hold a short, discomforting, symbolic, outdoor general strike to convey this lack of a threat. The general strike would be televised and broadcast to the aggressing nation. All over the victim country, more citizens than had ever appeared outdoors could take part. A precedent for how the citizens could demonstrate is found in high school marching bands that, at football games, form symbols meaningful to the adversary–citizens could form symbols, such as American eagles or Russian bears.

Part of the communication process should both draw upon existing bonds between the communicators and members of the adversary country and establish new bonds. For example, the communicators could re-establish past bonds made through people-to-people programs, such as high school exchanges, past relief to the adversary after disasters, and, with some of the opponent country's citizens, could initiate joint projects that reduce hostilities. In particular, the communicators should reach people in the adversary country with whom they have bonds and who have ties with the initiators of the attack and can influence the initiators to de-escalate. Nations at war customarily use propaganda to create hatred toward their adversary. To retain bonds, the defenders should use as much propaganda domestically and in the adversary nation to bring compassion and to avoid dehumanizing each other.

To counter the initiator's arresting and killing of domestic opposition, the defenders should encourage the opposition to use security procedures normally used by people plotting a *coup d'état*. The defenders can encourage the domestic opposition within the adversary country to ask their country's sympathetic military personnel to offer protection. To support this effort, the defenders should send money, supplies, and perhaps advisors to the domestic opposition by flying under the opponent's radar signals–where radar does not detect planes.

As their fourth strategy, the defenders should add more appropriate pressures than the inappropriate ones that may have helped cause the attack. But what can the defenders use besides the traditional embargo? One pressure would be to reveal the extent to which other countries oppose the attack. To achieve this revelation, the United Nations would need a computerized, instant capability in place to poll all countries. A spontaneous example of this has already occurred in a nuclear crisis. During the Cuban Missile Crisis, developing world countries telegraphed to Acting U.N. Secretary General U Thant that the crisis must stop. He informed Soviet Premier Nikita Khrushchev and U.S. President John F. Kennedy of this response. This proved to Khrushchev that whatever support for challenging the power of the United States he might have expected from the developing world–which he was trying to impress–did not exist. He then de-escalated the crisis right away, though for other reasons also. Some countries with little power actually helped make a superpower back down![18]

The United Nations can organize countries that oppose the attack to ostracize the adversary. The United Nations and these countries can reduce or remove the opponent's influence on them and within international organizations, but retain the adversary's right to listen and to speak to them. The defenders could also show how the attack could harm the persons and property of the opponent's nationals living abroad.

As mentioned, the defenders can employ economic pressures, one of which would be to cease trade. To avoid the opponent's taking desperate acts due to feeling cornered by this embargo, the defenders should continue to trade in goods essential to life. The defenders also can exert pressure on the adversary through international instruments, such as the World Bank, and foreign influences on the adversary's national bank.[19] Switzerland could break its rule of keeping some of its bank accounts anonymous and could freeze the accounts of the leaders of the aggressing country until they initiate a satisfactory conclusion to the conflict.

If the initiators of the attack demand capitulation enforced by the threat of further nuclear attack, the defenders should counterthreaten with the pressure tactics given here–all applied at once. To make the threat by the defenders clear and graphic, the United Nations in peacetime–before nuclear crises occur–should simulate their defense and broadcast it to the world.

The fifth strategy is that the defenders should encourage the initiator's domestic opponents, including top leaders, to enforce de-escalation–when there is enough strength to coerce. The defenders can encourage the domestic opposition to the initiators to depose, arrest, and replace these aggressors. To assist this opposition, the defenders can slip resources into the offending country. To depose the leaders, the opposition can use constitutional procedures, a standard coup, bribery with amnesty, or can use masses of unarmed citizens to seize the leaders nonviolently, although this seizing probably would cost many casualties. Nonviolence without many casualties, actually deposed the brutal dictator Nicolae Ceausescu in Romania when he ordered his troops to disperse a crowd that was becoming restive while listening to him, and the soldiers defied his order. Ceausescu fled and was killed.

At this point, as their last tactic, the defenders can offer attractive terms for peace.

In terms of the danger confronted–a nuclear attack that has begun–this set of strategies, showing how leaders might actually stop such an attack, carries nonviolent action and other elements of nonmilitary defense farther than has been done in such detail before. This possibility is hopeful and awesome!

B. Scenario

To show how an actual conflict might be de-escalated, I turn to a step-by-step application. Like most scenarios of nuclear attack, or even all of them, this one is not fully plausible. But it is plausible that nuclear attack is likely to happen someday, for history is full of surprising tragedies. Since scenarios are needed in order to consider ways to deal with a nuclear attack, let us make do with flawed scenarios. Many scenarios of attack that strategists have used to develop defenses have differed from the actual attacks that later occurred. But, many of these scenarios have been enough like the actual attacks to make the planned defenses effective.

Suppose that, a few years from now, the countries of Nuclemania and Dictatorius are having a dispute about which of them should have sovereignty over a disputed territory between them in which citizens from each of these two countries are mingled. Suppose that Nuclemania has nuclear weapons, but its army is small. Dictatorius has a large army but no nuclear weapons. After much wrangling over the territory, Nuclemania receives intelligence indicating that Dictatorius plans to attack the territory and seize it. Dictatorius has massed troops on the border of the territory. Nuclemania is led by a reckless dictator named N. D., who makes a vague threat to pre-empt the attack. Dictatorius does not believe that N. D. is serious until N. D. orders the Nuclemania military to fire a nuclear missile from a mobile launcher at Dictatorius's massed troops. Many casualties result. N. D. makes vague threats that Nuclemania will fire more missiles at Dictatorius's troops and military facilities if Dictatorius does not stop trying to seize the territory. The U.S. president considers intervening militarily, but does not do so because his term of office is nearly over, and his successor opposes this intervention (Chart 1, 1). The United Nations quickly polls its members and discovers that all but two oppose Nuclemania's use of nuclear weapons.

The Security Council concludes that the two populations (17) in the disputed territory are so hostile to each other that they cannot live together. The Council decides to recommend that Dictatorius have sovereignty over the territory on grounds that more citizens of Dictatorius live there and that Nuclemania's use of nuclear weapons is so serious that it outweighs Nuclemania's claim of sovereignty. Then, the Council secures pledges from members to establish a special fund to enable citizens of Nuclemania who live in the territory to resettle in Nuclemania, with good housing, good schools, and so on (4). The Council members hope that this decision will lead Nuclemania to withdraw its ultimatum and to agree to let Dictatorius have sovereignty over the territory. However, N. D. refuses and keeps the offer out of Nuclemania's media.

Imagine that the United Nations has an enormous data bank of names of people outside of Nuclemania who know citizens within. From among people listed in this data bank, the United Nations enlists volunteers with contacts in Nuclemania to communicate the message that an emigration solution to the crisis has been suggested, but that Nuclemania's leader will not accept it (5). The message ends with the suggestion that Nuclemania's people demonstrate to pressure their leader to accept the United Nation's solution (12). Some of the recipients of the message lead organizations that can provide structures for arranging opposition to the dictator (15). Some countries send representatives to Nuclemania's border to give citizens of Nuclemania the same message (5), to donate funds to help organize demonstrations, and to provide access to broadcasting facilities that can reach Nuclemania.

The Security Council passes a resolution calling for members to embargo, even to banish Nuclemania except for food, medicine, and communication facilities (19). The United Nations prevents smuggling by patrolling Nuclemania's borders.

The citizens of Nuclemania are afraid that the prevailing wind will shift and that fallout from new explosions will blow to them (21). The citizens also feel that their country's use of nuclear weapons is unacceptable, that the embargo will hurt, and that the leader of their country should be forced to resign. Only about three percent of the citizens are willing to demonstrate against their government, and most of them are willing only after they see many other citizens demonstrating (23). But that percentage of residents of the capital, plus others who can get there rapidly, forms a critical mass. (This is twice the percent of the people of Moscow who appeared in the largest street demonstration that successfully opposed the coup in 1991. By the way, the Moscow example contradicts the theory that nonviolence requires unity.)

The demonstrators surround the building where the head of state has his office.

Members of an elite corps of troops fire upon the demonstrators to disperse them. The demonstrators return again and again, retreating when fired upon. Then a corps member sees his brother shot and cries out against that killing. The news is passed by word of mouth among the corps members, and they redefine their work as slaughter and as unconstitutional. Some military units cross to the demonstrators' side, where they may be hit if the remaining troops fire. Most of the remaining soldiers refuse to continue to fire (and risk hitting their colleagues). Their commander, feeling some of the same reticence and realizing that N. D. no longer has a sufficient number of loyal troops, orders them to return to their barracks. Realizing that the crowd will attempt to dispose its dictator (23), N. D. escapes, which leaves the country in the hands of the second-in-command. Though no democrat, the new leader calls off the nuclear attacks, withdraws the ultimatum, and accepts the U.N. resettlement plan (24). The new leader tells Nuclemanians in the disputed territory that they will have to move to Nuclemania freely or be forced to do so. Most comply. Some elude the order but are few enough to cause no trouble, so they are overlooked.

C. General Forms of Strength as Domains of Life

The strategies, strategic objectives, and tactics on Chart 1 are based on more general forms of strength, which derive from two axioms. The first is that virtually everything has strength because nearly everything can be granted, denied, or foisted on others in order to exert influence. The second is that there is extraordinary power in a combination of types of strength relevant to nuclear attack.

As for the first axiom, Eduard Spranger, a German philosopher who wrote in the 1920s, provided a convenient, inclusive classification for organizing all this strength in terms of the domains of life from which the strategist can seek applications.[20] With some augmentation, these domains are the spiritual, moral, intellectual, emotional, social, political, economic, physical, and aesthetic forms. All apply to public policy, not just to the personal realm. Together they show the vastness of nonmilitary strength, some of which is already available.

Spiritual strength includes people's willingness to face death for a great cause. Joan of Arc is a traditional role model.

Moral strength can take the form of the taboo, such as the one that most people hold against the first-use of nuclear weapons. First-use would probably break a stronger taboo than the initiation of conventional attack does and could therefore bring forth stronger opposition, particularly from bystander countries.

Intellectual strength includes the power of ideas, such as those of Karl Marx, the man who worked alone in a library producing ideas that motivated people to overturn the social systems of one-third of the population of the world. (And it was an idea, albeit an old one–the free market economy–that overturned many of them!)

Emotional strength includes the power to turn hate into love–the center of Martin Luther King, Jr.'s influence–and what he showed us how to do. Bonding between citizens of antagonistic countries is more difficult, but it happens, as when a victim-nation blames elements of the aggressor government while feeling a common humanity with the rest of the aggressor nation.

Social strength includes ostracism, such as what English public schools have used for discipline, with extraordinary effectiveness. Social power also involves elitism, including the bestowing of honors, such as presidential medals and nobility titles (lordships and knighthoods in the British case). These symbols were started centuries ago to hold British society together and made many powerful people loyal to the Crown. As a result, overthrowing the government by civil war became extremely unlikely.

Political strength includes diplomacy, such as the Camp David talks during the Jimmy Carter presidency.

Embargoes exemplify economic strength. In the 1960s and in the 1970s, the United Nations organized an embargo that helped end the minority government rule by whites in Rhodesia (now Zimbabwe).

Physical strength is exemplified by blockades.

Aesthetic strength includes good writing and speaking. Messages urging people to oppose nuclear aggressors would have more effect if written by great writers than by bureaucrats. Aesthetic strength also includes the power of laughter, which is what cartoonists use to help depose leaders, as Thomas Nast showed us with his cartoons of Boss Tweed of New York, and as did the cartoonist who depicted Richard M. Nixon with a long nose sprouting like Pinocchio's. Had Charlie Chaplin satirized Adolf Hitler in *The Great Dictator* before censorship began in Germany, Chaplin, too, might have used the weapon of laughter to depose an evil leader. (Hitler himself understood the power of aesthetics. He did not choose to switch from a handlebar mustache to a short one only because he thought it looked better; he adopted it in imitation of the person who was probably the best known man in the world. That man was Chaplin!)[21] Once a country's public and its bureaucrats see a leader as ridiculous, it is difficult to accept that leader as an authority.

D. Specific Forms of Strength: Methodologies

When these domains of general strength are exerted as power, more than one tends to be used together in various methodologies. These methodologies remind us that much is known about how to make people behave. Let us apply this knowledge to the problem of nuclear aggressors. I will list some methodologies, mainly starting from those I will explain least to those with the most explanation.

The first set of methods is the one used to induce terrorists to release hostages.[22] Authorities wear down the terrorists, bribe them, and correct the injustices causing the terrorism, among other things. The second is the variety of procedures used in mounting a *coup d'état*.[23] Plotters co-opt members of the administration, including body guards and military commanders, send critical figures out of the capital, and so forth. The third is what authorities use to control the criminally insane, which would be applicable if the aggressor were mentally ill. In particular, this includes avoiding cornering the insane person. The fourth is the application to nonviolence of a selection of principles of military strategy, such as surprise, concentration of force at the adversary's weak points, and maintaining the center of graveness, which was Carl von Clausewitz's caution to preserve a country's last sources of strength more than its territory.[24] For nonmilitary defenders, the last sources of strengths could include the remaining communication facilities and the people in line to be head of state of the victim country, including secretly designated successors after known ones have been killed.

The fifth methodology is law, which can be viewed as a set of tools. As international law continues to move towards forbidding the first-use of nuclear weapons, that norm will become part of the belief system of many more people, some of whom may become leaders of nuclear states who then will be reluctant to make a nuclear attack.[25] If a leader were to publicly consider making a nuclear attack or to carry one out, the norm against the first-use would lead many people, probably including some of his or her colleagues, to oppose such an attack. Furthermore, legal means would be available for fellow nationals to depose the aggressor. All countries have such laws, even monarchies do: they provide for appointing a regent. Deposing happens: Anthony Eden, Leopoldo Galtieri (of Argentina), Khrushchev, and Nixon, among others, were deposed by their colleagues, in some cases because they committed aggression. The number of people initiating a nuclear war would be small and therefore not too difficult to depose; a large group, such as a legislature or a full military command, would be unlikely to decide to initiate nuclear war.[26] Legal tools are powerful.

The sixth methodology is the standard set of negotiation techniques, such as compromising between two bargaining positions.

If this fails, negotiators or a third party can turn to creative conflict resolution, the seventh methodology. This approach relies on cleverness, identifying similar cases of conflict, varying all possible factors, identifying what the parties already agree upon, and integrative (win/win) bargaining, among other things.[27] The Berlin Wall could be considered an example of integrative bargaining. The East won relief from the flow of population out of East

Germany. Though displeased at the time, the West won relief from a festering conflict and from the threat of the East to conquer West Berlin. The strength of creative conflict resolution comes partly from the self-enforcement that occurs when both sides gain satisfaction. Since a nuclear attack might be caused by a severe, reasonable need, such as a threat to security, the techniques of creative conflict resolution could help to identify this need and to satisfy it in an acceptable way (possibly in time to prevent the attack). Creative conflict resolution is at the heart of the effort of the negotiation stage of nonmilitary defense.

Nonviolence, the last methodology I will list, is at the heart of the stage in conflict when negotiations fail and the defenders decide to try to force their position on the adversary. Nonviolent action is defined as protest, non-cooperation, or intervention that does not kill or wound others and that is done in conscience with an attitude of compassion that seeks reconciliation with the opponents, while opposing some of their actions. Established procedures, such as voting, and routine diplomacy, though generally not violent are seldom considered to be nonviolent action.[28] When using nonviolence for defense, activists give up territory while defending lives and social institutions. By contrast, military defenders give up lives while defending territory and social institutions.[29] The nonviolent defenders seek to regain control of the lost territory; military defenders cannot regain any of the lives and some of the other destruction they have lost.

Nonviolence is not passivity, it involves force: embargoes exert power; massive demonstrations stopped tanks in the revolution of 1986 in the Philippines,[30] and helped drive Nicolae Ceausescu, the brutal dictator of Romania, out of power in 1989.[31]

Besides such tangible force, nonviolence can make use of the intangible aspects of strength Spranger identified, including the spiritual one. Spiritual influence can be an appeal to the opponent's religious beliefs, as well as to secular ones. The spiritual includes the realm of ultimate concern, which can command a higher loyalty than loyalty to a national leader. Possible loyalties include ideology, common decency, social class, and country ("Sweet Land of Liberty," Mother Russia). As well, some people have loyalty to the legitimacy of a cause, and this loyalty can lead to victory. A study of eighteen major twentieth century conflicts showed that "the party that believes it is in the right and communicates this belief to an opponent who has some doubts about the legitimacy of his own position nearly always wins."[32] .

Law commands high loyalty for many people. Commissioned military officers in the United States take an oath to obey lawful orders. The implication is that they should disobey unlawful ones. Enlisted men are instructed that "complicity in the commission of crimes against peace, against humanity, and war crimes is punishable."[33] Russian military officers take an oath swearing to obey the constitution, statutes, and their superior officers.[34] The implication is that, if an order conflicts with a statute or the constitution, the higher authority should be obeyed.[35] In defying orders by their superior officers who were leading the coup attempt of 1991 in Moscow, Soviet military men showed how strong this oath is. These provisions, reflect the Nuremberg principles. As a result of the Nuremberg trials, the Allied governments executed Nazis partly for failing to undertake civil disobedience![36] Failure to disobey an order to fire nuclear weapons could be treated even more seriously than the Nazi war crimes if the firing were a crime against humanity. Nations could now establish Nuremberg-style courts to try nuclear aggressors, with dramatic, moot trials held periodically. Nearly all countries have factions wishing to take power from the incumbents. The initiation of a nuclear attack could give a faction justification for usurping power. Foreign business people friendly to a faction could help finance a coup.

Identity is one more higher loyalty. In 1986, when President Ferdinand Marcos of the Philippines ordered pilots loyal to him to bomb a dissident army camp, they found 100,000 civilians surrounding it. The pilots defied Marcos saying later that they viewed their identity as protectors of civilians, not as butchers of them.[37]

Higher loyalties can lead supporters of an aggressor to defy or abandon the aggressor or to malinger. Leaders of the entities that are the object of higher loyalties can inspire disloyalty to the aggressive leader. If a higher loyalty is an ultimate concern, it can lead activists to risk their lives. This willingness gives nonviolence campaigns a spirit that is more important than weapons, just as in military campaigns.

Moral suasion, another of Spranger's domains, can also carry out the nonviolence paradigm of reducing the aggressor's support. This reduction can be achieved by showing that the opponent's claim that their pronouncements, purposes, and values are the same as those of the followers is false, or at least that the values are more extreme. For example, when soldiers from the Warsaw Treaty Organization invaded Czechoslovakia in 1968, Czechoslovakians indicated that their liberalization was a development of communism, not a rebellion against it, as the invading soldiers had been told.[38] Tyrants are not converted by nonviolent action, but their supporters are, or are stopped from carrying out their orders.[39] Often, the conversion of the supporters is caused by the tyrant's overreaction to the nonviolent activists' demonstrations, revealing that the tyrant was more of a butcher than had been realized. A nuclear attack would probably be an overreaction. Intangible nonviolence has power.

This conversion of supporters of tyrants is particularly well illustrated by the Iranian Revolution of 1978, which in tactics, though not in spirit by its leaders, was nearly all an application of nonviolent action. Late in the revolution, the Shah ordered Iranian soldiers to disperse a crowd of demonstrators. One soldier told a demonstrator to leave or be shot. The demonstrator bared his chest and said, "Shoot me," which the soldier did. Then the soldier repeated the order to a demonstrator who had seen this killing. The result was the same. Then the soldier and his colleagues realized that the demonstrators had an extraordinary level of commitment so the soldiers asked some demonstrators what they were protesting. Upon being told of the Shah's atrocities, these soldiers malingered and told other soldiers of the atrocities, helping to cause a ripple of malingering.[40] Thus, with the seventh largest military budget on earth, the Shah could not protect himself.[41] Actually, some of his generals asked for authority to massacre demonstrators.[42] Had they done so, the result might have been an end to the rebellion as at Tiananmen Square. The result might also have been a mass, uncontrollable uprising, had *jihad* been involved, leading demonstrators to be willing to die and soldiers unwilling to shoot their compatriots. As we will see, commanders of army divisions guarding Beijing defied their leader's request that they order their troops to shoot the demonstrators at Tiananmen Square.

Yet the risk of death or wounding in the Iranian Revolution was doubtless much less than had the struggle been a military one on both sides. Nonviolent action often has a much lower casualty rate than does military action. For example, India nonviolently achieved independence from a European country at a cost of far fewer deaths proportional to population than Algeria suffered when it violently achieved independence from a European country. The odds of surviving in India were about 4,000 times better than in Algeria.[43]

The most common objection to nonviolence is that it fails against a brutal opponent who is particularly willing to inflict death. This allegation is false; by demonstrations, defiance, and other means, nonviolence saved tens of thousands of Jews in many countries during the brutal Nazi era.[44] Besides, German generals said after World War II that, in many of the occupied countries, the nonviolent underground was more difficult to deal with than was the violent resistance because it baffled them and they had difficulty stopping it.[45]

Contrary to another common belief, many well-known American historical events involved nonviolent action: colonists intervened to form legislatures that acted as parallel governments in defiance of British colonial law. Later, slaves escaped through underground railroads, women demonstrated for suffrage, labor struck to secure the right to bargain collectively, civil rights activists improved conditions for minorities, protesters helped limit the escalation of the Vietnam War, and congress passed a resolution urging economic sanctions against the Soviet Union if it were to invade Poland to curb Solidarity.[46] Nonviolence has always been common in America.

The power and complexity of nonviolent action has been growing. In 1968, Czechoslovakians kept half-a-million Warsaw Treaty Organization troops from toppling the Czechoslovakian government–a feat that the Czechoslovakian military never could have achieved. This event represented progress: it was a complicated defense, not just a simple embargo or a domestic event, and it was organized by a government, not only by under-funded dissidents as has usually been the case in the past.[47] In 1980 and 1981, the Solidarity trade union in Poland, assisted by the United States and other countries, used nonviolence to prevent an attack that the Soviet Union had fully prepared and that a number of authoritative sources believe would otherwise have happened.[48] This case involved allies and, like the last, involved a superpower.[49] In 1991, the countercoup in the Soviet Union non-violently stopped a coup by leaders of the government, the military, and the secret police. This event counters the view that Russians were too irreligious and too inexperienced in nonviolence to employ it in a major way.

Of course, there are countercases and developments in methods of countering nonviolence. For instance, in 1989, in Tiananmen Square in China, nonviolent activists failed to achieve the freedoms they demanded. When, partly by fraternizing with troops, they did cause the local military commanders to refuse to commit troops to disperse them, the government countered by calling in troops from the provinces who did not speak the language of the demonstrators.[50]

Overall, however, nonviolence has developed well beyond what it was under Gandhi. Nonviolence will continue to become more powerful as more advanced nonviolent events occur; as the United Nations prepares for its use under its Charter's Article 41, which mandates nonviolent action; and as so-cieties more fully accept its value. In summary, nonviolence is powerful (ten Latin American dictatorships were overthrown nonviolently between 1931 and 1961);[51] characteristic of American, Islamic (recall the Palestinians' *Inti-fada* and the Pathans in Pakistan),[52] Russian, and many other cultures (what country has had none?); useful for defense (as in Poland); and useful against brutal and totalitarian forces (nearly all the Jews in Bulgaria, Denmark, and Finland were saved from the Nazis nonviolently).[53]

No one yet knows the potential of nonviolence for ending nuclear threats and attacks, however, a hint does exist. In his memoirs, Nixon admitted that his ultimatum to North Vietnam was that the United States would "take mea-sures of the greatest consequence and force" if, by 1 November 1969, there was not "major progress toward a solution to the war."[54] H. R. Haldeman, Nixon's Chief of Staff, claims that the ultimatum was a nuclear threat.[55] What else could "greatest force" mean? Nixon also wrote in his memoirs that he withdrew the ultimatum particularly because of the nonviolent demonstration by one-quarter-of-a-million people in Washington during the Vietnam Moratorium in October 1969. He wrote that this demonstration indicated that his ultimatum did not have popular support.[56] If Haldeman was right, non-violent action's efficacy in nuclear crises is not simply theory; it is history.

E. Relationships among the Forms of Strength

The relationship among the three levels of domains [see section 1C], methodologies [section 1D], and strategies [section 1A] can be seen as a hierarchy. For example, the economic domain (and others) includes nonviolence, to which the embargo is subordinate. The relationship can also be seen as a crosstabulation of the domains and the methodologies so as to generate strategies and tactics. For each domain, one asks, what strategies and tactics can be found within all the methodologies? For each methodology, one asks, what strategies and tactics can be found within each domain? Chart 2 presents this crosstabulation with some of the strategies and tactics in the earlier chart entered into the boxes of the columns into which they fit. The number of empty boxes suggests how many more strategies and tactics to end a nuclear attack could be found, perhaps enough to fill all the boxes, some of which would have many entries. This potential of the chart is intended to give the impression of the massive amount of nonmilitary strength that parties could aggregate.

F. Organization of the Strengths into a Defense

My second axiom is that there is extraordinary power in the application of a combination of Spranger's general domains of strength, the specific methodologies, and their application as strategies and tactics, as seen in Chart 2. This power can be grasped by examining how this combination would look if organized into a defense. As with military struggles, the organization would involve command, control, and communication.

The command might be given to defense departments of the countries that use nonmilitary defense or to a new department. The defense would be coordinated by the secretary general of the United Nations. Obviously, the victim country would act independently, as well as in coordination with other parties.

Control would be exercised through a network resembling the complicated, widespread network used to deal with fire, which has forest-fire prevention ads, fire drills, smoke detectors, fire stations, and so on.[57] This defense network would include (1) prevention, such as education to develop global loyalty, and (2) preparation, including rehearsals of everyone's role in the defense. The network would also involve (3) detection, and (4) reporting, including a worldwide emergency telephone number for reporting nuclear danger to the media and to the United Nations. Finally, a network would entail (5) treatment, including a permanent cadre to direct the masses of nonviolent activists who would act after a threat or attack. At best, this network would be worldwide, and thus would exist in the aggressing country, even

Chart 2: Crosstabulation of Domains and Methodologies to Produce Strategies and Tactics

Domains (Numbers and letters in parentheses refer to those in Chart 1)

Method-ologies	Spiritual	Moral	Intellectual	Emotional	Social	Political	Economic	Physical	Aesthetic
Nonviolent Action	Appeal to higher loyalties (D)	Divide opponent (III)	Communicate with adversary (5)	Ease opponent's fear (I)	Bond with opponent (G)	Send 50 prominent people to negotiate (2)	Remove inappropriate pressures (II)	Avoid nuclear response (1)	Broadcast pressure tactics (22)
Routine or Creative Negotiation		Appeal to common values (6)	Send 50 prominent people to negotiate (2)		Urge friends of adversary to seek peace (12)	Have UN poll countries on opposition to attack (17)	Negotiate grievances (4)		
Law		Stress law to government (6)			Stress law to friends of adversary (6)	Depose leader with constitutional law (23)			Aesthetically craft legal messages (5)
Military Creed					Stress soldiers' brotherhood (D)			Secure military support (16)	
Handling the Violent Insane	Use their values (6)						Avoid cornering opponent (19)		
Coup Procedures		Divide adversary (III)		Urge organizations to oppose initiators (15)				Use coup security tactics (14)	
Hostage-Release Methods						Satisfy legitimate grievances (3)		Show how attack harms opponents (21)	

though the leader of the country would try to suppress as much resistance as possible.

Obviously, not everyone in the world who could participate in seeking to end a nuclear attack would do so. A major reason for avoiding participation would be that individuals and nations could reap the benefits of de-escalation while letting others take the risk of acting against the aggressor. However, significant participation could result from giving benefits such as monetary incentives to participants only, paid by the victim country or by a multi-national escrow account. Participation could also result from compelling it by law (perhaps as part of a national-service program), from organizing (particularly by forming small groups and by bringing established organizations together), and from having participants drill in techniques of nonmilitary defense. At present, the public might not wish to pay to develop this network. If a nuclear attack does occur anywhere, the public will doubtless demand that a network be established.

Communication among defenders would be done in the standard diplomatic and military ways, including arrangements to act independently, as nuclear submarine crews can act if headquarters are destroyed.[58] In addition, vast means of communication with the opponent would be established as charted.

2. Further Ramifications of Nonmilitary Defenses

In this section, I report what little research has been done on nonmilitary responses to nuclear attack and conditions under which the defense might succeed or fail. Next, I report a poll showing the extent of support for the proposal by American voters and then some of the objections that have been made to the proposal as well as answers to them. Since the defense applies to nuclear terrorism as well as to a nuclear attack by a country, the section continues with consideration of some ways to counter such terrorism. The chapter ends with implementation possibilities for the proposal, a summary of it, and its significance.

A. Previous Research

Little research has been reported about how a nuclear threat or attack could be dealt with other than by counterstrike. What has been reported proposes partial measures. Stephen King-Hall proposed treating a threat by exposing it, by expressing disbelief that the opponent will actually carry out such a threat, by conducting propaganda against the opponent's ideology, and by threatening nonviolent action in response to the conventional attack expected to replace or accompany the nuclear attack. He was a knighted retired naval commander and thus was a member of the British establishment and was knowledgeable about military affairs.[59] Wilhelm Nolte proposed to defend against a nuclear and a conventional attack aimed at West Germany by exposing the nuclear threat, by bringing rural people to the cities, by performing nonviolent action there, and by carrying out conventional military defense in the countryside.[60] These programs might succeed, but it is worth seeking a broader, fully nonmilitary means to meet a nuclear crisis.

Herman Kahn and Howard Brembeck proposed nonmilitary, though not broad, plans to deal with nuclear crises. Kahn, at the end of his life, proposed banishing a nation that either threatened a nuclear attack or launched one. He also proposed banishing all nations that supported the aggressor.[61] He meant to bar trade, mail, influence, travel–everything possible. Brembeck has proposed using embargoes to enforce nuclear disarmament and to deal with any nation that used the weapons or avoided disarming.[62] Kahn and Brembeck's plans might succeed, but research reveals that embargoes tend to bring compliance when used against one's allies more than against one's enemies.[63] Still, Kahn and Brembeck proposed to institutionalize a worldwide embargoing system, which might succeed.

The Pentagon has briefly simulated nonmilitary defense against nuclear attack, but nuclear counterstrike always followed.[64] The results are classified.

B. Conditions of Failure and Success

There are conditions under which nonmilitary defense would have a small chance of succeeding. Most of the conditions that defeat military defense would also defeat nonmilitary defense, such as insufficient organization, insufficient overall strength as compared to the opponent's strength, or insufficient energy after an overwhelming number of casualties have been sustained. In addition, nonmilitary defense would be likely to fail under conditions particular to itself, such as the victim's being without communication with many members of the opposing side, and without sufficient participation by the victim's public. Nuclear attacks would seem to be less effectively met by this kind of defense than would nuclear threats.

Nonmilitary defense would probably succeed most often when a quick win/win bargain could be struck or when a nuclear crisis is drawn out over time. A major difference between nonmilitary and military defense is that, after failing, that is, after surrendering, the victim is more likely to have a chance to continue struggling if nonmilitary defense is used than if military defense is used. Furthermore, nonmilitary defense will continue to develop, reducing the likelihood of failure. And, again, it is too early to estimate the chances that nonmilitary defense will succeed; therefore, research on it should continue.

C. Support for the Proposal

Many Americans accept the concept of alternatives to counterstrike. Averaging two polls taken in 1988 shows that only forty-four percent of American voters favored counterstriking to deal with a nuclear attack on American military forces in combat. Fifty-one percent preferred using other means. (Five percent were uncertain.) The chief pollsters of presidential candidates George Bush and Michael Dukakis performed these polls; Americans Talk Security commissioned them.[65] Duane Cady, a philosopher, also accepts the concept of a nonmilitary alternative to nuclear counterstrike:

> In fact, nonmilitary defense not only may be plausible but also may be more likely [to be] effective in achieving security goals than the superpowers' present means of stockpiling nuclear weapons and threatening nuclear holocaust.[66]

A list of a range of experts, whose belief in the research is attested by their having helped fund it, is found at the end of this chapter.

D. Objections to the Proposal

An objection to the proposal for nonmilitary defense is that devising any response to nuclear attack would be useless because nothing can stop a limited nuclear attack from greatly escalating. Although a limited nuclear attack would be likely to escalate, this outcome is not one hundred percent certain. Therefore, governments should prepare ways to attempt de-escalation without counterstriking.

A further objection to the proposal of nonmilitary defense is that, if a country announces that it will not use nuclear counterstrike, other countries may make nuclear threats against that country. Since 1945, all countries without nuclear weapons have been in that position without suffering conquest by a nuclear threat, though if no country with nuclear arms could have been counted on to counterstrike, such conquests might have occurred. Besides, the defense does not require a pledge to avoid using nuclear weapons before, after, or concurrently with nonmilitary defense. Nonmilitary defense could be used with conventional military defense.

Another objection is that tyrants would have control over dissidents who want to avoid or to end a nuclear attack by their country. The history of nonviolence shows that when a critical mass of opposition is reached, tyrants lose control. The Philippine Revolution of 1986 and the East European revolts of 1989 through 1991 are examples.

E. Nuclear Terrorism

Nuclear terrorism is of particular concern. Three strategies stand out for prevention or for treatment if it happens. One is to strengthen the taboo against the first use of nuclear weapons. Already, this taboo may explain why terrorists have not made a nuclear attack: they would lose too many of the supporters they need for cash and for safe houses, and they might be assassinated by their colleagues who realize that a crackdown on terrorists in general would follow, even if the perpetrator of the attack were unknown.

The second antiterrorism strategy is to conduct principled foreign relations. It is stunning how many terrorist organizations have goals that are just. Thus, justice brings security. As Robert C. Johansen, a peace professor (irenologist) has written, "In our era as never before in history, what is ethically desirable to do in relating to one's neighbor converges with what is politically prudent for oneself."[67]

Third, the technical procedures for the identifying, seizing, and disarming of nuclear weapons should be more thoroughly funded instead of being reduced in funding, as has been the case.[68]

F. Implementation

Today, no major nuclear power is the enemy of another. This respite is a good time to take steps to prepare a safer defense against nuclear attack than counterstrike would be. Research agencies need to study the proposal further. This chapter is designed to show that such research on nonmilitary responses to nuclear attack is feasible. Then activists need to work to convince governments to adopt the defense, probably starting with countries such as New Zealand and Sweden that are small and have a progressive tradition. A beginning also might be made with countries that may be threatened with nuclear attack and that do not choose to adopt a nuclear defense. Japan is a possible example.[69] The activists should be encouraged by the opinion of Johan Galtung, the wise Norwegian peace researcher, that antinuclear activists were effective, for they made the illegitimacy of nuclearism clear.[70] Both the effectiveness of activism and the illegitimacy are encouraging. Finally, nuclear powers should engage in a worldwide effort to establish a system for dealing with nuclear crises, as suggested by the research.

G. Summary

An observation by Jonathan Zuck, a student of international affairs, summarizes the alternatives to nuclear counterstrike developed here to deal with nuclear threat or attack.[71] He notes that the world failed to prevent World War II because of too much tender action (appeasement at Munich) as well as too much tough action (excessive reparations demanded at Versailles). He concludes that a balance is needed, which is a concise way to describe what has been spelled out here; that is to say, remove some of the pressures that could cause a nuclear attack, and, if needed, add more appropriate pressures to de-escalate from it. More specifically, regarding the fear-based causes of a nuclear attack, tender nonmilitary defense could be the following: alleviate real and trumped-up fears, satisfy legitimate grievances, call upon interpersonal and interorganizational bonds, invoke loyalties higher than the loyalty to the initiators of the attack, and emphasize the antinuclear taboo, all of which could lead supporters to cease assisting the initiators. Coordinated with these measures, and particularly in regard to the illegitimate causes of a nuclear attack, tough nonmilitary defense could be the following: Reduce the aggressor's influence abroad, institute an embargo, further ostracize, cause domestic turmoil and opposition, refuse demands, employ civilian-based (nonviolent) defense against conventional attack, and encourage top leaders of the aggressing country to depose the initiators and accept attractive terms for de-escalation. Military action might be coordinated with these approaches. In addition, all other relevant forms of nonmilitary strength could be built up and combined.

H. Significance

Furthermore, the significance of the proposed nonmilitary defense in the event of nuclear threat or attack is that, if successful, the defense could accomplish the following:

(1) Supplement or eventually replace nuclear deterrence with a defense that is more likely to avoid the pressures that could cause a nuclear attack, including those leading to a pre-emptive attack.

(2) Increase the chance to de-escalate, in the event of a nuclear threat or attack.

(3) Facilitate nuclear arms-level reduction by providing a replacement before making deep reductions. This replacement would make it possible to deal with a party that cheats on a nuclear disarmament treaty by hiding some nuclear weapons, and then threatens with them. Having an alternative to nuclear counterstrike would make it possible to reduce the number of nuclear weapons, not only by treaty, but by unilateral action, as generally happens when a superior weapon supplants an older one. We live in an ideal and unique time for reduction or even abolition because no nation possessing the bomb is an enemy of another.

(4) Reduce nuclear proliferation by offering an alternative defense (demand side), not just by imposing a restriction of nuclear materials (supply side).

(5) Possibly reduce defense budgets. (It is too early to know the cost of nonmilitary defense.)

(6) Improve the means for meeting a conventional attack nonmilitarily, perhaps along with a reduced conventional military response, for the defense proposed here applies to such an attack as well as to a nuclear one.

(7) Reduce the number of wars by reducing the number of weapons parties hold, because, to some extent, weapons beg to be used.

(8) Reduce the amount of militarism in the world by preparing to struggle against the worst form of attack with nonmilitary means, thus encouraging nonmilitary struggle at lower levels.

(9) Through research, including simulation, test the limits of nonviolent action, now widely thought, without evidence, to be quite limited.

(10)Provide, at last, an answer to the parable of the tribes. This myth holds that if one out of a group of tribes is militaristic and conquers another tribe, the remaining ones will arm, become militaristic, and lose many of their peaceful values. If the other tribes prepare a nonmilitary defense and they succeed in defending themselves, they will not lose their freedom or their peaceful values.

Leo Tolstoy was right: war takes on a life of its own and cannot be subjected to much control. Nuclear attack would be amenable to even less control than would a conventional attack. But some control is possible, and, as in *War and Peace*, many partly coordinated actions in the direction of resistance could perhaps prevail. Often, a party will prevail because the slaughter has exhausted its opponent and nearly exhausted itself, which is a reason to consider nuclear counterstrike carefully before undertaking it. But, slaughter is not the only way to struggle. If a nuclear attack occurs, some of the surviving leaders will act rather than do nothing, and it would be well to consider and make possible their range of options beyond military ones.

Although the bomb cannot be uninvented, a more satisfactory defense may be found that, at least partly, can replace it.[72]

Notes

1. Letter from General George Lee Butler, former Supreme Commander of U. S. Strategic Air Command, 30 June 1998.
2. Bruce Russett, *Controlling the Sword* (Cambridge, Mass.: Harvard University Press, 1990), ch. 5.

3. Samuel P. Huntington, "The Clash of Civilizations?" *Foreign Affairs*, 72 (Summer 1993), pp. 22-28.

4. James Baker III, *The Politics of Diplomacy* (New York: G. P. Putnam and Sons, 1995), p. 359.

5. Louis R. Beres, *Mimicking Sisyphus: America's Countervailing Nuclear Strategy* (Lexington, Mass.: Heath, 1983).

6. J. David Singer, Political Science Dept., Correlates of War Project, University of Michigan (personal communication, April 1995).

7. Colonel Roger Mickelson, Assistant Department of Defense emergency planner (personal communication, August 1998).

8. Gene Sharp, *The Politics of Nonviolent Action* (Boston: Porter Sargent, 1973), ch. 1.

9. Gene Sharp, *Social Power and Political Freedom* (Boston: Porter Sargent, 1980), pp. 232 and 276.

10. Thomas Kuhn, *The Structure of Scientific Revolutions* (Chicago: University of Chicago Press, 1970), pp. 5-7.

11. Robert Osgood, *The Nuclear Dilemma in American Strategic Thought* (Boulder, Colo.: Westview, 1988), ch. 2.

12. Lawrence Freedman, "The First Two Generations of Nuclear Strategists," in *Makers of Modern Strategy*, ed. Peter Paret (Princeton, N.J.: Princeton University Press, 1986), p. 778.

13. "From the Political Arena," *NOD & Conversion*, No. 39 (December 1996), pp. 18-19; and General George Lee Butler, "National Press Club Remarks," Washington, D.C.: National Press Club (4 December 1996).

14. Karen J. Warren and Duane L. Cady, eds., *Bringing Peace Home: Feminism, Violence, and Nature* (Bloomington, Ind.: Indiana University Press, 1996).

15. Richard Betts, Brookings Institution, Washington (personal communication, spring 1998).

16. Roger Fisher, Harvard Law School (personal communication, fall 1985).

17. Edward B. Atkenson, Major General, U. S. Army Intelligence (personal communication, November 1988).

18. Richard W. Fogg, "How the United Nations Helped Stop a War," *United Nations Observer* (August 1981), p. 7.

19. Federal Reserve Bank of New York, *Annual Report* (1987), pp. 31-33; and Gearge Garry, *Money, Financial Flows, and Credit in the Soviet Union* (Cambridge, Mass.: Ballinger, 1977), pp. 138-139.

20. Eduard Spranger, *Types of Men* (Halle, Saale, Germany: Max Niemeyer, 1928).

21. John McCabe, *Charlie Chaplin* (Garden City, N.Y.: Doubleday, 1978), p. 190.

22. Thomas Strentz, "Law Enforcement Policy and Ego Defenses of the Hostage," *FBI Law Enforcement Bulletin* (April 1979), p. 2. See also Ben A. Franklin and David Binder, "Three Islamic Diplomats Bridge Gap to Gunmen," *The New York Times* (12 March 1977), p. A1.

23. Gregor Ferguson, *Coup D'État: A Practical Manual* (Poole, Dorset: Arms and Armour, 1987).

24. Anders Boserup and Andrew Mack, *War Without Weapons: Nonviolence in National Defense* (New York: Schocken, 1975), pp. 151-173.

25. International Court of Justice, Advisory Opinion, *Legality of the Threat or Use of Nuclear Weapons* (The Hague: 8 July 1996), section 105 (2) C, in "World Condemns Use of Nuclear Weapons," *The New York Times* (8 July 1996), p. A8.

26. Glenn Snyder and Paul Diesing, *Conflict Among Nations* (Princeton, N.J.: Princeton University Press, 1977), p. 511.

27. Richard W. Fogg, "Dealing with Conflict: A Repertoire of Creative, Peaceful Approaches," *Journal of Conflict Resolution*, 29:2 (June 1985), pp. 330-358. Also, Roger Fisher, Elizabeth Kepelman, and Andrea Kupferschneider, *Beyond Machiavelli* (Cambridge, Mass.: Harvard University Press, 1994).

28. Sharp, *The Politics of Nonviolent Action*, p. 64; and Theodore Herman, Peace Studies Dept., Colgate University, retired (personal communication, August 1999).

29. Johan Galtung, *The True Worlds* (New York: Free Press, 1980), p. 215.

30. Richard Deats, "The Revolution that Surprised the World," *Fellowship* (July/August 1986), pp. 3-5 (and personal communication).

31. David Binder, "Bucharest Battle," *New York Times* (23 December 1989) p. 1.

32. Snyder and Diesing, *Conflict Among Nations*, p. 498.

33. United States Department of the Army, *The Law of Land Warfare* (Washington: U. S. Government Printing Office, Field Manual #27-10, 1956), p. 178.

34. William Baxter, *Soviet Air Land Battle Tactics* (Novato, Calif.: Presidio Press, 1986), p. 55.

35. Victor Kremenuk, Deputy Director, U. S./Canada Institute, Moscow (personal communication, October 1988).

36. Philip Berrigan (personal communication, August 1998) .

37. Richard Deats, Fellowship of Reconciliation, Nyack, N.Y. (personal communication, May 1986).

38. Institute of History of the Czechoslovakian Academy of Sciences, *The Czech. Black Book*, ed. Robert Littell (New York: Praeger, 1969), pp. 9 and 197.

39. Gene Sharp, Program on Sanctions, Center for International Affairs, Harvard University (personal communication, November 1985).

40. Jerrold Green, *Revolution in Iran: The Politics of Countermobilization* (New York: Praeger, 1982), p. 121, and (personal communication, April 1988).

41. *Reader's Digest Almanac and Yearbook* (New York: Norton, 1980), p. 465.

42. Edward C. Luttwak, Center for Strategic and International Studies, Washington (personal communication, June 1993).

43. Sharp, *The Politics of Nonviolent Action*, p. 552.

44. Sharp, *Social Power and Political Freedom*, p. 81; and Ronald J. Sider and Richard K. Taylor, *Nuclear Holocaust and Christian Hope* (Downers Grove, Ill.: Intervarsity, 1982), p. 243.

45. Sir Basil Liddell Hart, "Lessons from Resistance Movements–Guerilla and Nonviolent," *Civilian Resistance as a National Defense*, ed. Adam Roberts (Baltimore, Md.: Penguin, 1969), p. 240.

46. *Congressional Quarterly Weekly Report*, 39:51 (December 1981), p. 252.

47. Sharp, *Social Power and Political Freedom*, p. 232.

48. Ryszard Kuklinski, Zbigniew Brzezinski, and Richard Pipes, "Special Report: Poland in Crisis, 1980-1981," *Orbis*, 42 (Winter 1988), pp. 3-48, particularly pp. 12

and 15; and Samuel Huntington, *The Strategic Imperative* (Cambridge, Mass.: Ballinger, 1982), p. 16.

49. Lawrence Weschler, *The Passion of Poland* (New York: Pantheon, 1982).

50. Bernard E. Trainor, "Civil War for Army?" *New York Times* (6 June 1989), p. A16.

51. Patricia Parkman, *Insurrection without Arms* (Ph.D. dissertation, Temple University, Philadelphia, 1980).

52. John Damis, "The Moroccan-Algerian Conflict over the Western Sahara," *Maghreb Review* 4:2 (1979), p. 53; and Eknath Easwaran, *A Man to Match His Mountains: Badshah Kahn, Nonviolent Soldier of Islam* (Petaluma, Calif.: Milgiri, 1984).

53. Sharp, *The Politics of Nonviolent Action*, p. 81; and Sider and Taylor, *Nuclear Holocaust and Christian Hope*, p. 243.

54. Richard M. Nixon, *The Memoirs of Richard Nixon* (New York: Grosset and Dunlap, 1978), p. 402.

55. H. R. Haldeman, *The Ends of Power* (New York: Times Books, 1978), pp. 82 and 83.

56. Nixon, *Memoirs*, p. 408.

57. Bill Ury, *Beyond the Hotline* (Boston: Houghton Mifflin, 1985).

58. Joseph S. Nye, Jr., Graham Allison, and Albert Carnesale, Jr., eds., *Fateful Visions: Avoiding Nuclear Catastrophe* (Cambridge, Mass.: Ballinger, 1988), p. 232.

59. Stephen King-Hall, *Defense in the Nuclear Age* (Nyack, N.Y.: Fellowship of Reconciliation, 1959).

60. Wilhelm Nolte, "Autonomous Protection," and "A Strategy to Avert War," in *Winning Peace: Strategies and Ethics for a Nuclear-Free World*, ed. Dietrich Fisher, Jan Oberg, and Welhelm Nolte (Philadelphia: Taylor Francis, 1989), chaps. 9 and 10, esp. p. 119.

61. Herman Kahn, "On Arms Control," *New York Times* (13 June 1982), sec. 6, p. 42.

62. Howard Brembeck, *Defense for a Civilized World* (Goshen, Ind.: Fourth Freedom Forum, 1988).

63. Gary C. Hufbauer and Jeffrey J. Schott, *Economic Sanctions Reconsidered* (Washington: Institute for International Economics, 1985).

64. Colonel Roger Mickelson, Assistant Department of Defense emergency planner (personal communication, August 1998).

65. Americans Talk Security, "A Series of Surveys of American Voters" (Washington: Americans Talk Issues Foundation), no. 6 (June 1988) p. 72, and no. 9 (October 1988) p. 81.

66. Duane Cady, *From Warism to Pacifism: A Moral Continuum* (Philadelphia: Temple University Press, 1989), p. 90.

67. Robert C. Johansen "A Policy Framework for World Security," in *World Security: Trends and Challenges at Century's End*, ed. Michael T. Klare and Daniel C. Thomas (New York: St. Martin's, 1991), p. 422.

68. Gary Taubes, "The Defense Initiative of the '90s," *Science*, 267:24 (February 1995), pp. 1096-1100.

69. Richard W. Fogg, "Center Devises and Will Broadcast a Nonmilitary Defense for Japan," *The Third Alternative* (Baltimore, Md.: Center for the Study of Conflict, Fall/Winter 1993), p. 1.

70. Johan Galtung, *Peace by Peaceful Means: Peace and Conflict, Development and Civilization* (Thousand Oaks, Calif.: Sage, 1996), p. 8.

71. Jonathan Zuck, "Nuclear Crises: The Prospects for Nonmilitary Crisis Management," a paper delivered at the First Annual Conference on Conflict Resolution, University of the South Pacific, Fiji Islands (January 1986).

72. For their comments, I wish to thank Edward B. Atkeson, Frank C. Benedict, Thomas Benson, Pat Birnie, Frank A. Camm, John Carley, Barry Childers, Linda Compton, Adam Curle, Chris Drennen, Steven David, Craig Davis, William DeMars, Marcus Dubber, Edmund T. Dubois, Jennifer D'Urso, Carol Ehrlich, Edward Ernst, Jerome D. Frank, William C. Gay, Robert Ginsberg, Ethel Hensley, Theodore Herman, Robert L. Holmes, Egbert Jahn, Victor Kremenuk, Anne Lundbaek, Careen Mayer, Roger W. Mickelson, Lauren Mitten, Robert Munnelly, Alan and Hannah Newcomb, Charles E. Pirtle, Earl C. Ravenal, Julie Rehmeyer, David Riesman, Gene Sharp, Amy Slaughter, Mark Sommer, Hugh Steinberg, John F. Taylor, Freyda Weis, Gale Whittier, Judith Willner, Antoni Wrega, and Jonathan Zuck. The Mary Reynolds Babcock Foundation and the New Land Foundation provided support. The value and importance of the research by the Center for the Study of Conflict, where this study was done, is demonstrated by the range, judgment, and eminence of some of our donors: The late Kenneth Boulding, former president of the American Association for the Advancement of Science, for scholarly support; Yvonne Logan, former president of the U. S. Section of the Women's International League for Peace and Freedom, for peace-movement support; Brockway McMillan, former Undersecretary of the U. S. Air Force, for military support; our congress member, who keeps all his donations anonymous, for political support; Hans Bethe, Nobel Laureate in physics, for support from an expert on the bomb.

Twelve

SOVEREIGNTY AND POSITIVE PEACE

Steven Lee

The assumption with which I begin is that nobody knows what is going on in the world. The demise of the Soviet Union has overturned so many familiar concepts and comfortable assumptions that the way forward is not clear. An initial celebratory optimism, captured in former U.S. President George Bush's notion of the "new world order," has given way to confusion and pessimism in the face of the violence and suffering we have witnessed in the past five years. If you will excuse what would surely be regarded by colleagues from other disciplines as professional hubris, I would argue that, despite what the social scientists think, it is chiefly philosophers who are in a position to make sense of our situation. The social scientists may do this best when the familiar concepts and comfortable assumptions apply, but at historical turning points they lose their sight. When at dusk the Owl of Minerva takes flight, it is philosophers who are able to discern its path. I believe that it falls largely to philosophical thought to make sense of the post-cold-war world, and that the philosophical community has an obligation to bend its best efforts in this direction. Philosophers must examine the familiar concepts and comfortable assumptions of the cold war to determine why they no longer fit and which ones should be adopted in their place. My discussion in this chapter is a halting step in this direction. I discuss two concepts, peace and sovereignty, in such a way as to help us better to understand the post-cold-war world. I think that it is lack of an adequate understanding of these concepts, among others, that is causing confusion about the new situation we face.

1. Positive Peace

To understand the notion of peace, we must first consider the distinction between positive and negative peace. Negative peace is usually defined as the absence of violence in the relations among nations. What more than this is there to positive peace? One common positive characterization of peace is the presence of justice in addition to the absence of violence.

But while it may be true that a state of positive peace would lead to the substantial elimination of injustice, it is a mistake to define positive peace in terms of justice, partly for reasons which will become clearer below. Because the notion of peace concerns the role of conflict in human affairs, whether positive or negative, it should be defined in terms of the notion of conflict.

Negative peace is the absence of violent conflict. It will not do to say that positive peace is the absence of all conflict, for that surely is a utopian dream.
Rather, keeping the definition in terms of conflict, I think that it is better to
define positive peace as the nonviolent resolution of conflict. War is the violent resolution of conflict, and peace is the nonviolent resolution of conflict. A
negative concept of peace requires simply the containing of conflict short of
violence, while a positive concept of peace requires successful efforts at resolving conflict in a nonviolent manner. (Because most major human
conflicts result from injustice, positive peace would lead to the substantial
elimination of injustice.)

There are good arguments for preferring a positive to a negative concept
of peace, and understanding these arguments will help us to understand the
post-cold-war world. But first let us note the problems with some arguments
purporting to show that peace should be defined negatively rather than
positively. One is an argument from ordinary usage. Ronald J. Glossop argues
that a positive concept of peace is not descriptively adequate, that a negative
concept better fits actual usage. A positive concept of peace "seems not to be
faithful to our normal use of the term."[1] Arguments from ordinary usage are
of questionable force, but I think that this argument can be met on its own
terms. All that one must do is to show that there are important areas of
ordinary discourse where "peace" is used in a positive way. Here is one.
Given that "war" is the contradictory of "peace," consider that the absence of
violent conflict between the United States and the Soviet Union was referred
to for over forty years as a "cold war."

Another argument purporting to show that peace should be defined
negatively is that defining peace positively confuses our thinking. According
to Glossop, a positive concept of peace

> actually interferes with our thinking clearly about issues of peace and
> justice and their interrelations [such that] we would be forced to over-
> look certain distinctions which must be made if we are to understand the
> problems involved in creating an ideal society.[2]

The idea seems to be that while we want both the absence of violent conflict
and the presence of justice, these are different goals, and it would confuse our
efforts to achieve them by running them together into a single notion of
peace. One example of this problem that Glossop seems to have in mind is the
following: Given that the level of injustice between adversarial nations is
sometimes sufficient, on just-war grounds, to justify one going to war against
the other, and sometimes not, if peace were defined as the absence of
injustice, we might have trouble distinguishing these two cases.

Consider a third, related argument.[3] The notion of justice, unlike the
idea of the absence of violent conflict, is not ideologically or culturally neu-

tral. We can agree with our adversaries on when violent conflict is absent, but not on when justice is present. Thus, if we identify peace under a positive concept, we may make it more difficult to achieve the desirable goal of putting an end to violent conflict.

These last two arguments are pragmatic in character. Each holds that carving up the world conceptually by employing a concept of positive peace, is an impediment to achieving the goals we wish to achieve. But whatever the strengths of these arguments, they each depend on defining positive peace as including the presence of justice, a definition I have rejected, and, in fact, these arguments are part of the reason for such a rejection. If the achievement of justice is seen as a likely but contingent outcome of positive peace, rather than as one of its defining conditions, the two arguments lose their force. Adversarial nations may not have a just relationship, nor even agree on a substantive notion of justice, but that does not stand in the way of their establishing mechanisms for nonviolently resolving their conflicts. Only by adversary nations making use of such mechanisms, whether or not they agree on a notion of justice, would they come to realize what justice between them amounted to, and be able to achieve justice in their relationship.

But I want to focus not on rebutting pragmatic arguments against adopting a positive concept of peace, but on presenting pragmatic arguments for adopting such a concept, and in so doing make connection with my theme about better understanding the post-cold-war world. To help in this, let me remind you of Plato's discussion of pleasure in the *Republic*. If we imagine a midpoint between pleasure and pain, Plato suggests, we can see that what most people regard as pleasure, namely, bodily pleasure, is really only the process of removing the pain of bodily deprivation, that is, the process of moving from pain to the absence of pain at the midpoint. But pain soon returns. In contrast, intellectual pleasure is a truer and more enduring form of pleasure, because it does not arise out of a state of pain, but is a process of movement beginning at the midpoint and rising to a state of full unalloyed pleasure. What most people call pleasure is simply the absence of pain, not genuine pleasure. We may call this Plato's concept of positive pleasure. My argument for a positive concept of peace is analogous to Plato's argument for a positive concept of pleasure. What most people call peace is simply the cessation of violent conflict, as what most people call pleasure is simply the cessation of pain. But the mere cessation of violent conflict is invariably followed, sooner or later, by its resumption, as the sad history of human warfare tells us, just as bodily satiation is followed again by the pain of deprivation. If we regard pleasure as the mere absence of pain, Plato tells us, we will never know enduring pleasure. Likewise, if we regard peace as the mere absence of violent conflict, we will never know enduring peace. Only if we establish mechanisms for the nonviolent resolution of conflict, can we have any assurance that violent conflict will not return. For Plato it was its enduringness that made intellectual pleasure the true form of pleasure. For us it is the enduringness of positive peace that makes it the appropriate concept of peace. For Plato, the reasons were metaphysical: the closer to the eternal and the unchanging something is, the truer it is. For us, the reasons are pragmatic: the more enduring peace is, the greater value or usefulness it has.

How does all of this relate to our understanding the post-cold-war world? The cold war, as its name suggests, was peace only in a negative sense. The United States and the Soviet Union remained implacable foes, negotiating only on the periphery of their differences. There was no real effort to resolve the basic conflict between them. This was not accidental. Nuclear weapons enforced this state of negative peace, and, indeed, kept the peace from becoming anything more than negative. Nuclear deterrence forestalled efforts to achieve substantial levels of cooperation between the superpowers. As Daniel Farrell has argued, nuclear weapons make international relations more like a Hobbesian state of nature, in that nuclear weapons establish a kind of equality of power among nations (in particular, those nations standing in a relationship of Mutual Assured Destruction or MAD), because such nations are equally capable of destroying one another.[4] Such equality is characteristic, in Thomas Hobbes's view, of individuals in the state of nature, but is not generally characteristic of nations, because conventional military power varies so widely among them. The vulnerability of nuclear antagonists to mutual destruction and the belief of each that it is preserved from destruction only by its own apocalyptic nuclear threats against the other create a climate in which enmity is seen as inescapable and lawlessness is seen as avoidable only through the maintenance of the threats. In this way, the cold war made positive peace seem impossible. At the same time, many saw nuclear weapons as very effective enforcers of negative peace, so that negative peace came to be regarded by some as all that was necessary.

Thus, with the end of the cold war, we are coming out of a time in which nations, the superpowers at least, perceived negative peace as peace simpliciter. Negative peace was seen as all that could be achieved, and perhaps as all that needed to be achieved. The nuclear peace did provide a certain level of stability in world affairs, which is why some regarded it as all the peace that was necessary. Now, with the end of the nuclear standoff, negative peace no longer provides that level of stability, and in many places in the world things seem to be becoming unstuck. Worse, because of our forty-year addiction to a nuclear negative peace, we cannot conceive how anything more than negative peace is possible. Such blindness has not affected all of the world: events in South Africa, the Middle East, and Northern Ireland show that some have used the opportunity created by the end of the cold-war freeze in international relations to move decisively toward a state of positive peace. But the message needs to get through more clearly for the United States, which has been so long subject to nuclear addiction and the mistaken assumptions to which it led. The United States must be more willing, for example, to negotiate in genuine good faith, differences over the division of the international economic pie, and to make real use rather than merely self-interested token or symbolic use of international organizations such as the United Nations. Of course, moves in this direction are strongly opposed, especially by those on the political right, as being a surrender of sovereignty. Thus, it is misunderstandings about sovereignty, as well as misunderstandings about peace, that get in the way of positive peace. So, my discussion must turn to a consideration of sovereignty.

2. Sovereignty

The notion of sovereignty presents a puzzle. In this section I explore this puzzle and one possible solution to it. The puzzle struck me in thinking about the implications of an argument made by Jonathan Schell in *The Fate of the Earth*.[5] Schell suggests that nuclear weapons have made national sovereignty obsolete and that we ought to admit this and abandon sovereignty in favor of a world government. The puzzle is that while nuclear weapons are said by Schell to make sovereignty obsolete, the political realities of sovereignty are seen by him to be the main stumbling block to the abolition of the weapons. If sovereignty is obsolete, it should no longer be a stumbling block.

Let me put the puzzle in a more general form. On one side, the notion of sovereignty figures prominently in our descriptions of the global political situation. The stumbling block sovereignty is said to pose to efforts to deal with nuclear weapons is one example of this. To take another example, a natural characterization of the political changes in Eastern Europe accompanying the demise of the Soviet Union is that a number of national political communities have vigorously asserted, sometimes by force of arms, their sovereignty. Against this is the claim, on the other side, that, as a result of the contemporary realities of global affairs, national sovereignty has become irrelevant, an anachronistic notion. These realities include not just the existence of nuclear weapons, but more importantly the accelerating pace of global economic integration and the increasingly widespread and detrimental global impact of humans on our earth's natural environment. These factors are said to have made sovereignty obsolete by making it impossible for states to control the effect of the actions of others on their institutions and their citizens.

In recent decades, states have tried to respond to these sovereignty-undermining factors by entering into mutual agreements with other states in an effort to mitigate or to control the negative pressures from outside their borders, agreements which form the substance of international law. But these agreements themselves seem to represent a loss of sovereignty. Because they involve states binding themselves in various ways, and hence partially losing control of their future actions, international agreements appear to exchange one form of constraint for another. Such exchanges may be in the states' best interest overall, but sovereignty seems to be lost in either case.

Thus, the notion of sovereignty seems continually important and at the same time increasingly irrelevant to an understanding of world affairs. From one perspective, sovereignty seems an enduring force in international relations, while from another perspective, its force seems spent. This is the puzzle. Before launching into the substance of my attempt to resolve it, I should make it clear that I am intending to speak at the descriptive rather than the prescriptive level. That is, I am trying to determine whether the notion of sovereignty is adequate in helping us to describe the realities in contemporary international affairs. I am not directly concerned with the question whether sovereignty ought to be retained. To make clear this difference, I should point out that there is an alternative way to understand Schell's argument. When he claims that nuclear weapons have made sovereignty obsolete, he might have meant not that these weapons have made sovereignty less descriptively adequate, but that they have made sovereignty less prescriptively adequate. It might mean that sovereignty is less morally defensible as a principle for organizing power; it is not empirically obsolete, but morally obsolete. Whatever Schell meant, there is a clear sense in which nuclear weapons and, to a greater degree, global economic integration and environmental impact have made the notion of sovereignty descriptively inadequate, and thus the puzzle remains at the descriptive level. I would not, defend the view that the descriptive and the prescriptive are completely independent of each other, but I have chosen to focus on the descriptive end of the descriptive/prescriptive continuum.

What is sovereignty? Paraphrasing a classic definition offered by John Austin, one can say that a state has sovereignty when there is a group in that state that the citizens of that state obey and that does not obey anyone else, inside or outside of the state. Such a group is the sovereign. The sovereign commands and is uncommanded. This reveals a divide in the theory of sovereignty: there is sovereignty *in* the state, the fact that the sovereign commands, and there is sovereignty *of* the state, the fact that the sovereign is uncommanded. The former may be referred to as internal sovereignty and the latter as external sovereignty. Internal sovereignty is power over others; external sovereignty is independence from interference by others. Most importantly, sovereignty, according to the traditional Hobbesian understanding, is *unlimited*. That is, if a group is sovereign, there is no other group, inside the state or out, which can limit that group in its internal exercise of power or in its external independence. The implication is that sovereignty, like pregnancy, is an all-or-nothing matter, that there is no such thing as partial sovereignty. It is this sense of sovereignty that generates the puzzle, for it seems to preclude our saying, as we might be inclined to say, that the contemporary global situation is one in which states have partially lost their sovereignty. Either there is a group at the head of the government of a state with unlimited power and independence, or there is not.

Some people would reject the idea that sovereignty involves the notion of unlimited power and independence. While acknowledging the role of the notion of unlimitedness in the historical definition of sovereignty, they would maintain that that definition long ago became irrelevant to the realities of power distribution in society. Instead, what people now mean by the term "sovereignty" is simply the power and that independence, however partial, that the central government of a state actually enjoys. On this view, my puzzle is itself anachronistic, nothing more than a confirmation of the wisdom of shifting the definition in this way. This may be a correct observation about how the term is in fact usually used, but it ought not to be used in this way. For unlimitedness distinguishes the specific notion of internal sovereignty from its genus, the notion of power, and unlimitedness distinguishes the specific notion of external sovereignty from its genus, independence. Thus, if this characteristic is abandoned, it is not clear why we need the notion of sovereignty at all. Why not then just talk about power and independence? In any case, I treat the concept of sovereignty as involving unlimitedness, and see if the puzzle with sovereignty so understood can be resolved. If it can be resolved we need not abandon the traditional definition and there is still room for the traditional concept of sovereignty, despite the contemporary realities of power distribution.

My concern is external sovereignty, the independence of the state in the context of the international community. The puzzle is a puzzle of external sovereignty; it concerns the question of a state's, and its sovereign's, independence from outside interference. But a similar problem arises regarding internal sovereignty, and theorists of sovereignty have made distinctions relevant to the solution of this problem. The problem in the case of internal sovereignty is that the power of sectors of civil society, most obviously the economic sectors, seems to have deprived government of the unlimited power that is the hallmark of internal sovereignty. Partly in response to this problem, theorists of sovereignty have distinguished between different types of sovereignty. Consider, for example, that there are laws a government lacks the power to enforce because, should they be enacted, they would be systematically ignored or disobeyed by the citizens. This suggests that we should distinguish between two types of sovereignty, legal sovereignty, which belongs to the government, and political sovereignty, which belongs to the people. More generally, there may be different types of sovereignty, located in different groups in society. The suggestion is not that we replace the notion of legal sovereignty with some other sort of sovereignty, but rather that we recognize that sovereignty is of different kinds. The different types of sovereignty are based on different types of power. This opens the possibility, despite the wide distribution of power in society, that a particular type of power may be held by a particular group in an unlimited way. Thus, the government may hold legal power in an unlimited way, and hence have legal sovereignty, in the traditional sense in which sovereignty involves the holding of unlimited power.

Consider again external sovereignty, which, on the traditional view, requires unlimited independence. The contemporary reality of international life is that there are actions taken by actors outside the state, that result in significant interference with the activities of individuals or institutions of that state. It is primarily through such actions that the independence of states is diminished, and it is through the growing number and efficacy of such actions, resulting especially from economic integration and environmental impact, that claims of unlimited independence are so obviously an illusion. So, the puzzle is, how can we speak of external sovereignty, understood as unlimited independence, in the face of this reality? The solution is to make a distinction, analogous to the one discussed above regarding internal sovereignty, between different types of independence, hence different types of external sovereignty. Most importantly, there is legal independence, which may remain unlimited even as other forms of independence decline. When legal independence is unlimited, the state has external legal sovereignty. Thus, external sovereignty, specifically, external legal sovereignty, can co-exist with loss of independence, so long as the type of independence lost is not legal independence.

Someone might object that, because states often take legal action in response to outside influences, as in the adoption of certain trade policies to counter foreign competition, legal independence is an illusion. But this is a mistake. The state retains the legal freedom to choose the form of response or not to respond at all. A domestic analogy makes this clear. A person normally retains individual autonomy, despite the fact that his or her actions are often in response to the impositions of others. But this analogy also suggests the limits to legal independence. In the individual case, if the imposition on the part of others grows too great, as in the gunman's "your money or your life," we regard it as coercive, resulting in a loss of the threatened party's autonomy. Likewise, when external pressures on a state grow too great, its legal independence is forfeited in substance, even if the forms of legal independence are retained. This is likely the case today with some third-world nations under economic pressure from the West.

One piece of the argument remains. Can external legal sovereignty be said to hold in the light of the existence of international law? As suggested earlier, there is an obvious connection between the growth in international law and the growth in the level of external pressures to which states are subject. The connection seems to be that states enter into international agreements in order to mitigate the outside pressure. States, by agreeing to provisions of international law, choose to create certain constraints on their own behavior, in order to reduce the external pressures, by getting other states to likewise constrain their behavior. Such agreements, in other words, exchange nonlegal constraints for legal constraints. But when a state is under legal constraints, it seems that its legal independence would be reduced, hence its external legal sovereignty annulled. I cannot in the brief space available do justice to this challenge, but simply point out that on one prominent view, international law differs from domestic or municipal law in that international law is a system dependent on recognition and agreement on the part of the parties it binds. On this view, international law, a form of agreement law, is not a denial of a state's legal sovereignty, but is rather an exercise of that sovereignty. This view is strengthened by consideration of the nature of the sanction consequent to the violation of international law. Instead of the normally coercive formal punishment of municipal law, there exists only informal, often unorganized, normally less than coercive reprisals on the part of other nations. But should the sanction rise to the point of coercion, however informal, it would indeed amount to a loss of legal sovereignty on the part of states.

This brings me to my final point, an attempt to consider the implications of the above for our understanding of the post-cold-war world. The virtue of the account I have offered is that it recognizes that state independence must be charted in at least two dimensions rather than one. Thus, I have distinguished legal independence from other types of independence. This provides a two-dimensional model for how states hold on to and lose independence, in contrast with a model that would see the loss of independence as gradual erosion in a single dimension. The advantage of the two-dimensional model is that it shows how states can exercise some control over the diminution of their independence, at least control over the form that diminution takes. In particular, as I argued above, states' retention and exercise of legal sovereignty allows them to trade the disorganized constraints from outside for the organized self-constraints of international agreements, the latter constraints being on the whole less burdensome. The contrast between these two models bears, I think, on what the future may hold. On the one-dimensional model, the expectation would be for an unorganized erosion of state independence to a chaotic mix of external power centers, a vision which supports the so-called "coming state of anarchy" in global political affairs. On the two-dimensional model, we may be more sanguine in our expectations. Eroding state independence can be largely orchestrated by the state itself in virtue of its retention of legal sovereignty in such a way as to foster the growth of world order through an expanding international treaty regime. This may lead eventually, when the constraints begin to become generally coercive, to a proto-world government. But whether or not the constraints develop to this extent, the fact that the constraints will take the form of international law means that the world will be a safer place. It will be safer because the extent of international law is reflective of the extent to which nations are in the habit of, and have available to them the means of, adjudicating their conflicts. In other words, the extent of international law is indicative of the opportunities available to achieve positive peace. Thus, the understanding of sovereignty I have outlined shows that the achievement of positive peace is within our grasp. It shows how we can in our post-cold-war future, despite the current chaos and uncertainty, achieve not only peace in our time, but peace in our children's time as well.

Notes

1. Ronald J. Glossop, *Confronting War* (Jefferson, N.C.: McFarland, 2nd ed., 1987), p. 10.

2. *Ibid.*

3. *Ibid.,* p. 19.

4. Daniel Farrell, "Hobbes and International Relations: the War of All against All," in *The Causes of Quarrel,* ed. Peter Caws (Boston: Beacon, 1989), pp. 64-77.

5. Jonathan Schell, *The Fate of the Earth* (New York: Avon Books, 1982).

SECTION III

DAY-TO-DAY PEACEMAKING FOR A JUST FUTURE

INTRODUCTION

Day-to-day peacemaking, even more than international and national peace-making efforts, entails a connection to social justice. Although social justice concerns are often analyzed in terms of personal and group moral rights and responsibilities, an analysis of social justice issues in terms of peacemaking requires a broader perspective. At times, this broader perspective takes on the form of a utopian vision of a just, peaceful society. At other times, it is expressed as a recognition and response to injustice that does not attempt an articulation of justice (distributive or otherwise).

As each of the chapters in Section III illustrates, day-to-day peacemaking requires a personal response. The response is mediated through an individual's relationship with others and an individual's capacity for action. At times, the day-to-day peacemaking becomes a model for global peacemaking. As Marilyn Fischer details, Jane Addams, for instance, used the daily tasks of women as both a model and a rallying cry for international social justice efforts as part of the peace process. In another chapter, Laura Duhan Kaplan argues that even everyday peacemaking needs to be critically assessed both internally and externally. The methods of philosophy, then, can help us to reconsider our daily activity and situate it within the larger picture for peace. They can also be used to analyze critically our current social justice and peacemaking activity. This later role of philosophy might help ensure the integrity and autonomy of all participants in the peacemaking process.

Similarly, as many of the chapters in this section point out, the methods of international and national peacemaking might be aptly applied to day-to-day conflict in need of peacemaking. Alison Bailey examines the power and politics of language of race while Sally J. Scholz and Ron Hirschbein each address the relation between global peacemaking required by war or other international conflict, and the peacemaking needed in local communities to combat verbal violence and gang warfare. Although we must recognize that such analogies between local and global conflict break down at some point, we ought not to overlook the potential to learn from each other as peacemakers, whether our focus is international or limited to the immediate community. We should also be cautioned not to overlook nontraditional and non-Western sources for knowledge about peacemaking and from peacemakers. As Gail M. Presbey points out, canonical philosophy has been remiss in its dismissal of African sources of peacemaking wisdom. The sages and queen mothers are peacemakers in their local communities and their insights into peacemaking provide a fuller, more vivid picture of the process of conflict resolution that also ensures the dignity of all parties in conflicts.

Section III opens with a theoretical call for day-to-day peacemaking. According to Fischer in "Jane Addams's Pragmatist Pacifism," Addams believed that international peacemaking was only a reality when concern for social justice accompanied it. After a brief discussion of the four stages of evolutionary ethics, Fischer presents Addams's unique blend of pragmatism and feminism. Addams's goal is to achieve a "new humanitarianism" that expands the moral domain of social democracy from the local level to the international level. This is achieved, in part, when individuals extend the sympathetic understanding they experience toward their neighbors to a broader social realm. Women in the early part of the twentieth century were situated to do that. Fischer offers, by way of example, the international food needs after World War I. As she states,

> Addams saw meeting international food needs as a channel through which the idealism and self-sacrifice that war generates could be turned to positive account....Addams wanted to use food as the medium for linking women's daily activity and affection to their understanding of and contribution to international needs.

In other words, daily activity was to serve as a model for global activity. Women traditionally meet the food needs of their family, friends, and neighbors. Addams's goal was to get women to perceive distant peoples with the same compassion with which they served those who were near.

This chapter sets the foundation for chapters that follow, in that it illustrates the need to see localized social justice activity as not only important but necessary to peacemaking efforts globally. In the next chapter Kaplan draws on some of the insights that come from the day-to-day activity of mothers. In her chapter, "Mothering as a Motivation for Pacifism: Theorizing from Inside and Out," Kaplan approaches an account of mothering as the basis for pacifism from two perspectives. The first is the view from within the experience, while the second examines the social construction of motherhood. Kaplan's phenomenological analysis of mothering specifies the aspects of the experience that might inform a peacemaking perspective. On the other hand, a critical analysis of the social construction of motherhood results in a realization that motherhood might also support a militarist, sexist, and racist society. Kaplan's conclusion draws on both perspectives claiming that motherhood might best be linked to pacifism insofar as the emotional experience of motherhood is tempered by the critical realization of social influences that sustain unjust social orders.

Drawing on the wisdom that comes with experience, Presbey's "Contemporary African Sages and Queen Mothers: Their Leadership Roles in Conflict Resolutions," illustrates another aspect of day-to-day peacemaking and encourages a cross-cultural examination of peacemaking. Presbey uses the stories of contemporary sages and queen mothers in Kenya and Ghana in arguing that theoretical and practical accounts of peacemaking have much to learn from the experience and practice of community conflict resolution in

Africa. The sage, a person who uses his or her "wisdom and insight for the ethical benefit of the community," embodies wisdom, intelligence, compassion, and reflection, while also serving as a moral role model for the community. These character traits are used in the *art* of conflict resolution. As Presbey notes, conflict resolution is an *art* rather than a *science* because successful mediation cannot be systematically taught. It is a subtle practice to which a person is drawn because of his or her gifts, and compassion for the members of the community. Presbey's chapter is important both because it focuses on interpersonal conflict resolution as peacemaking and because it challenges us to look beyond traditional Western philosophy for theoretical and practical models of peacemaking. It is also interesting to note the connection between the more practically-oriented chapters of Fischer, Kaplan, and Presbey and Joseph C. Kunkel's account in Section I, of the ethics of care as a theoretical model for peacemaking.

The final three chapters of the book make use of military analogies as a means of gaining insight into peacemaking, in order to respond to social injustice. In "Catcalls and Military Strategy," Scholz offers a framework for responding to some of the daily violence of sexism. Her argument is grounded on an analogy between the dehumanization that occurs as part of military strategy in war and the dehumanization that results from verbal violence. Both forms of dehumanization involve a sort of name-calling that labels the recipient of the call as a "morally inferior object." This labeling facilitates the ease with which violence may be inflicted on the so-named object. Verbal violence is part of the training for war and plays a similar role in social injustice or oppression. Scholz uses this analysis to propose a pacifist response to catcalls and similar forms of verbal violence.

"Race-Making as the Process of Enmification," by Bailey, examines arbitrary race-making social practices to expose the privilege that must be renounced for a real response to racial injustice to occur. The dominant group in society, Bailey argues, creates the racial distinctions. The classification of peoples into A and not-A, or white and nonwhite, arbitrarily creates a dominant or "norm" class opposed by a subordinate or morally inferior class. As Bailey points out, this process of enmification is not unlike the dehumanization of war. Like Scholz, Bailey then illustrates the ease with which violence and privilege are justified. Both these papers reveal the importance of examining the politics and power of language in our peacemaking and social justice efforts.

Similar to the two previous chapters, the final chapter in this volume draws on a militarist analogy and challenges our understanding of violence. In "Gangs and Nations: Parallels and Analogies," Hirschbein argues that there are numerous significant parallels between the motivation and activity of gangs, and that of nations or militaries. Hirschbein concludes that recognizing these parallels may assist our peacemaking efforts on the local level of gang politics as well as the international or interstate level. A clearer understanding of the pathos of gangbanging may enlighten our current conceptions of international conflict. Hirschbein makes use of first-person narratives from both military personnel and gang members. This method provides the reader with a conduit through which to view the emotional and psychological intensity of gang and military activity.

Section III emphasizes the many practical and theoretical challenges peacemakers confront. As philosophers and citizens, our attempts at peacemaking reach beyond ourselves and must not be stunted by inactivity. We daily face new threats to justice, personal integrity, and peace. The role of the peacemaker is to think, to feel, and to act. Our hope, in compiling these chapters, is that as we struggle to elucidate the activity of peacemaking we also endorse the activist community of peacemakers and continue to offer support, insight, and challenge.

Thirteen

JANE ADDAMS'S PRAGMATIST PACIFISM

Marilyn Fischer

Pacifism, political and industrial reform, and neighborhoods that nourish bodies and spirits are deeply interwoven in Jane Addams's vision of social democracy. Peace in international relations and peacemaking in daily activities are intimately connected and mutually supportive. I first briefly explain Addams's pragmatism and evolutionary theory of ethics, which provide a theoretical framework, and then describe how, for Addams, pacifism and day-to-day peacemaking are both integral to enacting social democracy.

1. Pragmatism and Evolutionary Ethics

Addams's philosophical commitments place her clearly within the classical American pragmatist tradition.[1] She was especially close to John Dewey, who served as a trustee of Hull House. Concrete experience and sympathetic understanding are foundational to Addams's philosophy. She founded Hull House as a pragmatist test, believing that the meaning and validity of her ideas could only be determined through concrete experience.[2] Addams writes, "A man who takes the betterment of humanity for his aim and end must also take the daily experiences of humanity for the constant correction of his process."[3] All through her writings, Addams tests ideas and concepts by their actual enactment in concrete experience, showing, for example, how inadequate it is to use the franchise as the measure of equality,[4] or to describe labor contracts as voluntary agreements between equals.[5] Similarly, Addams criticizes wealthy philanthropists, stating that because they lack the knowledge that can only be obtained by living with the poor, their altruism embodies a form of contempt.[6] With other pragmatists, Addams sees no division between reason and emotion; both are needed for understanding and for effective social action. Affections are shaped through daily interactions with individuals in all their quirks. Affection, guided by reason, leads to "sympathetic knowledge," which Addams calls "the only way of approach to any human problem."[7] Progress toward social justice requires that both social sentiments and social institutions be reshaped. Either alone will be ineffective.[8] Addams, like so many of her time, views human history in evolutionary terms, and includes ethical change in this pattern. As society evolves, so ethical ideals and codes should be adapted to fit the prevalent mode of social organization. Addams refers to four stages in ethical history.

The first stage she calls primitive, and associates it with instincts for security from attack and starvation,[9] instincts to respond with kindliness to neighbors' needs,[10] and to feed children and the helpless.[11] Some of these instincts are biological, shared by humans and animals;[12] others emerge historically. For example, Addams writes about how the instinct to feed children and the helpless came about one million years before the instinct for mass fighting.[13] These are powerful sentiments; in working for social change, these instincts should not be erased, but should be treasured and reshaped to meet the needs of the current age.

The next stage Addams names "individual ethics" and associates it with social contract theory and the natural rights tradition, which she refers to as eighteenth-century philosophy. The tradition's central character, natural man, she views as a highly abstract, lopsidedly rational apparition.[14] Although thinkers in this tradition conceive of ethics as universal and egalitarian, Addams criticizes its conception of ethical obligation as hierarchical and patriarchal.[15]

The third stage is social ethics, or social democracy. Addams views the city as a densely interconnected social organism. All persons and all social classes are equally and reciprocally interdependent; we need to reshape political, economic, and social institutions to reflect this interdependency. Our ethical values and codes should accord with this. In all of her work–at Hull House, and in national and international affairs–Addams aimed to "provide the channels in which the growing moral force of [people's] lives shall flow."[16] Addams's goal is a society in which all persons' creative potential can flourish, in which all may benefit from the goods of social living, and all may contribute.

The final stage Addams calls a new humanitarianism. This is the expansion of social democracy from neighborhoods and cities to the international level. As evidence that this stage is beginning to dawn, Addams points to international cooperative efforts to control diseases, to international postage services, and so on. But the strongest evidence of this new humanitarianism she finds in the daily interactions of her Hull House neighbors, representing, in 1889, eighteen nationalities, some of them from regions with historic animosities. In that squalid urban setting, Addams sees her neighbors working out cosmopolitan relations with sympathetic understanding. In this sturdy, concrete, daily evidence, Addams senses that "the modern world is developing an almost mystic consciousness of the continuity and interdependence of mankind."[17]

2. Addams's Pacifism in *Newer Ideals of Peace*

I develop Addams's arguments for pacifism in two parts: the first based on her 1906 book, *Newer Ideals of Peace*, and the second based on her writings during and after World War I. The two parts are continuous in terms of theory, although they differ in emphasis, as Addams's involvements moved from social and industrial amelioration in Chicago, to direct involvement with peace organizations and international institutions. This sequence illustrates how, for Addams, peacemaking efforts are knit into daily activities, and peace among nations is a clear and close extension of a just peace within neighborhoods, cities, and nations.

A glance down the table of contents of *Newer Ideals of Peace* reveals this is not a straight-forward antiwar tract. There are chapters on industrial legislation, the labor movement, and the importance of utilizing immigrants and women in city government. Addams presents the book as a direct response to William James's challenge to find a "moral equivalent of war." James was impressed with how war fosters manly, heroic virtues, in contrast to the insipid tone of peaceful, social evolution. To maintain these manly virtues James proposes to conscript the nation's young men and engage them in a fight against Nature as his moral equivalent of war.[18] Addams knew, from her own personal experience, and saw in the lives of other young people that women and men needed to participate widely in life, and contribute to the greater good. Addams agrees with James's crucial insight that people need to involve themselves in projects that call upon heroism, courage, and self-sacrifice, but that these virtues need to be redirected to peaceful ends.

The purpose of the book, Addams writes, is to suggest "newer, more aggressive ideals of peace."[19] Addams criticizes Leo Tolstoy's pacifism as a weak, dovelike creed.[20] She defines peace this way: "It is no longer merely absence of war, but the unfolding of life processes which are making for a common development."[21] Adopting a pacifist creed is inefficacious, without also working for deep changes in sentiments, institutions, and daily patterns of living.[22]

Her critique goes far beyond James. Rather than simply redirecting militarism from human blood to Nature, Addams sees militarism itself as the problem. Attaining peace requires that militarism, deeply embedded in social structures, behavior patterns, and emotional responses, be replaced with social democracy.

Addams's standard method of analysis is to point out how the institutions, opinions, and emotional responses of the day contain within them unhelpful strains from previous stages of ethical evolution, resulting in "maladjustment." For example, instincts of tribal loyalty from the primitive stage still persist into the present, making war analogous to school-yard bullying. The time for such adolescent bravado is long past.[23] Ideals from the stage of individual ethics sustain continued militarism in society. The individualism of John Locke and the rationalism of Immanuel Kant keep their distance from concrete experience and sympathetic understanding. Militarism in political and economic institutions is maintained because the enlightenment ideals which underlie them are "untouched by that worldly wisdom which counsels us to know life as it is."[24]

Addams sees this pattern in industry. Industry itself is a vast, organic social web, requiring intricate coordination of large numbers of people. This indicates that industry is ripe for social democracy. Yet, the patterns of capitalism, which concentrate ownership and decision-making in the hands of a few, are militaristic holdovers from the stage of individual ethics. Addams states this connection explicitly:

> Society regarded machinery as the absolute possession of the man who owned it at the moment it became a finished product, quite irrespective of the long line of inventors and workmen who represented its gradual growth and development....The possessor of the machine, like the possessor of arms who preceded him, regards it as a legitimate weapon for exploitation, as the former held his sword.[25]

Addams sees clearly the relation between capitalism and war, stating, "Unrestricted commercialism is an excellent preparation for governmental aggression."[26]

Addams was similarly troubled by developments in organized labor. She was strongly sympathetic to labor unions. Many unions held organizing meetings at Hull House; Addams was called upon frequently to negotiate labor disputes. She interprets the international labor movement as embodying a universal call for justice, and thus an indication of social democracy. Yet she was critical of organized labor as still embodying some militarism. She pointed to structural antagonism between labor and management, to labor's tendency to be more concerned with "fleshpots" rather than justice, and to increases in racial and class animosity that accompanied strikes as blacks and more recent immigrants were brought in as strike-breakers.[27] Before peace can be attained, these elements of militarism needed to be replaced.

In *Newer Ideals of Peace*, Addams's moral equivalent of war is "the new industrialism." This suggests changes far more encompassing than James's conscripts fighting against Nature. Addams welcomes industrialization, the diversity and tempo of city life. But there is much work to be done to bring social democracy to industry and civic affairs.

Addams finds her model for peace in the concrete experience of her immigrant neighbors. Together they go through the details of daily life—feeding their children, looking for work, dealing with garbage, disability, and death. Torn from their roots as rural European peasants, living at the edge of survival, Addams sees in them "unusual mental alertness."[28] Addams does not romanticize her neighbors; she readily acknowledges they possess a full range of human strengths and failings.

> It is not that they are shouting for peace–on the contrary, if they shout at all, they will continue to shout for war–but that they are really attaining cosmopolitan relations through daily experience.... [A]ll of the time, below their shouting, they are living in the kingdom of human kindness. They are laying the simple and inevitable foundations for an international order....[29]

Addams finds in her neighbors' daily interactions, patterns for peace that civic, industrial, national, and international relations would be wise to adopt.

In *Newer Ideals of Peace* Addams links women's potential contributions to peace to their involvement in civic and industrial affairs. As an argument for woman's suffrage, Addams states that women need this involvement in order to carry out their traditional responsibilities. Addams's argument is no call to woman as Victorian mother, ensconced in the household caring for her children. Addams understands women's traditional work anthropologically. In previous eras women were deeply involved in economic productive activity, and "women's work" included planting, harvesting, threshing, and weaving, in addition to nurturing the young and caring for the sick and the old. As industrialization moved more of these activities out of the household and into the factory, a woman's control of her family's well-being moved progressively out of her hands. Addams views city governance as enlarged housekeeping: caring for sewers, garbage disposal, food and water sanitation, building codes. All of these are modern, urban versions of traditional women's work.[30]

Women need to be involved in civic and industrial affairs, both because they have had centuries of experience with the daily details of providing for their families, and because in being excluded, they lose the educative effects of such participation.[31] This is a pragmatist account, with women's potential contributions to society understood in terms of what women actually do, and what they could do, day by day. Because of her critique of the enlightenment tradition and its vocabulary of rights, Addams does not frame her advocacy for women in terms of equal rights. And while Addams certainly hoped women's civic and industrial involvements would improve matters, she differed from those at the time who claimed that women's participation in public affairs would have an automatically civilizing effect. In *The Second Twenty Years at Hull House*, reflecting back on her work for woman's suffrage, Addams agrees with G. K. Chesterton in saying, "Many people have imagined that feminine politics would be merely pacifist or humanitarian or sentimental. The real danger of feminine politics is too much of a masculine policy."[32] Hierarchical relations among women troubled Addams. Because these relations are not based on sympathetic understanding and reciprocity, they are undemocratic and often exploitive. Addams saw how many culturally idolized Victorian mothers could be Victorian mothers precisely because they exploited other women–Addams's neighbors, primarily African Americans and recent immigrants–as domestic servants.[33] She points out the irony of middle class charity workers, themselves economically dependent women, urging her women neighbors to work toward self-sufficiency.[34] Pacifism as day-to-day peacemaking includes bringing relations among women into accord with social democracy. The link between pacifism and day-to-day peacemaking is clear in Addams's adaptation of the prophet Isaiah's famous quote. Addams concludes *Newer Ideals of Peace,*

> [Isaiah] contended that peace could be secured only as men abstained from the gains of oppression and responded to the cause of the poor; that swords would finally be beaten into plowshares and pruning-hooks, not because men resolved to be peaceful, but because all the metal of the earth would be turned to its proper use when the poor and their children should be abundantly fed.[35]

3. Pacifism and the First World War

Addams wrote extensively on pacifism during and after the First World War, particularly in *Women at The Hague, Peace and Bread in Time of War,* appropriate sections from *The Second Twenty Years at Hull House,* and in innumerable speeches and articles. In these works Addams's pragmatist perspective from *Newer Ideals of Peace* is carried explicitly to the international level. People's ethical ideals and commitments, their understanding of daily activity, and their emotional responses, need to be matched to the current level and complexity of social organization. These connections can only be created through concrete experience and sympathetic understanding. Since in the early twentieth century, economic, social, and political problems were international in scope, people's understanding of their daily activities and their emotional sentiments would also need to be of inter-national scope.[36] Addams believed that we need to think and feel internationally about what we do every day.

Addams had been involved in peace groups long before war broke out in Europe in August 1914. She hesitated to take leadership in an exclusively women's peace organization, yet when Emmeline Pethick Lawrence, Rosika Schwimmer, and Carrie Chapman Catt implored her to lead a women's peace meeting in January 1915, she agreed, writing to a friend, "In this case the demand has been so universal and spontaneous over the country that it seemed to me best to take it up."[37] The Woman's Peace Party, which later became the United States branch of the Women's International League for Peace and Freedom, grew out of this meeting.[38]

In April 1915, Addams chaired the Women's International Congress at The Hague, a remarkable assembly of women from neutral and belligerent nations. Addams remarked that for women from warring nations to participate in the congress was "little short of an act of heroism. Even to appear to differ from those she loves in the hour of their affliction has ever been the supreme test of a woman's conscience."[39]

Many women in these organizations believed that women have an inherently pacifist nature, and thus their responsibility and effectiveness regarding world peace issue from their natural, nurturing femininity. Some of Addams's statements seem to reflect these sentiments. In her 1915 address to the organizing conference of the Woman's Peace Party, Addams stated, "I do not assert that women are better than men...but we would all admit that there are things concerning which women are more sensitive than men, and that one of these is the treasuring of life."[40] In her account of the 1915 International Conference of Women at The Hague, Addams writes,

> [S]o women, who have brought men into the world and nurtured them until they reach the age for fighting, must experience a peculiar revulsion when they see them destroyed, irrespective of the country in which these men may have been born.

She adds,

> It was also said at the Congress that the appeals for the organization of the world upon peaceful lines may have been made too exclusively to reason and a sense of justice, that reason is only a part of the human endowment; emotion and deep-set racial impulses must be utilized as well–those primitive human urgings to foster life and to protect the helpless, of which women were the earliest custodians....[41]

Using these and similar statements, some writers have classified Addams with cultural feminists who regard women as having an innately pacifist, feminine nature.[42] Jean Bethke Elshtain states this explicitly:

> Addams's is a sophisticated statement of women as pacific Other, a variant on the Beautiful Soul, which she attempts to ground historically and anthropologically and to bring to bear on public discourse...presuming, for example, that the extension of suffrage to women would automatically humanize governments.[43]

However, Addams's statements are better understood in light of her pragmatism and commitment to social democracy, with day-to-day peacemaking a central part of that commitment. It is true that Addams uses the language of primitive instincts, but she does not restrict the term to biological or innate characteristics; instincts can be acquired and carried by culture to future generations. Sometimes Addams does associate with women instincts to feed and care for the helpless. But these statements need to be understood within her pragmatist framework. Addams knows well that human history has been heavily gendered, and that the concrete, daily experiences of women and men continue in this pattern. In the passage where she speaks of women experiencing revulsion when the sons they have nurtured die in battle, she makes an analogy to the revulsion an artist-soldier feels when ordered to destroy an architectural treasure.[44] Who we are and what we feel are shaped by what we do, through concrete, daily experience.

Addams values the caretaking women do, and believes this activity and its attendant emotional shaping are important to the process of establishing peace. Thus, women should participate fully in international affairs. This is not because women are "beautiful souls," or have an innately pacific nature; it is because of women's daily life patterns. This is parallel to Addams's frequent statements about how her impoverished Hull House neighbors in their daily lives had crafted patterns of understanding that cross tribal loyalties. Those working in international affairs could learn much from the lives and sympathies of those Addams calls "humble peoples."[45]

Addams does associate militarism with men. But again, this is based on their concrete, daily experiences of functioning in militaristic relations in commerce, industry, and politics, and not because they possess a sex-linked militaristic nature. Throughout Addams's writings there are many references to men repulsed by war's brutality, to women who have militaristic impulses, and to privileged women, who, with militaristic spirit, treat the poor with contempt.

Fundamental to Addams's opposition to the war was her commitment to bringing social democracy to the international arena, as well as to neighborhoods, cities, and nations. Traveling through Europe during and after the war, Addams witnessed war's brutality directly. She writes, "War itself destroys democracy wherever it thrives and tends to entrench militarism."[46] Using the perspective of evolutionary ethics, Addams explains how war reverses the slow, gradual process of fostering the tolerance, understanding, and affection upon which genuine consent, and hence, genuine democracy, must be based. Primitive impulses of kindliness and pity for the helpless are "burned away"; divisions based on exclusive tribal loyalty are exacerbated.[47] In this light the whole notion of war making "the world safe for democracy" is an oxymoron. Regardless of how noble a nation's initial reasons for entering war may have been, they are quickly forgotten, as subsequent atrocities become justification for continuing the brutality.[48] Addams charts how this backward evolution continues long after the hostilities officially cease. She links the continuing war mentality, reinforced by the sour aftermath of the Bolshevik revolution, to setbacks in child labor legislation, protection of civil liberties, and other attempts at social reform.[49]

During and after the war, Addams worked with Herbert Hoover's Department of Food Administration and the Friends Service Committee to find funding and food for the starving in Europe.[50] Addams saw meeting international food needs as a channel through which the idealism and self-sacrifice that war generates could be turned to positive account. These programs provided an opportunity to enlarge the scope of primitive instincts of care and tribal loyalty from the national to the global level. Addams saw food programs as potential sources for creating links of action and sympathetic understanding among people all over the world.

Addams particularly wanted to speak to women's groups; to feed the hungry, women's contributions were vital. Like others, she encouraged women to conserve their families' food carefully, to make more available for the starving in Europe. But her theoretical understanding of this involvement runs deep. Historically, women's concrete relation to food has been humane rather than commercial, to keep families alive, rather than as simply a commodity for profit.[51] Addams wanted to use food as the medium for linking women's daily activity and affection to their understanding of and contribution to international needs. Addams criticized the League of Nations for failing to take on meeting food needs as a central task. Instead of adopting this vital purpose through which great need and sustaining emotion could be joined, the League substituted instead the shorn, political rationalism of eighteenth century philosophy.[52]

In *Newer Ideals of Peace* a new industrialism built upon social democracy was Addams's proposed moral equivalent for war. During and after the war Addams focused her energies on creating organizations that could resolve international disputes and provide channels for international cooperation. In both her earlier and later writings international peace and daily activities are linked within her vision of social democracy, created through sympathetic understanding, and leading to a welcoming solidarity for all.

Notes

1. See Charlene Haddock Seigfried, *Pragmatism and Feminism* (Chicago: Chicago University Press, 1996), pp. 73-79.

2. Jane Addams, "A Function of the Social Settlement," in *On Education*, ed. Ellen Condliffe Lagemann (New Brunswick, N.J.: Transaction, 1994), p. 77.

3. Jane Addams, *Democracy and Social Ethics* (New York: Macmillan, 1907; reprint ed., Cambridge, Mass.: Harvard University Press, 1964), p. 176.

4. Jane Addams, *Philanthropy and Social Progress* (1893; reprint ed., Montclair, N.J.: Patterson Smith, 1970), p. 3.

5. Jane Addams, *Newer Ideals of Peace* (New York: Macmillan, 1906), pp. 41-43.

6. *Ibid.*, pp. 48-49.

7. Jane Addams, *A New Conscience and an Ancient Evil* (New York: Macmillan, 1912), p. 11.

8. Addams, *Newer Ideals*, pp. 8-9.

9. Jane Addams, *Peace and Bread in Time of War* (1922; reprint ed., New York: Garland, 1972), p. 202.

10. Addams, *Democracy,* pp. 19-20.

11. Addams, *Peace and Bread*, p. 75.

12. Jane Addams, Emily G. Balch, and Alice Hamilton, *Women at The Hague* (1915: reprint ed., New York: Macmillan, 1972), p. 130.

13. Addams, *Peace and Bread*, p. 75.

14. Addams, *Newer Ideals*, p. 60.

15. Marilyn Fischer, "Philanthropy and Injustice in Mill and Addams," *Nonprofit and Voluntary Sector Quarterly,* 24:4 (Winter 1995), p. 286.

16. Addams, *Democracy*, p. 152.

17. Jane Addams, *The Second Twenty Years at Hull House* (New York: Macmillan, 1930), p. 7.

18. William James, "The Moral Equivalent of War," in *Nonviolence in America: A Documentary History*, ed. Staughton Lynd and Alice Lynd (Maryknoll, N.Y.: Orbis, 1995), pp. 65-75.

19. Addams, *Newer Ideals*, p. 3.

20. *Ibid.*, pp. 3-4.

21. Jane Addams, "What Peace Means," in *Jane Addams on Peace, War, and International Understanding,* 1899-1932, ed. Allen F. Davis (New York: Garland, 1976), p. 11.

22. Jane Addams, "The New Internationalism," in *Jane Addams on Peace*, ed. Davis, p. 59.

23. Addams, *Newer Ideals*, p. 211.

24. *Ibid.,* p. 32.

25. *Ibid.*, p. 149.

26. *Ibid.*, p. 223.

27. Jane Addams, *A Modern Lear* (1912; reprint ed., Chicago: Jane Addams's Hull-House Museum, 1994), pp. 14-15, 22, 140 and 141.

28. *Ibid.,* p. 14.

29. *Ibid.*, p. 18.

30. *Ibid.*, pp. 183ff.

31. *Ibid.*, p. 184.

32. Addams, *Second Twenty Years*, p. 110.

33. Addams, *Democracy*, ch. 4.

34. *Ibid.*, ch. 2.

35. Addams, *Newer Ideals*, pp. 237-238.

36. Addams, *et al.*, *Women at The Hague*, pp. 135ff.

37. Quoted in Harriet Hyman Alonso, *Peace as a Women's Issue* (Syracuse, N.Y.: Syracuse University Press, 1993), p. 62.

38. See Alonso, *Peace as a Women's Issue;* and Carrie A. Foster, *The Women and the Warriors* (Syracuse, N.Y.: Syracuse University Press, 1995).

39. Addams, *et al.*, *Women at The Hague*, p. 125.

40. Addams, "What War is Destroying," p. 63.

41. Addams, *et al.*, *Women at The Hague*, pp. 128-130.

42. See Josephine Donovan, *Feminist Theory* (New York: Continuum, 1991), pp. 54-61; and C. Roland Marchand, *The American Peace Movement and Social Reform, 1898-1918* (Princeton, N.J.: Princeton University Press, 1972), ch. 6.

43. Jean Bethke Elshtain, *Women and War* (New York: Basic Books, 1987), p. 235.

44. Addams, *et al.*, *Women at The Hague*, p. 128.

45. Addams, *Peace and Bread*, pp.111ff; and Jane Addams, "War Times Challenging Woman's Traditions," in *Jane Addams on Peace*, ed. Davis, p. 136.

46. Addams, *et al.*, *Women at The Hague*, p. 77.

47. Addams, *Peace and Bread*, pp. 4 and 112.

48. Addams, *et al.*, *Women at The Hague*, p. 85.

49. Addams, *Second Twenty Years,* pp. 157ff.

50. Addams, *Peace and Bread*, ch. 4; and *Second Twenty Years,* ch. 5.

51. Addams, *Peace and Bread,* p. 82.

52. *Ibid.*, pp. 208ff.

Fourteen

MOTHERING AS A MOTIVATION FOR PACIFISM: THEORIZING FROM INSIDE AND OUT

Laura Duhan Kaplan

An old Jewish joke:

> A married couple with a troubled marriage comes to see the Rabbi. First, the husband tells the Rabbi his view of the problems and their causes. The Rabbi listens thoughtfully, and then says, "You're right!" The wife, angered by this, then tells her version. The Rabbi again listens carefully and says, "You're right!" An observer pulls the Rabbi aside and says, "Rabbi! You just told him he was right, and then you told her she was right. How can they both be right?" The Rabbi answered, "You know, you're right!"

In this chapter, I would like to let two opposing sides of a debate be right simultaneously. I shall evaluate the claim that mothering provides a good foundation for pacifism from both inside mothering and outside of mothering. The inside view will show that powerful emotions and the thoughts they stimulate can motivate mothers to work towards peace. The outside view will remind us, however, that emotions, including the emotions of mothering, are at least partially socially constructed. Since these emotions are constructed in a warist, racist, and sexist society, they pull mothers away from pacifist praxis. After presenting the inside and outside views, I suggest that pacifist mothers can be motivated by the inside view while at the same time critically evaluating their practice in light of the truths offered by the outside view.

1. Defining "Inside" and "Outside" Views

My conception of "inside" and "outside" views is strongly affected by phenomenological philosopher Paul Ricoeur's discussion in *Freud and Philosophy* of two types of hermeneutics, two approaches to interpreting texts and social practices.[1] Ricoeur calls the first hermeneutic a hermeneutic of "recollection" and the second a hermeneutic of "suspicion." A hermeneutic of recollection inspires an interpreter to remember that any social practice, no matter how bizarre it may seem to an outsider, has meaning for the practitioners. The interpreter's task is, first of all, to suspend amazement that anyone could be so naive as to accept uncritically (what appears to an outsider to be) the surface meaning of the practice. The interpreter's second task is to practice along with the practitioners and try to be moved by the meanings they find. Ricoeur's example of such a hermeneutic is the study of the phenomenology of religion, in which an investigator "believes with the believer" in order to understand the nature of the sacred. I call a view constructed through a hermeneutic of recollection an "inside" view because it presents the data of consciousness and because it represents the experiences of those involved in a practice. In this chapter, when I answer from "inside" mothering, I describe some of the profound changes in my philosophy of life that seem to have descended upon me since giving birth, as well as the connections I have made between these new views and the rationales for pacifism.

A hermeneutic of suspicion inspires an interpreter to assume that a practice has a meaning other than the one practitioners are aware of, a meaning that is invisible to the practitioners for important reasons. The interpreter's theory about why the true meaning of the practice is hidden from the practitioners provides a key that will crack the code of the self-deception, allowing practitioners to see whose interests are served by the masking of the truth and why. Ricoeur's examples of this kind of hermeneutic include Marxist theory, in which economic power relations color our conceptions of ourselves and the world; and Freudian theory, in which the instinctive motivations for our actions are hidden from our egoconsciousness. I call a view of a practice constructed using a hermeneutic of suspicion an "outside" view because, in denying the veracity of a person's conscious representation of the practice, it has to rely on correlations between aspects of the practice and material conditions. Further, such a view usually begins as a view articulated by observers situated outside of the practice. In this chapter, when I speak from "outside" mothering, I suggest that the meanings I ascribe to mothering are not inherent in mothering itself. Instead, powerful groups have defined mothering in ways which benefit them, and these definitions structure my experience of the practice. This challenges the claim that mothering can motivate women towards pacifism, as pacifism purports to be an ethical principle that orients people in the world. If the very things that ground my maternal pacifism are illusions, then my principles are not firmly grounded, and are subject to change through social manipulation. The key to cracking the code constructed by these social definitions of mothering comes from feminist and multicultural hermeneutics, the former influenced by a Marxist emphasis on deconstructing capitalist ideology.

Below I present an inside view and an outside view, and conclude by revising the inside view in response to the critique from outside.

2. A View from Inside Mothering

At the time of this writing, I have only been a mother for sixteen months (plus an expectant mother for nine), but already my metaphysical, ethical, and epistemological experiences are changing.

Less than twenty four hours after giving birth, I lay in bed with my newborn, bathed in afternoon sunlight and exhausted euphoria, and imagined the human race passing by on the sidewalk in front of my house. My imagination drew on the diagrams that show the evolution of hominids through the prehistoric eras, or the relative proportions of body parts through the human life cycle, with their drawings of the human body at various stages of uprightness, ascending and descending in height. I saw generations of humanity pass by simultaneously: children accompanied by the teenagers they become, the adults they mature into, the elders they become, and, again, the children they grandparent, all together in a steps and stairs parade. I saw that all humanity participates in the same parade, enmeshed in connections that are so trivial as to be meaningless to the observer but so basic as to set the very categories of experience for the participants. Now, when I look at a person, I see each one as a freeze frame in the parade of humanity; my mind's eye adds a family. I have come to realize that everybody is connected to others; at the very least, everyone is somebody's child.

For every person, there at least exists a mother, who, if she had the luxury of caring for them, learned from them about the fragility of life, the pain of hope, the possibility of a new relationship to the unknowns of life and the force we imagine controls them, God. I, who was brought up to believe, and do believe, that God helps those who help themselves, now know a new sense of helplessness, which, at its best moments, is transformed into wonder. Two weeks after giving birth I wrote the following short essay, which I called "When you wish upon a star."

Sometimes when I hold my two week old daughter against me after nursing her, we listen to the tape of lullaby songs my husband made for her. The nursery is semi-dark, we are semi-naked, I feel her skin against mine as she begins to doze, her face relaxing, her head drooping. Quietly, I sing along with the tape, barely whispering in her ear.

"If your heart is in your dreams/no request is too extreme/anything your heart desires/will come to you....When you wish upon a star/your dreams come true."

My eyes tear up and I sob quietly, being careful not to wake her or shake her.

Why do I cry? Perhaps because she is so precious, even though she's hardly anything or anyone yet. The mystery of it colors and scents my days, transforming the fragmented tedium of infant care chores into a peaceful routine.

But why does the song "When you wish upon a star" make me cry? The lyrics seem like one of those sweet lies we devise for children. Yet it seems now that my dreams have come true. I have my husband, my job, health, happiness, and now Hillary. Perhaps I cry because I don't know what the song says is true. Was my heart in my dreams? Does that mean I worked hard to make them come true? Does hard work make a difference? Or is it only a sweet lie that wishing makes it so?

And I cry because I don't know what I dare wish for Hillary. Even wishing that she grow up healthy over the next two years, that her development unfold normally, seems to be asking too much. What if it didn't happen? Of course, if it didn't happen, then the next wish would be that she perform to her capacity, that she be happy, and that my husband and I cope peacefully. Even that would be okay.

But as I think, "Even that would be okay," my eyes fill with tears again, my body shakes, my nose runs. I just cannot fathom the future–it is deep, deeper, deepest. I get a tiny vision of what it might look like for the three of us to be happy together and it hurts too much. I cry at my good fortune and at the fear of losing it, because all is fortuitous and fragile. Why is it so scary to hope?

Meanwhile, Hillary winks and blinks, cracks a smile, snorts, sighs, and snuggles against me. She is still learning how to fall asleep.

Am I crying tears of joy?

Sixteen months later, I truly do not know what kind of tears I was crying. Even the intense joys of mothering are gifts of grace which appear without warning on my daughter's person: her mischievous kiss, designed to divert me from disciplining her; her generous sharing of her toys with a (surprisingly, to her) disinterested cat; her systematic attempt to learn the difference between a cookie and a cracker. But my sense of helplessness in the face of the universe is balanced by a new self-mastery. Or perhaps it is the opposite of self-mastery, more like a letting go of self. Sara Ruddick writes that "a single, typical day [of mothering] can encompass fury, infatuation, boredom, and simple dislike."[2] Yet in the face of those feelings, there is a job to be done, the job of loving the object of those feelings. Is it possible to love someone who angers you, bores you, and makes you dislike them? Yes, if love becomes a practice, rather than a feeling. Yes, if love becomes what Immanuel Kant calls a "duty" rather than an "inclination."[3] This does not mean I do not enjoy loving: sometimes I do, sometimes I do not. But always when I assess the meaning of my life against the standard of solidity, I feel or think that practicing love has created something in the world equal to what it took from me, though leaving me exhausted. But how does one practice love in the face of unpleasant feelings? I have learned to do so by developing a new relation to my feelings: they have become the background music to a day's work. My own desires are irrelevant to successful completion of the aims of the work. And, oddly, continuing the work in the face of feelings of frustration (as my self-mastery is not perfect) gives me a new sense of competence.

Perhaps it is easy to see how these new metaphysical sensibilities can motivate a mother to care about peace. If everyone is connected, the wounding of one person touches off a network of suffering. If everyone is someone's child, every death rips an irreparable wound in a parent's heart and every enemy demon has a great deal in common with you. If control over the sources of our joys is just past the horizon of our reach, then avarice and greed seem like wasteful exercises. And if love can be practiced even when it contradicts our feelings, then it is possible to love in the face of propaganda to the contrary, and it is possible to love even those who threaten violence. The moral imperatives of mothering are so strong, that if they could be linked to a peace politics, surely we would have an example of William James's "moral equivalent of war."[4]

It is hard for me to believe that preservative love, fostering growth, and social training, which are the basic aims of mothering as identified by Ruddick,[5] are anything but universal aims. And because the lessons that I am learning from trying to achieve those aims are so intense, it is hard to believe that those lessons are not universal. Perhaps it is because their onset coincided with a biological event. Or perhaps there is some validity to the type of intuition René Descartes sometimes calls "the light of nature."[6] Because I am so certain of my own devotion, because it gradually crept up on me yet hit me like a ton of bricks, I am simply certain that intense devotion to one's child is a cultural invariant. I am certain even though I know persons within my own culture who have not felt that devotion. Odd: I am a thoughtful person, trained in and a trainer in critical thinking. Has mothering turned my brain into sentimental mush or can I guarantee "by the light of nature" that I share a basic orientation with all mothers?

3. A View from Outside Mothering

When I speak frankly from inside mothering, it becomes clear that powerful emotions direct my thoughts. However, in turning my thoughts towards pacifism, it may be the case that I have given a one-sided picture of the emotions of mothering. For example, Victoria Davion has written that preservative love, one of the basic aims of mothering identified by Ruddick, can motivate mothers to engage in violence if they believe it will protect their children.[7] While Davion's essay evokes the image of a one-on-one conflict, her point is easily applicable to war. If a mother believes that a war is for defensive purposes, or that waging and winning it will afford her child a safer life, then that mother may well condone a war. If Davion is right, then the emotions of motherhood lead away from as well as towards pacifism. How can we untangle this contradiction in order to identify what is valuable in maternal pacifism? One method may be to examine the nature of emotion in general, and the emotions of motherhood in particular, in order to see how those emotions are constructed and, therefore, how they may be constructively directed.

Alison Jaggar has argued that emotions are at least partially socially constructed, offering at least four reasons for her claim.

(1) Children are taught appropriate emotional responses to situations, for example, fear of strangers.

(2) Cultural differences exist in what is recognized as an expression of a particular emotion.

(3) Emotions involve judgments that involve concepts that are intertwined with the "linguistic resources" of a culture.

(4) Encouraging the expression or suppression of certain emotions (such as anger) among particular groups can serve social aims, such as the maintenance of an oppressive hierarchy.[8]

Jaggar's theory of emotion can function as a hermeneutic of suspicion for questioning the authenticity of my emotion as a mother. Her first three reasons show that my consciousness of my emotion as immediate and universal is not consistent with a social scientific view of the genesis of emotional attitudes and styles. Her fourth reason suggests that the powerful emotions I associate with motherhood may have been artificially encouraged because they help to maintain some group's position on a social hierarchy.

Following Jaggar's suggestion, I shall call into question three specific aspects of my inside view of the experience of mothering. For each, I will speculate about the powerful social interests that are served by my identifying that experience with mothering. I will question whether I can serve those interests and still be committed to pacifism. As I am able to confirm only a correlation, and not a causal structure, between the emotion and the social hierarchy, these speculations should be taken as questions to be entertained by pacifist mothers, not as facts to be catalogued by social scientists. Three aspects of my experience seem to me to be at least partially socially constructed. They are my beliefs that (1) the joys of mothering are gifts of grace, (2) the struggle to be a full-time caretaker is spiritually fulfilling, and (3) the universal experience of mothering is shared by all mothers.

The view that the joys of mothering are gifts of grace and not the fruits of hard labor may, in some cases, be attributed to a woman's generally religious outlook on life. However, I believe that the construction of mothers as passive rather than active participants in a process also contributes to the view. This construction of mothers has been exploited and extended by the obstetrical profession, as acceptance of this construction by women furthers their reliance on this surgical specialty. Mainstream obstetrical practice constitutes a large and well-paid industry, a significant portion of which is devoted to education, that is, convincing women that birth cannot proceed safely without obstetrical intervention. In an obstetrically managed birth, a woman is treated as a passive nonparticipant just as she is entering motherhood. Often the birthing woman is reduced to a body and the body is denied any wisdom of its own. An artificial script is imposed on labor, which specifies incorrectly the normal order and duration of events. If a baby is "late," that is, looks like it may come more than two standard deviations outside the mean arrival time, labor is induced with pitocin, an artificial hormone. "*They* induced me," mothers say. If the waters do not break by mid-first stage labor (which they are not particularly supposed to do), an amniotomy is performed. "*They* broke my waters," mothers say. If the cervix does not dilate at an even rate, a cesarean is recommended. "*They* did a C-section," mothers say. Physicians, nurses, and now mothers assume that the birthing mother wants an epidural anesthetic, and that without it she will be unable to enjoy what some feminist authors have called "birthing labor,"[9] pain that is endured out of love for a family. On the bright side, at least mothers who choose pain relief say "*I* had an epidural." But for the most part, the birthing mother is constructed as passive by obstetrical practice. Obstetricians who deliver the baby even speak as if they bring new life into the world, while the mother is merely the vessel.[10] I am not resorting to hyperbole here, but reporting on normal everyday discourse about birthing.

If the image of mothers as passive recipients of children is pushed by those who want to sell mothers unnecessary goods, then there is good reason to suspect that the image is grounded in the fantasy of the advertisers, rather than in the experience of the mothers. In other words, there exists good reason to suspect that the image is a false one. And yet the correlative view that the joys of motherhood are gifts of grace was an important foundation for my maternal pacifism. That view made the striving for earthly goods that leads to war appear futile, and life appear more precious as it appeared more fragile. Perhaps, then, this is not a way of thinking about motherhood that can ground a serious pacifism, for a serious ethical commitment should not be founded on a lie designed to exploit the believer!

The view that the struggle to be a full-time caretaker is spiritually fulfilling is also an important component of my maternal pacifism. The image of spiritual development that I construct for myself includes training in the practice of unconditional love. However, Adrienne Rich's work in *Of Woman Born* suggests that the spiritual fulfillment I claim comes from motherhood may be more of a rationalization than a reality.[11] According to Rich, a false yet persuasive view of the meaning of mothering that developed during the rise of capitalism obscures the reality that mothering is both demanding and devalued. The falsehood finds expression in the myth that the full-time mother-homemaker has the most fulfilling life. Rich shows how the institution of motherhood is entangled with the public-private distinction that is associated with liberal political philosophy.[12] This distinction, she argues, which sets up the home as a private place of refuge "from the brutal realities of work and struggle" is a "creation of the Industrial Revolution."[13] In order to justify paying women low wages, capitalists encouraged the view that woman's proper place was not in productive labor, that in fact woman's proper place was to care for the wage-earner. The results of this view for women, Rich says, were disastrous. The myth forestalled any examination and amelioration of the difficult life of working-class women by declaring that they resided in a pleasant refuge. It separated women from one another, wedding each to a single home, and leading to their powerlessness as well as loneliness. And the myth also allocated to women the responsibility for being perfectly loving, forgiving, emotional, and charmingly irrational.

Perhaps, as I imagine I am developing spiritually by working as a mother, I am in fact merely living out the role of a social subordinate who may not express anger against a status quo, but who may only express love, acceptance, and admiration for her oppressors. If this is the case, then my maternal pacifism has a shaky foundation, as it is grounded not on genuine emotion but on a mask that may hide negative and violent emotions. Worse yet, if Rich is right, then my maternal pacifism becomes a reaffirmation of my confinement to the domestic sphere, undercutting any public impact that my declaration of pacifism could have.

Another important component of my maternal pacifism was the view that mothers everywhere could easily come to share it, because the lessons I am learning from mothering are universal. However, Alison Bailey, drawing on the work of Patricia Hill Collins, has noted that mothers of different cultures and classes experience mothering differently.[14] For example, what Bailey calls "racial/ethnic" mothers may see the core of their "motherwork" as ensuring the survival of children in dangerous neighborhoods; teaching children a positive identity in a dominant culture that offers them only negative self-images; and empowering themselves to retain control over their children's lives. While this may look like a variant of Ruddick's "preservative love, fostering growth and social training," simply to rename racial/ethnic motherwork in Ruddick's terms obscures the reality of the different forms that preservative love and social training must take in oppressive situations. Elizabeth Spelman has suggested that middle-class white feminists avoid looking at racial differences so that they can avoid asking themselves what role they play in the maintenance of white supremacy.[15] Perhaps my feeling that the lessons of mothering are powerful, persuasive and universal does reflect an unwillingness to admit the existence of differences between equals. Perhaps it expresses a false hope that all good mothers share what I, admittedly an affluent intellectual living in a safe neighborhood, deem important and ethical. If that is the case, then my vision that maternal pacifism has the potential for creating a mass moral equivalent to war rests upon a studied denial of the importance of the experience of other races, classes, and ethnic groups, groups who may not experience mothering as a foundation for pacifism. And a denial of the consciousness of others has been shown to lead away from, rather than towards, nonviolence. If the implications of Bailey's, Collins's, and Spelman's views are correct, then maternal pacifism has the potential to defeat itself, if actual political events call for pacifist mothers to sacrifice so that others may benefit.

4. Revising Maternal Pacifism from the Outside In

In section two of this chapter, I articulated a version of maternal pacifism drawn from inside my experience of mothering. In Section Three, I presented three criticisms drawn from a larger social perspective outside of my immediate experience. Collectively, these three criticisms can be understood to say that a pacifism grounded in the emotions of mothering is a product of false consciousness. The beliefs that form the foundation for maternal pacifism are at least partially the result of manipulations of women by the medical establishment, capitalists, and white supremacists. This does not bode well for pacifist mothers, for it implies that we do not realize how embedded our lives are in the very activities that lead to war, that is, exploitation and domination. Although we believe that we are calling for pacifism, the substance of our lives affirms warism. And we cannot see it, unless we are receptive to an outside viewer who can decode our beliefs for us.

This critique has devastating implications, some of which are radically inconsistent with my experience of mothering. Like all outside critiques of a practice, the critique suggests that no mother can see the world clearly and for herself. If she did, she would recognize that mothers implicitly, and sometimes explicitly, teach hate along with love. She would recognize that mothering only creates new opportunities for manipulation and self-deception. But, speaking from the inside view, characterized by the deep conviction that my experience is valid, I know that mothers, even privileged mothers, are not simply dupes playing out false scripts. Mothers, of all social classes, are mediators between ideals and realities, between inside views of their goals and outside critiques stating what is really possible. When raising their children, they direct and redirect; when acquiring resources or services to care for their children, they bargain and reassess. Mothers committed to pacifism can use these same skills to respond to the critique from outside, viewing it as a reality check on the functionality of their commitment to pacifism.

Therefore, I choose to accept the critique as a set of cautions that should inform my work as a mother. From the critique, I have learned that simply giving birth and raising children does not, in itself, constitute pacifist praxis. Simply mothering in conventional ways can lead away from peace, training children to be comfortable with violence, injustice, and war. Constant vigilance on a mother's part is required if her mothering behaviors and motherly lessons are not to deteriorate into the merely conventional, if opportunities to expose and improve the status quo are not to be missed in the name of her own children's welfare, if an overly romantic view of the importance of her work is not to blind her to the diversity among mothers. I do not pretend to have mastered either this vigilance or the critical self-consciousness needed to sustain it; I only claim to have set it forth as an ideal. Mediating between the ideals of justice and the realities of preservative love is not easy, but the difficulty of the task is not, for me, sufficient to warrant rejecting it as an ideal.

Notes

1. Ricoeur, *Freud and Philosophy: An Essay on Interpretation* (New Haven, Conn.: Yale University Press, 1970), pp. 20-36.

2. Sara Ruddick, *Maternal Thinking: Toward a Politics of Peace* (New York: Ballantine, 1989), p. 70.

3. Immanuel Kant, *Grounding for the Metaphysics of Morals,* in *Classics of Western Philosophy*, ed. Steven M. Cahn (Indianapolis, Ind.: Hackett, 2nd ed., 1977), pp. 925-976.

4. Willian James, "The Moral Equivalent of War," in *War and Morality*, ed. Richard Wasserstrom (Belmont, Calif.: Wadsworth, 1970), pp. 4-14.

5. Ruddick, *Maternal Thinking,* pp. 65-123.

6. René Descartes, *Meditations on First Philosophy*, trans. Donald A. Cress (Indianapolis, Ind.: Hackett, 1979), p. 38.

7. Victoria Davion, "Pacifism and Care,*"* *Hypatia,* 5:1 (1992), pp. 90-100.

8. Alison M. Jaggar, "Love and Knowledge: Emotion in Feminist Epistemology," in *Women, Knowledge, and Reality: Explorations in Feminist Epistemology*, ed. Ann Garry and Marilyn Pearsall (Boston: Unwin Hyman, 1989), pp. 129-155.

9. Ruddick, *Maternal Thinking,* p. 50.

10. See Kathryn Allen Rabuzzi, *Mother with Child: Transformations through Childbirth* (Indianapolis, Ind.: Indiana University Press, 1994).

11. Adreinne Rich, *Of Woman Born: Motherhood as Experience and Institution* (New York: Norton, 1976).

12. *Ibid.*, pp. 46-52.

13. *Ibid.*, pp. 49-50.

14. Alison Bailey, "Mothering, Diversity, and Peace Politics," *Hypatia,* 9:2 (1994), pp. 188-198.

15. Elizabeth V. Spelman, *Inessential Woman: Problems of Exclusion in Feminist Thought* (Boston: Beacon, 1988).

Fifteen

CONTEMPORARY AFRICAN SAGES AND QUEEN MOTHERS: THEIR LEADERSHIP ROLES IN CONFLICT RESOLUTIONS

Gail M. Presbey

The German philosopher, Heinrich Beck, suggests that only by our attempt to understand other world cultures, and thereby to understand the underlying causes of today's misunderstandings and conflicts, will the global community reach a point where world peace will be truly possible. Mogobe Ramose and Jameson Kurasha, two African contributors to Beck's recent book, attempt to explain African concepts and values in such a way that mutual understanding between Africans and non-Africans will be enhanced. Northerners in Europe and the United States may come to realize that the ideas of an African culture may be more conducive to harmony and peace, both within and between societies.[1] A careful study of conflict resolution in Africa, therefore, can help us doubly. By learning from those who resolve conflict, whether on the interpersonal, community, or inter-community level, we gain helpful tools for peacemaking in our own contexts. And by learning more about African approaches to conflict resolution, we further the intercultural understanding that Beck sees as so important to world peace.

Only recently have academic philosophers begun to hear voices from outside the Euroamerican tradition. By sheer force of habit, we turn to the great European philosophers of the past for the wisdom and insight to deal with our contemporary problems. But how often do we think of turning to Africa? I was first drawn to Kenya by what I heard about a sage philosophy project started by H. Odera Oruka of University of Nairobi. He was convinced that many thinkers of great wisdom hold positions of respect in their rural African communities, and he insisted that the academic world would learn much by seeking them out and drawing on their wisdom. In my research I went with Odera Oruka to rural Kenya, and met several impressive persons, mostly men, with much to say about resolving conflicts and restoring peace to their communities. Often, they had general theories founded on much first-hand experience. In Ghana, I found similar cases, except that women often took charge of reconciling opponents. They did so in their roles as queen mothers. Queen mothers are part of the Akan traditional governance system. While chiefs are elected to rule their communities, queen mothers are elected to take charge of what is especially considered to be the women's sphere of communal life, particularly marriages and the marketplace. Elections happen from within a pool of candidates eligible by heredity.[2]

In both cases, whether East or West Africa, I found tradition to be very much alive. While African society has problems and influences unique to this time, tradition remains flexible and ever-changing without losing its identity. The wise persons I met and interviewed saw themselves as part of a tradition, but were in their own ways keen thinkers and innovative contributors to this tradition.

These sages' conflict resolution and peacemaking practices have much to teach us in the United States. While much of their practical advice may be learned abstractly in textbook or workshop form in training course for mediators, the sages make the message real and personal by illustrating with their own experiences. They embody the subtle qualities necessary to make mediations and arbitrations successful. Indeed, we may again come to believe that successful conflict resolution is more an art than a science if we listen as they describe their artful, and skillful, way of getting parties to reconcile. The rural and village life that makes this kind of resolution possible is waning, and the impersonality of neighborhoods and rise of urban settings challenges the social network that kept both problems and their solutions local. However, since the sages have many reservations about the influences of Western values on Africa, much of what they say provides a valuable criticism of ourselves and helps suggest remedies for our antagonism, greed, and neglect of personal and group responsibility.

1. Researching the Sages

This chapter is based on interviews with several persons distinguished in their communities for wisdom and peacemaking. Several had taken part in Odera Oruka's sage philosophy project. As he explains, a sage is a person who uses his or her wisdom and insight for the ethical benefit of the community:

> The mere philosopher looks for pure knowledge and tries to express knowledge, but the sage cares about knowledge, and adds to knowledge morality, the moral spirit. He aims at the ethical betterment of the community that he lives in.[3]

Odera Oruka wanted to make the voices of individual sages heard, as he complained that anthropologists too often presented Africa as a place of unanimous and anonymous group wisdom. His book, *Sage Philosophy: Indigenous Thinkers and Modern Debate on African Philosophy,* included commentary on the group beliefs and customs of the Luo, as well as providing excerpts of twelve interviews of sages from different locations in Kenya. This chapter follows his suggestions by giving accounts of the personal messages of the sages as well as commenting on common themes to be found among them. While the sages are each unique in their personalities and presentations, there are similarities in their approaches to resolving conflict.

This chapter therefore draws upon the wisdom of several sages from Kenya, from both Western and Nyanza Provinces. [4] The sages, such as Nyando Ayoo of Sega and Wanyonyi Manguliechi of Kimilili, are regularly sought out to resolve conflicts in their communities. Ali Mwitani Masero of Kakamega District, in addition to counseling, is a traditional healer. While most of the sages included in Odera Oruka's study, and known to his research assistants such as Chaungo Barasa of Bungoma (whose help was indispensable to me in this project), were elder men, Odera Oruka made a point of saying that being elder or male was not a requirement of sagacity. Barasa (included as a young male sage in the *Sage Philosophy* book) introduced me to three women, Jones Lozenja Makindu, Rose Vugusa Masadia, and Ellyshaba Majinga, all of Maragoli, Western Province, who are included in the study. Nevertheless, the overwhelming majority of sages in Odera Oruka's study were men. I found it helpful to balance the study by inclusion of women from Ghana. I was able to interview several queen mothers from Ghana who had a similar social role to the sages—counseling people in disputes, resolving conflicts, with the difference being that they held official titles of power in their communities, and held courts where disputes were resolved. I think that when we look at Odera Oruka's definition of a sage, we recognize that many queen mothers are indeed sages; and I do not mean to suggest, by referring to them as queen mothers, that they are not sages. The queen mothers I interviewed, Nana Ama Adobea II of Aseseso and Nana Amma Serwah of Kokofu, were from the Akan community of Ghana. Nana Latebea, also interviewed, is an Akan female chief (*Akyeampim-Hemeaa*) of Adukrom, in Okere, Ghana. She holds a political position occupied by males.[5]

Whereas the sages interviewed in Kenya did not all have official political positions as did the queen mothers in Ghana, both parties would express their position as being somewhere in between mediation and arbitration. Mediation has been considered the introduction of a third party who helps the two parties to come to agreement between themselves.[6] Arbitration occurs when a person is given official power to make a decision, which the person makes carefully after consulting both parties. While the sages may not have official authority to enforce their decisions, they nevertheless often give advice that they expect to be taken and followed by both parties—a sign of arbitration. For example, Masero defends his practice of telling people advice, for he explains that often what they think is best in the situation is wrong. On the other hand, the queen mothers who hold official elected positions in their communities are given jurisdiction over several spheres of community activity such as the marketplace. However, Adobea explains that as a queen mother she does not have the power to dissolve marriages. Her official role is only to consult with the family members and give her advice, and then it is up to the families to act upon it so her role often seems more like a mediator than an arbiter.

Despite the differences between the three ethnic groups, geographically separated by a few thousand miles in East and West Africa, there is enough in common among the groups to help conflict mediation and arbitration to flourish. As Jay Folberg and Alison Taylor explain, "The use of mediation is favored in cultures where conflict itself is unacceptable...."[7] In such cultures, face-saving is necessary. As Gary L. Welton reveals, disputes most appropriate for community mediation are with parties that have an ongoing relationship–a characteristic of the small rural communities in which the sages and queen mothers are set. "Because of the nature of their interdependence, they are most likely to experience continuing difficulties, leading to ever-increasing levels of conflict. Hence, they will be more motivated to seek a mutually satisfying agreement."[8]

While Welton made his comments in a general fashion, several studies on Africa note the dynamic of interdependence enforcing stick decisions by traditional political bodies. For example, Marco Bassi notes in his study of the Borana of northern Kenya that assemblies are able to impose fines because to avoid payment would be to cut oneself off from all relations with the clan. Boranas would add, "How could you live without the clan?"[9] However, Bassi notes that the main purpose of the Borana judicial system is not to impose fines, but to reduce social tension and resentment.

> When a quarrel is discussed in the context of an assembly, there is always a first phase of clarification, during which each side's position is explained and latent tension is slowly dissolved, eventually leading to a reciprocal understanding.[10]

That the communities covered here have an active practice of mediation helps in its success. As Folberg and Taylor explain, "How a potential participant perceives the offer of mediation and relates to the goals, process steps, and mediator's role and techniques has a great deal to do with the ethnic and socioeconomic lessons the person has learned before mediation."[11] Although their study includes a chart which rates the reactions of ethnic groups to factors involved in mediation (such as the need for outside help, interpersonal conflict, mediator's credentials, mediator's role, techniques), the chart does not include Africans among its groups studied (although it does include African-Americans).[12]

These common themes were found in the approach of sages and queen mothers to conflicts:

(1) A concern and love for others and a genuine interest in resolving conflicts. These qualities inspired sages to get involved, and to see problems through to their practical resolutions. Such concern and love were fruits of morally exemplary lives. Such lives, in turn, gained the sages or queen mothers respect and caused their advice to be taken seriously.

(2) The importance of gaining the confidence of both parties to a dispute, and listening closely and with compassion to each side's story. Listening was followed by deep reflection where God would inspire the solution, which often involved an innovative interpretation of tradition.

(3) The need to be a prophetic voice, pointing to the root causes of conflict within the community. Examples are materialism, jealousy, and intolerance.

2. Concern and Love for Others

A big question regarding Kenyan sages is, how did they become sages? To an extent it is a self-elective position. A person becomes a mediator because he or she cares about the people who are harmed by conflict. Such a caring nature is often attributed to the fruit of upbringing and nurturing by loving parents. What follows is a selection of the stories and descriptions provided by the Kenyan sages regarding their philosophy and practice of compassion.

Makindu sums up her philosophy by the exhortation to love others, and she suggests that loving others is wisdom in itself. If a person did so, jealousy (what she considers to be the biggest obstacle to wisdom) would not arise. She also asserts that love could stop the political conflicts in Uganda, Ethiopia, and Rwanda. She displays her love of others through showing kindness to those in need. As one example of this, back in 1974 when there had been an influx in her area of Ugandan refugees, she mediated between community members, the local chief, and the refugees, to come up with a solution to their problems. She asked the chief if the refugees could live on her compound; when he granted permission, she raised funds for the construction of dormitories for four hundred children and ninety parents.

A friend of Makindu, Masadia, in agreeing that the message of loving others should be spread, added that people should never isolate the person who promotes hate. Instead, people should bring that person close, so that they can find out his or her problem. Is it money? hunger? jealousy? Only on such a basis can a person be understood with compassion and be approached with helpfulness instead of fear.

From his earliest days, Ayoo, now in his nineties, would give food and a place to stay to all in need, even to "mad people walking naked." In running his business (a "hotel" in Sega, near the border of Uganda), he habitually gave free meals to those with no money. As Odera Oruka described Ayoo, "He was a person who liked and enjoyed giving people things." Ayoo said he came to Sega in response to God's call. He was often castigated for filling a woman's role (showing compassion and feeding people).

Masero says his caring nature aids him in resolving disputes. As he explains, "This drive to help others is derived from my father who used to do the same, so much so that he even took in destitutes and, with my mother's support, brought them up and even gave them land." He has taken in a young girl named Habiba, whose mother died at childbirth. He expects that those who have been helped will later help others as well.

But Masero's abilities were developed gradually, and in the beginning, he was thought to be mad. As he explains, "At one time before my healing mission, I was strangely sick (or possessed) and I stayed in the wilderness like an animal for six months not even wanting to see people...." But he emerged from the isolation with a renewed interest in others and an ability to help them both physically and psychologically. This conviction of being especially called to help others fuels his drive to help others. As he explains, "I do not feel like I have special powers; I do not even understand myself because once there is a problem, I feel listless and disturbed until I find a solution to the same." One can notice, in the sage's self-description, a moral theory motivated by the injunction "not to turn away from someone in need." Carol Gilligan calls such an ethics the "ethics of care," a perspective on morality embraced by many women but few men (at least where her study was done, in the United States). One who sees mending relationships as of utmost importance, due to our status as interdependent beings, will know that relationships require listening and efforts at understanding different points of view.[13] Many feminist authors have developed Gilligan's ideas further and have been exploring a feminist ethics of care. Sandra Harding noted that there are many parallels (what she called a "curious coincidence") between feminist episte-mologies and African epistemologies. African and African-American thinkers argued that Africans as a whole are more caring, more relational, and not as coldly abstract as Europeans. Harding finds many problems in making broad generalizations about "all Africans" and "all women."[14] I would agree that such sweeping generalizations cannot be accurately upheld. But here I only argue that sages are particularly known for their caring. Indeed, caring is a virtue that sages cannot do without. Harding notes that whether persons are caring or not is influenced by history and social status. The sages, we can say, are in a social context where caring is possible, and where it is still admired.

Manguliechi explains that he was not always accepted by the community, especially when he was younger. As he explains,

> Most older men would scorn me and dismiss me as too young to counsel and too inexperienced to understand the intricacies of cultural heritage. But through consistency and the power of God's talent, they came to accept my position and acknowledge the fact that I had the capacity to do what I was doing.[15]

Because of his success, he has been appointed Chairman of the Council of Counselors in the whole of Kimilili Division. So, the self-selection that begins by persons volunteering their time and concern because of their spontaneous care for others, eventually becomes recognized as possessing moral authority and even official title. As Manguliechi explains, the most intransigent cases that cannot be solved by other mediators are often referred to him. "Once I put my interpretation of such situations to the parties concerned and the resolution of such a crisis, I am listened to and heeded without contradiction whatsoever."

In Ghana, queen mothers are elected by community leaders from a small pool of women eligible by heredity. As Kwabena Antwi-Boasiako explains in his novel, *The Hidden Agenda*, women who actively campaign for the position, as in the United States style of democracy, are seen to be ambitious and therefore lacking in essential qualities of trust and integrity needed to carry out their duties.[16] In this context elections model the Platonic ideal of searching for the best person who becomes willing to lead as a service to others and not for any sense of self-aggrandizement. This point is illustrated well by the story given by Nana Ama Adobea regarding her recruitment as a queen mther. She had lived in London with her husband for ten years, and had only recently come back to Ghana at the time she was chosen. Her mother was still alive, but she was getting old. The seat of queen mother is hereditary, but she had seven sisters. Tradition picks the oldest daughter, but the elders of the community can consult, weighing the character of the daughters, and make their own choice. She got wind that they wanted to choose her. She said no! When asked why she did not want to be queen mother, she said she was an independent woman, and a businesswoman, and she also liked her leisure. She lived abroad, and she did not know much about traditions. The elders went to talk to her husband. She had already told her husband to refuse the offer. But unbeknownst to her, her husband accepted it, drank the Schnapps which sealed the case. The day she went to her village and saw all her sisters there, she still did not know it would be her. Suddenly ten big strong men came and picked her up on the chair in which she was sitting. They smeared a white clay on her face and slaughtered a goat. That made it final: she was declared queen mother. She was shocked and stunned. Hoping to get away, she took off her clothes, causing men to run and hide their faces. Then she ran back to Accra. It took six months for the elders to convince her that it was a good thing, and she finally accepted being queen mother. Now she likes it, but it is a demanding job. She had to go through a ceremony in which she dressed in clothes of mourning, and promised her community that she would serve them selflessly until her death.

Adobea has about one thousand women in her community, and she is in charge of all their affairs. She oversees the marketplace, all ceremonies with women (rites of passage for young women, marriages), and every weekend she goes to her village to hear cases. She provides her service out of true concern and compassion for those in her community. While her community members would insist that she has been divinely chosen for this role, even the religious skeptic can agree that she has responded to her role with self-sacrifice and concern for others.

Serwah insists that keeping oneself morally upright is the main "weapon of success" as a queen mother, for it is then people respect you. You will be able to convince people to forgive each other, because of your influence. As Kwesi Yankah explains, elderhood is more a challenge than a privilege in Akan society, because one must lead a morally exemplary life. In addition, Serwah notes that there is the respect and dignity accorded the stool (on which she sits), and so people find it difficult to "walk over her." The stool itself is sacred, and as Yankah explains, while one is seated on it one is able to be an intermediary between the human and spirit worlds, gaining wisdom of the ancestors.[17]

3. Resolving Disputes

A major social role for Makindu involves marriage counseling. As she explains, her procedure is to approach the wife first. (Many people assume that the woman is in the wrong). Despite a bias against women, men will listen to her. She goes in a sincere way, and does not accuse either party. When approaching men who are reluctant to cooperate, and who say that women are stupid, she will agree with them, but will ask, what "stupid thing" had been said or done on this occasion? In this way she draws information out of both parties so that she can understand the situation. She then explains the usefulness of their loving each other, in hopes that based on a mutual understanding, they can reconcile their differences.

A key part of her role in settling domestic disputes is in educating women about how some of their own actions reinforce the notion that women are inferior to men. For example, statements like, "If I were a man, I'd do this..." increase the bias that men are better. Women also sometimes praise what is evil in the man, and therefore provoke him to aggressive actions. By counseling women that they are equal to men, she enables them to gain their self-esteem and break out of a negative cycle of mistreatment.

To resolve disputes, Manguliechi listens to both parties and assesses the nature of the problem at hand. He then points out the source of the problem, and the wrongs of each party, if any. Then he passes judgment, in the light of his assessment of the issues at stake. He must take time to reflect on issues, especially those that are not simply taken care of by Bukusu society traditional norms and rules. Manguliechi appeals to Bukusu rules, but, as he explains, they are wide-reaching and so have something to say on any topic. This leaves a lot of latitude for interpretation. His special talent is to know what aspect of the tradition to call upon in any given situation, so that the problem can be resolved. However, he consistently insists that his talent for dispute settlement comes from God's power, not his human ability.

One example of a dispute resolution took place in 1992 between two brothers. One brother accused the other of killing his child. However Manguliechi reminded them that in Bukusu tradition, a person only calls someone a thief if he or she has been caught in the act of stealing. Since there was no physical act by the accused brother against the child, neither poisoning, cutting, nor spearing, Manguliechi suggested that the brother could not have been responsible for the death. The brothers heeded his advice. While the brothers earlier had not been speaking to each other, Manguliechi ordered them to prepare a meal, to eat together, and after eating, to shake hands and declare that their disagreement was over. Ever since, the accord has stayed in place. The genius portrayed in this case is not only in encouraging one brother to give up a superstitious account of the death of his child, but also in devising a ritual, so that the brothers could concretely act out their reconciliation. Such actions reinforce a change in attitude.

Another dispute involved a case in 1994, when a motorist had knocked down a pedestrian, who died as a result. The family of the deceased had demanded payment of sixty head of cattle, referring to the Bukusu traditional practice of cattle compensation for murder. After investigating and pondering, Manguliechi made a case that the motorist had killed only inadvertently, and not deliberately. Therefore, the fine in cattle should be reduced to ten heads of cattle, a sum to which both parties agreed.

Masero explains that people come to him first and foremost because he is a unifier and he brings together those who have disagreed or have had misunderstandings. Besides responding to people who seek him out, he also involves himself in conflicts that he witnesses.

For example, there was a dispute between a father and a son. The son wanted the father to help him pay a dowry for a wife, but the father refused, saying the son was still young and needed to work and acquire property. The son then insisted he wanted to sell a piece of land to which he was entitled, that was presently part of the father's farm. The father, however, insisted that the farm had not been subdivided yet, and so the son had no property of his own. In the case, Masero explained that the father was in the right. However the question was, how to reconcile the two parties. Family members had gotten involved and had made matters worse by being divisive. So Masero approached each party individually and listened with sympathy. He then brought them together and the matter was settled amicably. He explains that,

> Where there is a quarrel or misunderstanding, I do not just wish to intervene but I take time to reflect on the causes of the situation. I befriend both parties individually and speak to both separately as if I side with them. In this way, I grasp the causes of the quarrel and then call them together with other people and advise them in the light of my findings on the facts of the case.[18]

Key to his ability to resolve issues is his knowing how to prod people in conversation to get at the heart of an issue, instead of skirting the major points.

Masero has solved other disputes as well. Being a traditional healer, he noticed that the healers in his area had rivalry among themselves which involved some trying to discredit the others in an attempt to win more clients. Masero explained to them that they had to work together to combat diseases such as diabetes and hypertension in ways that modern doctors could not. Lack of mutual understanding would hinder their collective ability to deal with diseases. Masero was then instrumental in involving the district health office who convened a seminar in traditional healing in which those who attended were awarded certificates.

Serwah explains that her role is to make peace within her society. For example, if people are sent to the police for offenses such as not paying debt, they can request the queen mother to intervene. She invites elders to help her do the mediation. She also notes that queen mothers play an active role in preventing wars.

In marriage conflicts, Serwah explains that she begins by meeting privately with each of the partners. She allows each side to make a case, then counsels each of them. Before people decide to bring their problems to her, they must discern that she is wise and intelligent, that she can listen carefully and make a good judgment. In all cases, she must be careful in her choice of words; even if someone provokes her, she should not respond antagonistically.

Serwah explains that to be an effective and fair arbiter, it is best to have all three of the following attributes: (1) Intelligence (*Adwene*), which is the ability to argue well, to make a point with justification; (2) Wisdom (*Nyanso*), which is a form of circumspection that properly places individuals in the context of their larger life and actions; and (3) Reflection or Deep Thinking (*Badwenma*), which is the ability to listen carefully, to sort out truths from statements made to please or flatter one's listeners, or to look good in their eyes. A reflective person can detect inconsistencies of character in the speaker.

Adobea explains that when she and other traditional rulers hear cases in traditional courts, "the results are encouraging in most cases, as the methods used are natural laws 'being human and making human decisions,' and not strictly sticking to technicalities as in the case of law courts."

Latebea says a person must speak and listen carefully when hearing cases. A person must sit down quietly, and think before he or she talks. When approaching someone regarding winning cooperation on some matter, do not say, "Hey you, do this..."; instead, quietly say, "I beg you to..." and give reasons for your request. Otherwise, the person may abuse you. Such a reflective speaker knows how to handle people, and talk to them. This is a sign of true education. Her comments especially reflect Akan social practices which hold politeness and face-saving at high value. As Yankah explains in *Speaking for the Chief*, the spoken word is seen by the Akan to have a potency because of its immediate impact. There is a risk involved in face-to-face communication, so face-threatening acts must be warded off by the use of indirection, politeness, and deference.[19]

4. Prophetic Voice

In addition to handling interpersonal conflicts, Manguliechi has pondered the general causes of the problems he encounters. He sees his social role as not only resolving individual disputes as they arise, but also as speaking in public about virtues and vices in general. Like Makindu, he cites jealously and envy as the root cause of most conflicts. Jealousy causes antagonisms and suspicions within society. Jealousy starts when those who have a lot boast about it, thereby engendering the envy of the have-nots. He sees the pursuit of power on the national level (the vying of the parties) as another example of desire for wealth and self-aggrandizement. Drunkenness is an added variable that can lead to confrontation, since the drunk person can escalate minor squabbles into full fledged conflicts. As Manguliechi explains:

> To do away with these societal conflicts, I always preach to people about the necessity of doing away with jealousy, envy, and bitterness and vengefulness against others, and I stress the need for unity as a prerequisite to social peace and progress, as envy and greed can only bring turmoil to all. I seek to reach all by arguing that we are the ones who bring evil to ourselves. For instance, if a person is rained upon she or he ought not to blame the rain as it rains on he who sees. Before it rains, clouds are formed and a person who sees them should seek shelter; and just before it starts raining, it thunders for those with ears to hear also to seek shelter, if they had no eyes to see the clouds. In my counseling about the evils of society, I proceed along this symbolism.[20]

Here in Manguliechi's testimony we see other key aspects of his social role as the resolver of conflicts: the counseling against strong negative emotions, the counseling of others to be aware of what they are doing and to look before they leap, and insisting on individual responsibility for social ills.

Masero also pinpoints jealously, especially among neighbors, as the key cause of conflict. For example, if someone has a large, productive sugarcane plantation, a neighbor who is jealous may let his cattle into the plantation, leading to animosity. Others gossip about petty things or get exceedingly angry when owed small sums of money.

Ayoo believed that people of this generation were spoiled by betrayals due to jealousy. People would begin accusing others. In contrast, God cares for all people, and so there is no real cause for jealousy. Ayoo cites people's ambition to be famous as another source of problems. Odera Oruka elaborates on the point made by Ayoo by explaining *tamaa* spirit (a Kiswahili word for greed): "When someone else sees something nice, he/she says 'Oh! What can I do? So-and-so now has this. We are finished.'" Such an attitude leads to self-castigating.

Ayoo is convinced that "through calm spirit (*chuny mangich*) a person acquires something. But restless spirit (*chuny malieth*) is not good....Cruelty brings poverty but humility brings wealth." His wife Dorka agrees that whenever her husband gave their things away out of generosity, it brought more wealth.

Majinga, an oral historian in her nineties, believes it is not enough to intervene in a marriage or in a young woman's life once there is a problem. She echoes Makindu's concern for young girls and women growing up with confidence in themselves. She sparks this confidence in others by reciting stories from the local oral tradition that present role models for women in relying upon their own abilities and insight, as well as pulling together to help each other in times of trouble. For example, one story told of a mother with four daughters, who suspected that two travelers asking for hospitality intended to harm her daughters. Using her cunning intelligence, she told her daughter to fetch water for the visitors, while secretly telling her not to return. When the daughter did not come back, she sent the second to look for her, and then the third, until in this way she successfully protected all her daughters from harm. Such stories, Majinga explains, encourage women to feel solidarity amongst themselves so that they turn to each other for help instead of feeling helpless and turning to men. There would be fewer cases of women abused in marriages if women were first encouraged to be self-reliant and confident about themselves.

5. The Sages and the Art of Conflict Resolution

Community mediation training guides and studies are filled with advice for mediators, including manifesting such attributes as confidentiality, neutrality, and subtle nonverbal behavior such as inclining a person's head forward in a listening attitude. A good mediator must aid negotiators in impression management and face-saving, be familiar with tactics to move a party off a currently held position and onto a new position, build trust, and be able to establish an agenda or priorities. The success of a mediation may depend on other subtleties such as timing of their interventions with the parties, monitoring language intensity of the mediation, and being able to pick up on language ambiguities which disputants would use to hint at alternatives for settlement and mediators themselves would use to initiate proposals without controlling parameters of the solution. Tailoring tactics to several types of disputes may increase effectiveness; for example, face-saving and pressure tactics were found to be good methods for high-hostility situations, but counter-productive in low-hostility contexts.[21]

Such comprehensive studies are steps to understanding the success of attempts at conflict resolution. Paul V. Olczak and others suggest that a dialogue between scientists and practitioners of conflict resolution is needed. Answering the question, "Does community mediation work?" is a complicated matter. The success of mediations can be improved as the subtleties of approaches and tactics are made more manifest through studies. But is mediation an art or a science?[22] Careful studies may help to improve the teaching of mediation, insofar as it can be learned from a handbook, by providing a clearer grasp of the general principles. Yet, given the attention to circumstance required, it may be that the successful practice of mediation should still be considered an art. The sages are special and unique because they, through endless experience and reflection, have become the sorts of persons who can effectively mediate conflicts. They embody the wisdom that can only be catalogued, but not easily reproduced, by scientists. We can only benefit by studying their example.

I suggest that much of what Folberg and Taylor say about "celebrity mediation" may be an added factor in the context of sages and queen mothers. They explain that the novelty of a celebrity or a public figure as mediator often helps parties that were formerly inflexible become willing to engage in conflict resolution, especially if the dispute becomes public. As they explain, "[F]ew disputants wish to appear unreasonable in the spotlight of public attention."[23] While the sages and queen mothers are not film and television celebrities, they are indeed well-known in their communities. Their mediation draws widespread attention to a dispute. Even without newspapers or radio publicity, all the people who matter soon come to know about the dispute–all the rural neighbors with whom the disputants expect to live for the rest of their lives. The spotlight of attention falls on the sage's decision, and the respect given the sage or queen mother in the community aids powerfully in its enforcement.

A pressing need to resolve many political and ethnic conflicts exists in Africa today.[24] Paulin J. Hountondji notes that many Africans feel passive and fatalistic when confronted with malfunctioning systems and bureaucracies. Many wait helplessly in government offices to see if their petition will be heard or paperwork processed. When hospitals are careless and cause health damage, people say, "This commotion will not bring the dead person back." Such an attitude about so many services ends up lowering people's resistance to bad systems. They feel disempowered.[25] It is heartening to know that a rich heritage of expertise in conflict resolution is to be found in Africa. It remains to be seen how this resource would be best tapped to solve current problems. It could be tapped indirectly, through the people's acquisition of skills and tactics to be used in negotiations (by observing and studying sages and queen mothers). Or, it could be tapped more directly by the recruiting of local talent and experience for use in the process of conflict resolution itself. The need is great, so no opportunity should be lost. Community involvement in articulating needs and negotiating for their fulfillment must go beyond the rural setting to urban institutions.

The usefulness of learning from the sages and queen mothers is not limited to the African context, as their insights and example of living reconciliation is valuable to us all wherever we may be. In the industrialized countries, the sages can remind us that mediation needs to be popularized. The possibility of resolving conflict through mediation must be incorporated into our daily thinking. While there are mediation centers in many states in the United States, mediation has not yet effectively become a part of culture. African sages and queen mothers are well known as a resource grieving parties can seek. Most individuals in Africa can remember times when persons they knew had conflicts resolved in that way. There is a need to popularize mediation, so that it becomes part of our culture. When people begin to seek out conflict resolution as a solution to their personal problems, they may become more experientially convinced that there are better ways to solve disputes than violence, control, and force. The more this conviction grows, the more we are on our way to a more peaceful world.

Notes

1. Moboge Ramose, "Specific African Thought Structures and Their Possible Contribution to World Peace," and Jameson Kurasha, "The African Concept of Personality as a Possible Contribution to Global Reconciliation," *Kreativer Friede durch Begegnung der Weltkulturen*, ed. Heinrich Beck (New York: Peter Lang, 1995).

2. Kwesi Yankah, *Speaking for the Chief: Okyeame and the Politics of Akan Royal Oratory* (Bloomington, Ind.: Indiana University Press, 1995), pp. 70-71.

3. Kai Kresse, "Philosophy Needs to Be Made Sagacious: An Interview with H. Odera Oruka," 16 August 1995 at the University of Nairobi, *Issues in Contemporary Culture and Aesthetics*, 3 (April 1996), Jan van Eyck Academie, Maastricht, The Netherlands. See also H. Odera Oruka's Introduction in *Sage Philosophy: Indigenous Thinkers and Modern Debate on African Philosophy*, ed. H. Odera Oruka (Nairobi: African Center for Technology Studies Press, 1991), pp. 9-10.

4. Nyando Ayoo interviewed by the author, in Sega, Nyanza Province, Kenya, and Martine Outa, Barasa Nyango, and Dorka Nyando, interviewed by author in Sega, on 19 November 1995, translated on site by H. Odera Oruka, and later retranslated by Oriare Nyarwath. (Tape and transcript are in possession of the author.) Jones Lozenja Makindu, Ellyshaba Majinga, and Rose Vugusa Masadia interviewed by the author, in Maragoli, Western Province, Kenya, on 12 May 1996, assisted and translated by Chaungo Barasa. Wanyonyi Manguliechi interviewed by the author in Western Province, Kenya, 7 October 1995, translated on site by Chaungo Barasa. (Tape and transcript are in possession of the author.) Ali Mwitani Masero interviewed by the author in Western Province, Kenya, 6 October 1995, translated on site by Chaungo Barasa, and later retranslated by Shadrack Wanjala Nasong'o. (Tape and transcript are in posession of the author.)

5. Nana Ama Adobea II was interviewed in English in Aburi, Ghana in May 1996 and later provided written comments. Nana Latebea was interviewed in English in Accra in July 1996. Nana Amma Serwah was interviewed in Kokofu, Ghana on 6 July 1996, translated by Joseph Osei. (Tape and transcript are in posession of the author.)

6. Karl A. Slaikeu, *When Push Comes to Shove: A Practical Guide to Mediating Disputes* (San Francisco: Jossey-Bass, 1996).

7. Jay Folberg and Alison Taylor, *Mediation: A Comprehensive Guide to Resolving Conflicts without Litigation* (San Francisco: Jossey-Bass, 1986), p. 321.

8. Gary L. Welton, "Parties in Conflict: Their Characteristics and Perceptions," *Community Mediation: A Handbook for Practitioners and Researchers*, ed. Karen Grover Duffy *et al.* (New York: Guilford, 1991), p. 105.

9. Marco Bassi, "Institutional Forgiveness in Borana Assemblies," *Sociology, Ethnology Bulletin* [Ethiopia], 1:2 (March 1992), pp. 50-60.

10. *Ibid.*, p. 53.

11. Folberg and Taylor, *Mediation*, p. 318.

12. *Ibid.*, pp. 322-323.

13. Carol Gilligan, *In A Different Voice: Psychological Theory and Women's Development* (Cambridge, Mass.: Harvard University Press, 1982).

14. Sandra Harding, *The Science Question in Feminism* (Ithaca, N.Y.: Cornell University Press, 1986), pp. 165-190.

15. Manguliechi (interview by author).

16. Kwabena Antwi-Boasiako, *The Hidden Agenda* (Accra: Anima Publications, 1995).

17. Kwesi Yankah, *The Proverb in the Context of Akan Rhetoric: A Theory of Proverb Praxis* (New York: Peter Lang, 1989), pp. 73 and 75.

18. Masero (interview by author).

19. Yankah, *Speaking for the Chief*, pp. 10-11.

20. Manguliechi (interview by author).

21. Peter J. Carnevale *et al.* "Mediator Behavior and Effectiveness in Community Mediation," in *Community Mediation: A Handbook for Practitioners and Researchers*, ed. Karen Grover Duffy *et al.* (New York: Guilford, 1991), pp. 120-124.

22. Paul V. Olczak *et al.*, "Toward a Synthesis: the Art with the Science of Community Mediation," in *Community Mediation*, ed. Duffy *et al.,* pp. 329-343.

23. Folberg and Taylor, *Mediation*, p. 140.

24. See David R. Smock and Chester A. Crocker, eds., *African Conflict Resolution: the U. S. Role in Peacemaking* (Washington: United States Institute of Peace Press, 1995); and David R. Smock, ed., *Making War and Waging Peace: Foreign Intervention in Africa* (Washington: United States Institute of Peace Press, 1993).

25. Paulin J. Hountondji, "Daily Life in Black Africa," in *The Surreptitious Speech: Présence Africaine and the Politics of Otherness, 1947-1987*, ed. V.Y. Mudimbe (Chicago: University of Chicago Press, 1992), pp. 344-364.

Sixteen

CATCALLS AND MILITARY STRATEGY

Sally J. Scholz

All oppression creates a state of war.
Simone de Beauvoir[1]

If, like Beauvoir, we recognize that oppression "creates a state of war," then perhaps we can look to peacemaking models used in response to war as guides in our day-to-day response to manifestations of oppression. That is, by understanding war and the peacemaker's response to it, we can better understand how the violence of oppression functions and propose a peacemaker's response to that injustice. In what follows I make use of an analogy between the dehumanization that occurs as part of military strategy in war and the dehumanization that results from verbal violence. By focusing on one type of verbal violence, catcalls, I show that the dehumanization or objectification that results from verbal violence contributes to the war of an oppressive system. Finally, I use this analysis to propose a pacifist response to catcalls and similar forms of verbal violence. This pacifist response draws on our obligation as peacemakers to ensure not merely the absence of war but the presence of justice. I begin with a brief presentation of a basic military conception of strategy.

1. Military Strategy

The primary focus in this section on military strategy is on the process of dehumanization (also called psychological violence by some). A process of dehumanization is among the first steps of an active military campaign. Such a process also provides a model by which other forms of verbal violence, such as catcalls, might be analyzed.

Generally speaking, "strategy" is defined as,

> the art and science of developing and using political, economic, psychological and military forces as necessary during peace and war, to afford the maximum support to policies, in order to increase the probabilities and favorable consequences of victory and to lessen the chances of defeat.[2]

Strategy includes the procedures for maneuvering personnel and resources into the most advantageous position prior to engaging in battle. These preliminary procedures form part of the game-plan that is used both to ready the offensive forces for the fight and to best incapacitate the opponent.

Dehumanization of the opponent is a crucial aspect of the preliminary procedures in preparation for the violence of war. Soldiers have often described their perception of the enemy as nothing short of "thingness." Indeed, some have relayed stories in which they were taught to dehumanize the enemy so as to better be able to kill them. The dehumanization process usually begins on a level of language. The enemy is given a new name as part of the process. The name facilitates a new identity for those so named in the minds of the aggressors. This identity is the identity of an object that in turn justifies the moral inferiority ascribed to this enemy group. Noted military historian D. G. Kehl details this process in the following quotation:

> The implication is that one is perfectly justified in killing prisoners and civilians because the enemy is morally inferior and therefore not worthy to live. War, in fact any kind of conflict, invariably involves stereotyping, false categorizing ("good guys" vs. "bad guys") and dehumanization....What is fundamental about violence is that the basic right of the dignity of human personhood is violated. Even before physical violence is done to him, psychological violence is done in that his right to dignity is violated when he is considered morally or ethnically inferior, and so unfit to live.[3]

Although the violence may take place in the mind of the aggressor, it is nonetheless inflicted on the victim. The impact of the psychological violence is in the stripping of personhood from the enemy and this dehumanization facilitates the ease with which physical violence may then be inflicted. The only real defense to dehumanization of this sort, aside from engaging in battle, is an indirect defense to humanize both the aggressor and the perceived enemy.

Sissela Bok notes the role of dehumanization in military strategy when she quotes Joseph de Maistre:

> A friendly young man...brought up to recoil from violence and from blood, can be led with the greatest of ease to seek out and destroy those whom he is told to regard as enemies: "The blood that flows all around him only incites him to spill his own and that of others. By degrees he grows inflamed and will come to experience the *enthusiasm of carnage*."[4]

Notice that Bok's "friendly young man" is told whom to regard as an enemy. There need be no personal animosity on the part of the attacker in order for him/her to inflict harm. All that is needed is some sort of permission or compulsion. In addition, Maistre presents a description of the incendiary nature of violence. Once violence has gained social recognition if not social approval, it sparks an inferno of legitimated attacks.

Betty A. Reardon echoes Maistre in the following description of the readiness differing parties have to use violence against each other:

> Such readiness appears to derive from two sources: first, permission or social and/or political legitimization to carry out the violent and aggressive impulses, and second, dehumanization of the other in the relationship. The reinforcement of otherness, coupled with rationalizing the lesser worthiness of the other, facilitates the alienation that can push competitive but inequitable relationships into violent conflict.[5]

With the process of dehumanization in motion, the next step in effective military operations is to spatially locate and limit the free mobility of your opponent, both physically and psychologically.[6] The goal is to cage the enemy and cut off the enemy's supply sources or support systems. This provides the attacker with a potentially weak and certainly immobile victim upon which to prey.

As Kehl mentioned, the purpose of good strategy is to provide the best groundwork and justification for the violence that is necessary to conquer the opponent. Or, if the preliminary strategy was effective in itself, physical violence may not be necessary as the opponent will be too powerless to put up a struggle. Incapacitating the enemy is the final goal and all of the means used are violent. Thus, following the violence of dehumanization, violence might take the form of cultural violence, such as exclusion from decision-making procedures in matters that affect a person's life, or the constant threat of physical violence, and physical violence.

The dehumanization that occurs as part of military strategy, followed by immobilization and physical violence, provides a good model for analyzing forms of verbal violence.[7] In the next section I look at one example of verbal violence: catcalls. Catcalls, like the enemy name-calling described above, function to dehumanize. The analogy between the dehumanization of catcalls and the dehumanization within military strategy offers some insight into the peacemaker's role and responsibility with regard to the verbal violence of catcalls. The peacemaker's response relies on the notion that catcalls are only a small part of the oppression of sexism.

2. Catcalls and Verbal Violence

A catcall is a street remark, usually sexual, and most often directed at women from unknown men. Although I primarily focus on catcalls that are targeted at women, many other social groups experience similar acts of verbal violence that also might contribute to immobilization and further violence. Catcalls contribute to the dehumanization found in a sexist, misogynist, or patriarchal society. Similar forms of verbal violence or hate speech might be found to contribute to a racist, heterosexist, classist, ageist, or ablest society. Our analysis of peacemaking with regard to catcalls might serve as a guide for peacemaking in these other forms of verbal violence or oppression as well.

Catcalls are a part of the strategy of the war within patriarchy. They are an effective psychological tool that aids unintentional and intentional "policies" that keep women from, for example, attaining positions of authority in the work-place for which they are qualified and walking without fear in public areas day and night. Catcalls, like the dehumanization that occurs in military strategy, serve to dehumanize both the woman to whom a call is aimed and women as a social group.

The victim of a catcall is dehumanized via objectification and, often in the objectification, is fragmented. She becomes a "nice piece of ass" or perhaps just a "cunt." In whatever manner the caller refers to the woman, she becomes nothing more to the caller than an object. She is given a new label and identity by the catcaller in the same manner that the military renames its opponents. In the act of catcalling the caller has removed the callee's active determination of her identity in the relationship to the caller. Just as Kehl describes the psychological violence of war efforts, the recipient of a catcall or similar form of verbal violence has his or her "right to dignity" violated and is considered "morally inferior." As bell hooks says, "As objects, one's reality is defined by others, one's identity created by others, one's history named only in ways that define one's relationship to those who are subject."[8] Sandra Bartky echoes this in *Femininity and Domination*, saying, "objectification occurs independently of what women want; it is something done to us against our will."[9] For both the enemy in military strategy and victims of oppression this activity deprives individuals and social groups of their capacities for self-determination. Because of objectification, the choices for daily or life projects, plans, activities, and self-definitions are limited. Dehumanization of catcalls has facilitated immobilization.

Linguist Deborah Cameron argues that "the most important effect of street remarks...is that they are a way of controlling public space and defining women as intruders within it."[10] Catcalls remind women of our vulnerability while simultaneously underscoring the patriarchal structure in which they occur. That is, catcalls serve as a verbal representation of the predominance men have in public space. In addition, before and while women move from one situation or location to another they must think about safety factors. This added precaution not only takes up time and energy that could be used in more productive ways but may also cause the woman to choose to curtail her activity so as to minimize her vulnerability. Catcalls serve as a verbal reinforcement or reminder of the potential of being attacked. As Cameron notes,

> for women, these practices create a certain reality in and of themselves: they are, in fact, a form of social control and definition....In other words, the proliferation of terms that function as sexual slurs on women's reputations is used as a weapon to keep women in line.[11]

The words and phrases of catcalls encase women in a cultural context wherein sexual violence is an all too common phenomenon.

The verbal violence of catcalls quickly changes to intimidation of physical violence or physical violence itself: "At times, self-consciousness can shade into actual fear; for many street remarks are not ambiguous but clearly hostile."[12] As many victims and survivors of sexual violence may attest, words do indeed cause harm.

Catcalls and other forms of verbal violence dehumanize not only the individual victim but also the social group to which the victim belongs. Catcalls target individuals insofar as they are members of a social group; catcalls are generally based on negative stereotypes or derogatory labels of a group. The individual is victimized because she or he is labeled as object. The group is victimized because it receives the status of moral inferiority. It is as a member of the inferiorized group that an individual is marked by the dominant group. As Iris Young comments, the knowledge of an individual's status within a traditionally oppressed group itself functions to dehumanize and immobilize: "The oppression of violence consists not only in direct victimization, but in the daily knowledge shared by all members of oppressed groups that they are liable to violation, solely on account of their group identity."[13] In addition to the potential for physical violence, women suffer from the violence of the internalized identity garnered from catcalls. In other words, a person begins to see him or herself as inferior: "Internalization of Otherness means that one has come to identify oneself through the eyes of the dominant group in society."[14] The dominant group has consciously or unconsciously determined and prescribed this identity, believing it correctly labels those they subordinate. As a subordinate other, a woman may fear violence, and violence done to the objectified other is rarely questioned and may even be accepted or justified. This was historically the case with domestic violence wherein the wife/victim was considered her husband's property, an object he owned and rightfully controlled.

Bartky uses phenomenology to describe her experience of a catcall in *Femininity and Domination: Phenomenology of Oppression*. Her description is worth quoting at length as it reveals the elements of dehumanization or objectification, immobilization, and the violence of oppression described above:

[F]ragmenting perception, which is so large an ingredient in the sexual objectification of women, serves to maintain the dominance of men. It is a fine spring day, and with an utter lack of self-consciousness, I am bouncing down the street. Suddenly I hear men's voices. Catcalls and whistles fill the air. These noises are clearly sexual in intent and they are meant for me; they come from across the street. I freeze. As Sartre would say, I have been petrified by the gaze of the Other. My face flushes and my motions become stiff and self-conscious. The body which only a moment before I inhabited with such ease now floods my consciousness. I have been made into an object. While it is true that for these men I am nothing but, let us say, a "nice piece of ass," there is more involved in this encounter than their mere fragmented perception of me. They could, after all, have enjoyed me in silence. Blissfully unaware, breasts bouncing, eyes on the birds in the trees, I could have passed by without having been turned to stone. But I must be *made* to know that I am a "nice piece of ass": I must be made to see myself as they see me. There is an element of compulsion in this encounter, in this being-made-to-be-aware of one's own flesh; like being made to apologize, it is humiliating. It is unclear what role is played by sexual arousal or even sexual connoisseurship in encounters like these. What I describe seems less the spontaneous expression of a healthy eroticism than a ritual of subjugation.[15]

Bartky's experience was one of being "petrified by the gaze," of being "turned to stone." Her humanity was replaced by thingness; she was a victim of objectification. In addition, with these phrases, she describes how the catcall immobilized her, stripped her of her free movement. Not only do her motions "become stiff and self-conscious" her body can no longer be easily inhabited. The catcall has taken her free subjectivity and left in its place other-defined objectivity.

Finally, as if the violence described in the previous paragraph were not enough, the catcall manifests itself as a "ritual of subjugation." That is, as a ritual it is an outward sign or ceremony prescribed according to a rule or custom, in this case, patriarchy or even misogyny. The subjugation occurs on a multiplicity of levels ranging from fear of walking alone thereby forcing a person to "play it safe: walk with an escort," to sexual harassment in the work-place, to sexual violence, and more.

Prior to moving on to the final section of this chapter wherein I discuss the task of peacemaking in response to catcalls, it might be worth noting the connection some have drawn between sexism and a war culture. In *Sexism and the War System*, Reardon argues that the "fundamental willingness to use violence against others on which warfare depends is conditioned by early training and continuous socialization in patriarchal society."[16] Men, according to Reardon, are conditioned to use violence in the form of competition among equals and as a means of keeping inferiors (be they the enemy or women) oppressed. Women, on the other hand, are socialized to believe that violence is a normal part of human relations, or Reardon says, as "a fundamental given of the human condition."[17] The oppression of women is seen as a sort of training ground for military activity. By attributing a causal connection between patriarchy and the war system, Reardon claims that the subjugation of women is due to and necessary for preparedness in battle:

> At base, because men are conditioned to be warriors and women to be wives and mothers, there is a social expectation that warfare will take place on battlegrounds, in board rooms, at professional conventions, in the marketplace, and any locus where men compete. Because men always must be ready to do battle, society gives them tacit permission to practice in more private, even intimate, settings, and conspires through sex-role separation to produce the "intimate enemy," the fundamental relationship that makes possible many subsequent enemy relations.[18]

If catcalls function to dehumanize women in much the same manner that enemy labeling functions in military strategy, then we should also be able to look to pacifist responses to military aggression for assistance in formulating our response to the verbal violence of catcalls.

3. A Pacifist Response

In this final section I explore the application of pacifist principles to the verbal violence of catcalls. I begin with a brief discussion of varieties of pacifism, apply a form of humanizing pacifism to catcalls, and illustrate it with an example. I end with a discussion of the need for systemic as well as immediate responses to verbal violence.

Pacifistic responses to war vary a great deal. Duane Cady, in *From Warism to Pacifism: A Moral Continuum*, outlines several stances taken in opposition to war.[19] The pacifist responses range from absolute pacifism, which opposes violence of any kind, to selective conscientious objection or just war theory, which may oppose any given war for moral or religious reasons. In addition, Cady aptly illustrates how attempts to overcome warism are interconnected with attempts to overcome other social evils such as racism and sexism. Most of the pacifist stances entail actively working to end injustice, whether the injustice occurs in the form of war or oppression. The pacifist, then, is called to respond not only to the immediate situation of war but also to the social structures that legitimate war and other injustice. We need not, in other words, "be content with informal, guerrilla-style resistance" to catcalls.[20]

Our response to catcalls emphasizes the need to address the issue on a systemic or structural level and aims for not merely an absence of verbal violence but a "positive peace." In *Feminist Perspectives on Peace and Peace Education*, Birgit Brock-Utne clearly delineates the differences and conditions for positive and negative peace. Negative peace is merely the absence of war. Positive peace, she argues, is "the absence of indirect violence."[21] Positive peace includes the absence of structural violence such as the patriarchal societal conditions that allow and even encourage actions that degrade an individual or social group like women while another individual or social group privileges from their oppression.

For catcalls both in their immediacy and as a part of an unjust social structure, positive peace entails a pacifist response to the catcall that fits with or enhances the ideal of a social structure free of oppressive power relations. Passively accepting the social structure that allows catcalls to exist and even encourages, or at least does not actively discourage, such behavior can only keep women locked in the cage of fear which helps keep patriarchy or misogyny in place.

Peacemaking should ensure that the dehumanization of verbal violence is confronted in such a way that neither the victim nor the perpetrator is further dehumanized. Paulo Freire, in *Pedagogy of the Oppressed*, offers a model for such humanizing action. He explains that the oppressed must humanize the oppressor as well as themselves. Both the oppressed and the oppressors are "manifestations of dehumanization."[22] One of the reasons it is so central to liberation, according to Freire, that both oppressed and oppressor be humanized (and that the oppressed facilitate the humanization) is that "oppressive reality absorbs those within it and thereby acts to submerge men's [*sic*] consciousness."[23] The oppressed have the clearest understanding of oppression while the oppressors may be blinded by their privileged status. This is one of the reasons the oppressed must help the oppressor throw off the oppression. It cannot, however, be the sole responsibility of the oppressed according to Freire. Consider the following example of such liberating positive peacemaking in action.

A group of college-age men yelled a variety of different catcall things at a colleague from across four lanes of traffic. The distance is no doubt significant, as not having to look someone in the face and using the anonymity of a group of people facilitates the dehumanization process. My colleague was sufficiently miffed at their blatant dehumanization of her that she crossed the street, yelling "Hey, what's your name?" At which point they "took off running."

This example aptly displays a humanizing response to the dehumanizing catcall. The woman in the example asked the callers to identify themselves.

Such an action allows two things to occur: by asking the question she humanizes herself in the eyes of the callers. That is, an object cannot inquire. An object may have some sort of reflexive reaction but an inquirer must be a subject. Her question also humanizes the callers. The callers are asked to identify themselves not by how others see them, not as anonymous within the group of catcallers, but by how each male sees himself as individual–by his name. In addition, by answering the question my colleague posed, the callers may be faced with the question of whether they accept the responsibility for their actions. By leaving themselves unidentified, on the other hand, the callers are able to hide in anonymity or in the "group mentality."

Immediate responses to catcalls, like my colleague's in the above example, must be carefully considered so as not to legitimate the behavior of catcalls or the social structure (power structure) that allows them to exist. Instead of dehumanizing both parties, or contributing to the violence of the situation by responding in a verbally violent manner, we must reclaim our embodied subjective humanity. We must, in other words, disarm the catcaller by responding in a humanizing way.

The group of men who catcalled my colleague dehumanized her *via* their catcall but also are themselves dehumanized. Their consciousness is absorbed in an unjust social structure that may not necessarily encourage catcalls but nonetheless legitimates their continued existence. Patriarchy has so clouded their social existence that they may not even realize that catcalls are violent. This is also why it is instructive to see catcalls as part of a larger social structure and to respond to catcalls both in their immediacy and in a more systemic fashion.

Politicization of catcalls brings to light the problem while also placing it within the wider problem of sexism. The use of public forums to both identify the problem of catcalls and address the culture that they reinforce is one way to politicize catcalls. This entails challenging a system, in this case a misogynist system, that allows oppression of any form to continue. So as to not contribute to the violence of the situation, our challenge to the system should be careful not to engage any of the dehumanizing methods of the oppressor. As Freire explains,

> The struggle begins with men's [*sic*] recognition that they have been destroyed. Propaganda, management, manipulation–all areas of domination–cannot be the instruments of their rehumanization. The only effective instrument is a humanizing pedagogy in which the revolutionary leadership establishes a permanent relationship of dialogue with the oppressed.[24]

Two historical examples of humanizing systemic pacifist responses to verbal violence against women are the Anti-Flirt Club and the Take Back the Night

March. The Anti-Flirt Club was formed in Washington, D.C. in 1920. It was an organization of female office workers determined to "combat street harassment of women."[25] The 1970s saw the beginning of "Take Back the Night." "Take Back the Night" is an annual march on college campuses around the country. Through this public forum, we inform the community that we, as men and women, will not continue to accept violence in our midst. Both of these programs helped to bring the issues of verbal and physical violence against women to light. Movements such as these express the problem and provide a challenge to public space that excludes or oppresses women by trying to reclaim safe public space for everyone. As Dolores Hayden explains,

> A political program to overcome the "thereness" of women and win all female and male citizens, and their children, access to safe public urban space requires that the presence of women (and their children) in public space be established as a political right.[26]

Catcalls, and similar forms of verbal violence against individuals and oppressed groups, contribute to the perpetuation of a socially constructed image of members of a social group. Verbal violence allows cultural and physical violence to continue to be inflicted on that group. In our struggles for liberation on every front–warism, sexism, racism, heterosexism, ageism, ableism–we must remain critical of those social structures that allow or perpetuate the conditions for the possibility of oppressive practices. In other words, passive acceptance of oppressive behaviors as "cultural phenomena" about which "nothing can be done" only serves to legitimate those behaviors thereby perpetuating the violence and dehumanization for all of society. Our particularized focus to end violence on one front must be seen as "part of an overall struggle to end violence."[27] As Reardon points out, we must add a time dimension to the revolutionary phrase "think globally, act locally." That is, "think futuristically, act daily."[28]

Notes

1. Simone de Beuvoir, *The Second Sex*, trans. H. M. Parshley (New York: Bantam, 1952), p. 675.

2. United States Joint Chiefs of Staff, *Dictionary of Military and Assorted Terms* (Washington, 1986), p. 346.

3. D. G. Kehl, "War Must Be Governed by Laws," in *War and Human Nature: Opposing Viewpoints*, ed. David L. Bender and Bruno Leone (St. Paul, Minn.: Greenhaven, 1983), p. 105.

4. Sissela Bok, *A Strategy for Peace: Human Values and the Threat of War* (New York: Pantheon, 1989), p. 11.

5. Betty A. Reardon, *Sexism and the War System* (New York: Teachers College Press, 1985), p. 40.

6. Lesley J. McNair, "War Is Kill or Be Killed," in *War and Human Nature*, ed. David L. Bender and Bruno Leone (St. Paul, Minn.: Greenhaven, 1983), pp. 108-111.

7. See Birgit Brock-Utne, *Feminist Perspectives on Peace and Peace Education* (New York: Pergamon, 1989), pp. 141-149.

8. bell hooks, *Talking Back: Thinking Feminist, Thinking Black* (Boston: South End, 1989), p. 42.

9. Sandra Bartky, *Femininity and Domination: Studies in the Phenomenology of Oppression* (New York: Routledge, 1990), p. 27.

10. Deborah Cameron, *Feminism and Linguistic Theory* (New York: St. Martin's, 1992), p. 107.

11. *Ibid.*, p. 109.

12. *Ibid.*, p. 107.

13. Iris MarionYoung, *Justice and the Politics of Difference* (Princeton, N.J.: Princeton University Press, 1990), p. 62.

14. Josephine Donovan, *Feminist Theory: The Intellectual Traditions of American Feminism* (New York: Continuum, 1992), p. 136.

15. Bartky, *Femininity and Domination*, p. 27.

16. Reardon, *Sexism and the War System*, p. 38.

17. *Ibid.*

18. *Ibid.*, p. 51. See also Linda Bird Francke, *Ground Zero: The Gender War in the Military* (Needham Heights, Mass.: Simon and Schuster, 1997).

19. Duane Cady, *From Warism to Pacifism: A Moral Continuum* (Philadelphia: Temple University Press, 1989).

20. Cameron, *Feminism and Linguistic Theory*, p. 105.

21. Brock-Utne, *Feminist Perspectives on Peace*, p. 43.

22. Paulo Freire, *Pedagogy of the Oppressed*, trans. Myra Bergman Ramos (New York: Herder and Herder, 1968), p. 33.

23. *Ibid.*, p. 36.

24. Freire, *Pedagogy of the Oppressed*, p. 55.

25. Dolores Hayden, *Redesigning the American Dream* (New York: W. W. Norton, 1984), p. 213.

26. *Ibid.*, p. 212.

27. bell hooks, *Feminist Theory: From Margin to Center* (Boston: South End, 1984), p. 125.

28. Reardon, *Sexism and the War System*, p. 86.

Seventeen

RACE-MAKING AS THE PROCESS OF ENMIFICATION

Alison Bailey

> War and aggression, like racism and sexism are systematic....
> Those women who are white and define themselves as feminist
> must consciously and actively divorce themselves from the privileges
> afforded them as a result of racism so that we all might have a better
> chance at unity that would actually challenge white male privilege and its
> system of thought and action (patriarchal monopoly capitalism).
> Zala Chandler[1]

> To address not only racial oppression, but also class
> exploitation and even militarism, the idea that it is
> desirable or unavoidable to be white must be exploded.
> David Roediger[2]

To argue that peacemakers should be attentive to racism labors the obvious. Contemporary peace movements in the United States have roots in abolitionist, suffrage, labor, and civil rights struggles; and these movements have almost always made connections between peace and social justice. In this chapter, I address a less obvious connection between racism and militarism by exploring the claim that the construction of racial identities in the United States follows the militaristic logic of enemy construction. If militarism and racism are inconceivable without a clearly defined image of a hated "other," then peacemaking requires a critique of racial construction and of the privileges racial classification is meant to generate and sustain. The project of understanding how racial identities are constructed, then, is directly related to the project of peacemaking. This chapter has two basic objectives. The first is to explain the political construction of the racial category "white" in the United States as part of a process of enmification, or enemy-making. The next is to make visible the similarities between the construction of races and the construction of enemies by exploring two defining features of privileged identities–purity and indistinguishability–and to explain how these features are central to the processes of racial construction and enemy making.

1. Illusive Nature of "White" Identities

The illusive nature of white racial identity is, in part, the product of the essentialist views of race that ground ordinary racial discourse. In the United States the racial category "white" was conceived as an abstract category beyond "color." The fact that one counts as "colored" if one is not white indicates that whiteness is defined as either void of color or in opposition to color. Labeling so-called "nonwhites" as "colored" is an example of what Donna Haraway calls the God trick; it places whites in a racial category beyond and above color designation and constitutes for itself the power to name others.[3] This power hides the embodied nature of whiteness as an unmarked marker of racial privilege. Remarking on the disembodied gaze that signifies the unmarked positions of "man" and "white," Haraway insists on "the embodied nature of all vision," and that we must reclaim

> the sensory system that has been used to signify a leap out of the marked body and into a conquering [aperspectival] gaze from nowhere. This is the gaze that mythically inscribes all the marked bodies, that makes the unmarked category claim the power to see and not be seen, to represent while escaping representation.[4]

The politics of whiteness is marked by an interdependent set of characteristics that grow from this aperspectival posture. If one does not recognize white as a color, then one cannot be "colored white." I use this term intentionally to embody the gaze, to call attention to whiteness as both a standard against which racial lines are drawn and as a marker of privilege.

The historic absence of any discussion critical of "whiteness" in racial discourse suggests that whiteness acts as a nondefined (invisible) definer of color. When whiteness is not racialized we fail to see clearly the role it plays in maintaining hegemonic systems of power. Either we understand whiteness as a colorless, vacuous, formless, neutral, metacultural or metaracial identity without content, or we retreat to discussions of white ethnicity in hopes of giving whiteness some content. White people working in the peace movement who are unaware of or unwilling to understand themselves as racialized–colored white–adopt a disembodied posture which excludes them as members, participants, and perpetuators of a racialized culture. Placing whiteness outside of the racial spectrum ignores the centrality of whiteness in the formation of race and gender identities; this gives white people the privilege to address the racial dimensions of peace issues at a comfortable distance. Whites participate in political struggles and movements as missionaries, providers of services, and allies to struggle, but failure to make the connections between white privilege and the oppression of persons of color obscures the institutionalized nature of racism. This objectivist stance obscures the interactive relationships among all of our lives and prevents white activists from seeing "oppressions as interlocking systems shaping everyone's experience and identity."[5]

Since whiteness is encoded in systems of racial classification in the United States, discussions of white identity must begin with an inquiry into the nature of racial classification itself. In ordinary language, so-called "races" are understood as categories of human beings based on average differences in physical traits transmitted genetically; but traits do not a race make, traits are only traits. There are no racial essences that give meaning to the concept race, and there are no necessary and sufficient conditions for racial membership. A light complexion, ability to digest lactose, straight hair, or fine facial features occur in nature, but the notion that this particular group of traits collectively comprises a "race" that is metaphysically divisible from other races is an ideological construction pure and simple. Human genetic variation is the result of a seamless continuum of genetic change across the globe. The vast majority of human genetic variation occurs within populations not between them and only some six percent are accounted for by "race."[6] If races are not natural kinds and are instead socio-political constructs, then it makes more sense to talk about racial classifications than it does to talk about race.

It seems fairly obvious that to be racially classified as white means more than just being classified as Caucasian. As Marilyn Frye states: "The concept of whiteness, is not just used...it is *wielded*"; to be white is to be a member of an exclusive club whose membership is closely guarded.[7] History illustrates this point. The first European colonists in the Americas had no concept of themselves as "white." Legal documents from Virginia initially referred to whites as Christians and, toward the mid-seventeenth century, as Englishmen.[8] The choice of "Christian" or "English" as group designations reflects a binary (A/not-A) construction of identity; to be Christian was to be not-heathen. When referring to indigenous populations, English colonists at Jamestown and in Maryland used the terms "savages" and "pagans" respectively. Since all non-Englishmen were clearly identified as Irish, Scots, Dutch, or French, the designations Neger or Negro were most likely national designations.[9] Before the 1660s, class and race prejudice were difficult if not impossible to distinguish. Indentured servitude was common for both Africans and Europeans, and the contempt behind descriptions of both groups does not appear to differ. Some white servants were reduced to slavery upon arrival to the colonies, some were sold to the Powatan people, and at one point there was even a controversial plan to send Irish girls to Jamaica for breeding purposes. Thus, it is likely that the operative distinctions and prejudices among colonists were based on class rather than race.[10]

The racial category "white" was established as a legal concept shortly after Bacon's Rebellion in 1676. Its purpose was to strategically separate servants of European and African descent who united against the colonial elite during the later part of the seventeenth century. Although this designation was not the result of Bacon's Rebellion alone, there is sufficient historical evidence to suggest that the category "white" developed as a response to the fear of servant uprisings against wealthy landowners. Elite Virginians felt threatened by the possibility that servants, slaves, and disappointed freedmen would make a common cause and rise up against the landowning class. After the Servant's Uprising of 1663, Bacon's Rebellion, and the 1683 Tobacco Riots, there was a concerted effort among members of the House of Burgesses in Virginia to draw up statutes aimed at dividing white and black labor. When servant rebellions temporarily subsided, a steady stream of racially specific legislation regulating marriage, baptism, illegitimate births, and periods of indenture convinced white servants and white freedmen that it was in their interest to grant alliances along visible signs of skin tone rather than along class lines as they had in the past.[11] Slavery slowly became a permanent and inheritable condition for Africans, while Europeans were freed upon the expiration of their indenture. In Virginia the word "white" began appearing in legal documents around 1682 as a direct result of new legislation enforcing the hereditary bond servitude of Negroes, anti-miscegenation laws, and new anti-Negro attitudes.[12] By the early eighteenth century the idea of a homogeneous white race was adopted as a political means of generating cohesion among European explorers, traders, migrants, and settlers of North America.[13]

But the boundaries of the category "white" were not set once and for all in the late seventeenth century. One of the most striking features of racial classification is its elasticity. Like all racial categories, "white" is an ambiguous concept whose boundaries as a racial designation are never fixed. The political nature of whiteness as an exclusive club requires that the boundaries of racial classification be constantly re-invented as new candidates for whiteness arise. It is possible for persons to change their race according to where they are, when they are there, and what they are doing. Persons of mixed race, for example, have been able to change their racial classification by crossing a geographical boundary. In 1785, Virginia legally classified as Negro all those persons having one black parent or grandparent. This allowed mulattos to be legally white if their ancestry was less than one-fourth black; crossing over into South Carolina, however, meant being legally classified as mulatto.[14] In 1930, Virginia adopted the one-drop rule, and the statute exempted individuals having one fourth or more Indian blood and less than one-sixteenth Negro blood. These individuals were members of their tribe while on reservations, but were classified as "colored" while off the reservation.[15]

While some states have had general racial classification statutes, others have legislated racial classifications for particular activities such as marriage or education. This means that racial classification changes with activity. The Kentucky case of *Mullins v. Belcher* (1911), for instance, held that a child having one-sixteenth Negro blood could not attend a white school. Nevertheless, other legislation dictated that any person who looks white and has white phenotypic characteristics is not classified as mulatto under Kentucky anti-miscegenation statutes.[16] So it was possible for a person to be classified as black when attending school, but white when signing marriage papers. Thus, racial categorization is not a neutral means of classification; it is a privilege-generating taxonomy that shifts historically to preserve the unearned advantages associated with being classified as white. The constant gerrymandering of racial boundaries demonstrates that to be white "is to be a member of a self-defining kin group whose membership line is closely guarded."[17]

The principal mechanism of complex systems of domination, such as racism or heterosexism, is to structure the world so that privileges are invisible to those who stand to benefit from them. Just as most men or most heterosexuals are carefully taught not to recognize privileges that come with being male or being heterosexual, so whites are taught not to acknowledge the unearned advantages granted with being classified "white." The systemic and unexamined nature of what it means to have dominant group privilege is made clearer by Peggy McIntosh's metaphor of the "invisible knapsack" given to persons who are members of the group "white." White privilege, she argues,

[is] an invisible package of unearned assets that I can count on cashing in each day, but about which I was "meant" to remain oblivious. White privilege is like an invisible weightless knapsack of special provisions, assurances, tools, maps, guides, code books, passports, visas, clothes, compass, emergency gear, and blank checks. [18]

It is worth highlighting some of the common examples of white privilege in this sense. Briefly, some of these privileges include:

I can, if I wish, arrange to be in the company of people of my race most of the time.

I can be sure that my children will be given curricular material that testifies to the existence of their race.

I am never asked to speak for all the people of my racial group.

I can dress any way I want and not have my appearance explained by the perceived tastes of my race.

Whether I use checks, credit cards, or cash I can be fairly sure that my skin color will not count against the appearance of my financial reliability.

In most instances I can be assured of having the public trust.[19]

In this way whiteness is an invisible package of unearned assets that white people can count on cashing in each day, but about which they were meant to remain oblivious.

The maintenance of whiteness as a position of structural advantage lies in the silence surrounding its invisibility, vagueness, imprecision, and instability. Because white survival does not depend upon constant awareness of invisible knapsacks, most whites are not in a structural position to see the affects of racialization on their lives. For the white race to exist, the boundaries have to shift constantly to exclude undesirable identities. Maintaining the fictitious boundaries designed to protect white purity, however, requires the vilification of other so-called "nonwhite" identities.

2. Other-Making and the Logic of Privileged Identity Construction

To understand race-making as a process of enmification, we need to unpack the logic underlying race-making as a form of privileged identity construction. In *Faces of the Enemy*, Sam Keen explores what he calls a phenomenology of the hostile imagination. Keen defines human beings as *homo hostilis*, a hostile enemy-making species, driven to construct enemies as scapegoats for the unconscious remnants of our own hostility and hatred.[20] The confrontations we engage in are compulsive rituals by which we continue to try to irradicate the parts of ourselves we despise. Our best hope for survival, he suggests, is to change the way we have been taught to think about enemies. In short, we need to examine carefully the construction of the eyes through which we see those we cast as "other," foreign, or unlike ourselves. However, I would argue that this examination is incomplete if it focuses on how we see the "other" while avoiding a critical examination of the invisible privileges generated by the activity of other-making.

The majority of nations, racial/ethnic groups, tribes, classes, and cultures create a social solidarity and membership in part by systematically fashioning themselves against feared tribes and nations. Group identity is fashioned largely by dividing the world into a basic A/not-A antagonism, and assigning a superior value to the A side of the dichotomy. One of the primary functions of this hostile divisive ontology is to rationalize war and violence, to justify harms, and to dismiss injustices against persons or groups we view as significantly unlike ourselves. It is worth spelling out in detail the features and consequences of adopting an organizing principle which divides the world into us/them, white/"colored," male/female, or civilized/savage.

The logic of oppositional (A/not-A) identity formation is at the heart of all complex systems of domination such as racism, sexism, heterosexism, classism, ageism, and militarism. Central to this logic is the idea that A identities are stable, normal, and generic human selves. Essentialist views of race, grounding racial classification in the United States, and construction of enemies in war propaganda, share this oppositional logic. On the A/not-A model, categories like "white," and "man," are central signifiers, so white women, and both men and women of color, have negative identities as "not-white," "not-man," or "not white/man." The underlying feature of the A/not-A logic focuses attention on a stable center that is held in place by what spins at a safe distance around it. The language that accompanies the construction of enemies and so-called nonwhites is an exclusionary language that places the "generic" subject as male, European/white, peaceloving, democratic, or civilized at the center of inquiry. The construction of subjects along the A/not-A dichotomy insures that A identities have privileged status. Since authority is a mark of privileged subjectivity, its preservation requires a safe distance to be maintained between this "A self" and "not-A other." As the history of "white" as an unstable racial category illustrates, it is only through this distancing process that boundaries of racial classification could be drawn and re-drawn as patterns of immigration challenged established racial boundaries and new candidates for whiteness arose. The nature of privileged subjects is made clearer by focusing on two themes inherent in this logic: the purity of the A-identity and the indistinguishablity of not-A identities.

3. Purity and Contamination

The purity and contamination dichotomy is operative in the construction of both races and enemies. Naomi Scheman's work on the construction of privileged identities has this to say about the role of purity in maintaining boundaries between subjects:

> The epistemic project of the privileged (or those who seek to join their ranks) has been: first, to distance themselves sufficiently from the contaminating influences of the body so that what they believe will come to have the status of knowledge (because it will either be replicated by those who similarly abstract themselves from anything that could lead them to think differently or will be challenged by those who can be dismissed because they've failed to purify themselves).[21]

The assignment of privileges to persons on the basis of racial markers can only work if racial boundaries are rigidly maintained. One way to preserve boundaries is to create a distance between oneself and others by portraying them as dirty, animalistic, savage, or violent. White purity/supremacy, for example, is based on the degradation of black bodies. The so-called "contaminating effect" of the blood of darker races is evident in the strong asymmetry in the rules of racial inheritance. The rule of hypodescent declares that if person P has one black parent, grandparent, or great-grandparent, regardless of person P's phenotype, person P is nonwhite. But it does not follow that if person P has any white parent, grandparent, or great-grandparent, person P is categorized as white. One black family member is sufficient to negate the whiteness (purity) of P's line of descent. Anything short of pure whiteness is "colored." The asymmetrical nature of kinship for white people and people of color highlights the importance of racial purity and posits whiteness as a position of structural advantage. Being white comes with a set of legislated social and structural privileges which many whites believe are acquired solely by merit.

Current racial categories on United States census and most university affirmative action forms still reflect this logic. The descendants of one white person and any nonwhite identity (for example, Asian, black, Latino) will always be a hyphenated American. In all mixed race identities the one drop that determines identity is the nonwhite drop regardless of race or ethnicity. The language of purity and contamination is still present in the discourse of liberal whites who "don't see color" or "are not racist." One example of this occurred during a national press conference when Caspar Weinberger told reporters that when he looked at Colin Powell he saw "not a 'black' man, but a man."[22] Behind this popular phrase is, I believe, a fear that any acknowledgment of race can be interpreted as being racist, as contaminating. In this respect purity seems to presuppose color blindness.

A similar process is at work in enemy-making which is often done along racial or ethnic lines. Like the white race, the Aryan race as such does not exist. The construction of an Aryan identity, however, was integral to Nazi Germany's construction of a new national enemy. In *Mein Kampf*, Adolf Hitler marks out this new identity by describing so-called inferior races in the discourse of disease and impurity. Paraphrasing Hitler's views, Robert W. Rieber and Robert J. Kelly explain that Hitler sought a cure for an era infected with sickness and disease. He identified the cause of this contamination as the pollution of the pure Aryan race with the inferior, degenerate blood of Jews and Slavs.[23] A contaminating other was necessary for the construction of a pure Aryan identity. The contaminating impact of these groups extended beyond the Aryan gene pool; it was also reflected in the perception that these groups culturally polluted the body politic. By portraying Jews in particular as "inferior races," which "plagued" the nation, Nazi ideology succeeds in making Jews appear as what they are not–dangerous, greedy, and a threat to the nation. The iconography of Nazi war propaganda depicts the Jew as "physically repugnant, as sexually ravenous and hideous, as obese or unaesthetically thin and frail,...as something even lower than an animal." In a classic act of enmification, this "defenseless minority was turned into a public 'enemy' as a means of providing a sense of vitality to a policy that was rationally and morally bankrupt, and as a means of uniting and mobilizing a disorganized and disheartened populace."[24]

The purity of white identity is also sustained culturally. In the United States, whites have historically maintained their race privilege by projecting onto recent immigrants and persons of color all corrupting habits and influences that detract from their whiteness.[25] For example, in *From Sundown to Sunup*, George Rawick argues that one of the reasons racism grew so quickly in eighteenth-century America was that blackness came to symbolize all that accumulating capitalists had given up, but still desired. As whites increasingly adopted a world view that attacked holidays, saved time, eschewed contact with nature, bridled sexuality, postponed gratification, and separated work from the rest of life, these discarded habits became attached to peoples of color who were seen as closer to nature, less moral, more bodily, hypersexual, pleasure seeking, and lazy because they took time off from work, and were not time conscious. In Rawick's words:

> The racist like the reformed sinner, creates a pornography of his former life....In order to insure that he will not slip back into the old ways or act out half-suppressed fantasies, he must see a tremendous difference between his reformed self and those whom he formerly resembled.[26]

If well-integrated, psychologically stable individuals are aware of their own vices, then they do not need an enemy onto which evils are projected. The process of enmification, however, projects onto opponents all of one's corrupting habits and influences. From a psychological standpoint of the A identity, enemy-making, like race-making, is an

> emotional catharsis and outpouring of oneself in an unusual way; one's least desirable traits and dispositions are projected onto another, transferred to the enemy, so that the presence of the enemy means the dissolution of those unsavory characteristics that may have previously defined oneself.[27]

Addressing the process by which cold war paranoia divided the world into the good guys, who were righteousness and pure, and the bad guys, who were characterized by the attributes of savageness, hostility, and evil, Keen remarks:

> [Paranoia] begins with a splitting of the "good" self, with which we consciously identify and which is celebrated by myth and media, from the "bad" self, which remains unconscious so long as it may be projected onto the enemy. By this slight of hand, the unacceptable parts of the self–its greed, cruelty, sadism, hostility...are made to disappear and are

recognized only as qualities of the enemy. Paranoia reduces anxiety and guilt by transferring to the other all the characteristics one does not want to recognize in oneself.[28]

Paranoia allows A identities to see and to acknowledge only those aspects of the enemy's behavior which confirm common stereotypes. Thus in the United States press we hear about the mining of the Red Sea, the cruelty of the Serbs, and the tyranny of Saddam Hussein, but nothing of our mining of Nicaraguan harbors, our role in international arms trafficking, or the tyranny of United States corporate imperialism abroad. Whatever the A identity considers to be bad, wrong, taboo, distasteful, forbidden, or inhumane will be used to construct images of the enemy. During World War II, it was rumored that Nazis cannibalized children. During the Gulf War Hussein was said to have been a brutal womanizer who slept with young women and then had them executed. Keen's survey of war propaganda across the globe highlights common themes constructing the enemy as rapist and desecrator of women and children, criminal committer of atrocities and torture, enemy of God, barbarian, greedy and wasteful, and beast-like.

4. Indistinguishability of Not-A Identities

A second feature common to the construction of racialized subjects and enemies is the idea that membership in the not-A category means that a person's identity is indistinguishable from other items in the not-A group. The logic of opposition does not distinguish between not-A identities. It does not fashion these distinct racial identities into autonomously defined categories. That is, the construction of most not-A racial categories is rarely left up to those who occupy them. To be part of the not-A (nonwhite) category is to be part of a hodgepodge of undifferentiated, formless, undeliniated items that are only related insofar as they share the ontological status not-A. To make this point Frye gives a humorous example using the category "vanilla."

> If, for instance, "vanilla" is assigned as the A, then not-A includes not only strawberry, chocolate, and peppermint ripple but also triangles, the square root of two, the orbit of Haley's comet, and all of the shoes in the world. All of these are not vanilla, and *as not* vanilla, they are indistinguishable. The vanilla/not-vanilla dichotomy makes no distinction within the realm of not-vanilla. [29]

Likewise the formless, undifferentiated pile of nonwhite identities might include black, Mexican, Vietnamese, Winnebago, or people who look white and speak with "foreign" accents. So this view does not split the world into two equal piles. It splits everything into "white" and an undifferentiated heap of "other" identities "that all look alike" and do not fit the white category. One effect of undifferentiation is that bodies of color are understood to be interchangeable, as indistinguishable from one another. The perceived indistinguishability between African Americans, or between Mexicans, justifies their exploitation as low paid domestics, fieldworkers, service providers, and caregivers. As laborers they are interchangeable and their expedibility is justified.

The construction of enemies also relies on indistinguishability. The object of warfare is to destroy the enemy and to do this we systematically create a faceless enemy by blurring the distinctions between individuals and thinking of them only as "the enemy." As Keen explains:

> Almost all works on war refer to the enemy obliquely. A strange silence pervades political, military and popular thought on this matter. Our reluctance to think clearly about the enemy appears to be an unconscious conspiracy. We systematically blur distinctions and insist that the enemy remain faceless, because we are able to perpetuate the horror of war, to be the authors of unthinkable suffering only when we blind ourselves to what we are doing. Traditionally we have maintained this practice of unthinking by creating dehumanizing stereotypes of the objects of our violence....[30]

The enemy becomes a flexible not-A category in which we may assign any threat about which we do not wish to think clearly. Facelessness is a precondition for destruction. The imagination of *homo hostilis* systematically destroys our natural human tendency to identify with others. A healthy imagination would, at best, lead us to the recognition that those we are fighting against are very much like ourselves, and, at worst, lead us to recognize that we ought to discriminate between combatants and non-combatants. The hostile imagination makes both identification with the enemy and distinction between enemies impossible. The failure of William Calley, the lieutenant in charge of the U. S. Platoon at the My Lai Massacre, to see women and children as illegitimate targets of violence is a striking instance of this. In Calley's own words:

> I was ordered to go in there and destroy the enemy....I did not sit down and think in terms of men, women, and children. They were all classified the same, and that was the classification that we dealt with, just as enemy soldiers.[31]

The project of understanding how racial identities are constructed is directly related to the project of peacemaking. If militarism and racism are inconceivable without a clearly defined image of a hated "other," then peacemaking requires a critique of the logic of enemy construction that privilege-generating systems of racial classification are meant to sustain. It is also important to recognize that social change can be brought about without enmification. Mohandas Gandhi and Martin Luther King, Jr. were both able to alter the social structure of entire nations without resorting to the process of enemy making. Neither Gandhi nor King demonized their oppressors by turning them into enemies in the minds of their followers. For Gandhi, it was not the British people who quelled India's independence movement. Instead, the problem lay in the fact that the British failed to appreciate the extent to which Indians had internalized liberal principles of democracy, and thought that these principles should apply to themselves. The British were not the problem, colonialism was. Likewise, King avoided the process of enemy-making by refusing to demonize whites by calling them racists. He simply argued that the values of autonomy, liberty, and equality should be applied equally and without reservation to all Americans regardless of color. White Americans were not the problem, racism was.[32] In both cases there is an agreement that the values of liberal democracy are good values, but that selective application of these values falls short of their initial goals. Our best hope for survival, then, is to change the way we have been taught to think about enemies; and, an integral part of this project requires that we understand race-making as a privilege-generating and enemy-making process of classification.

Notes

1. Zala Chandler, "Antiracism, Antisexism, and Peace (Sapphire's Perspective)," in *Rocking the Ship of State: Toward a Feminist Peace Politics,* ed. Adrienne Harris and Ynestra King (Boulder, Colo: Westview, 1989), pp. 32-33.

2. David Roediger, *Toward the Abolition of Whiteness* (New York: Verso, 1994), p. ix.

3. Donna Haraway, "Situated Knowledges: The Science Question in Feminism and the Privilege of Partial Perspective," *Feminist Studies,* 14:3 (Fall 1988), pp. 575-599.

4. *Ibid.*, p. 581.

5. Ruth Frankenburg, *White Women, Race Matters: The Social Construction of Whiteness* (Minneapolis, Minn.: University of Minnesota Press, 1993), p. 10; and Ann Russo, "We Cannot Live without Our Lives: White Women, Antiracism, and Feminism," in *Third-World Women and the Politics of Feminism,* ed. Chandra Talpade Mohanty, Ann Russo, and Lourdes Torres (Bloomington, Ind.: University of Indiana Press, 1991), pp. 299-300.

6. Richard Lewontin's 1972 study cited in James Shreeve, "Terms of Estrangement," *Discover* (November 1994), p. 60.

7. Marilyn Frye, "On Being White: Thinking toward a Feminist Understanding of Race and Race Supremacy," *The Politics of Reality: Essays in Feminist Theory* (Freedom, Calif.: Crossing, 1983), p. 115.

8. William Walter Hening, *The Statutes at Large: Being a Collection of All the Laws of Virginia*, vols. 1-3, (New York: R. and W. and G. Bartow, 1823); Virginia, House of Burgesses, *Journals of the House of Burgesses of Virginia, 1619-1658*, ed. H. R. McLlwaine (Richmond, Vir.: Colonial, E. Waddey, 1915); Winthrop D. Jordan. *White over Black: American Attitudes toward the Negro, 1550-1812* (Chapel Hill, N.C.: University of North Carolina Press, 1968), pp. 94-97; and Theodore Allen, *The Invention of the White Race: Racial Oppression and Social Control*, vol. 1 (New York: Verso, 1994), pp. 10-11.

9. Lerone Bennett, Jr., *The Shaping of Black America* (Chicago: Johnson, 1975), pp. 5-20.

10. *Ibid.;* and Edmund S. Morgan, *American Slavery, American Freedom: The Ordeal of Colonial Virginia* (New York: W. W. Norton, 1975), pp. 235-249 and 325-328.

11. Hening, *Statues*, vol. 2, pp. 26, 119, 170, 260, 283, 490, and 491, and vol. 3, pp. 87, 88, 251, 304, 450, 453, and 495.

12. *Ibid.*, vol. 2, p. 515.

13. Theodore Allen, *The Invention of the White Race*, pp. 1-24; David R. Roediger, *The Wages of Whiteness: Race and the Making of the American Working Class* (New York: Verso, 1991), pp. 3-40; Jordan, *White over Black;* and Lerone Bennett, Jr., *Before the Mayflower: A History of Black America* (Chicago: Johnson, 6th ed., 1987).

14. F. James Davis, *Who Is Black?: One Nation's Definition* (University Park, Penn.: Pennsylvania State University Press, 1993), pp. 34-35.

15. Charles S. Mangum, Jr., *The Legal Status of the Negro* (Chapel Hill, N.C.: The University of North Carolina Press, 1940), p. 6; and Davis, *Who Is Black?*, p. 9.

16. *Mullins V. Blecher*, 142 Ky. 673, 143 S. W. 1151 (1911) and *Theophanis V. Theophanis*, 244 Ky. 689, 57 S. W. (2d) 957 (1932); and Mangum, *The Legal Status of the Negro*, p. 12.

17. Frye. "On Being White," pp. 114-115.

18. Peggy McIntosh, "White Privilege and Male Privilege: A Personal Account of Coming to See Correspondences through Work in Women's Studies," *Race, Class, and Gender: An Anthology*, ed. Margaret L. Andersen and Patricia Hill Collins (Belmont, Calif.: Wadsworth, 1991), p. 71.

19. *Ibid.*, pp. 71-72.

20. Sam Keen, *Faces of the Enemy: Reflections of the Hostile Imagination*, ed. Anne Page (San Francisco: Harper and Row, 1986), pp. 11 and 25.

21. Naomi Scheman, *Engenderings: Constructions of Knowledge, Authority, and Privilege* (New York: Routledge, 1993), p. 193.

22. Cornel West, "The Importance of Black History Month" (talk given at Illinois Weslayan University in Bloomington, Ill, on 1 February 1997).

23. Robert W. Rieber and Robert J. Kelly, "Substance and Shadow: Images of the Enemy," in *The Psychology of War and Peace: Images of the Enemy*, ed. Robert W. Rieber (New York: Plenum, 1991), p. 23.

24. *Ibid.*

25. Marilyn Frye, "White Woman Feminist," *Willful Virgin: Essays in Feminism, 1976-1992* (Freedom, Calif.: Crossing, 1992), pp. 147-169.

26. George Rawick, *From Sundown to Sunup: The Making of the Black Community* (Westport, Conn.: 1972), pp. 132-133. Cited in David R. Roediger, *The Wages of Whiteness,* p. 95.

27. T. Sheehan, *The First Coming* (New York: Random House, 1986), cited in Reiber and Kelly, *The Psychology of War and Peace,* p. 16.

28. Keen, *Faces of the Enemy,* p. 19.

29. Marilyn Frye, "The Necessity of Differences: Constructing a Positive Category of Women," *Signs: Journal of Women, Culture, and Society,* 21:4 (Summer 1996), p. 999.

30. Keen, *Faces of the Enemy,* p. 24.

31. Cited in *ibid.,* p. 25.

32. Robert W. Rieber and Robert J. Kelly, "Substance and Shadow," p. 14.

Eighteen

GANGS AND NATIONS: PARALLELS AND ANALOGIES

Ron Hirschbein

What most folks miserably fail to realize is that our wars
are no less complicated than world wars....Some causes are
righteous and in accord with human nature, while others are
reactionary and repressive. Gang wars fall somewhere in between.
Former Crip, "Monster" Kody Scott[1]

Street gangs in the military? To the embarrassment of the Pentagon,
the answer is definitely yes. A *Newsweek* investigation shows that
gang activity has been reported in all four branches of the armed
services and at more than 50 major military bases around the nation.
Newsweek, 24 July 1995[2]

Academic studies of peacemaking tend to concentrate on international
conflict. This is appropriate given the ongoing regional wars that plague
humanity. Unfortunately, this preoccupation with averting and resolving
international conflict overlooks the gang warfare that kills thousands in
American inner-cities. A more robust notion of peacemaking invites a sober
appreciation of the fatal attraction of gangs that, according to "Monster"
Kody Scott, "Recruit more people than the...United States Armed Forces do."[3]
Accordingly, in order to facilitate peacemaking in the inner-city, two
questions that are the subject of this chapter must be resolved: Why are gangs
attractive to inner-city youth? And, what is the nature of gang warfare in
theory and practice?

Scott was called "Monster" because his brutality shocked seasoned
gangsters. This chapter critiques his narrative response to these issues. In his
autobiographical saga there are striking parallels between gangs and nations.
Specifically, he likens his war against the Bloods (a rival gang) with wars
between nation-states (especially the Vietnam War). This chapter aims to
understand whether Scott's comparisons are truly parallels, or merely
analogies–tendentious comparisons that exaggerate similarities while
concealing differences.

The views of national leaders are not helpful in this matter: they are not
in the habit of likening themselves to gangsters. Such appellations are re-
served for adversaries: George Bush dubbed Saddam Hussein a gangster; and

in 1962 Fidel Castro called John F. Kennedy a gangster (among other things) during the Cuban Missile Crisis. (A variety of political actors and analysts referred to leaders in the recent Balkan civil war as "gangsters.") The popular press is predictable: gangs get bad press because they engage in "senseless killing"; however, as the Persian Gulf conflict illustrates, the American media generally regards killing orchestrated by American governing elites as patently sensible.

The ethos of national leaders differs markedly from gangster "attitude." If I may be permitted an anecdotal indulgence: I felt comfortable conversing over coffee and Christmas cookies at the home of a former Director of the Lawrence Livermore Laboratory. I suspect that a visit with the Crips would be less congenial. And yet, I am haunted by a possibility explored by sociologist Stjepan Mestrovic in his *Barbarian Temperament*. Contrasting the myth of progress and enlightenment with the real atrocities perpetrated by modern governing elites, he suggests:

> In a very real sense, all of the human animal's profound education...culture, and technical competence has not bettered nor tamed his or her aggression, brutality and destructiveness. And, one could make a case for the claim that things are getting progressively worse.[4]

In other words, beneath a veneer of civilized gentility, elites remain barbaric. Compared to twentieth-century massacres and holocausts, the wars of the past seem almost nostalgic. I entertain the possibility that Scott's tropes are not hyperboles. Let us examine his account of the attraction of gangs.

1. Fatal Attraction

> To be in a gang in South Central...is the equivalent of growing up in Grosse Pointe, Michigan, and going to college: everyone does it. Those who don't aren't part of the fraternity.[5]

According to Scott, gangs exist because, like international warfare, they are a well-established institution. In the inner-city, belonging to a gang is as natural as other unquestioned practices such as driving on freeways or shopping in suburbia. Like other ascendant institutions, gangs survive and prosper by meeting diverse needs. What are they?

In Scott's narrative, economic factors play a surprisingly minor role in accounting for the institutionalization of gangs. Gangsters are not above stealing cars and dealing drugs to make money. As sociologist M. S. Jankowski argues, their "anti-social" behavior differs little from the machinations of certain corporate elites; he cites a gangbanger's diatribe:

I act like they do in the big time, no different. There ain't no corporation that acts with morals...and I ain't about to either....They sell a two-cent bolt to the government for $30 and don't blink an eye. They get caught, but they ain't sorry, they're just sorry they got caught.[6]

A crucial difference exists: gangs are illegal. Popular media coverage overlooks wholesale legal violence and obsesses on relatively small-scale illegal violence. Sensationalizing the retail mayhem fomented by illegal gangs distracts attention from perfectly legal, momentous mayhem: corporations that deal nicotine and alcohol–thereby creating massive suffering and social problems–are treated differently from gangsters hustling illegal drugs. Likewise, "shrewd investors" play the stock market, while "degenerates" shoot craps in the ghetto.

Scott acknowledges these economic factors, but stresses that gangbangers do not live by contraband alone. They gamble for higher stakes: he and his comrades were consumed with making history, not money. It is noteworthy that political analyst Richard Barnet reaches the same conclusion in his account of American national security managers.[7] *Monster* is the saga of cadres of young men struggling to make a name for themselves–to gain respect–on the mean streets of the inner-city. Again, drawing comparisons with the international realm, Scott argues that gangs are a response to the Balkanization of America, a burgeoning ethnic intolerance and hatred that foments a pathological group mentality: "An atmosphere is developing here similar to that in Bosnia and Herzegovina due to the failure of positive multicultural existence."[8]

Responding to this American-style Balkanization, gangs–not unlike official military organizations–offer security, brotherhood, status, and rites of passage into manhood. Recollecting his triumphant return from battle, Scott shares a cherished memory: "When I went back among my troops I saw pride, love and admiration in their faces....I felt like a world champion, a liberator...."[9] Such pride and bonding parallel the experience of combatants. As William Broyles, Jr., a Vietnam veteran, observes:

> The enduring emotion of war, when everything else had faded, is comradeship. A comrade...you can trust with anything, because you trust him with your life....Unlike marriage [war is] a bond that cannot be broken by a word, by boredom or divorce, or by anything other than death.[10]

However, Scott stresses that gangbanging is not merely an attempt to nurture and express virtues such as pride, admiration, and love. To paraphrase William James's gloss on war, revealing the horror of gang warfare does no good; that is its main attraction. Gangbanging punctuates the monotony of ghetto life by offering illicit excitement, what Vietnam veterans call "the Jazz." It offers what Sigmund Freud deemed the supreme pleasure: the sudden, unexpected release of long-repressed, forbidden impulses. Scott favors us with numerous expressions of such intoxicating desublimation:

> I lived for the power surge of playing God, having the power of life and death in my hands. Nothing I knew could compare with riding in a car with three other homeboys with guns, knowing that they were as deadly and courageous as I was.[11]

Scott's revelation was not unlike Broyles's perverse epiphany in Vietnam:

> The love of war stems from the union, deep in the core of our being, between sex and destruction...love and death. War may be the only way in which most men touch the mythic domains in our soul....[It is] the initiation into the power of life and death. It is like lifting off the corner of the universe and looking at what's underneath.[12]

Nevertheless, a crucial difference between gangs and nations must be reiterated, a polar opposition that may reveal the primary attraction of gangs– their illicit nature. To paraphrase James once again: it does no good to indict the illegitimacy of gangbanging–that is its main attraction! Sociologist Richard Sennett's penetrating study of charismatic authority concludes that, for diverse reasons, illicit leadership is more seductive than staid authority bearing the imprimatur of legitimacy.[13] Consider the heroic narratives that resonate through time–sagas of young heroes defying elders, risking every-thing, and working wonders in history. Jason's death-defying adventures are the template for countless derivative dramas; Solon's law-giving is the stuff of classrooms and educational television. Likewise, Dwight D. Eisenhower's relatively peaceful administration is represented as lackluster and uneventful; Kennedy's imprudent risks are enshrined as "Camelot." In a like manner, inner-city youth have little incentive to fight for legitimate governments. Illicit gangs are more appealing. As Scott allows: "I knew...that the total lawlessness was alluring, and that the sense of importance, self-worth, and raw power was...intoxicating beyond any other high on the planet."[14]

This is not to suggest that gangsters are disinclined to joining the military. Much to the dismay of the powers-that-be, gangbangers enlist, but their reasons are far from patriotic. A recent United States Justice Department symposium convened by Janet Reno concluded that military service provides an opportunity for gangbangers to purloin weapons beyond their wildest dreams: "Some gangs have access to highly sophisticated personal weapons such as grenades, machine guns, rocket launchers and military explosives."[15] This "kid in the candy store" appeal of the Armed Services' arsenals presents a host of problems for those who would maintain martial discipline: turf battles on aircraft carriers and gang-related attacks on military bases are not unusual. And, a recent Air Force manual expands upon telltale signs of gang membership, and even offers a glossary of gangbanging cant and gestures.[16]

Unhappily, the fatal attraction of gangbanging is not limited to the mean streets, the prisons, and the military. The youth culture emulates, even celebrates, the ethos of gangbanging. Even college students find certain "gangsta" affectations irresistible. Gangsters are not the only ones who adorn reversed baseball hats *de rigueur,* and wear baggy shorts. Could it be that the widespread appeal of "Gangsta Rap" reveals the appeal of illicit heroes?

2. Gangbanging: Theory and Practice

We plotted...most of the night trying to decide on which act would...grab their attention. We pondered castration, blinding, sticking a shotgun up the victim's rectum, and cutting off his ears....After all, killing him would be too easy, too final. No, we wanted him to live, to be a walking reminder of our seriousness.[17]

Finding apologists for atrocities committed by nation-states is not difficult. My Lai was an "unfortunate incident," as was burying Iraqi soldiers alive in the land war in Kuwait. Killing countless Iraqi civilians was merely "collateral damage" (a term that sounds no worse than a bad credit report). Unlike nations that enjoy a monopoly on interpretive practices, gangs lack apologists–let alone influential theorists–to justify their conduct. Scott is no latter-day Thomas Aquinas proffering a summa on gangbanging. However, Scott's moral sensibility is far from seamless. In places he depicts inner-city gangsters as cruel nihilists lacking any moral horizon whatsoever. He claims that this lack of a moral code differentiates ghetto gangs from older mobs. This deficit is seen as the result of the devaluation, if not the destruction, of Afro-American culture.

[Italian gangsters] overstood [*sic*] their heritage and their relation to the world as European people. We, on the other hand, were just Crips with no sense of anything before us or where we were headed. We were trapped behind the veil of cultural ignorance without even knowing it.[18]

Yet, like a philosopher, Scott cannot resist the temptation to rationalize his actions. His rationalizations combine vintage political realism with an over-determined, quasi-Freudian account of group pathology. At times, he sounds like a mainstream realist attributing simple, transparent motives to social actors thrown into an anarchist situation not of their making. His perspective is akin to the *Realpolitik* of officials such as James Woolsey, former Director of the CIA, who admonishes that–through no fault of the United States–it is a jungle out there. The "Soviet dragon" has been slain but, he says, "We live now in a jungle filled with a bewildering variety of poisonous snakes, and in many ways the dragon was easier to keep track of."[19] Accordingly, the United States must remain the strongest, cleverest political animal.

Likewise, Scott explains that the Crips must remain strong and cunning:

> My activity gravitated around a survival instinct: kill or be killed. Conditions dictated that I evolve or perish. I did not start this cycle, nor did I conspire to create conditions [for]...murder. My participation came as second nature.[20]

Unlike Woolsey, Scott suggests there is a pathology inherent in the collective mentality endemic to gangs and nations, the perverse power of what Freud called the "Oldest Psychology." This mentality is the most ancient, universal, and irresistible force acting upon our species. As Freud explains:

> The individual in a group is subjected through its influence to what is often a profound alteration of his mental activity. His liability to affect becomes extraordinarily intensified, while his intellectual ability is markedly reduced.[21]

Scott's account of himself equivocates between *Realpolitik* and intoxicating group pathology. At times he insists that he was thrown into a milieu that virtually required gangbanging for survival. He also depicts gangs as a seductive, cult-like experience that distorted his thought, emotions, and behavior. In the end, his narrative becomes a lamentation in which he takes responsibility for his actions and claims that he could have done otherwise. The combat narratives of many a warrior labor under the same vacillation. The freedom/determinism controversy cannot be resolved here. But it is reasonable to conclude that the conflicts typical of our twisted and cruel century do not bring out the best in our species.

The dirty wars fought in Indochina, the Balkans, and the streets of Los Angeles, corroborate Freud's apprehension regarding collective pathology. These conflicts are not merely the continuation of diplomacy by other means. As Scott urges, they are a perverse form of expression, a "pretext" for making an indelible statement:

> Our homie...was shot, and while he lay in the street, mortally wounded, the gunmen came back around the corner in a white van....They ran his head over and continued on. The occupants in the van had also shot two other people...both civilians.[22]

Finding parallel accounts of atrocities committed on a more massive international scale is not difficult: to list but a few instances, Indochina, East Timor, Iraq, Rwanda, and the Balkans. Like the apologists in the service of nation-states, gangsters rationalize their atrocities against the innocent and defenseless. Scott offers obligatory regrets about civilian casualties, but he justifies such carnage as an inevitable aspect of combat, or as a strategy essential for demoralizing the enemy.

Other parallels between gangs and nations are worth noting briefly. Like soldiers, gangsters have uniforms, basic training, and cadence calls. Like nations, they make opportunistic alliances based upon the dictum, "My enemy's enemy is my friend," and, they take and torment prisoners. Like soldiers crazed by the brutal absurdity of their predicament, gangsters are consumed by revenge or "payback." Scott cites the exhortation of the mother of a slain gangster:

> You were his homeboys, his friends, and because of this I have called you two over here to tell you personally...I don't want to ever see you again if you can't kill them motherfuckers that killed my boy....Do something to avenge my son's death![23]

This "talking the talk" is archetypal combat discourse heard at My Lai or South Central Los Angeles. However, Scott stresses a salient and tragic difference between his experience and that of Vietnam veterans:

> In Vietnam when a soldier was wounded badly...he was sent home. Home was a place where there was peace. No real danger of the 'Cong existed stateside. The war was ten thousand miles away. In contrast, our war is where we live. Where do we go when we've been wounded bad, or when our minds have been reduced to mincemeat by years, not months, of constant combat?[24]

There is another salient difference that eludes Scott. To paraphrase Bertrand Russell, for every person shot by gangsters, a million have been shot by governments. True, the general public does not bestow legitimacy upon gangs. And, unlike governments, gangs do not have unlimited access to the means of destruction. However, in the postmodern context, a realm in which conceptual and national boundaries blur, the difference between gangs and nations is not as clear and distinct as many would like to believe. Perhaps a more robust understanding of chaotic inner-cities will encourage a fuller account of the international anarchy that plagues the planet; the converse may also be true. Consider the admission of Smedley Butler, former Commandant of the United States Marine Corps:

I spent thirty-three years and four months...as a member...of the Marine Corps....I spent most of my time being a high-class muscle man for Big Business, for Wall Street, and for the bankers. In short, I was a racketeer for capitalism....Looking back on it, I feel I might have given Al Capone a few hints. The best he could do was operate his racket in three city districts. We Marines operated on three continents.[25]

Notes

1. Sanyika Shakur, aka Monster Kody Scott, *Monster: The Autobiography of an L. A. Gang Member* (New York: Penguin, 1993), p. 8.

2. Gregory Vistica, "'Gangstas' in the Ranks," *Newsweek*, 126:4 (24 July 1995), p. 48.

3. Scott, *Monster,* p. 70.

4. Stjepan Mestrovic, *The Barbarian Temperament* (New York: Routledge, 1993), p. 177.

5. Scott, *Monster*.

6. Cited in Joe Wilson, "Corporate Ethics and Gang Culture," *San Francisco Chronicle* (11 September 1996), p. A16.

7. Richard Barnet, *Roots of War* (New York: Penguin, 1973).

8. Scott, *Monster,* p. 382.

9. *Ibid.*, p. 155.

10. John Broyles, Jr., "Why Men Love War," in *Making War/Making Peace,* ed. Francesca Cancian and James Gibson (Belmont, Calif.: Wadsworth, 1990), p. 32.

11. Scott, *Monster,* p. 226.

12. Broyles, "Why Men Love War," p. 33.

13. Richard Sennett, *Authority* (New York: Alfred Knopf, 1980).

14. Scott, *Monster,* p. 70.

15. Cited in Vistica, "'Gangstas' in the Ranks," p. 49.

16. *Ibid.*, p. 48.

17. Scott, *Monster,* pp. 72-73.

18. *Ibid.,* p. 209.

19. Quoted in John Prados, "Woolsey and the CIA," *The Bulletin of the Atomic Scientists,* 49:6 (July/August, 1993), p. 34.

20. Scott, *Monster,* p. 138.

21. Sigmund Freud, *Group Psychology* (New York: W. W. Norton, 1961), p. 52.

22. Scott, *Monster,* p. 29.

23. *Ibid.*, p. 49.

24. *Ibid.*, p. 104.

25. Cited in Richard Edward, Michael Reich, and Thomas Weisskopf, *The Capitalist System* (Englewood Cliffs, N.J.: Prentice-Hall, 3rd ed., 1972), p. 486.

BIBLIOGRAPHY

Abrams, R. H. *Preachers Present Arms.* New York: Round Table, 1933.

Addams, Jane. *A Modern Lear.* Chicago: Jane Addams's Hull-House Museum, 1994.

_____. "A Function of the Social Settlement." In *On Education*, ed. Ellen Condliffe Lagemann. New Brunswick, N.J.: Transaction, 1994.

_____. *Twenty Years at Hull House.* Urbana, Ill.: University of Illinois Press, 1990.

_____. "What War is Destroying." In *Jane Addams on Peace, War, and International Understanding: 1899-1932*, ed. Allen Davis. New York: Garland, 1976.

_____. "What Peace Means." In *Jane Addams on Peace, War, and International Understanding: 1899-1932*, ed. Allen Davis. New York: Garland, 1976.

_____. "War Times Challenging Woman's Traditions." In *Jane Addams on Peace, War, and International Understanding: 1899-1932*, ed. Allen Davis. New York: Garland, 1976.

_____. "The New Internationalism." In *Jane Addams on Peace, War, and International Understanding: 1899-1932*, ed. Allen Davis. New York: Garland, 1976.

_____. *Peace and Bread in Time of War.* New York: Garland, 1972.

_____. *Democracy and Social Ethics.* Cambridge, Mass.: Harvard University Press, 1964.

_____. *Second Twenty Years at Hull House.* New York: Macmillan, 1930.

_____. *A New Conscience and an Ancient Evil.* New York: Macmillan, 1912.

_____. *Newer Ideals of Peace.* New York: Macmillan, 1906.

Addams, Jane, Emily G. Balch, and Alice Hamilton. *Women at The Hague.* New York: Macmillan, 1972.

Addams, Jane, *et al. Philanthropy and Social Progress.* Montclair, N.J.: Patterson Smith, 1970.

Allen, Theodore. *The Invention of the White Race: Racial Oppression and Social Control.* New York: Verso, 1994.

Alonso, Harriet Hyman. *Peace as a Women's Issue.* Syracuse, N.Y.: Syracuse University Press, 1993.

Antwi-Boasiako, Kwabena. *The Hidden Agenda.* Accra, Ghana: Anima Publications, 1995.

Baier, Annette. "Claims, Rights, Responsibilities." In *Prospects for a Common Morality*, ed. Gene Outka and John P. Reeder, Jr. Princeton, N.J.: Princeton University Press, 1993.

_____. "Trust and Antitrust." *Ethics*, 96 (1985-86), pp. 231-260.

_____. "What Do Women Want in a Moral Theory?" *Nous*, 19 (1985), pp. 53-63.

Bailey, Alison. "Mothering, Diversity, and Peace Politics." *Hypatia*, 9:2 (Spring 1994), pp. 188-198.

_____. *Mothers, Birthgivers, and Peacemakers: The Problem of Maternal Thinking in Feminist Peace Politics.* Ph.D. dissertation, Department of Philosophy, University of Cincinnati, 1993.

Bailey, Sidney D. *War and Conscience in the Nuclear Age.* New York: Saint Martin's, 1987.

Bainton, Roland. *Christian Attitudes toward War and Peace.* Nashville, Tenn.: Abingdon, 1960.

Baker, James. *The Politics of Diplomacy.* New York: G. P. Putnam and Sons, 1995.

Bamba, Nobuya, and John F. Howes, eds. *Pacifism in Japan: The Christian and Socialist Tradition.* Vancouver: University of British Columbia Press, 1978.

Bartky, Sandra Lee. *Femininity and Domination: Phenomenology of Oppression.* New York: Routledge, 1990.

Bassi, Marco. "Institutional Forgiveness in Borana Assemblies." *Sociology, Ethnology Bulletin* [Ethiopia], 1:2 (March 1992), pp. 50-60.

Baxter, William. *Soviet Air Land Battle Tactics.* Novato, Calif.: Presidio, 1986.

Beauvoir, Simone de. *The Second Sex,* trans. H. M. Parshley. New York: Bantam, 1952.

Bennett, John C., ed. *Nuclear Weapons and the Conflict of Conscience.* New York: Charles Scribner's, 1962.

Bennett, Lerone, Jr. *Before the Mayflower: A History of Black America.* New York: Penguin, 1988.

_____. *The Shaping of Black America.* Chicago: Johnson, 1975.

Beres, Louis R. *Mimicking Sisyphus: America's Countervailing Nuclear Strategy.* Lexington, Mass.: Heath, 1983.

Berrigan, Daniel. *The Dark Night of Resistance.* New York: Doubleday, 1971.

Bok, Sissela. *A Strategy for Peace: Human Values and the Threat of War.* New York: Pantheon, 1989.

Boserup, Anders, and Andrew Mack. *War without Weapons.* London: Frances Pinter, 1974.

Boulares, Habib. *Islam: The Fear and the Hope.* London: Zob Books, 1990.

Boulding, Elise. "The Pacifist as Citizen." In *Pacifism and Citizenship: Can They Coexist?,* ed. Kenneth M. Jensen and Kimber M. Schraub. Washington: Institute of Peace, 1991.

Boutros-Ghali, Boutros. *An Agenda for Peace.* New York: United Nations, 1992.

Bove, Laurence F., and Laura Duhan Kaplan, eds. *From the Eye of the Storm: Regional Conflicts and the Philosophy of Peace.* Amsterdam: Rodopi, 1995.

Boyer, Robert. *Atrocity and Amnesia: The Political Novel since 1945.* New York: Oxford University Press, 1985.

Brembeck, Howard. *Defense for a Civilized World.* Goshen, Ind.: Fourth Freedom Forum, 1988.

Breytonbach, Breyton. *End Papers: Essays, Letters, Articles of Faith, Workbook Notes.* New York: Farrar, Straus, and Giroux, 1986.

Brock, Peter. *Freedom from Violence: Sectarian Nonresistance from the Middle Ages to the Great War.* Toronto: University of Toronto Press, 1991.

_____. *Studies in Peace History.* York, England: William Sessions, 1991.

Brock-Utne, Birgit. *Feminist Perspectives on Peace and Peace Education.* New York: Pergamon, 1989.

Brown, Robert McAfee. *Making Peace in the Global Village.* Philadelphia: Westminster, 1981.

Broyles, Jr., John. "Why Men Love War." In *Making War/Making Peace,* ed. Francesca Cancian and James Gibson. Belmont, Calif.: Wadsworth, 1990.

Buber, Martin. *I and Thou,* trans. Ronald Gregor Smith. New York: Charles Scribner's Sons, 2nd ed., 1958.

Burns, E. L. M. *Between Arab and Israeli.* Toronto: Clarke, Irwin, 1962.

Cadoux, Cecil J. *The Early Church and the World.* Edinburgh: T. and T. Clark, 1955.
_____.*The Early Christian Attitude to War.* London: Headley Brothers, 1919.
Cady, Duane. *From Warism to Pacifism: A Moral Continuum.* Philadelphia: Temple University Press, 1989.
Cameron, Deborah. *Feminism and Linguistic Theory.* New York: St. Martin's, 1992.
Card, Claudia. "Caring and Evil." *Hypatia,* 5:1 (Spring 1990), pp. 101-108.
Carnevale Peter J., *et al.* "Mediator Behavior and Effectiveness in Community Mediation." In *Community Mediation: A Handbook for Practitioners and Researchers,* ed. Karen Grover Duffy, *et al.* New York: Guilford, 1991.
Chandler, Zala. "Antiracism, Antisexism, and Peace (Sapphire's Perspective)." In *Rocking the Ship of State: Toward a Feminist Peace Politics,* ed. Adrienne Harris and Ynestra King. Boulder, Colo.: Westview, 1989.
Chatfield, Charles. *For Peace and Justice: Pacifism in America, 1914-1941.* Knoxville, Tenn.: University of Tennessee Press, 1971.
Chodorow, Nancy. *The Reproduction of Mothering.* Berkeley, Calif.: University of California Press, 1978.
Cooper, John. "The Psychology of Justice in Plato." *American Philosophical Quarterly,* 14:2 (April 1977), pp. 151-157.
Curtin, Deane, and Robert Litke, eds. *Institional Violence.* Amsterdam: Rodopi, 1999.

Daly, Lloyd. *Aesop without Morals: The Famous Fables and a Life of Aesop.* New York: Thomas Yoseloff, 1963.
Damis, John. "The Moroccan-Algerian Conflict over the Western Sahara." *Maghreb Review,* 4:2 (1979), p. 53.
Davion, Victoria. "Pacifism and Care." *Hypatia,* 5:1 (Spring 1990): pp. 90-100.
Davis, F. James. *Who Is Black?: One Nation's Definition.* University Park, Penn.: Pennsylvania State University Press, 1993.
Debs, Eugene. *Writings and Speeches.* New York: Hermitage, 1948.
Deming, Barbara. *Prisons that Could Not Hold.* San Francisco: Spinsters Ink, 1985.
Department of the Army, United States of America. *The Law of Land Warfare.* Washington: U.S. Government Printing Office, Field Manual #27-10, 1956.
Derrida, Jacques. "Racism's Last Word." In *"Race," Writing, and Difference,* ed. Henry Louis Gates, Jr. Chicago: The University of Chicago Press, 1986.
Descartes, René. *Meditations on First Philosophy,* trans. Donald A. Cress. Indianapolis: Hackett, 1979.
Donovan, Josephine. *Feminist Theory: The Intellectual Traditions of American Feminism.* New York: Continuum, 1992.
Dorfman, Ariel. *Last Waltz in Santiago: And Other Poems of Exile and Disappearance,* trans. Edith Grossman. New York: Penguin, 1988.
Droba, D. D. "Churches and War Attitudes." *Sociology and Social Research,* 16:4 (July-August 1932), p. 550.

Easwaran, Eknath. *A Man to Match His Mountains: Badshah Kahn, Nonviolent Society of Islam.* Petaluma, Calif.: Milgiri, 1984.
Edward, Richard, Michael Reich, and Thomas Weisskopf. *The Capitalist System.* Englewood Cliffs: Prentice-Hall, 2nd ed., 1972.
Eisler, Riane. *The Chalice and the Blade.* New York, Harper Collins, 1988.

Ellsberg, Robert, ed. *By Little and by Little: The Selected Writings of Dorothy Day.* New York: Alfred A. Knopf, 1983.

Elshtain, Jean Bethke. *Women and War.* New York: Basic Books, 1987.

Etzioni, Amitai. *The Spirit of Community: Rights, Responsibilities, and the Communitarian Agenda.* New York: Crown, 1993.

Farmer, Paul. *The Uses of Haiti.* Monroe, Maine: Common Courage, 1994.

Farrell, Daniel. "Hobbes and International Relations: The War of All against All." In *The Causes of Quarrel,* ed. Peter Caws. Boston: Beacon, 1989.

Feinberg, Joel. *Social Philosophy.* Englewood Cliffs, N.J.: Prentice-Hall, 1993.

Ferguson, Gregor. *Coup D'État: A Practical Manual.* Poole, Dorset: Armes and Armour, 1987.

Fischer, Marilyn. "Philanthropy and Injustice in Mill and Addams." *Nonprofit and Voluntary Sector Quarterly,* 24:4 (Winter 1995), pp. 281-292.

Fisher, Dietrich, Jan Oberg, and Wilhelm Nolte. *Winning Peace: Strategies and Ethics for a Nuclear-Free World.* Philadelphia: Taylor Francis, 1989.

Fisher, Roger, Elizabeth Kepelman, and Andrea Kupferschneider. *Beyond Machiavelli.* Cambridge, Mass.: Harvard University Press, 1994.

Fisher, Roger, William Ury, and Bruce Patton. *Getting to Yes: Negotiating Agreement without Giving In.* New York: Houghton Mifflin, 2nd ed., 1991.

Fogg, Richard W. "Dealing with Conflict: A Repertoire of Creative, Peaceful Approaches." *Journal of Conflict Resolution,* 29:2 (June 1985), pp. 330-358.

_____."How the United Nations Helped Stop a War." *United Nations Observer* (August 1981), p. 7.

Folberg, Jay, and Alison Taylor. *Mediation: A Comprehensive Guide to Resolving Conflicts without Litigation.* San Francisco: Jossey-Bass, 1986.

Forcey, Linda. *Mothers of Sons.* New York: Praeger, 1987.

Foster, Carrie A. *The Women and the Warriors.* Syracuse, N.Y.: Syracuse University Press, 1995.

Frankenburg, Ruth. *White Women, Race Matters: The Social Construction of Whiteness.* Minneapolis, Minn.: University of Minnesota Press, 1993.

Freedman, Lawrence. "The First Two Generations of Nuclear Strategists." In *Makers of Modern Strategy,* ed. Peter Paret. Princeton, N.J.: Princeton University Press, 1986.

Freire, Paulo. *Pedagogy of the Oppressed,* trans. Myra Bergman Ramos. New York: Herder and Herder, 1968.

Freud, Sigmund. *Group Psychology.* New York: W. W. Norton, 1961.

_____. *Why War?* In *Collected Papers,* ed. James Strachey and Joan Riviere. London: Hogarth and Institute of Psycho-Analysis, 1957.

_____. *Civilization and Its Discontents.* In *The Standard Edition of the Complete Psychological Works of Sigmund Freud,* ed. James Strachey, with Anna Freud (24 vols.). London: Hogarth and Institute of Psycho-Analysis, 1953-1966.

Freund, Norman. *Nonviolent National Defense: A Philosophical Inquiry into Applied Nonviolence.* Lanham, Md.: University Press of America, 1989.

Friedman, Marilyn. *What Are Friends for?: Feminist Perspectives on Personal Relationships and Moral Theory.* Ithaca, N.Y.: Cornell University Press, 1993.

Friedrich, Carl Joachim. *Inevitable Peace.* New York: Greenwood, 1948.

Frye, Marilyn. "The Necessity of Differences: Constructing a Positive Category of Women." *Signs: Journal of Women, Culture, and Society,* 21:4 (Summer 1996), pp. 991-1010.

———. *Willful Virgin: Essays in Feminism.* Freedom, Calif.: Crossing, 1992.

———. "On Being White: Thinking toward a Feminist Understanding of Race and Race Supremacy." In *The Politics of Reality: Essays in Feminist Theory.* Freedom, Calif.: Crossing, 1983.

Gallie, W. B. *Philosophers of Peace and War: Kant, Clausewitz, Marx, Engels, and Tolstoy.* Cambridge, U.K.: Cambridge University Press, 1978.

Galtung, Johan. *Peace by Peaceful Means: Peace and Conflict, Development and Civilization.* Thousand Oaks, Calif: Sage, 1996.

———. *The True Worlds.* New York: Free Press, 1980.

Gandhi, M. K. *Nonviolent Resistance (Satyagraha).* New York: Schocken, 1961.

Garry, George. *Money, Financial Flows, and Credit in the Soviet Union.* Cambridge, Mass.: Ballinger, 1977.

Gauthier, David. *Morals by Agreement.* Oxford: Clarendon, 1986.

Gay, William, C. "Militarism in the Modern State and World Government: The Limits of Peace through Strength in the Nuclear Age." In *From the Eye of the Storm: Regional Conflicts and the Philosophy of Peace,* ed. Laurence F. Bove and Laura Duhan Kaplan. Amsterdam: Rodopi, 1995.

———. "The Prospect for a Nonviolent Model of National Security." In *On the Eve of the 21st Century: Perspectives of Russian and American Philosophers,* ed. William C. Gay and T. A. Alekseeva. Lanham, Md.: Rowman and Littlefield, 1994.

Gay, William C. and T. A. Alekseeva, eds. *On the Eve of the 21st Century: Perspectives of Russian and American Philosophers.* Lanham, Md.: Rowman and Littlefield, 1994.

Gilligan, Carol. *In a Different Voice: Psychological Theory and Women's Development.* Cambridge, Mass.: Harvard University Press, 1982.

Giroux, Henry. *Border Crossings: Cultural Workers and the Politics of Education.* New York: Routledge, 1992.

Glossop, Ronald J. *Confronting War: An Examination of Humanity's Most Pressing Problem.* Jefferson, N.C.: McFarland, 3rd ed., 1994.

———. *World Federation?* Jefferson, N.C.: McFarland, 1994.

Gordimer, Nadine. *Burger's Daughter.* New York: Viking, 1979.

Gosling, J. C. B. *Plato.* London: Routledge and Kegan Paul, 1973.

Green, Jerrold. *Revolution in Iran: The Politics of Countermobilization.* New York: Praeger, 1982.

Greene, Maxine. *The Dialectic of Freedom.* New York: Teachers College Press, 1988.

Haldeman, H. R. *The Ends of Power.* New York: Times Books, 1978.

Hallie, Philip. "From Cruelty to Goodness." In *Vice and Virtue in Everyday Life,* ed. Christina Sommers and Fred Sommers. New York: Harcourt Brace, 1997.

———. *Lest Innocent Blood Be Shed.* New York: Harper and Row, 1979.

Hampshire, Stuart. *Innocence and Experience.* Cambridge, Mass.: Harvard University Press, 1989.

Haraway, Donna. "Situated Knowledges: The Science Question in Feminism and the Privilege of Partial Perspective." *Feminist Studies,* 14:3 (Fall 1983), pp. 575-599.

Harding, Sandra. *The Science Question in Feminism.* Ithaca, N.Y.: Cornell University Press, 1986.

Harnack, Adolf. *What Is Christianity?* New York: Harper and Row, 1957.

Harris, Adrienne, and Ynestra King, eds. *Rocking the Ship of State: Toward a Feminist Peace Politics.* Boulder, Colo.: Westview, 1989.

Hart, Basil Liddell. "Lessons from Resistance Movements–Guerrilla and Nonviolent." In *Civilian Resistance as a National Defense: Nonviolent Action against Aggression,* ed. Adam Roberts. Baltimore, Md.: Penguin, 1969.

Hartsock, Nancy. "The Feminist Standpoint: Developing the Ground for a Specifically Feminist Historical Materialism." In *Discovering Reality,* ed. Sandra Harding and Merrill Hintikka. London: D. Reidl, 1983.

Heilbroner, Robert L. *Behind the Veil of Economics.* New York: W. W. Norton, 1988.

Held, Virginia. *Feminist Morality: Transforming Culture, Society, and Politics.* Chicago: University of Chicago Press, 1993.

Hening, William Walter. *The Statutes at Large: Being a Collection of All the Laws of Virginia* (3 vols.). New York: R and W and G. Bartow, 1823.

Hick, John. *An Interpretation of Religion: Human Responses to the Transcendent.* New Haven, Conn.: Yale University Press, 1989.

Hill, Janice. "Letter to a Political Prisoner." In *Of the Heart and the Bread: An Anthology of Poems for Peacemakers,* ed. Brandywine Peace Community. Swarthmore, Penn.: Plowshares, 1985.

Hoagland, Sarah Lucia. "Some Concerns about Nel Noddings' *Caring.*" *Hypatia,* 5:1 (Spring 1990), pp. 109-114.

hooks, bell. *Talking Back: Thinking Feminist, Thinking Black.* Boston: South End, 1989.

_____. *Feminist Theory: From Margin to Center.* Boston: South End, 1984.

Hountondji, Paulin J. "Daily Life in Black Africa." In *The Surreptitious Speech: Présence Africaine and the Politics of Otherness, 1947-1987,* ed. V. Y. Mudimbe. Chicago: University of Chicago Press, 1992.

Houston, Barbara. "Caring and Exploitation." *Hypatia,* 5:1 (Spring 1990), pp. 115-119.

Hufbauer, Gary C., and Jeffrey J. Schott. *Economic Sanctions Reconsidered.* Washington, D.C.: Institute for International Economics, 1985.

Huntington, Samuel P. "The Clash of Civilizations?" *Foreign Affairs,* 72:3 (Summer 1993), pp. 22-49.

_____. *The Strategic Imperative.* Cambridge, Mass.: Ballinger, 1982.

Inge, W. R. *Christian Ethics and Modern Problems.* New York: G. P. Putnam's Sons, 1930.

Jaggar, Alison M. "Caring as a Feminist Practice of Moral Reason." In *Justice and Care: Essential Readings in Feminist Ethics,* ed. Virginia Held. Boulder, Colo.: Westview, 1995.

_____. "Love and Knowledge: Emotion in Feminist Epistemology." In *Women, Knowledge, and Reality: Explorations in Feminist Epistemology*, ed. Ann Garry and Marilyn Pearsall. Boston: Unwin Hyman, 1989.

James, William. "The Moral Equivalent of War." In *Nonviolence in America: A Documentary History*, ed. Staughton Lynd and Alice Lynd. Maryknoll, N.Y.: Orbis, 1995.

Johansen, Robert C. "A Policy Framework for World Security." In *World Security: Trends and Challenges at Century's End*, ed. Michael T. Klare and Daniel C. Thomas. New York: St. Martin's, 1991.

Jordan. Winthrop D. *White over Black: American Attitudes toward the Negro, 1550-1812*. Chapel Hill, N.C.: University of North Carolina Press, 1968.

Kant, Immanuel. "Idea for a Universal History with a Cosmopolitan Intent." In *Perpetual Peace and Other Essays*, trans. Ted Humphrey. Indianapolis: Hackett, 1983.

_____. *Perpetual Peace and Other Essays*, trans. Ted Humphrey. Indianapolis: Hackett, 1983.

_____. *Grounding for the Metaphysics of Morals*. In *Classics of Western Philosophy*, ed. Steven M. Cahn. Indianapolis: Hackett, 2nd ed., 1977.

Kaplan, Laura Duhan, and Laurence F. Bove, eds. *Philosophical Perspectives on Power and Domination: Theories and Practices*. Amsterdam: Rodopi, 1997.

Keen, Sam. *Faces of the Enemy: Reflections of the Hostile Imagination*. San Francisco: Harper and Row, 1986.

Kehl, D. G. "War Must Be Governed by Laws." In *War and Human Nature: Opposing Viewpoints*, ed. David L. Bender and Bruno Leone. St. Paul, Minn.: Greenhaven, 1983.

King, Jr., Martin Luther. *Where Do We Go from Here: Chaos or Community?* New York: Harper and Row, 1967.

_____. *Why We Can't Wait*. New York: New American Library, 1964.

_____. *Stride toward Freedom*. San Francisco: Harper and Row, 1958.

King-Hall, Stephen. *Defense in the Nuclear Age*. Nyack, N.Y.: Fellowship, 1959.

Kohlberg, Lawrence. *The Philosophy of Moral Development*. San Francisco: Harper and Row, 1981.

Kresse, Kai. "Philosophy Needs to Be Made Sagacious: An Interview with H. Odera Oruka." *Issues in Contemporary Culture and Aesthetics*, 3 (April 1996).

Kretzmann, John P., and John L. McKnight. *Building Communities from the Inside Out: A Path toward Finding and Mobilizing a Community's Assets*. Evanston, Ill.: Northwestern University Press, 1993.

Kuhn, Thomas. *The Structure of Scientific Revolution*. Chicago: University of Chicago Press, 1970.

Küng, Hans, and Karl-Joseph Kuschel, eds. *A Global Ethic: The Declaration of the Parliament of the World's Religions*. New York: Continuum, 1994.

Kunkel, Joseph. "Somalia: Humanitarian Aid or Business as Usual?" In *From the Eye of the Storm: Regional Conflicts and the Philosophy of Peace*, ed. Laurence F. Bove and Laura Duhan Kaplan. Amsterdam: Rodopi, 1995.

Kurasha, Jameson. "The African Concept of Personality as a Possible Contribution to Global Reconciliation" In *Kreativer Friede durch Begegnung der Weltkulturen*, ed. Heinrich Beck. New York: Peter Lang, 1995.

Lao Tsu. *Tao Te Ching*, trans. Stephen Mitchell. New York: Harper Perennial, 1988.

Lecky, W. E. H. *History of European Morals*, vol. 2. New York: D. Appleton, 1929.

Lee, Umphrey. *The Historic Church and Modern Pacifism*. Nashville, Tenn.: Abingdon-Cokesbury, 1943.

Lentricchia, Frank. *Criticism and Social Change*. Chicago: University of Chicago Press, 1983.

Lerner, Michael. *The Politics of Meaning: Restoring Hope and Possibility in an Age of Cynicism*. New York: Addison-Wesley, 1996.

Lever, Janet. "Sex Differences in the Complexity of Children's Play and Games." *American Sociological Review*, 43 (1978), pp. 471-483.

———. "Sex Differences in the Games Children Play." *Social Problems*, 23 (1976), pp. 478-487.

Lilienthal, Alfred. *The Zionist Connection*. New York: Dodd, Mead, 1978.

Little, David. "The Nature and Basis of Human Rights." In *Prospects for a Common Morality*, ed. Gene Outka and John P. Reeder, Jr. Princeton, N.J.: Princeton University Press, 1993.

Lötter, HPP (Hennie). *Injustice, Violence, and Peace: The Case of South Africa*. Amsterdam: Rodopi, 1997.

Luther, Martin. *Works*, vol. 3. Washington: Carnegie Institution, 1917.

MacGregor, G. M. C. *The New Testament Basis for Pacifism*. London: James Clarke, 1936.

Maduro, Otto. *Religion and Social Conflict*. Maryknoll, N.Y.: Orbis, 1982.

Mangum, Jr., Charles S. *The Legal Status of the Negro*. Chapel Hill, N.C.: University of North Carolina Press, 1940.

Marchand, C. Roland. *The American Peace Movement and Social Reform, 1898-1918*. Princeton, N.J.: Princeton University Press, 1972.

Marsden, George M. *Religion and American Culture*. New York: Harcourt Brace, 1990.

Martin-Baro, Ignacio. *Writings for a Liberation Psychology*, ed. Adrienne Aron and Shawn Corne. Cambridge, Mass.: Harvard University Press, 1994.

Mayer, Peter, ed. *The Pacifist Conscience*. New York: Holt, Rinehart, and Winston, 1966.

McCabe, Hohn. *Charlie Chaplin*. Garden City, N.Y.: Doubleday, 1978.

McIntosh, Peggy. "White Privilege and Male Privilege: A Personal Account of Coming to See Correspondences through Work in Women's Studies." In *Race, Class, and Gender: An Anthology*, ed. Margaret L. Andersen and Patricia Hill Collins. Belmont, Calif.: Wadsworth, 1991.

McNair, Lesley J. "War Is Kill or Be Killed." In *War and Human Nature: Opposing Viewpoints*, ed. David L. Bender and Bruno Leone. St. Paul, Minn.: Greenhaven, 1983.

McNeal, Patricia. "Catholic Conscientious Objection during World War II." *The Catholic Historical Review*, 61:2 (1975), pp. 222-242.

Melton, J. Gordon, ed. *The Encyclopedia of American Religious Creeds*. Detroit, Mich.: Gale Research Company, 1988.

———. *Encyclopedia of American Religions*. Wilmington, N.C.: McGrath, 1978.

Mestrovic, Stjepan. *The Barbarian Temperament*. London: Routledge, 1993.

Metz, Johann Baptist. *The Emergent Church*, trans. Peter Mann. New York: Crossroad, 1986.

Mill, John Stuart. *Utilitarianism*. Indianapolis: Hackett, 1979.

Morgan, Edmund S. *American Slavery, American Freedom: The Ordeal of Colonial Virginia*. New York: W. W. Norton, 1975.

Nagle, William J., ed. *Morality and Modern Warfare*. Baltimore, Md.: Helicon, 1960.

Nelson-Pallmeyer, Jack. *The School of Assassins: The Case for Closing the School of the Americas and for Fundamentally Changing U.S. Foreign Policy*. Maryknoll, N.Y.: Orbis, 1997.

Nixon, Richard. *The Memoirs of Richard Nixon*. New York: Grosset and Dunlap, 1978.

Noddings, Nel. "A Response." *Hypatia,* 5:1 (Spring 1990), pp. 120-126.

_____. *Caring: A Feminine Approach to Ethics and Moral Education*. Berkeley, Calif.: University of California Press, 1984.

Normandeau, A., and B. Leighton. *A Vision of the Future of Policing in Canada*. Ottawa, Ont.: Police and Security Branch, Soliciter General Canada, 1990.

Nye, Joseph S., Graham Allison, and Albert Carnesale, Jr., eds. *Fateful Visions: Avoiding Nuclear Catastrophe*. Cambridge, Mass.: Ballinger, 1988.

Oates, Stephen B. *Let the Trumpet Sound: The Life of Martin Luther King, Jr.* New York: Harper and Row, 1982.

Odera Oruka, H., ed. *Sage Philosophy: Indigenous Thinkers and Modern Debate on African Philosophy*. New York: E. J. Brill, 1990.

Olczak Paul V., *et al.* "Toward a Synthesis: The Art with the Science of Community Mediation." *Community Mediation: A Handbook for Practitioners and Researchers*, ed. Karen Grover Duffy, *et al.* New York: Guilford, 1991.

Omaar, Rakiya. "One Thorn Bush at a Time." *New Internationalist*, 256 (June, 1994), pp. 8-10.

Osgood, Robert. *The Nuclear Dilemma in American Strategic Thought*. Boulder, Colo.: Westview, 1988.

Parkman, Patricia. *Insurrection without Arms*. PhD Dissertation, Temple University, Philadelphia, 1980.

Piscatori, James, ed. *Islamic Fundamentalisms and the Gulf Crisis*. Chicago: American Academy of Arts and Sciences, 1991.

Pollitt, Katha. "Are Women Morally Superior to Men?" *The Nation*, 225:22 (28 December 1992), pp 799-807.

Prados, John. "Woolsey And The CIA." *The Bulletin of the Atomic Scientists*, 49:6, (July/August, 1993), pp. 33-39.

Quigley, Thomas E., ed. *American Catholics and Vietnam*. Grand Rapids, Mich.: William B. Eerdmans, 1968.

Rabuzzi, Kathryn Allen. *Mother with Child: Transformations through Childbirth*. Indianapolis: Indiana University Press, 1994.

Ramose, Moboge. "Specific African Thought Structures and Their Possible Contribution to World Peace." In *Kreativer Friede durch Begegnung der Weltkulturen,* ed. Heinrich Beck. New York: Peter Lang, 1995.

Ramsey, Paul. *War and the Christian Conscience: How Shall Modern War Be Conducted Justly?* Durham, N.C.: Duke University Press, 1961.

Rawls, John. *A Theory of Justice.* Cambridge, Mass.: Harvard University Press, 1971.

Reardon, Betty. *Sexism and the War System.* New York: Teachers College Press, 1985.

Reardon, Betty, and E. Norland, eds. *Learning Peace.* Albany, N.Y.: State University of New York Press, 1994.

Rich, Adrienne. *Of Woman Born: Motherhood as Experience and Institution.* New York: Norton, 1986.

Ricoeur, Paul. *Freud and Philosophy: An Essay on Interpretation.* New Haven, Conn.: Yale University Press, 1970.

Rieber, Robert W., and Robert J. Kelly. "Substance and Shadow: Images of the Enemy." *The Psychology of War and Peace: Images of the Enemy,* ed. Robert W. Rieber. New York: Plenum, 1991.

Rieff, David. *Slaughterhouse: Bosnia and the Failure of the West.* New York: Simon and Schuster, 1995.

Roberts, Adam, ed. *Civilian Resistance as a National Defense.* Baltimore: Penguin, 1969.

Roediger, David R. *Toward the Abolition of Whiteness.* New York: Verso, 1994.

_____. *The Wages of Whiteness: Race and the Making of the American Working Class.* New York: Verso, 1991.

Rogers, Carl. *On Becoming a Person: A Therapist's View of Psychotherapy.* Boston: Houghton Mifflin, 1961.

Rosenwasser, Penny. *Voices from a Promised Land.* Willimantic, Conn.: Curbstone, 1992.

Ruddick, Sara. "Fierce and Human Peace." In *Just War, Nonviolence, and Nuclear Deterrence: Philosophers on War and Peace,* ed. Duane L. Cady and Richard Werner. Wakefield, N.H.: Longwood Academic, 1991.

_____. *Maternal Thinking: Toward a Politics of Peace.* New York: Ballantine, 1989.

Russett, Bruce. *Controlling the Sword.* Cambridge, Mass.: Harvard University Press, 1990.

Russo, Ann. "We Cannot Live without Our Lives: White Women, Antiracism, and Feminism." In *Third-World Women and the Politics of Feminism,* ed. Chandra Talpade Mohanty, Ann Russo, and Lourdes Torres. Bloomington, Ind.: University of Indiana Press, 1991.

Scanlon, T. M. "Utilitarianism and Contractualism." In *Utilitarianism and Beyond,* ed. Amartya Sen and Bernard Williams. Cambridge, U.K.: Cambridge University Press, 1982.

Schell, Jonathan. *The Fate of the Earth.* New York: Avon, 1982.

Scheman, Naomi. *Engenderings: Constructions of Knowledge, Authority, and Privilege.* New York: Routledge, 1993.

Schindler, Colin. *Ploughshares into Swords.* London: Y. B. Tauris, 1991.

Seigfried, Charlene Haddock. *Pragmatism and Feminism.* Chicago: Chicago University Press, 1996.

Sennett, Richard. *Authority.* New York: Alfred Knopf, 1980.

Shakur, Sanyika. *Monster: The Autobiography of an L. A. Gang Member.* New York: Penguin, 1993.

Sharp, Gene. *Social Power and Political Freedom.* Boston: Porter Sargent, 1980.

———. *The Politics of Nonviolent Action.* Boston: Porter Sargent, 1973.

Sharp, Gene, and Bruce Jenkins. *Civilian-Based Defense: A Post-Military Weapons System.* Princeton, N.J.: Princeton University Press, 1990.

Sheehan, T. *The First Coming.* New York: Random House, 1986.

Shreeve, James. "Terms of Estrangement." *Discover,* 15:11 (November 1994), pp. 56-58.

Shridharani, K. *War without Violence.* New York: Garland, 1972.

Sibley, Mulford Q., and Philip E. Jacob. *Conscription of Conscience.* Ithaca, N.Y.: Cornell University Press, 1952.

Sider, Ronald J., and Richard Taylor. *Nuclear Holocaust and Christian Hope.* Downers Grove, Ill.: Intervarsity, 1982.

Silone, Ignazio. *Bread and Wine,* trans. Eric Mosbacher. New York: New American Library, 1986.

Slaikeu, Karl A. *When Push Comes to Shove: A Practical Guide to Mediating Disputes.* San Francisco: Jossey-Bass, 1996.

Smock, David R., ed. *Making War and Waging Peace: Foreign Intervention in Africa.* Washington: United States Institute of Peace, 1993.

Smock, David R., and Chester A. Crocker, eds. *African Conflict Resolution: The U.S. Role in Peacemaking.* Washington: United States Institute of Peace, 1995.

Snyder, Glenn, and Paul Diesing. *Conflict among Nations.* Princeton, N.J.: Princeton University Press, 1977.

Socknat, Thomas P. *Witness against War: Pacifism in Canada, 1900-1945.* Toronto: University of Toronto Press, 1987.

Somerville, John. "Democracy and the Problem of War." In *Moral Problems in Contemporary Society: Essays in Humanistic Ethics,* ed. Paul Kurtz. Englewood Cliffs, N.J.: Prentice-Hall, 1969.

Spelman, Elizabeth V. *Inessential Woman: Problems of Exclusion in Feminist Thought.* Boston: Beacon, 1988.

Sperry, Willard L., ed. *The Religion of Soldier and Sailor.* Cambridge, Mass.: Harvard University Press, 1945.

Spranger, Eduard. *Types of Men.* Halle, Saale, Germany: Max Niemeyer, 1928.

Steinberg, Warren. *Masculinity: Identity, Conflict, and Transformation.* Boston: Shambhala, 1993.

Taheri, Amir. *Holy Terror: Inside the World of Islamic Terrorism.* Bethesda, Md.: Adler and Adler, 1987.

Tannen, Deborah. *You Just Don't Understand: Women and Men in Conversation.* New York: Ballantine, 1990.

Taubes, Gary. "The Defense Initiative of the '90s." *Science,* 267:4 (February 1995), pp. 1096-1100.

Tertullian, *Apology.* In *The Ante-Nicene Fathers,* vol. 3, ed. Alexander Roberts and James Donaldson. New York: Christian Literature, 1890.

———. *The Chaplet.* In *The Ante-Nicene Fathers,* vol. 3, ed. Alexander Roberts and James Donaldson. New York: Christian Literature, 1890.

_____. *On Idolatry.* In *The Ante-Nicene Fathers*, vol. 3, ed. Alexander Roberts and James Donaldson. New York: Christian Literature, 1890.

Tharoor, Shashi. "Peace-Keeping: Principles, Problems, Prospects." *Naval War College Review*, 47:2 (Spring 1994), pp. 9-22.

Theophrastus. *Characters*, trans. J. N. Edwards. New York: G. P. Putnam, 1929.

Thucydides. *The Complete Writings of Thucydides: The Peloponnesian War*, trans. Richard Crawley. New York: Random House, 1951.

Tillich, Paul. "The Nuclear Dilemma: A Discussion." *Christianity and Crisis*, 21:19 (November 1961), pp. 203-204.

Tolstoy, Leo. *The Kingdom of God Is within You: Or, Christianity Not as a Mystical Teaching but as a New Concept of Life*, trans. Leo Wiener. New York: Farrar, Straus, and Cudahy, 1961.

Tong, Rosemarie. *Feminine and Feminist Ethics.* Belmont, Calif.: Wadsworth, 1993.

Tronto, Joan. "Women and Caring: What Can Feminists Learn about Morality from Caring?" In *Justice and Care: Essential Readings in Feminist Ethics*, ed. Virginia Held. Boulder, Colo.: Westview, 1995.

_____. *Moral Boundaries: A Political Argument for an Ethic of Care.* New York: Routledge, 1993.

United Nations. "Universal Declaration of Human Rights." In *Basic Documents of Human Rights*, ed. Ian Brownlie. Oxford: Clarendon, 1971.

United States Joint Chiefs of Staff. *Department of Defense Dictionary of Military and Associated Terms.* Washington: U.S. Government Printing Office, 1986.

Ury, William. *Beyond the Hotline: How Crisis Control Can Prevent Nuclear War*, ed. Martin Linsky. Boston: Houghton Mifflin, 1985.

Vistica, Gregory. "'Gangstas' in the Ranks." *Newsweek*, 126:4 (24 July 1995), p. 48.

von Clausewitz, Carl. *On War*, ed. and trans. Michael Howard and Peter Paret. Princeton, N.J.: Princeton University Press, 1976.

Walker, Margaret Urban. "Moral Understandings: Alternative 'Epistemology' for a Feminist Ethics." In *Justice and Care: Essential Readings in Feminist Ethics*, ed. Virginia Held. Boulder, Colo.: Westview, 1995.

Warren, Karen J. "A Feminist Philosophical Perspective on Ecofeminist Spiritualities." In *Ecofeminism and the Sacred*, ed. Carol J. Adams. New York: Continuum, 1993.

Warren, Karen J., and Duane Cady, eds. *Bringing Peace Home: Feminism, Violence, and Nature.* Bloomington, Ind.: Indiana University Press, 1996.

_____. "Feminism and Peace: An Overview." *American Philosophical Association Newsletter on Feminism and Philosophy*, 93:1 (Spring 1994), pp. 39-41.

Warren, Karen J., and Jim Cheney. "Ecological Feminism and Ecosystem Ecology." *Hypatia*, 6:1 (Spring 1991), pp. 179-197.

Washington, James M., ed. *A Testament of Hope: The Essential Writings of Martin Luther King, Jr.* San Francisco: Harper and Row, 1986.

Wasserstrom, Richard, ed. *War and Morality.* Belmont, Calif.: Wadsworth, 1970.

Watson, G. R. *The Roman Soldier.* Ithaca, N.Y.: Cornell University Press, 1969.

Weil, Simone. *Waiting for God*, ed. Leslie Fiedler. New York: Harper Colophon, 1951.

Wells, Donald A., ed. *An Encyclopedia of War and Ethics.* Westport, Conn.: Greenwood, 1996.

Welton, Gary L. "Parties in Conflict: Their Characteristics and Perceptions." In *Community Mediation: A Handbook for Practitioners and Researchers,* ed. Karen Grover Duffy, *et al.* New York: Guilford, 1991.

Weschler, Lawrence. *The Passion of Poland.* New York: Pantheon, 1982.

Whitehead, Alfred North. *Process and Reality.* New York: Free Press, 1969.

Wilson, Joe. "Corporate Ethics and Gang Culture." *San Francisco Chronicle* (11 September 1996), p. A16.

Wittner, Lawrence S. *Rebels against War.* Philadelphia: Temple University Press, 1984.

Woodward, Beverly. "Nonviolent Struggle, Nonviolent Defense, and Nonviolent Peacemaking." *Peace and Change,* 7:4 (Fall 1981), pp. 62-63.

Yankah, Kwesi. *Speaking for the Chief: Okyeame and the Politics of Akan Royal Oratory.* Bloomington, Ind.: Indiana University Press, 1995.

_____. *The Proverb in the Context of Akan Rhetoric: A Theory of Proverb Praxis.* New York: Peter Lang, 1989.

Young, Iris Marion. *Intersecting Voices: Dilemmas of Gender, Political Philosophy, and Policy,* Princeton, N.J.: Princeton University Press, 1997.

_____. *Justice and the Politics of Difference.* Princeton, N.J.: Princeton University Press, 1990.

Zahn, Gordon C. "Catholic Opposition to Hitler: The Perils of Ambiguity." *Journal of Church and State,* 13: 3 (Autumn 1971), pp. 413-425.

ABOUT THE AUTHORS

ALISON BAILEY is an Associate Professor at Illinois State University where she teaches philosophy and women's studies. She is the author of *Posterity and Strategic Policy: A Moral Assessment of U. S. Strategic Weapons Options*, 1989, and several articles on feminist peace politics. Her current research addresses questions related to the construction of privileged identities, moral responsibility, and resistance. Her articles on these topics appear in *Hypatia*, and the *Journal of Social Philosophy*, and in two edited volumes *Philosophical Perspectives on Power and Domination* (VIBS, 1997), and *Whiteness: Feminist Philosophical Reflections*, 1999. She and Paula Smithka are currently coediting the forthcoming VIBS volume: *Community, Diversity, and Difference: Implications for Peace*.

MARILYN FISCHER is an Associate Professor of Philosophy at the University of Dayton. She has published in the *Journal of Social Philosophy*, the *Journal of Value Inquiry*, and a number of interdisciplinary journals. Her research focuses on political philosophy, particularly philosophical issues in philanthropy, and on music and culture. She is currently writing a book on Jane Addams's theory of social democracy.

RICHARD WENDELL FOGG directs the Center for the Study of Conflict, located at 5846 Bellona Avenue, Baltimore, Maryland 21212. His publications include: "Reagan Can now Try on the Mantle of Peace," *Chicago Sun Times* (14 May 1985), and "Teaching Nonviolent Power to Children," in *Ways Out: The Book of Changes for Peace*, edited by Gene Knudsen-Hoffman, 1988. His major achievement has been to conceive of a nonmilitary defense against a nuclear attack that has begun. Fogg is a member of the Consortium on Peace, Research, Education, and Development; and of Concerned Philosophers for Peace.

WILLIAM C. GAY is Professor of Philosophy and Chair of the Department of Philosophy at the University of North Carolina at Charlotte. He specializes in war and peace studies, social and political philosophy, and continental philosophy. With T. A. Alekseeva, he is coauthor of *Capitalism with a Human Face: The Quest for a Middle Road in Russian Politics*, 1996, and coeditor of *On the Eve of the 21st-Century: Perspectives of Russian and American Philosophers*, 1994. With Michael Pearson, he is coauthor of *The Nuclear Arms Race*, 1987. He is editor of *Concerned Philosophers for Peace Newsletter* (since 1987), was CPP President (1993), and served as CPP Executive Director (1996-1999). He has published widely on issues of peace, justice, and nonviolence.

LEO GROARKE is Professor of Philosophy at Wilfrid Laurier University. He is the author and editor of a number of books and many articles on a wide variety of topics in the history of ideas, applied ethics, political philosophy, and argumentation theory. His most recent book is *The Ethics of the New Economy: Restructuring and Beyond,* 1998, and his most recent articles include "Can Capitalism Save Itself? Some Ruminations on the End of Capitalism," "Realism, Restructuring, and Amalgamation," "Two Solitudes: Professional Ethics and the Nonprofessional," and "Pornography, Censorship, and Obscenity Law in Canada." He is a member of Concerned Philosophers for Peace, Transparency International, the Canadian Philosophical Association, and the International Society for the Study of Argumentation.

RON HIRSCHBEIN has served as a visiting research philosopher at the University of California, San Diego, as a visiting professor in Peace and Conflict studies at the University of California, Berkeley, and as a visiting professor at the United Nations University in Austria. He currently heads a program in War and Peace Studies at California State University, Chico. In addition to numerous articles on international politics and military strategy, he has published three books: *Newest Weapons/Oldest Psychology: The Dialectics of American Nuclear Strategy,* 1991; *What If They Gave a Crisis and Nobody Came?: Interpreting International Crises,* 1997; and *Voting Rights: The Devolution of American Politics,* 1999.

THOMAS A. IMHOFF is an Associate Professor of Philosophy and a staff member with the Center for Applied and Professional Ethics at California State University, Chico. His publications include: "Bureaucracy and the Subversion of Democracy," in *Contemporary Philosophy,* and, with Thia Wolf and Lauren Wright, "Collaborative Role-Play and Negotiation: A Cross-Disciplinary Endeavor," *Journal for Advanced Composition.*

LAURA DUHAN KAPLAN is Associate Professor of Philosophy and Coordinator of Women's Studies at the University of North Carolina at Charlotte, where she teaches a variety of interdisciplinary courses. She is author of *Family Pictures: A Philosopher Explores the Familiar,* 1998; editor of the forthcoming *Philosophy and Everyday Life: A Narrative Introduction;* and coeditor with Laurence F. Bove of *Philosophical Perspectives on Power and Domination,* (VIBS, 1997), and *From the Eye of the Storm: Regional Conflicts and the Philosophy of Peace,* (VIBS, 1995). She is the current President of Concerned Philosophers for Peace.

JOSEPH C. KUNKEL is Professor of Philosophy at the University of Dayton where he teaches courses in American pragmatism, ethics, ethics of war, and philosophy of peace. He is editor of the Philosophy of Peace special series and an associate editor of VIBS under Rodopi. He is coeditor with Kenneth Klein of *Issues of War and Peace: Philosophical Inquires*, 1989, and *In the Interest of Peace: A Spectrum of Philosophical Views*, 1990, and author of numerous essays that apply ethical standards to national and international situations involving violence and war. He has been a member of Concerned Philosophers for Peace since its inception in 1981, served as Executive Secretary from 1989 to 1995, and President in 1997.

STEVEN LEE received his Ph.D. in philosophy from York University in 1978 and is currently Professor of Philosophy at Hobart and William Smith Colleges. For a number of years, he has been writing and teaching on the ethical and conceptual implications of contemporary social and technological change. Currently, he is working on the question of how this change has affected the notion of sovereignty. He has also worked on the moral implications of nuclear weapons. He has published *Morality, Prudence, and Nuclear Weapons*, 1993. He is a former president of Concerned Philosophers for Peace.

MARY LENZI is Assistant Professor of Philosophy at the University of Tennessee-Knoxville. She received her Ph.D. from the University of Pennsylvania in Ancient Greek philosophy. Her articles on Platonic cosmology, political philosophy, and psychology appear in *The Monist*, and *The Analytic Freud: Psychoanalysis and Analytic Philosophy* (forthcoming). She is co-editor and contributing author with John Kultgen of *Problems of Democracy*, a forthcoming volume in the Philosophy of Peace special series in VIBS.

ROBERT LITKE is a Professor of Philosophy at Wilfrid Laurier University. He is a long-time member of Concerned Philosophers for Peace and a frequent contributor to CPP's annual conferences. He is coeditor with Deane Curtin of *Institutional Violence*, 1999, a volume in this Philosophy of Peace special series in VIBS.

MAR PETER-RAOUL is Assistant Professor of Religious Studies at Marist College. She is the Founder and Co-Projectkeeper of the Marist Praxis Project. She is coeditor, with Linda Rennie Forcey and Robert Frederick Hunter, of *Yearning to Breathe Free: Liberation Theologies in the United States*, 1990. She is a member of Concerned Philosophers for Peace, has published a number of articles in VIBS volumes, and was selected as a 1999 Coolidge Fellow by the Association of Religion and Intellectual Life.

GAIL M. PRESBEY has been a Fulbright Senior Scholar at the University of Nairobi, in the Department of Philosophy. She is presently affiliated with the University of Detroit Mercy. Her coedited introductory text, *The Philosophical Quest: A Cross-Cultural Reader*, is in its second edition. She has published articles in *Research in African Literature, American Philosophical Association Newsletter for Philosophy and the Black Experience*, as well as other journals and anthologies. She is a member of the American Philosophical Association Committee on International Cooperation.

JUDITH PRESLER is an Associate Professor of Philosophy at the University of North Carolina at Charlotte. Her interests in philosophy of peace focus upon the implications for peace of political and ethical theories. Recently published is her chapter, "Plato's Solution to the Problem of Political Corruption," in *Philosophical Perspectives on Power and Domination*, edited by Laura Duhan Kaplan and Laurence F. Bove, 1997. Other chapters in books forthcoming are "Genocide and Moral Philosophy," "Desegregation: Lessons for Peace," and "Problems for Democracy: The Procedural Republic."

JERALD RICHARDS is Professor of Philosophy at Northern Kentucky University. He teaches courses in ethics, social and political philosophy, philosophy of peace and war, and philosophy of nonviolence. He has published articles on such peace-related topics as nuclear deterrence, just war morality, nonviolence, the Gulf War, Gandhi, and criminal punishment.

SALLY J. SCHOLZ is Assistant Professor of Philosophy at Villanova University. She has published articles on systemic oppression, domestic violence, ethics, and feminist theory. She has published in *The Thomist, Teaching Philosophy, The Journal of Social Philosophy*, and numerous other venues. Her current research focuses on language in the thought of Simone de Beauvoir and on the role of language in social solidarity. In her research, she seeks to locate the intersection between philosophy and experience.

DONALD A. WELLS is Emeritus Professor of Philosophy for the University of Hawaii at Hilo. He was a Kent Fellow, a Ford Foundation Post-Doctoral Fellow, and a Rockefeller Foundation Fellow at Bellagio. He is the author of *God, Man, and the Thinker: Philosophies of Religion*, 1962; *The War Myth*, 1967; *War Crimes and Laws of War*, 2nd ed., 1991; *The Laws of Land Warfare: A Guide to the U.S. Army Manuals*, 1992; and editor of *An Encyclopedia of War and Ethics*, 1996. Wells is a member of the American Philosophical Association, Concerned Philosophers for Peace, and the Society for the Philosophical Study of Marxism.

INDEX

VIBS

The **Value Inquiry Book Series** is co-sponsored by:

American Maritain Association
American Society for Value Inquiry
Association for Process Philosophy of Education
Center for Bioethics, University of Turku
Center for International Partnerships, Rochester Institute of Technology
Center for Professional and Applied Ethics, University of North Carolina at Charlotte
Centre for Applied Ethics, Hong Kong Baptist University
Centre for Cultural Research, Aarhus University
College of Education and Allied Professions, Bowling Green State University
Concerned Philosophers for Peace
Conference of Philosophical Societies
Gannon University
Global Association for the Study of Persons
Institute of Philosophy of the High Council of Scientific Research, Spain
International Academy of Philosophy of the Principality of Liechtenstein
International Center for the Arts, Humanities, and Value Inquiry
International Society for Universal Dialogue
Natural Law Society
Philosophical Society of Finland
Philosophy Born of Struggle Association
Philosophy Seminar, University of Mainz
R.S. Hartman Institute for Formal and Applied Axiology
Russian Philosophical Society
Society for Iberian and Latin-American Thought
Society for the Philosophic Study of Genocide and the Holocaust
Society for the Philosophy of Sex and Love
Yves R. Simon Institute.

Titles Published

1. Noel Balzer, *The Human Being as a Logical Thinker.*

2. Archie J. Bahm, *Axiology: The Science of Values.*

3. H. P. P. (Hennie) Lötter, *Justice for an Unjust Society.*

4. H. G. Callaway, *Context for Meaning and Analysis: A Critical Study in the Philosophy of Language.*

5. Benjamin S. Llamzon, *A Humane Case for Moral Intuition.*

6. James R. Watson, *Between Auschwitz and Tradition: Postmodern Reflections on the Task of Thinking.* A volume in **Holocaust and Genocide Studies.**

7. Robert S. Hartman, *Freedom to Live: The Robert Hartman Story,* edited by Arthur R. Ellis. A volume in **Hartman Institute Axiology Studies.**

8. Archie J. Bahm, *Ethics: The Science of Oughtness.*

9. George David Miller, *An Idiosyncratic Ethics; Or, the Lauramachean Ethics.*

10. Joseph P. DeMarco, *A Coherence Theory in Ethics.*

11. Frank G. Forrest, *Valuemetrics$^\aleph$: The Science of Personal and Professional Ethics.* A volume in **Hartman Institute Axiology Studies.**

12. William Gerber, *The Meaning of Life: Insights of the World's Great Thinkers.*

13. Richard T. Hull, Editor, *A Quarter Century of Value Inquiry: Presidential Addresses of the American Society for Value Inquiry.* A volume in **Histories and Addresses of Philosophical Societies.**

14. William Gerber, *Nuggets of Wisdom from Great Jewish Thinkers: From Biblical Times to the Present.*

15. Sidney Axinn, *The Logic of Hope: Extensions of Kant's View of Religion.*

16. Messay Kebede, *Meaning and Development.*

17. Amihud Gilead, *The Platonic Odyssey: A Philosophical-Literary Inquiry into the* Phaedo.

18. Necip Fikri Alican, *Mill's Principle of Utility: A Defense of John Stuart Mill's Notorious Proof.* A volume in **Universal Justice.**

19. Michael H. Mitias, Editor, *Philosophy and Architecture.*

20. Roger T. Simonds, *Rational Individualism: The Perennial Philosophy of Legal Interpretation.* A volume in **Natural Law Studies.**

21. William Pencak, *The Conflict of Law and Justice in the Icelandic Sagas.*

22. Samuel M. Natale and Brian M. Rothschild, Editors, *Values, Work, Education: The Meanings of Work.*

23. N. Georgopoulos and Michael Heim, Editors, *Being Human in the Ultimate: Studies in the Thought of John M. Anderson.*

24. Robert Wesson and Patricia A. Williams, Editors, *Evolution and Human Values.*

25. Wim J. van der Steen, *Facts, Values, and Methodology: A New Approach to Ethics.*

26. Avi Sagi and Daniel Statman, *Religion and Morality.*

27. Albert William Levi, *The High Road of Humanity: The Seven Ethical Ages of Western Man,* edited by Donald Phillip Verene and Molly Black Verene.

28. Samuel M. Natale and Brian M. Rothschild, Editors, *Work Values: Education, Organization, and Religious Concerns.*

29. Laurence F. Bove and Laura Duhan Kaplan, Editors, *From the Eye of the Storm: Regional Conflicts and the Philosophy of Peace.* A volume in **Philosophy of Peace.**

45. Alan Soble, Editor, *Sex, Love, and Friendship: Studies of the Society for the Philosophy of Sex and Love, 1977-1992.* A volume in **Histories and Addresses of Philosophical Societies.**

46. Peter A. Redpath, *Wisdom's Odyssey: From Philosophy to Transcendental Sophistry.* A volume in **Studies in the History of Western Philosophy.**

47. Albert A. Anderson, *Universal Justice: A Dialectical Approach.* A volume in **Universal Justice.**

48. Pio Colonnello, *The Philosophy of José Gaos.* Translated from Italian by Peter Cocozzella. Edited by Myra Moss. Introduction by Giovanni Gullace. A volume in **Values in Italian Philosophy.**

49. Laura Duhan Kaplan and Laurence F. Bove, Editors, *Philosophical Perspectives on Power and Domination: Theories and Practices.* A volume in **Philosophy of Peace.**

50. Gregory F. Mellema, *Collective Responsibility.*

51. Josef Seifert, *What Is Life? The Originality, Irreducibility, and Value of Life.* A volume in **Central-European Value Studies.**

52. William Gerber, *Anatomy of What We Value Most.*

53. Armando Molina, *Our Ways: Values and Character,* edited by Rem B. Edwards. A volume in **Hartman Institute Axiology Studies.**

54. Kathleen J. Wininger, *Nietzsche's Reclamation of Philosophy.* A volume in **Central-European Value Studies.**

55. Thomas Magnell, Editor, *Explorations of Value.*

56. HPP (Hennie) Lötter, *Injustice, Violence, and Peace: The Case of South Africa.* A volume in **Philosophy of Peace.**

57. Lennart Nordenfelt, *Talking About Health: A Philosophical Dialogue.* A volume in **Nordic Value Studies.**

58. Jon Mills and Janusz A. Polanowski, *The Ontology of Prejudice.* A volume in **Philosophy and Psychology.**

73. Peter A. Redpath, *Masquerade of the Dream Walkers: Prophetic Theology from the Cartesians to Hegel.* A volume in **Studies in the History of Western Philosophy.**

74. Malcolm D. Evans, *Whitehead and Philosophy of Education: The Seamless Coat of Learning.* A volume in **Philosophy of Education.**

75. Warren E. Steinkraus, *Taking Religious Claims Seriously: A Philosophy of Religion,* edited by Michael H. Mitias. A volume in **Universal Justice.**

76. Thomas Magnell, Editor, *Values and Education.*

77. Kenneth A. Bryson, *Persons and Immortality.* A volume in **Natural Law Studies.**

78. Steven V. Hicks, *International Law and the Possibility of a Just World Order: An Essay on Hegel's Universalism.* A volume in **Universal Justice.**

79. E. F. Kaelin, *Texts on Texts and Textuality: A Phenomenology of Literary Art,* edited by Ellen J. Burns.

80. Amihud Gilead, *Saving Possibilities: A Study in Philosophical Psychology.* A volume in **Philosophy and Psychology.**

81. André Mineau, *The Making of the Holocaust: Ideology and Ethics in the Systems Perspective.* A volume in **Holocaust and Genocide Studies.**

82. Howard P. Kainz, *Politically Incorrect Dialogues: Topics Not Discussed in Polite Circles.*

83. Veikko Launis, Juhani Pietarinen, and Juha Räikkä, Editors, *Genes and Morality: New Essays.* A volume in **Nordic Value Studies.**

84. Steven Schroeder, *The Metaphysics of Cooperation: The Case of F. D. Maurice.*

85. Caroline Joan ("Kay") S. Picart, *Thomas Mann and Friedrich Nietzsche: Eroticism, Death, Music, and Laughter.* A volume in **Central-European Value Studies.**

86. G. John M. Abbarno, Editor, *The Ethics of Homelessness: Philosophical Perspectives.*

87. James Giles, Editor, *French Existentialism: Consciousness, Ethics, and Relations with Others.* A volume in **Nordic Value Studies.**

88. Deane Curtin and Robert Litke, Editors, *Institutional Violence.* A volume in **Philosophy of Peace.**

89. Yuval Lurie, *Cultural Beings: Reading the Philosophers of* Genesis.

90. Sandra A. Wawrytko, Editor, *The Problem of Evil: An Intercultural Exploration.* A volume in **Philosophy and Psychology.**

91. Gary J. Acquaviva, *Values, Violence, and Our Future.* A volume in **Hartman Institute Axiology Studies.**

92. Michael R. Rhodes, *Coercion: A Nonevaluative Approach.*

93. Jacques Kriel, *Matter, Mind, and Medicine: Transforming the Clinical Method.*

94. Haim Gordon, *Dwelling Poetically: Educational Challenges in Heidegger's Thinking on Poetry.* A volume in **Philosophy of Education.**

95. Ludwig Grünberg, *The Mystery of Values: Studies in Axiology,* edited by Cornelia Grünberg and Laura Grünberg.

96. Gerhold K. Becker, Editor, *The Moral Status of Persons: Perspectives on Bioethics.* A volume in **Studies in Applied Ethics.**

97. Roxanne Claire Farrar, *Sartrean Dialectics: A Method for Critical Discourse on Aesthetic Experience.*

98. Ugo Spirito, *Memoirs of the Twentieth Century.* Translated from Italian and edited by Anthony G. Costantini. A volume in **Values in Italian Philosophy.**

99. Steven Schroeder, *Between Freedom and Necessity: An Essay on the Place of Value.*

100. Foster N. Walker, *Enjoyment and the Activity of Mind: Dialogues on Whitehead and Education.* A volume in **Philosophy of Education.**

101. Avi Sagi, *Kierkegaard, Religion, and Existence: The Voyage of the Self.* Translated from Hebrew by Batya Stein.